CIM
STUDY TEXT

Advanced Certificate

Marketing Operations

First edition June 1999
Second edition May 2000

ISBN 0 7517 4107 8 (previous edition 07517 4087 X)

British Library Cataloguing-in-Publication Data
A catalogue record for this book
is available from the British Library

Published by

BPP Publishing Limited
Aldine House, Aldine Place
London W12 8AW

www.bpp.com

Printed in Great Britain by
WM Print Ltd
Frederick Street
Walsall
West Midlands WS2 9NE

All our rights reserved. No part of this publication may be reproduced, stored in a retrieval system or transmitted, in any form or by any means, electronic, mechanical, photocopying, recording or otherwise, without the prior written permission of BPP Publishing Limited.

We are grateful to the Chartered Institute of Marketing for permission to reproduce in this text the syllabus, tutor's guidance notes, and past examination questions.

©
BPP Publishing Limited
2000

Contents

	Page
HOW TO USE THIS STUDY TEXT	(v)
SYLLABUS	(x)
TUTOR'S GUIDANCE NOTES	(xiii)
THE EXAM PAPER	(xiv)
STUDY CHECKLIST	(xvii)

PART A: THE MARKETING PLANNING PROCESS: AN OVERVIEW
1 Conducting a marketing audit   3
2 Developing marketing objectives and strategies   33
3 Implementing the marketing plan   63

PART B: THE MARKETING MIX
4 The background to promotional operations   91
5 Promotional operations in practice   107
6 Product, price and place operations   148

PART C: MANAGING MARKETING RELATIONSHIPS
7 Relationships with customers and suppliers   205
8 Relationships with the wider public and society   222

PART D: MARKETING OPERATIONS IN CONTEXT
9 Business-to-business marketing   241
10 Services marketing   253
11 Charity and not for profit marketing   266
12 International marketing   273

ILLUSTRATIVE QUESTIONS   295

SUGGESTED ANSWERS   298

LIST OF KEY CONCEPTS   327

INDEX   328

ORDER FORM

REVIEW FORM & FREE PRIZE DRAW

HOW TO USE THIS STUDY TEXT

Aims of this Study Text

To provide you with the knowledge and understanding, skills and applied techniques required for passing the exam

The Study Text has been written around the CIM syllabus (reproduced below, and cross-referenced to where in the text each topic is covered) and the CIM's Tutor's Manual.

- It is **comprehensive**. We do not omit sections of the syllabus as the examiner is liable to examine any angle of any part of the syllabus - and you do not want to be left high and dry.

- It is **on-target** - we do not include any material which is not examinable. You can therefore rely on the BPP Study Text as the stand-alone source of all your information for the exam.

To allow you to study in the way that best suits your learning style and the time you have available, by following your personal Study Plan (see below)

You may be studying at home on your own until the date of the exam, or you may be attending a full-time course. You may like to (and have time to) read every word, or you may prefer to (or only have time to) skim-read and devote the remainder of your time to question practice. Wherever you fall in the spectrum, you will find the BPP Study Text meets your needs in designing and following your personal Study Plan.

To tie in with the other components of the BPP Effective Study Package to ensure you have the best possible chance of passing the exam

Recommended period of use	Elements of BPP Effective Study Package
3-12 months before exam	**Study Text** Acquisition of knowledge, understanding, skills and applied techniques
1-6 months before exam	**Practice and Revision Kit (9/2000)** Tutorial questions and helpful checklists of the key points lead you into each area. There are then numerous examination questions to try, graded by topic area along with realistic suggested solutions prepared by marketing professionals in the light of the Examiner's Reports. The September 2000 edition will include the December 1999 and June 2000 papers.
1-6 months before exam	**Success Tapes** Audio cassettes covering the vital elements of your syllabus in less than 90 minutes per subject. Each tape also contains exam hints to help you fine tune your strategy.

How to use this Study Text

Settling down to study

By this stage in your career you may be a very experienced learner and taker of exams. But have you ever thought about *how* you learn? Let's have a quick look at the key elements required for effective learning. You can then identify your learning style and go on to design your own approach to how you are going to study this text - your personal Study Plan.

Key element of learning	Using the BPP Study Text
Motivation	You can rely on the comprehensiveness and technical quality of BPP. You've chosen the right Study Text - so you're in pole position to pass your exam!
Clear objectives and standards	Do you want to be a prizewinner or simply achieve a moderate pass? Decide.
Feedback	Follow through the examples in this text and do the Action Programme and the Quick quizzes. Evaluate your efforts critically - how are you doing?
Study Plan	You need to be honest about your progress to yourself - do not be over-confident, but don't be negative either. Make your Study Plan (see below) and try to stick to it. Focus on the short-term objectives – completing two chapters a night, say - but beware of losing sight of your study objectives
Practice	Use the Quick quizzes and Chapter Roundups to refresh your memory regularly after you have completed your initial study of each chapter

These introductory pages let you see exactly what you are up against. However you study, you should:

- **read through the syllabus and teaching guide** - this will help you to identify areas you have already covered, perhaps at a lower level of detail, and areas that are totally new to you

- **study the examination paper section**, where we show you the format of the exam (how many and what kind of questions etc).

How to use this Study Text

Key study steps

The following steps are, in our experience, the ideal way to study for professional exams. You can of course adapt it for your particular learning style (see below).

Tackle the chapters in the order you find them in the Study Text. Taking into account your individual learning style, follow these key study steps for each chapter.

Key study steps	Activity
Step 1 *Chapter Topic List*	Study the list. Each numbered topic denotes a **numbered section** in the chapter.
Step 2 *Setting the Scene*	Read it through. It is designed to show you **why the topics in the chapter need to be studied** - how they lead on from previous topics, and how they lead into subsequent ones.
Step 3 *Explanations*	Proceed **methodically** through the chapter, reading each section thoroughly and making sure you understand.
Step 4 *Key Concepts*	**Key concepts** can often earn you **easy marks** if you state them clearly and correctly in an appropriate exam.
Step 5 *Exam Tips*	These give you a good idea of how the examiner tends to examine certain topics – pinpointing **easy marks** and highlighting **pitfalls**.
Step 6 *Note taking*	Take **brief notes** if you wish, avoiding the temptation to copy out too much.
Step 7 *Marketing at Work*	Study each one, and try if you can to add flesh to them from your **own experience** - they are designed to show how the topics you are studying come alive (and often come unstuck) in the **real world**.
Step 8 *Action Programme*	Make a very good attempt at each one in each chapter. These are designed to put your **knowledge into practice** in much the same way as you will be required to do in the exam. Check the answer at the end of the chapter in the **Action Programme review**, and make sure you understand the reasons why yours may be different.
Step 9 *Chapter Roundup*	Check through it very carefully, to make sure you have grasped the **major points** it is highlighting
Step 10 *Quick Quiz*	When you are happy that you have covered the chapter, use the **Quick quiz** to check your recall of the topics covered. The answers are in the paragraphs in the chapter that we refer you to.
Step 11 *Illustrative questions*	Either at this point, or later when you are thinking about revising, make a full attempt at the **illustrative questions**. You can find these at the end of the Study Text, along with the **answers** so you can see how you did.

How to use this Study Text

Developing your personal Study Plan

Preparing a Study Plan (and sticking closely to it) is one of the key elements in learning success.

First you need to be aware of your style of learning. There are four typical learning styles. Consider yourself in the light of the following descriptions, and work out which you fit most closely. You can then plan to follow the key study steps in the sequence suggested.

Learning styles	Characteristics	Sequence of key study steps in the BPP Study Text
Theorist	Seeks to understand principles before applying them in practice	1, 2, 3, 7, 4, 5, 8, 9, 10, 11 (6 continuous)
Reflector	Seeks to observe phenomena, thinks about them and then chooses to act	
Activist	Prefers to deal with practical, active problems; does not have much patience with theory	1, 2, 8 (read through), 7, 4, 5, 9, 3, 8 (full attempt), 10, 11 (6 continuous)
Pragmatist	Prefers to study only if a direct link to practical problems can be seen; not interested in theory for its own sake	8 (read through), 2, 4, 5, 7, 9, 1, 3, 8 (full attempt), 10, 11 (6 continuous)

Next you should complete the following checklist.

Am I motivated? (a) ☐

Do I have an objective and a standard that I want to achieve? (b) ☐

Am I a theorist, a reflector, an activist or a pragmatist? (c) ☐

How much time do I have available per week, given: (d) ☐

- the standard I have set myself
- the time I need to set aside later for work on the Practice & Revision Kit
- the other exam(s) I am sitting, and (of course)
- practical matters such as work, travel, exercise, sleep and social life?

Now:

- take the time you have available per week for this Study Text (d), and multiply it by the number of weeks available to give (e). (e) ☐
- divide (e) by the number of chapters to give (f) (f) ☐
- set about studying each chapter in the time represented by (f), following the key study steps in the order suggested by your particular learning style.

This is your personal **Study Plan**.

Short of time?

Whatever your objectives, standards or style, you may find you simply do not have the time available to follow all the key study steps for each chapter, however you adapt them for your particular learning style. If this is the case, follow the Skim Study technique below (the icons in the Study Text will help you to do this).

Skim Study technique

Study the chapters in the order you find them in the Study Text. For each chapter, follow the key study steps 1-2, and then skim-read through step 3. Jump to step 9, and then go back to steps 4-5. Follow through step 7, and prepare outline Answers to the Action Programme (step 8). Try the Quick Quiz (step 10), following up any items you can't answer, then do a plan for the illustrative question (step 11), comparing it against our answers. You should probably still follow step 6 (note-taking).

Moving on...

However you study, when you are ready to embark on the practice and revision phase of the BPP Effective Study Package, you should still refer back to this Study Text:

- as a source of **reference** (you should find the list of key concepts and the index particularly helpful for this)
- as a **refresher** (the Chapter Roundups and Quick Quizzes help you here).

A note on pronouns

On occasions in this Study Text, 'he' is used for 'he or she', 'him' for 'him or her' and so forth. Whilst we try to avoid this practice it is sometimes necessary for reasons of style. No prejudice or stereotyping according to sex is intended or assumed.

Syllabus

SYLLABUS

Aims and objectives

- To build on the knowledge of marketing fundamentals which the student is already expected to have gained

- To encourage students to test and apply modern marketing theory to the understanding and solution of practical marketing problems and situations. This will enable them to perform effectively in any single functional area of marketing at junior management level

- To provide students with a sound understanding of the process of marketing planning (analysis, strategy and implementation) and underpinning knowledge for the Diploma subject Planning and Control

- To provide students with a sound understanding of the marketing mix tools that contribute towards the effective implementation of marketing strategy

- To be able to evaluate the relative effectiveness and costs of elements of the promotional mix providing underpinning operational knowledge for the Integrated Marketing Communications module at Diploma level

- To encourage students to explore the multiple relationships which need to be formed and maintained to enable successful and ongoing marketing exchange

- To demonstrate the need to adapt marketing operations in a variety of contexts; business-to-business, services, not-for-profit and international

Learning outcomes

On successful completion of this unit students will be able to:

- Conduct a basic marketing audit considering internal and external factors

- Understand the process of marketing planning at an operational level

- Understand the need to integrate marketing mix tools to achieve effective implementation of plans

- Select an appropriate integrated mix (4Ps or 7Ps) for a particular marketing context

- Select and justify the use of one or more promotional techniques for a particular marketing context

- Demonstrate the adaptation of marketing operations principles in a variety of contexts

- Understand and appreciate the marketing operations process and how it can be delivered through multiple relationships

- Communicate ideas effectively in a variety of formats; report, article, presentation

Syllabus

Indicative content and weighting	Covered in chapter

1 The marketing planning process: an overview (15%)

1.1 Conducting a marketing audit — 1
- Analysis of an organisation's marketing environment
  Macro: political, legal, economic, socio-cultural, technological
  Micro: market size/trends, customers, competitors, suppliers, distributors, publics
- Analysis of organisation's internal capabilities
  Financial resources, human resources, manufacturing, operations, R&D and marketing (strategy, mix, organisation, systems, productivity)
- SWOT analysis and key issues

1.2 Developing marketing objectives and strategies — 2
- Marketing objectives as simple goal statements, links to mission statement
- How marketing strategy defines target markets (from segmentation bases and profiles), differential advantage and desired brand positioning
- GAP analysis

1.3 Implementing the marketing plan — 3
- Implementation barriers
- Allocation of budgets, tasks, responsibilities
- Control implications
- Alternative ways of organising marketing activities; by function, product, region, types of customer, matrix
- Internal marketing implications; gaining commitment for the plan

2 The marketing mix (50%)

2.1 Promotional operations (20%) — 4, 5
- Theories of communication: single step, two step and multi-step communication models, adoption models
- Advertising techniques: campaign planning, developing creative and media briefs, message content, evaluation
- Sales promotion techniques: objectives, mechanics (sampling, price-offs, in pack etc), evaluation
- Public relations techniques: establishing publics, press relations, lobbying, crisis management, evaluation
- Sponsorship: objectives, types (sport, arts, community etc), evaluation
- Personal selling techniques (sales force, sales support and sales literature)

2.2 Pricing operations (10%) — 6
- The importance of price and its determinants
- Pricing models for decisions based on cost competition and demand (including basic break-even analysis, marginal costing and price elasticity).
- Pricing objectives and methods (cost-plus, perceived-value, competitive parity etc)
- Adapting the price (discounts, promotions, product-mix etc)

Syllabus

		Covered in chapter
2.3	Product operations (10%)	6

- The nature of products, components and life cycles
- Brand management; brand values, brand planning and threats to the brand
- Product portfolio, product mix (product line breadth and depth)
- New product development (idea generation, screening, concept development and testing, marketing strategy, business analysis, launch, evaluation and development)

2.4 Place operations (10%) — 6

- Distribution channels; consumer and business-to-business, new direct channels of distribution such as the internet.
- Criteria to select and evaluate alternative channels of distribution

3 Managing marketing relationships (15%)

3.1 Relationships with customers — 7

- Defining the concept, types of relationships; degree of importance
- The recognition of distributors, intermediaries, agents and franchisees as customers
- Customer retention planning; relationship marketing mix
- Managing customer relationships
- Key account management techniques

3.2 Relationships with outside suppliers — 7

- Briefing, working, control and review of agencies and consultancies (specifying needs/time span/budgets)
- Working with distributors, franchisees and agents; building relationships and controlling performance

3.3 Internal marketing relationships — 7

- The concept, organisational structures and cultures
- Effective internal marketing techniques (recruitment, training, communication, cross-functional team working etc)

3.4 Relationships with the wider public and society — 8

- The importance of marketing ethics and social responsibility
- Ethics for marketing executives and within the marketing mix
- Codes of ethics
- Social responsibility issues: consumer, community, green
- Proactive, reactive or passive strategies to social responsibility

4 Marketing operations in context (20%)

4.1 Industrial/business to business marketing applications — 9

- Distinguishing characteristics of business versus consumer markets
- Business buyer behaviour, factors affecting buying decisions and buying process
- Marketing mix differences (service components, bid and negotiated pricing, role of personal selling, use of distributors and agents)

Syllabus

Covered in chapter

4.2 Services marketing — 10
- Basic characteristics (intangibility, inseparability, perishability, heterogeneity)
- Extended marketing mix (people, process, physical evidence)
- Importance of service quality

4.3 Charity and not for profit marketing — 11
- Objectives differ from consumer/industrial markets
- Target markets (donors, volunteers, clients)
- Marketing mix differences (product, usually ideas and services rather than goods, short distribution channels, approach to pricing, promotion emphasis on PR and fact to face fund raising)
- Performance hard to measure

4.4 International marketing. — 12
- Identifying marketing information needs
- Marketing environment, managing the differences
- Structure choices: exporting, licensing, joint ventures, trading companies, direct ownership
- Necessary adaptations to the marketing mix

TUTOR'S GUIDANCE NOTES

The following is BPP's summary of the Tutor Manual produced by the CIM for this subject.

Students should understand three key aspects of marketing operations:

- The **processes** of marketing
- Marketing **relationships**
- The **context** of the operations.

Marketing **relationships** exist between the firm and the wide range of stakeholders who contribute to market dynamics. These include consumers, suppliers, distributors, employees and the wider public. Understanding is required of how relationships are formed and maintained.

Marketing operations take place within the **context** of the industry, the market and the organisation. Each aspect may impose its own constraints upon the development of marketing plans.

The Marketing Operations paper builds upon the content of the Marketing Fundamentals syllabus.

The syllabus has been changed to reduce the coverage of analysis and organisation issues in marketing planning while increasing the emphasis on the tactical aspects of the marketing mix. Promotional Practice now forms 20% of the syllabus, rather than being a subject in its own right. This reflects the importance of marketing communications and forms a basis for consideration of the strategic aspects of the subject at Diploma level.

The exam paper

THE EXAM PAPER

Assessment methods and format of the paper

	Number of marks
Section A: one minicase study with compulsory questions	40
Section B: any three questions from six (equal marks)	60
	100

Time allowed: 3 hours

Analysis of past papers

You should note that the syllabus weightings have changed since the exam in December 1998. The new syllabus applies from December 1999 onwards.

December 1999

Part A

1 Air Products and Chemicals is a leading supplier of gases and related equipment
   (a) Differences between industrial and consumer markets
   (b) Composition of a decision making unit: persuading its members

Part B

2 Notes on brand positioning
3 Report on a marketing opportunity
   or
   Report on sales promotion techniques
4 Presentation on developing marketing orientation
   or
   Outline contents of paper on new product development
5 Draft presentation on services marketing
6 Magazine article on briefing and managing outside suppliers
7 Report on impact of marketing environment on marketing mix in two foreign countries

June 1999

Part A

1 Ford and Honda's International Organisation, new international structures
   (a) Review of centralisation versus decentralisation strategies
   (b) Marketing mix implications of globalised versus customised strategies

Part B

2 Future macro/micro environments and their impact upon the marketing plan
3 Segmentation bases for consumer and business-to-business markets
4 Application of Ansoff's growth strategies and evaluation process
5 Roles and responsibilities of assistant Product Manager, Branch Manager, Marketing Manager and Marketing Director
6 Characteristics of a training service and the services marketing mix
7 Social responsibility with local and national examples

The exam paper

December 1998

Part A

1 Cafédirect
   (a) Social responsibility strategies
   (b) Code of ethical trading
   (c) Ethical differentiation

Part B

2 Segmentation
3 Outline marketing plan
4 Sales force control
5 Advertising agency selection
6 Excellence in marketing operations
7 Internal marketing

June 1998

Part A

1 Guinness Worldwide, new international markets
   (a) Information required on emerging markets to assess relative attractiveness
   (b) Market entry methods and the advantages/disadvantages of Guinness's current approach in Asia

Part B

2 Factors to take into account when conducting a market opportunity analysis
3 Outline contents of a detailed marketing plan. Likely benefits of this plan
4 Options for marketing organisation together with the strengths and weaknesses of each option
5 Write a case history on a not-for-profit organisation which illustrates marketing operations excellence
6 Notes on workshop to outline the distinctive characteristics of a service, solutions for dealing with these and examples
7 Draft an article on alternative strategies for dealing with social responsibility issues, with examples

December 1997

Part A

1 *Compulsory mini-case:* European Retail Market Entry - Levi's
   (a) The marketing environment: aspects to monitor for entry into European clothing market
   (b) Outline marketing plan for opening 300 stores across Europe in the next 10 years

Part B

2 Segmentation, targeting and positioning: a case history of an example of your choice
3 The marketing audit elements and how it can be used to identify strengths, weaknesses, opportunities and threats
4 Role of an assistant product manager: key tasks using a company examples of your choice
5 Briefing agencies for the provision of a marketing service for mobile phones and accessories in over 1,000 retail outlets

6 Business to business marketing: differences between consumer markets and how these influence the marketing mix
7 Green issues: how a proactive approach affects marketing strategy and programmes

June 1997

Part A

1 Compulsory mini-case: Customer service strategy for the TSB Retail Bank
   (a) Key principles of service quality and how to improve strategy
   (b) Structure and outline contents of an integrated marketing plan

Part B

2 Internal capability: strengths and weaknesses relative to a marketing opportunity
3 Marketing environment changes and their influence on the marketing mix
4 Constraints on marketing decisions: legal and non-legal
5 Marketing organisation: product, sales and marketing led orientations
6 Competitive tendering guidelines for a new market entry
8 International market research: types and sources of information

December 1996

Part A

1 Compulsory mini-case: charity marketing and the International Red Cross
   (a) Distinctive characteristics of marketing for the Red Cross charity as compared to a commercial organisation
   (b) The marketing environment: monitoring and influence on marketing strategy and programme development
   (c) Market segmentation: bases for consumer and business markets and for Red Cross donors

Part B

2 Ansoff's matrix: strategic alternatives
3 Social influences on consumer buying behaviour
4 Marketing management roles: differences between marketing, product and brand managers
5 Briefing a sales promotion agency
6 International marketing options and selection factors
7 Marketing information systems: components and the contribution of IT

Study checklist

STUDY CHECKLIST

This page is designed to help you chart your progress through the Study Text, including the Action Programme and illustrative questions. You can tick off each topic as you study and try questions on it. Insert the dates you complete the chapters Action Programme and questions in the relevant boxes. You will thus ensure that you are on track to complete your study before the exam.

	Text chapters Date completed	Action programme Number	Date completed	Illustrative questions Number	Date completed

PART A: THE MARKETING PLANNING PROCESS: AN OVERVIEW

1 Conducting a marketing audit		1, 2, 3, 4, 5, 6		1	
2 Developing marketing objectives and strategies		1, 2, 3, 4, 5, 6		2	
3 Implementing the marketing plan		1, 2, 3, 4, 5, 6, 7		3, 4, 5	

PART B: THE MARKETING MIX

4 The background to promotional operations		1, 2		6	
5 Promotional operations in practice		1, 2, 3, 4, 5, 6, 7		7	
6 Product, price and place operations		1, 2, 3, 4, 5, 6, 7, 8, 9, 10, 11, 12		8, 9, 10, 11	

PART C: MANAGING MARKETING RELATIONSHIPS

7 Relationships with customers and suppliers		1		12	
8 Relationships with the wider public and society		1, 2, 3		13	

PART D: MARKETING OPERATIONS IN CONTEXT

9 Industrial/business to business marketing		1, 2		14	
10 Services marketing		1, 2, 3, 4		15	
11 Charity and not for profit marketing		1, 2		16	
12 International marketing		1, 2		17	

Part A
The marketing planning process: an overview

1 Conducting a Marketing Audit

Chapter Topic List	Syllabus reference
1 Setting the scene	-
2 Marketing planning and strategic planning	1.1
3 Strategic planning	1.1
4 Situation analysis - an introduction	1.1
5 Using SWOT analysis	1.1
6 Internal appraisal	1.1
7 Environmental analysis - the macro-environment	1.1
8 Environmental analysis - the micro-environment	1.1
9 Conducting a marketing audit	1.1

Learning Outcome

Students will be able to conduct a basic marketing audit considering internal and external factors.

Key Concepts Introduced

- Marketing planning
- Strategic planning
- Company mission statement
- Situation analysis
- Business environment

Examples of Marketing at Work

- The launch of Mars Light
- Ericsson
- Opportunities
- Advertising
- Monitoring

Part A: The marketing planning process: an overview

1 SETTING THE SCENE

1.1 The marketing audit is the theme of this chapter but we need some background before we talk about it. Marketing in its widest sense is an important aspect of business strategy and we will set the marketing audit within the context of corporate strategic planning. Section 2 deals with the relationship between marketing planning and strategic planning.

1.2 Section 3 gives an overview of the whole strategic planning process. This is then amplified in sections 4 to 8 which deal with the information which must be collected for rational corporate planning to take place. Section 5 deals with the technique known as SWOT analysis.

1.3 Once you understand the overall process of corporate planning, the idea of the marketing audit should fall into place and this is dealt with in detail in section 9.

1.4 Be aware that terminology is sometimes used loosely. We have taken a fairly narrow approach to the marketing audit. Some people will use the term to refer to a much wider strategic appraisal, really corresponding to what we have called situation analysis. There is no reason why you should not make up your own mind about this, but take care in the exam to define your terms clearly and to make your overall meaning clear.

2 MARKETING PLANNING AND STRATEGIC PLANNING   12/97, 12/98

> **Key Concept**
> **Marketing planning** is defined by *Dibb, Simkin, Pride, Ferrell*:
> 'The marketing planning process *combines* the organisation's overall marketing strategy *with* fundamental analyses of trends in the marketing environment; company strengths, weaknesses, opportunities and threats, competitive strategies; and identification of target market segments. Ultimately the process *leads to* the formulation of market programmes or marketing mixes *which facilitate* the implementation of the organisation's strategies and plans.
> The emphases in key words (which are added by us) highlight the nature of the process.

> **Key Concept**
> **Strategic planning** sets or changes the **objectives** of an organisation. **Tactical planning** is concerned with decisions about the efficient use of an organisation's resources to achieve these objectives.

2.1 Although marketing has in the past been seen as a separate distinct activity with a primarily **tactical** role to play in business development, this view is largely being replaced by the recognition that marketing has a key **strategic role**.

2.2 The corporate audit of product/market strengths and weaknesses, and much of its external environmental analysis is directly informed by the marketing audit. The marketing department is probably the most important source of information for the development of corporate strategy, and represents the starting point for developing the marketing plan and identifying the key marketing controllables which can be manipulated in pursuit of objectives.

2.3 Marketing planning is thus subordinate to corporate planning but makes a significant contribution to it and is concerned with many of the same issues.

1: Conducting a marketing audit

2.4 **Corporate strategic plans** aim to guide the overall development of an organisation. Specific **marketing strategies will be determined within these boundaries**. To be effective, these plans will be interdependent with those for other functions of the organisation.

- The **strategic** component of marketing planning focuses on the direction which an organisation will take in relation to a specific market, or set of markets, in order to achieve a specified set of objectives.

- Marketing planning also requires an **operational** component which defines tasks and activities to be undertaken in order to achieve the desired strategy.

> **Exam Tip**
> The relationship between marketing and corporate planning was examined as a ten-mark part of the Snapple mini-case set in June 1996.

2.5 EXAMPLE - MARKETING PLANNING

ABZ Ltd is a privately-owned, UK-based industrial manufacturing company with an annual turnover of around £700 million and pre-tax profits of £70 million. Although primarily UK-orientated, the business has enjoyed considerable success in a large proportion of European markets and has made more limited gains further afield.

Reorganisation of the Marketing Function: Year 1

ABZ had recently reorganised its sales and marketing functions. Previously, the marketing function had a primarily tactical role, dealing with the promotional requirements of the business. Pricing strategy was handled by the finance function while new product development was dealt with by a bespoke team of personnel who did not feed directly into the marketing area. Following the reorganisation, a more extensive marketing department was developed around a series of product groups, each headed by a marketing manager with overall responsibility for marketing strategy development.

Marketing Planning Objectives : Year 1

The marketing director at ABZ was enthusiastic about market planning, believing that it would help the business capitalise on its resources to take advantage of new opportunities and to prioritise core target markets. The marketing director realised that ABZ's relative inexperience of formal marketing planning meant it would need to limit its efforts during the first year to developing a plan for the UK market (55% of ABZ's business). Objectives were set for first phase of marketing planning.

- To review the company's strengths and weaknesses.
- To analyse the wider marketing environment and key environment trends for ABZ's business.
- To obtain information on key customers.
- To understand the sales and contribution of different customer segments and reappraise priorities.
- To begin gathering competitor information.
- To develop detailed marketing programmes for UK markets and broad guidelines for other European markets.

Part A: The marketing planning process: an overview

Marketing Planning Objectives : Year 2

The basic planning objectives remained the same with the intention of broadening the analysis to include more markets in Europe and the rest of the world. A particular focus was to develop a more extensive understanding of ABZ's competitive environment. The structure of the planning programme continued as before with a combination of training days, advice sessions and regular review days for receiving feedback from the others. This was vital in planning the overall product portfolios as some products were partial substitutes for others.

Marketing Planning Objectives : Year 3

The marketing planning was progressing well, so this year ABZ's last two remaining product teams were included in the process. Once again, the analysis was combined to a limited number of customer groups and markets. For the first time it was possible to use the sales and financial contribution analysis carried out in year 2 to identify exactly what the priorities should be.

At this stage in the marketing planning, the marketing director needed to consider the changing needs and expertise of the product teams. Although most mangers were now comfortable carrying out a range of analyses and taking strategic decisions, the recruits in the two new product teams needed some induction.

A brief refresher course was set up and arrangements were made for the new teams to each work in conjunction with another team. This allowed the more experienced managers to transfer their expertise to the others.

In order to reinforce the status of the planning programme, the original product teams were tasked with reviewing the performance of last year's plan and updating the customer, competitor and environmental analyses.

Measuring the rewards

It is difficult directly to attribute success in the market place exclusively to a programme of marketing planning. However, the marketing director at ABZ was convinced that the planning programme had measurably improved the business' financial performance. Measures of market share across the four customer groups which began the marketing planning programme had, by the end of year 3, risen by an average of 4%. A number of additional benefits, both tangible and intangible, were also being attributed to the planning programme. In all cases these benefits were either directly or indirectly aided by improved interpersonal relationships.

- A new division, geared to the needs of one particular customer group, had been developed.
- A total of six new products had been launched.
- Greater control over the regions was possible than ever before.
- More control over new product development, pricing and promotional activity was one of the most visible outcomes of the planning exercise.
- A significant contribution to team building had been made.

Long Range Planning, 30/1, Dibb, S., pp. 53-63, 1997

3 STRATEGIC PLANNING

3.1 Stages in strategic planning

Development of the organisation's mission statement
↓
Statement of objectives
↓
Situation analysis
↓
Strategy development
↓
Specific plans
↓
Implementation

This section gives an overview of this process. Various aspects of situation analysis form the remainder of the chapter.

> **Key Concept**
> The **company mission statement** says what an organisation is aiming to achieve through the conduct of its business. The purpose is to provide the organisation with *focus* and *direction*.

3.2 The corporate mission depends on a variety of factors. **Corporate history** will often influence the markets and customer groups served - thus, in the banking sector Credit Agricole retains strong links with its farming depositors, while Coutts concentrates on high income consumers in its retail banking activities.

3.3 The commonest approach to the corporate mission relies on the company's product and market scope. The mission statement then rests on customer groups, needs served and technology employed.

3.4 A mission statement should not be too limiting; it should indicate the scope of future developments. A clear mission statement enables future growth strategies to rely on distinctive competences and to aim for synergies by dealing with similar customer groups, similar customer needs or similar service technologies. It would be insufficient for a bank to identify its mission as being 'banking' - it would be more appropriate to identify that mission as being, for example, 'meeting consumer needs for financial transactions.'

3.5 If mission statements are too narrow they tend to blinker management thinking. British Rail were accused of getting the mission statement wrong for decades in seeing themselves as being in the business of 'running a rail network'. Their image of their business, it is claimed, resulted in failure to respond strategically to the development of motorways, the growth of car ownership and the developing domestic airline network.

3.6 Arguably, it would have been more appropriate to see themselves as being in the business of 'transporting people and freight throughout Britain', since this would have given them a different view of threats and opportunities.

3.7 A good mission statement should be concise. It should clearly answer the question, 'what business are we in?'. Financial or profit dimensions can be left out as these are contained much more specifically in the corporate objectives.

Part A: The marketing planning process: an overview

Statement of objectives

3.8 Objectives are part of the planning process **both at the corporate and at the market level**. Corporate objectives define **specific goals for the organisation as a whole**. This may be expressed in such terms as profitability, return on investment, growth of asset base and earnings per share. They will permeate the planning process and be reflected in the objectives for marketing and other functional plans.

3.9 Clearly, the objectives specified for marketing will be subordinate to those specified at the corporate level. An important component of the marketing planning process is the translation of corporate (often financial) objectives into **market specific marketing objectives**. Examples are targets for the size of the customer base, growth in the usage of certain facilities, gains in market share for a particular product type. Any objectives must conform to three criteria; they must be **achievable**, they must be **consistent** and they must be **stated clearly** and preferably quantitatively.

Primary and secondary objectives

3.10 Although profitability must be the primary objective for a profit-making commercial organisation, there are different ways of measuring profitability. *Argenti* cited the creation of customers, servicing society, providing employment and maximising profits as various objectives, and concluded that an objective must be expressed in a particular way.

- It must identify the beneficiaries.
- It must state what the nature of the benefit is to be.
- It must state the size of the benefit.

3.11 When a company sets itself a **primary objective** such as growth in profits, it will then have to develop **strategies** by which this primary objective can be achieved. An objective must then be set for each individual strategy. Many **secondary objectives** may simply be targets by which the success of a strategy can be measured.

Trade-off between objectives

3.12 When there are several strategic objectives, some might be achieved only at the expense of others. For example, a company's objective of achieving increased turnover might have adverse consequences for cash flow.

3.13 In a trade-off between secondary objectives when strategies are formulated, a choice will have to be made. Secondary objectives will range from short-term to long-term and there might be a need to make trade offs between short-term and long-term objectives.

3.14 **Managerial performance is usually judged by short-term achievements.**

- Middle and senior management are criticised if they do not achieve budgetary aims.
- The board of directors of a public company are expected to achieve a certain growth in profits and EPS each year. Failing this, the share price will be marked down, and the board will be criticised for poor corporate results.

3.15 The emphasis on short-term achievements creates pressure for managers to **sacrifice longer term aims** in order to achieve short-term targets. Ideally, an organisation should try to control such trade-offs, to ensure that the most suitable decisions are taken in each situation.

1: Conducting a marketing audit

> **Action Programme 1**
> Give examples of decisions which might be made to achieve short-term objectives at the expense of long-term objectives.

Situation analysis

> **Key Concept**
> **Situation analysis** involves a thorough study of the broad trends within the economy and society, and a comprehensive analysis of markets, consumers, competitors and the company itself.

3.16 Environmental factors will affect the mission statement and the identification of objectives, but once strategic objectives are established, a much more comprehensive analysis is necessary as a basis for overall and market specific strategies. This analysis is considered further in the remaining parts of this chapter.

Strategy development

3.17 The process of strategy development links corporate level plans and market level plans. In developing strategy, most large organisations will be required to make important **resource allocation** decisions. This process of resource allocation is a key component of corporate strategy and it indicates the direction in which specific markets or products are expected to develop. It therefore provides direction for the development of **market level plans**.

Specific plans

3.18 **Market specific plans** express the organisation's intentions concerning particular markets, or in some cases, particular products. These are linked to the corporate plan through the statement of objectives and the resource allocation component in strategy development. Situation analysis at the market level can provide information on patterns of competition, consumer behaviour and market segmentation, as an input to the development of marketing objectives and market specific strategies.

3.19 Market specific variables, typically under the control of the marketing department, are product, price, promotion and place. The development of the marketing mix aims to ensure that the product is appropriate to the market in terms of its features, its image, its perceived value and its availability.

3.20 Marketing expenditure will depend on resource allocation decisions at corporate levels, but any marketing plan will include, as a matter of course, a statement of the budget required and the way it is to be spent.

Implementation

3.21 This involves identifying the specific tasks to be performed, the allocation of those tasks to individuals and putting in place a system of control. The implementation procedure may also include some elements of contingency planning. The market is always evolving so even the most well formed marketing plan will need to be changed and certain planned activities may turn out to be inappropriate or ineffective.

Part A: The marketing planning process: an overview

Marketing at Work

The launch of Mars Light

'Chocolate confectionery manufacturers spent £89 million last year convincing consumers to buy their products. It worked and the UK spent £3.4 bn on everything from Kit-Kat to Mars Bar and Cadbury's new great hope the Fuse Bar - a five per cent year on year growth.

This is substantial growth in a market which has changed little in 20 years. The top 20 brands would be familiar to anybody who had spent the past two decades in outer space. This has led to perennial accusations of a lack of innovation in the market.

Now one of those manufacturers - one which has always prided itself on full-blooded, full-fat chocolate bars - is entering virgin territory to launch a low-fat Mars Bar, Mars Light. The official Mars line is that the technology now exists to produce a low-fat bar that can deliver the same taste as the main brand.

"Mars never said that it would not enter the low-fat market on principle", says a Mars source, "but it has not previously been able to deliver the values of the top-selling brand in a low-fat format. Now it can."

Cynical observers suggest that it is a desperate move by Mars to stimulate the Mars Bar, which has been losing market share in recent years from six per cent in 1994 to 5.6 per cent last year, according to IRI Infoscan. Advertising support behind the brand has also been reduced. Critics accuse the company of lacking "real ideas" and instead taking the easy option of extending a brand, risking cannibalisation of the main brand, or worse, undermining its positioning, rather than launching a new one.

All of which Mars denies. "**Mars is always looking for new product ideas to extend the market - the total sector is continuing to grow in a difficult climate where people appear to have traditional tastes,**" says Mars head of external relations Gordon Storey. "We would not be launching Mars Light if we were simply going to steal consumers from the main brand."

If you look at the success it has had with Milky Way Lite, the US version of Mars Light, and the growth in the low-fat confectionery market, Mars may be making a wise move. It is also significant that the Mars Bar is the first mainstream countline brand to move into the low-fat sector.

"This is a colossal opportunity," says one source who has worked closely with Mars in the past. "Mars is a commercial company that will not let dogma get in the way of exploiting a good marketing opportunity. The brand was built on the 'work, rest and play' slogan but the tag has become iconic and the brand will not be damaged by moving away from either the tag or developing a low-fat variant." Mars Light will be launched in regional tests after Easter. If successful, it will be rolled out nationally later this year.'

Marketing Week, January 31 1997

4 SITUATION ANALYSIS - AN INTRODUCTION

4.1 Corporate situation analysis considers the company's resources and performance and the environment in which it exists. A resource audit needs to consider how well or how badly resources are being used, and whether or not the organisation's systems are efficient.

4.2 **Corporate resources** are sometimes described as the **five Ms**.

- **Men and women:** its human resources and organisation
- **Money:** its financial health
- **Materials:** supply sources and products
- **Machines:** the production facilities, its fixed assets, capacity etc
- **Markets:** its reputation, position and market prospects

4.3 In addition to this list it is also necessary to remember the less obvious **intangibles** like goodwill, brand names, patents, trademarks and development work in progress.

1: Conducting a marketing audit

> **Action Programme 2**
>
> For each of the five Ms identified above, give examples of the types of question which you would wish to ask in order to obtain information for use in an internal analysis.

4.4 The company's capabilities and performance must also be considered. Together with the audit of resources, these items make up the **internal appraisal**.

4.5 Every organisation operates under resource constraints. A **limiting factor** is anything which limits the activity of an entity. An entity seeks to optimise the benefit it obtains from the limiting factor. Finance seems always in limited supply, but there could well be other other factors which restrict the effective use of what finance is available.

- Shortages of suitable plant, skilled labour or raw materials
- A restricted distribution network which may be inadequate for a national market coverage
- Inadequate design and development capacity

4.6 In strategic planning, once limiting factors have been identified, planners need to develop plans which make use of the resources that are actually available, in order to counter this problem.

External factors

4.7 Environmental analysis is a consideration of what factors in the **external environment are relevant**, in conjunction with a realistic assessment of **how the external environment is changing**.

> **Exam Tip**
>
> A June 1997 question asked how a group of friends interested in model aircraft can turn their hobby into a genuine marketing opportunity for custom-made remote control cars. You were asked to relate the group's strengths and weaknesses to the marketing opportunity.
> A good approach is to identify and list what you consider to be all the critical areas for *any* company seeking to exploit a new marketing opportunity. Using this as a checklist so that you miss nothing out, you can note the strengths and weaknesses in each of these areas side by side. You could have adopted the sort of report format shown at the end of Section 5. (For example, what are the firm's strengths and weaknesses in marketing research?)
> For really good marks, identify which strengths and weaknesses are most important. You will show the examiner that you are able to prioritise.

5 USING SWOT ANALYSIS   6/98

5.1 Information about the current position and environment needs to be *assessed*. One of the most useful tools for sorting and analysing information is a **SWOT analysis. SWOT stands for strengths, weaknesses, opportunities and threats**. SWOT analysis is a management tool which can be used in a wide variety of situations. *Its value is as a technique to help you sort information* and it does not, in itself, provide ready made answers.

- **Strengths and weaknesses analysis** involves looking at the organisation itself and its product/service range. It is an **internal appraisal**.
- An analysis of **opportunities and threats** is concerned with the business environment.

Part A: The marketing planning process: an overview

Effective SWOT analysis does not simply require a categorisation of information, but also requires some *evaluation* of the relative importance of the various factors.

> **Action Programme 3**
>
> Give a brief explanation of what is meant by each of the four terms represented by the acronym SWOT.

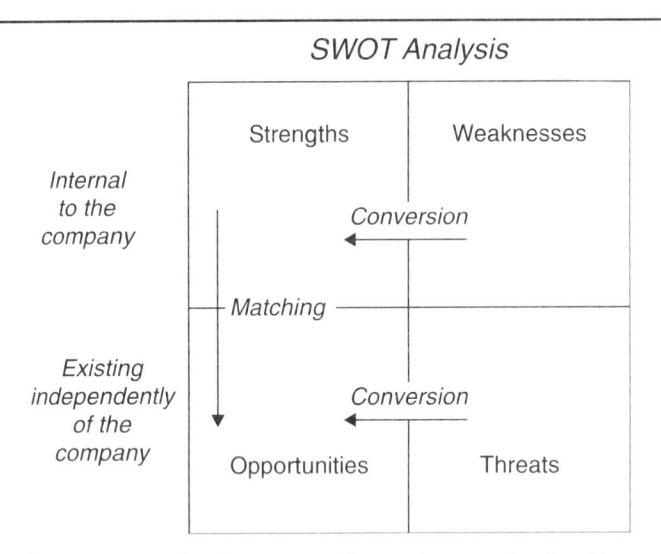

SWOT Analysis

	Strengths	Weaknesses
Internal to the company	↓	← Conversion
	— Matching —	
Existing independently of the company	↓	← Conversion
	Opportunities	Threats

5.2 SWOT analysis is often presented using a cruciform chart, as in the diagram above.

6 INTERNAL APPRAISAL

6.1 An **internal appraisal** seeks to identify the following.

(a) **Strengths** which the company should seek to exploit.
(b) **Weaknesses** in the company's present skills and resources.

6.2 **Aspects of the internal appraisal**

(a) **A study of past accounts and the use of ratios**. By looking at **trends**, or by comparing ratios (if possible) with those of other firms in a similar industry, it might be possible to identify strengths and weaknesses in major areas of the business.

(b) **Product position and product-market mix.** Existing products and those in a late stage of development should be reviewed for market performance and potential. the overall balance of the product portfolio should be considered.

(c) **Cash and financial structure**. If a company intends to expand or diversify, it will need cash to acquire subsidiaries or for investing in new capacity.

(d) **Cost structure**. If a company operates **with high fixed costs and relatively low variable costs**, high volumes of production and sale might be required to break even. In contrast, a company with low fixed costs should be able to operate at a lower breakeven point.

(e) **Managerial ability**. Management may well overestimate their own ability or be unable to form a useful evaluation.

6.3 Typically, the analysis would use information from all areas of company activity.

(a) **Marketing**
- Success rate of new product launches
- Advertising: evaluating advertising strategies and individual campaigns
- Market shares and sizes: is the organisation in a strong or weak position?
- Portfolio of business units: new, growth, mature and declining markets
- Sales force organisation and performance
- Service quality
- Customer care strategies: nature of markets targeted

(b) **Products**
- Sales by market, area, product groups, outlets
- Margins and contributions to profits from individual products
- Product quality
- Product portfolio: age and structure of markets
- Price elasticity of demand and price sensitivity of demand for products

(c) **Distribution**
- Delivery service standards - lead times for competitors and products
- Warehouse delivery fleet capacity
- Geographical availability of products

(d) **Research and development (R & D)**
- R & D projects in relation to marketing plans
- Expenditure on R & D relative to available assets
- Evaluation of R & D in new products/variations on existing products
- Appropriateness of R & D workload and schedules to competitor activity

(e) **Finance**
- Availability of short term and long term funds, cash flow
- Contribution of each product to cash flow
- Returns on investment from individual products
- Accounting ratios to identify areas of strength or weakness in performance

(f) **Plant, equipment and other facilities**
- Age, value, production capacity and suitability of plant and equipment
- Valuation of all assets
- Land and buildings: location, value, area, use, length of lease, book value
- Achievement of 'critical mass' of output capacity (economies of scale)
- Asset evaluation: age, condition, quality

(g) **Management and staff**
- Age profile
- Skills and attitudes
- State of industrial relations, morale and labour turnover
- Training and recruitment facilities
- Manpower utilisation
- Management team strengths and weaknesses

(h) **Organisation**
- Organisation structure in relation to the organisation's needs
- Appropriateness of management style and philosophy
- Communication and information systems

Part A: The marketing planning process: an overview

(i) **Raw material and finished goods stocks**

- The sources and security of supply
- Number and description of items
- Turnover periods
- Storage capacity
- Obsolescence and deterioration
- Pilfering, wastage

6.4 The analysis of opportunities and threats involves the following.

- The environment within which the firm operates
- The profit-making potential of the organisation
- The capacity of the organisation to exploit identified opportunities
- Strength of competition and its capacity to exploit opportunities

6.5 The opportunities might involve product development, market development, market penetration or diversification. Realism is particularly important in the evaluation process.

Action Programme 4

Give examples of political, economic, social and technological factors which might offer opportunities or be a source of threats.

Marketing at Work

Ericsson

'People want new phones and they buy Nokia. Ericsson doesn't have anything particularly new available,' mumbles a salesman in a mobile telephone store in one of Stockholm's more upmarket shopping districts.

Such comments are not new to Ericsson's Sven-Christer Nilsson. After a year as chief executive of the Swedish telecommunications equipment maker, he is having to live with the consequences of what analysts say is the company's failure to read the mobile handset market.

After reporting strong quarterly profits growth for 16 consecutive quarters, it was the quietly spoken Mr Nilsson who had to announce this year that the upward trend had broken in the fourth quarter of 1998.

Last week his task was even bleaker. While rival Nokia of Finland reported a near-doubling of profits, Ericsson had to admit that its profits had halved. Moreover, the company warned that it did not expect full-year earnings per share to reach the same level as in 1998.

The immediate cause of the problem was pinpointed as a drop in sales and profits of its mobile handset division. Even though volumes increased by 37 per cent, Ericsson products slipped inexorably down-market and were unable to extract the premium margins enjoyed by Nokia.

Mr Nilsson says the weak result has been caused by the nature of the mobile phone product life cycle, with an ageing model range sliding down to the middle and lower segment of the market. 'To me it is not acceptable to have this result, but at least we know why. There will be shorter product cycles in the future,' he said.

Bo Edvardsson, an analyst with Fischer Partners, said: 'Primarily he is paying for old sins he took over. The problem is that Ericsson did not have the urgency it needed in the handset business.'

Nicholas George, Financial Times, 27 April 1999

Example: report

6.6 In the next two sections, we look at macro-environmental and micro-environmental factors in more detail, but first, here is an example of the type of report which might be produced following the environmental analysis.

Strengths

(a) Marketing, products and markets
- Products A, B and C are market leaders
- Product D, new product launch, high profit potential
- Good brand images
- Good relations with suppliers and dealers
- Good packaging and advertising appeal

(b) Production
- New factory in North West, fully operational for next year
- Thorough quality inspection standards

(c) Finance
- £0.5 million cash available from internal resources
- Further £2.0 million overdraft facility, so far unused

(d) Management and staff
- High skills in marketing areas of packaging, sales promotion, advertising and sales generally
- Good labour relations, except at one plant which has low productivity

Weaknesses

(a) Marketing
- Products X, Y and Z contribute no profit.
- Products P, Q and R are declining and will lose profitability in three years.
- Sales of product D are dependent upon a high level of sales of complementary products (for example razor blades and razors).
- No new products, except for D, have been successfully launched in the last two years.

(b) Research and development
- No major new products have been derived from R & D for two years. Becoming too dependent on acquisition for additions to product range
- Little control over R & D budget

(c) Production
- Plant at most factories has an average age of 8.7 years
- New developments could threaten ability to compete
- High level of spoiled goods on lines 3, 7, 9 at one location
- Low productivity on all lines at one plant

(d) Management and staff
- Poor labour relations at plant with low productivity
- Senior executives approaching retirement with no clearly recognisable successor
- Success of the organisation too dependent on senior executive charisma

Opportunities

(a) Political
- Deregulation of the distribution market in the UK has allowed competitors to enter the marketplace, previously the domain of the state-owned monopoly supplier. This increases our range of potential customers in the UK and makes us less dependent on exports
- Removal of EU trade barriers has increased the size of the marketplace

Part A: The marketing planning process: an overview

- Expansion into Eastern Europe will enable access into new markets

(b) Economic
- Relatively weak state of sterling is helping exports
- UK economy coming out of recession, so customer confidence ('feel-good factor') improving

(c) Social
- We have an excellent 'green' image already and can capitalise on this. Our reliance on US markets has contributed to our being well ahead in this area
- We are well thought of as a local employer through our attention to social responsibility issues

(d) Technological issues
- Our new marketing database will allow good targeting of customers, especially as new companies set up following deregulation
- UK/US standards are being adopted in Asian markets, so we can compete there with existing products

(e) Competition
- Our reputation as a key supplier of the former state-owned monopoly gives us a head start against new start-up competitors

Threat

(a) Political
- Lack of agreement on standardisation across Europe means that French/German derived standard may be adopted in preference to ours (UK/US agreed).
- Black market in certain Eastern European states needs to be overcome in some way, given our ethical stance.
- Uncertainty in run up to UK general election will affect the development of the sector in the UK.

(b) Economic
- Any strengthening of sterling resulting from improvement of UK economic position will make exports less attractive on price alone.
- Increased competition from suppliers based on Pacific Rim makes it difficult for us to compete on price there and in the US.

(c) Social
- Increased focus on health and safety from EU is increasing cost of compliance and related overheads.
- Cost of maintaining green image, important in UK and US, will damage our potential in Eastern Europe where some competitors (and customers) are unconcerned with such issues.

(d) Technological
- Our main competitors control their distribution process more fully than we do in this area, as they have invested in new computer systems.

(e) Competition
- The two competitors to the former state-owned monopoly which were awarded licences first have merged, thereby pooling their R&D resource. There are suggestions that they will develop or buy their own manufacturing operation rather than buy from companies like us.

7 ENVIRONMENTAL ANALYSIS - THE MACRO-ENVIRONMENT

12/97, 6/99, 12/99

> **Key Concept**
> The **business environment** comprises all the economic, political, social, cultural, legal, technological and demographic influences acting on the markets within which the organisation operates. It also encompasses influences on customers and the behaviour of competitors in these markets. All these factors have an impact on the performance of the organisation, but cannot be controlled by management actions.

7.1 'The essence of formulating competitive strategy is relating a company to its environment .... Every industry has an underlying structure or set of fundamental economic and technical characteristics ... The strategist must learn what makes the environment tick.'

(Porter, Competitive Strategy)

The wider macro-environment may be analysed under the headings below

- Political
- Economic
- Social
- Technological

The mnemonic is PEST.

The political environment

7.2 The political environment includes the **legal environment**, which is dealt with below.

7.3 **Other areas under political influence in a mixed economy.**

- The government **controls** much of the economy, being the nation's largest supplier, employer, customer and investor. The aerospace and defence industries are particularly vulnerable to shifts in political decisions.
- **Nationalism** can impact in various ways. Shipping and airline industries have been affected as many countries build up their own fleets. Other effects include resistance to the power exercised by multinationals in some countries, and policies which insist on nationals being given positions of responsibility where multinational companies are operating.

Political change

7.4 Changes in political ideology have profound implications for business. For example, in the UK under 'Thatcherism', small business enterprise and competition were championed. Public sector firms were privatised and services put out to competitive tender. Wide ranging changes affected many business sectors.

7.5 **Political factors**

- The possible impact of political change on the organisation
- The likelihood of change taking place and the possible need for contingency plans
- What needs to be done to cope with the change ('scenario planning')

7.6 **The legal system** may be though of as part of the political environment. It lays down the framework for business with rules about business structure and ownership, such as the Companies Act. It regulates business relationships with contract law and guarantees individual rights with employment law. There is a wide range of regulations dealing with

Part A: The marketing planning process: an overview

general business activities such as health and safety regulations, rules about emissions into the environment and planning regulations.

Marketing at Work

Opportunities

Until the mid-1980s, the US gas industry was regulated and comfortable. The regulatory framework had created a monopoly franchise where gas and pipeline companies were almost guaranteed a healthy return on their investments.

So when the government set out to remove price controls, most of the interstate pipeline companies fought the loss of local monopolies.

But Enron, the Houston energy company, saw an opportunity. Instead of fighting deregulation, it explored what would happen if the market moved to a flexible system.

True, interstate pipelines would lose local monopolies, reducing the value of their local pipelines. But deregulation would also mean gas could be purchased from anywhere in the country and sold anywhere else. At the time, the cost of gas varied dramatically: it was much more expensive in New York and California than in Oregon and Idaho.

Enron set out to create the first national market for gas, allowing it to buy gas where it was cheap and sell it where it was expensive. It worked with government agencies to push for deregulation. It then purchased regional gas pipelines across the US, to create a national network.

That allowed Enron to buy the lowest cost gas from numerous sources across North America and to operate with the best spreads in the industry. Enron became the largest transporter of natural gas in North America, and its customers benefited from more reliable delivery and a price reduction of up to 40 per cent.

All industries, from traditional to modern, are subject to external trends that emerge over time. Think of the rise of the internet, the migration from mainframes to servers, the global movement toward protecting the environment, or pressures for deregulation in transport, telecommunications and utilities.

These changes shape the industrial landscape and are powerful sources of new market space. Yet many companies respond incrementally and passively as events unfold. Some even fight to stop the arrival of a new reality, as Enron's competitors did.

To profit from change - rather than be its victim - companies must use these trends to unlock value. The key is not to focus on projecting the trend itself, as many managers tend to do, but to assess how the trend will change the value a company is able to deliver to customers. Cisco Systems recognised that the world was hampered by slow data exchanges and incompatible computer networks. Demand for network computing was exploding, especially as the internet took off and the number of web users doubled roughly every 100 days. So Cisco could clearly see that the problem of slow data exchanges and incompatible computer systems would inevitably worsen.

To get ahead of this trend, Cisco designed routers, switches and other networking devices that offered customers fast data exchanges in a seamless computing environment. Today, more than 80 per cent of internet traffic flows through Cisco products, and its margins in this new market are in the 60 per cent range.

Financial Times, 10 June 1999

The economic environment

7.7 The general state of the economy influences prospects for all businesses. Generally, economic growth produces a benign environment with healthy demand for most goods and services.

7.8 Regional variations in growth rate will result in **differential demand**. If growth is accompanied by an increase in the size of the public sector, funded by higher taxation, then increased demand may manifest itself in public sector areas, such as demand for new school buildings, roads or more police cars.

1: Conducting a marketing audit

7.9 Economic influences

- The rate of inflation
- Unemployment and the availability of manpower
- Interest rates
- The balance of trade and foreign exchange rates
- The level and type of taxation
- The propensity to save within the community
- The availability of credit

Action Programme 5

Give examples of economic influences at an *international* level.

7.10 Increased demand during periods of expansion will create a planning need to satisfy demand. In times of recession, contracting demand will place the emphasis on cost-effectiveness, continuing profitability, survival and competition. The strategic planning process depends heavily on economic forecasts and information about economic trends.

Economic trends - regional, national and international

7.11 Three levels of economic trend analysis need to be considered; regional (area) trends, national trends and international trends.

7.12 The **local** geographical environment is important, whether it is in a growth area full of modern thriving commerce, such as Milton Keynes, or an area of decay. This will affect wage rates, availability of labour, disposable income of local consumers, and the provision of roads and other services.

7.13 Relevant **national** economic trends may include the prospects for growth, price inflation, unemployment, international trade, the balance of payments and taxation levels.

7.14 These must be located within the context of **world trends**. These can have an important influence on the future of any company with plans to trade abroad, whether in buying imports or selling as exporters. More and more markets are being opened to international competition, throughout Europe and also in the rest of the world.

7.15 EXAMPLE

The European Union has been implementing a single market. These changes have a number of implications.

(a) Many **technical barriers** to the free movement of goods between countries in the EU have been removed. Barriers are created by differences in areas such as product safety standards and food laws, for example on food labelling.

(b) EU rules open up the market for **goods purchased by governments** of member countries, by making sure that all companies in the Community have an equal chance to seek individual public contracts.

Part A: The marketing planning process: an overview

(c) Harmonisation measures in the provision of **financial services** include common regulations for banks and banking activities and removal of barriers preventing the provision of cross-border insurance services.

(d) Measures are being taken to liberalise **transport services**, so as to increase competition. Liberalisation measures are being applied to road haulage, shipping and civil aviation.

7.16 Before the Single European Market a domestic UK firm had a home market of some 56 million people but since 31 December 1992 it has grown to 350 million. The single market is still developing; for example, aviation has only been deregulated recently.

The social environment

7.17 Social change involves changes in the nature, attitudes and habits of society. Social changes are continually happening, and **trends** can be identified.

- **Rising standards of living** may result in wider ownership of items like automatic dishwashers, microwave ovens, compact disk players and sailing boats.
- **Society's changing attitude to business** tends to increase companies' obligations and responsibilities with respect to environmental protection and ethical conduct.
- An increasing proportion of people are employed in clerical, supervisory or management jobs.

Cultural changes

7.18 Cultural variables are particularly significant for marketing in foreign countries. Some cultural factors are shown on the chart on the following page.

7.19 Language differences have clear marketing implications. For example, brand names have to be translated, often leading to entirely different (and sometimes embarrassing) meanings in the new language.

7.20 Cultural differences may affect business in a variety of ways.

- Design of goods
- Trading hours
- Distribution methods

1: Conducting a marketing audit

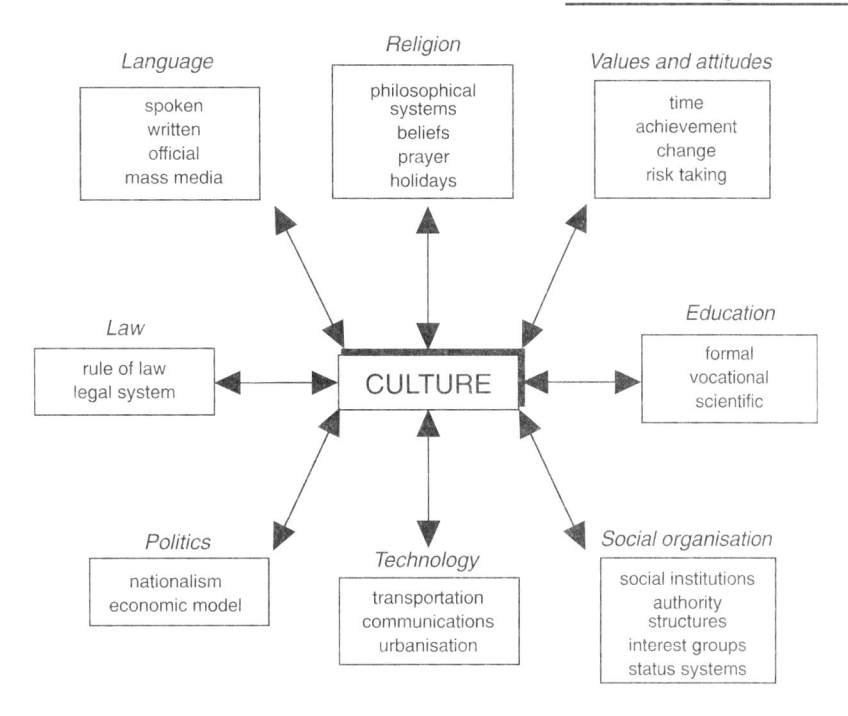

```
    Language              Religion          Values and attitudes
   ┌─────────┐       ┌──────────────┐       ┌──────────────┐
   │ spoken  │       │ philosophical│       │    time      │
   │ written │       │   systems    │       │ achievement  │
   │ official│       │   beliefs    │       │   change     │
   │mass media│      │   prayer     │       │ risk taking  │
   └─────────┘       │   holidays   │       └──────────────┘
                     └──────────────┘
                            
      Law                                         Education
   ┌─────────┐                                 ┌──────────┐
   │rule of law│ ◄───────► CULTURE ◄─────────► │  formal  │
   │legal system│                              │vocational│
   └─────────┘                                 │scientific│
                                               └──────────┘
    Politics              Technology           Social organisation
   ┌─────────┐       ┌──────────────┐       ┌─────────────────┐
   │nationalism│     │transportation│       │social institutions│
   │economic model│  │communications│       │    authority     │
   └─────────┘       │ urbanisation │       │    structures    │
                     └──────────────┘       │  interest groups │
                                            │   status systems │
                                            └─────────────────┘
```

The impact of culture

Socio-economic groups

7.21 Marketing interest stems from the observable fact that members of particular groups have similar lifestyles, beliefs and values which affect their purchasing behaviour. Socio-economic classification involves taking factors such as occupation, education and income into account.

Family

7.22 Family background is a very strong influence on purchasing behaviour. Family structure is changing in most of the developed world. There are more single person and single parent households due to increased divorce rate and population ages. The traditional nuclear family represents a relatively small proportion of all families.

The technological environment

7.23 **How technological change has affected business.**

- **The type of products or services that are made and sold.** Within consumer markets we have seen the emergence of home computers and internet services; industrial markets have seen the emergence of robots, new databases and teleworking.

- **The way in which products are made.** Modern automated systems of design and manufacture have revolutionised manufacturing.

- **The way in which services are provided.** Call centres and internet trading have expanded widely.

- **The way in which markets are identified.** Database systems make it easier to analyse the market place. New types of marketing strategy, and new organisational structures, have been developed.

Part A: The marketing planning process: an overview

7.24 The effects of technological change are wide-ranging.

- Cuts in costs may afford the opportunity to reduce prices.
- The development of better quality products and services provides greater satisfaction.
- Products and services that did not exist before.

Marketing at Work

Advertising

'This year will be an important one for Europe's advertising industry as agencies and marketers take stock of the rapid developments that are reshaping commercial communications.

The past few years have seen significant political, economic and legislative restructuring across the continent. At the same time, the information revolution has continued to grab headlines, with Internet development and digitalisation becoming major preoccupations.

Europe's advertising industry will undoubtedly be transformed by these forces. But the question of how the new technology can best be used to generate genuine communications benefits for clients and worthwhile levels of revenue for agencies remains unresolved.

Although less obviously newsworthy than the Internet, these closed communications systems will revolutionise the international communications activities of all major multinational companies and transform the information flow between agencies and their clients.

They should allow regional and global networks to forge closer internal communications links and pave the way to more durable cross-border client/agency relationships.

Marketing Week, January 24 1997

---

8 ENVIRONMENTAL ANALYSIS - THE MICRO-ENVIRONMENT 12/97

8.1 An analysis of the company's particular markets may be set within the context of the wider environment. This micro-environmental analysis concentrates on customers and competitors.

The nature of competition is a key element in the environment of commercial organisations. There are four main issues.

- Identifying the competitors
- The strength of the competition
- Characteristics of the market
- The likely strategies and responses of competitors to the organisation's strategies

8.2 **Intensity of competition** within an industry will affect the profitability of the industry as a whole. Intensity of competition is related to three main factors.

(a) **Whether there is a large number of equally balanced competitors**. Markets involving a large number of firms are likely to be very competitive, but when the industry is dominated by a small number of larger firms, competition is likely to be less intense.

(b) **The rate of growth in the industry**. Fast growth is likely to benefit a larger number of firms, and so their rivalry will be less intense. Rivalry is intensified where growth is slow or stagnant.

(c) **Whether fixed costs are high**. If fixed costs are high, and variable costs are a relatively small proportion of the selling price, high volumes are necessary. It is tempting for firms to compete on price, even though this may mean a failure to cover fixed costs and make an adequate return in the longer run.

8.3 Competition can have effects ranging between two extremes.

(a) It may **help the industry expand**, stimulating demand for new products and advertising.

(b) It may **leave demand unchanged**, so that individual competitors will simply be spending more money, charging lower prices and so making lower profits. The only benefits involve maintaining market share

Competitive moves/response models

8.4 In competitive markets, firms are influenced by the actions of competitors and are likely both to respond and to take expected competitor responses into account in the formulation of their own strategy. Price wars often result in falling profits for all firms and the only group to benefit are the customers who gain the short-term advantage of lower prices.

8.5 Assessing the likely industry response is an important dimension in the process of strategic planning. Two aspects are important.

- What moves might others make and how will that affect our business?
- How might others react to our strategies?

8.6 *Porter* identifies three broad categories of competitor responses.

(a) **Neutral moves** cause no real offence, and are co-operative or at least non-threatening.

- **Hospitable moves** are visible but cause no real threat.
- **Blind spot moves** are not recognised or perceived to be important perhaps because the firm is not felt at that time to be real competition.

(b) **Offence moves** are calculated to improve the firm's position and therefore may well elicit a response from competitors.

- **Superior strength moves** come from a privileged position, for example, location or technical superiority. The firm must enjoy clear superiority for such an approach to be effective.
- **Asymmetric cost moves**, where matching the move involves a substantial cost. Firms may be prepared to make short-term losses to gain strategic advantage.

(c) **Defensive moves** are made to protect the firm's position, for instance preventing other firms actually entering into battle.

- **Readiness moves** are moves made in anticipation of competition.
- **Leverage moves** are moves made so that the firm is ready to retaliate should it be necessary.

Marketing at Work

Monitoring

The consequences of not monitoring can be illustrated with two examples. EverReady lost market leadership in the battery market by not monitoring and then reacting slowly to Duracell's alkaline product launch. Estimation of competitive retaliation was clearly not conducted by Cadbury's when they launched the Aztec bar against the might of Mars. Due to Mars' aggressive response, the launch failed.

Part A: The marketing planning process: an overview

Schemes for assessing competitors

8.7 *Wilson, Gilligan and Pearson* suggest five key questions for the initial assessment of competitors.

- Who are we competing against?
- What are their objectives?
- What strategies are they pursuing, with what success?
- What strengths and weaknesses do they possess?
- How are they likely to behave, especially to offensive moves?

8.8 Porter's **competitive response profile** looks in detail at an individual competitor.

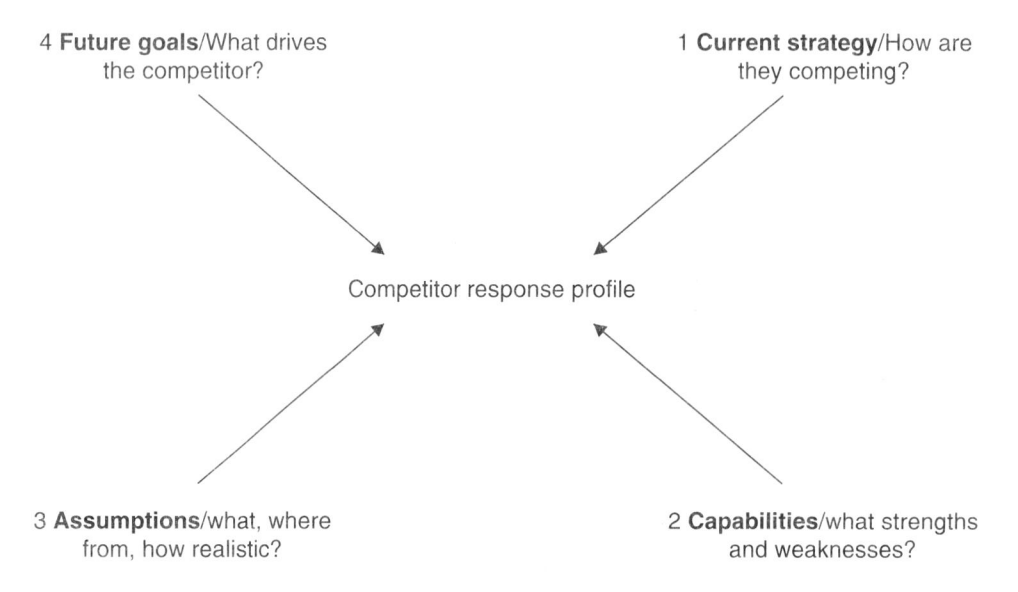

```
4 Future goals/What drives          1 Current strategy/How are
    the competitor?                      they competing?
                    ↘           ↙
              Competitor response profile
                    ↗           ↖
3 Assumptions/what, where           2 Capabilities/what strengths
    from, how realistic?                and weaknesses?
```

Understanding these four dimensions enables a detailed response profile to answer six key questions.

- Is the competitor satisfied with its current position?
- What moves is the competitor likely to make?
- In what segments is the competitor most vulnerable?
- What would provoke serious retaliation from this competitor?
- Where are we most vulnerable to attack from this competitor?
- What can we do to better defend ourselves?

Customer analysis

8.9 **Consumer behaviour** can be defined as the behaviour that consumers display in searching for, purchasing, using, evaluating and disposing of products. It provides the foundation knowledge which guides subsequent marketing strategy.

Factors affecting customer behaviour

8.10 A number of factors influence the consumer buying process.

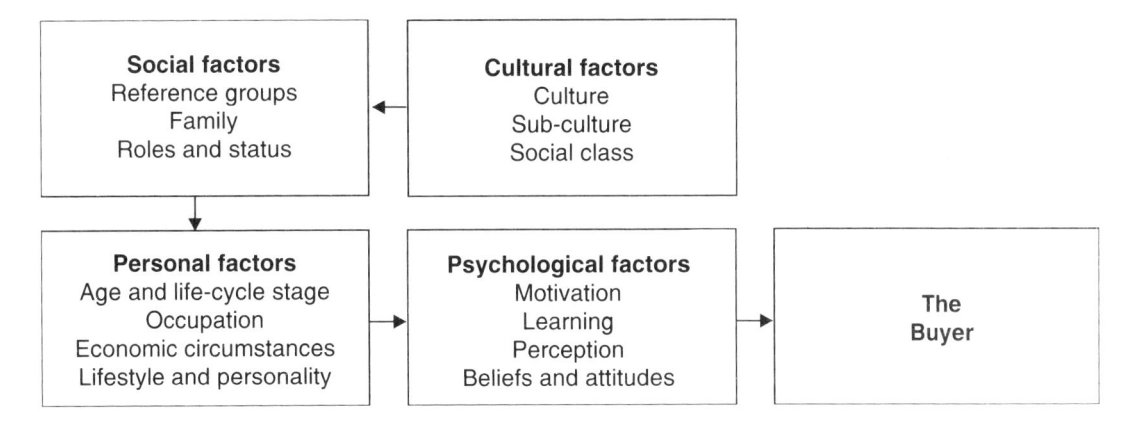

1: Conducting a marketing audit

```
┌─────────────────────────┐      ┌─────────────────────────┐
│     Social factors      │      │    Cultural factors     │
│    Reference groups     │ ◄────│        Culture          │
│         Family          │      │       Sub-culture       │
│    Roles and status     │      │      Social class       │
└───────────┬─────────────┘      └─────────────────────────┘
            │
            ▼
┌─────────────────────────┐      ┌─────────────────────────┐      ┌──────────────┐
│    Personal factors     │      │  Psychological factors  │      │              │
│ Age and life-cycle stage│      │       Motivation        │      │     The      │
│       Occupation        │ ────►│        Learning         │ ────►│    Buyer     │
│ Economic circumstances  │      │       Perception        │      │              │
│ Lifestyle and personality│     │  Beliefs and attitudes  │      │              │
└─────────────────────────┘      └─────────────────────────┘      └──────────────┘
```

8.11 **Cultural factors** exert the broadest and deepest influence on consumer behaviour. The culture in which we live, to a large extent, determines our **values, beliefs and perceptions**. **Buying behaviour** is also affected by subculture and social class. Mature consumers buy the majority of consumer durables and spend a large amount on financial services and leisure products. They also expect high levels of service and are generally more loyal if they receive this. Different social classes also display distinct brand preferences in areas such as clothing, decorative products and cars. Differences occur in media preferences and language which need to be considered in marketing communication strategy.

8.12 A consumer's behaviour is also influenced by **social factors**. People are influenced in their buying by the groups they are members of, called associate groups, and by the groups whose behaviour they reject, called disassociate groups. Marketers, in planning their target market strategy, should try to identify the reference groups and the key individuals whose behaviours and lifestyles are followed. For example, many football stars are used in advertising to appeal to the male youth market, Gary Lineker for *Walker's Crisps* and Eric Cantona for *Nike* products. Many people are influenced in their purchases by their colleagues at work and by membership groups outside of work. For example, the *Co-operative Bank* has attracted a number of environmentalists and members of the Liberal Democrats due to its 'green' positioning.

8.13 A buyer's decisions are also influenced by **personal factors**.

- One of the better known approached to market segmentation is *Wells and Gubar's* **family life cycle model**. This proposes that as we move through different phases of our lives, we buy different products and services and change out priorities.

- **Occupation** also influences consumption patterns.

- A person's **lifestyle** also influences what is deemed important to purchase, where they search for information on those goods; and how they make the purchase decision. For the seven lifestyle groups have been identified, including, Self Explorers, Conspicuous Consumers and Survivors.

8.14 Finally **psychological factors** such as motivation, learning, perception, beliefs and attitudes influences the consumer buying process.

8.15 A consumer's buying process is the result of the complex interplay of cultural, social, personal and psychological influences. The marketing planner is unable to influence many of these factors. They are useful, however, in segmentation terms and they can suggest how to develop a successful positioning concept and marketing mix to generate a strong and favourable consumer response.

Part A: The marketing planning process: an overview

Models of customer behaviour

8.16 Models attempt to express simply the fundamental elements of a complex process. They provide a means for the marketing manager to understand the buying process in order to develop strategies which fit the analysis. Here is an example of a well known theoretical model, the **Howard-Sheth model** of consumer behaviour.

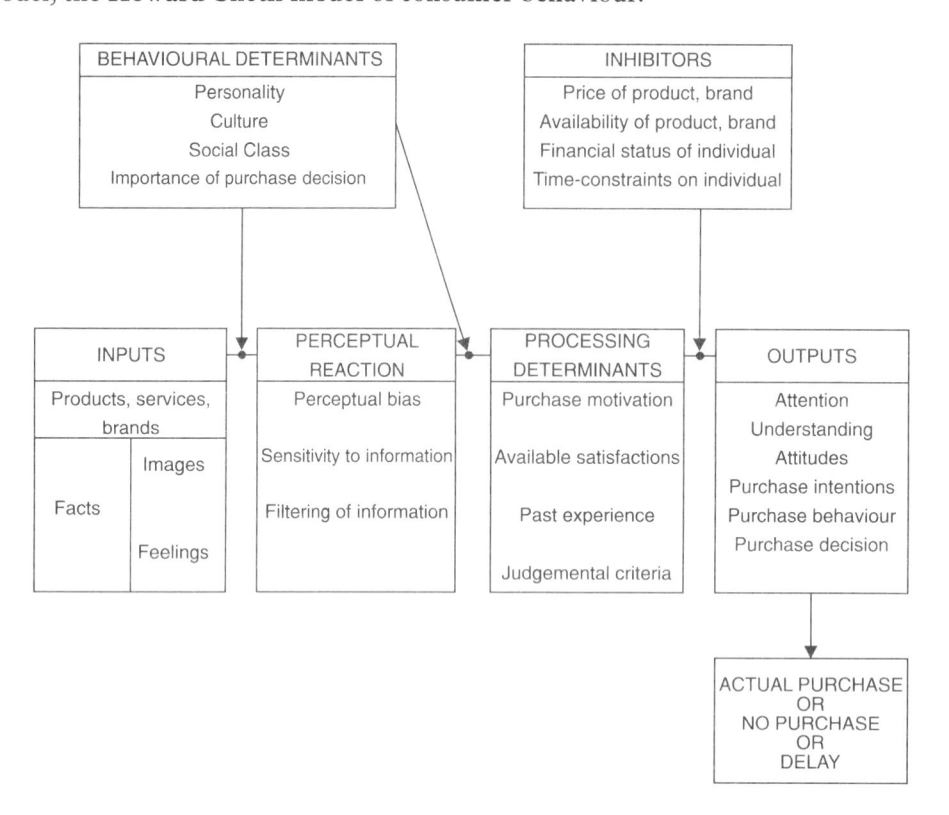

BEHAVIOURAL DETERMINANTS		INHIBITORS
Personality		Price of product, brand
Culture		Availability of product, brand
Social Class		Financial status of individual
Importance of purchase decision		Time-constraints on individual

INPUTS	PERCEPTUAL REACTION	PROCESSING DETERMINANTS	OUTPUTS
Products, services, brands	Perceptual bias	Purchase motivation	Attention
			Understanding
Images	Sensitivity to information	Available satisfactions	Attitudes
Facts			Purchase intentions
	Filtering of information	Past experience	Purchase behaviour
Feelings			Purchase decision
		Judgemental criteria	

ACTUAL PURCHASE
OR
NO PURCHASE
OR
DELAY

Exam Tip

Unlike many of the functions of the business, marketing is directed not inwards but outwards, towards the customer. Marketers therefore have to consider their **environment**.

Take the example of Daewoo, the subject of the 40-mark case study examined in December 1995. Part (a) of the mini-case offered you 10 marks to show why Daewoo's executives need to understand market trends and in (b) offered a further 15 marks to identify which parts of the marketing environment should be monitored most closely.

(Part (c) brought these issues into the marketing planning process, the subject of Chapter 3.)
So, how should you go about tackling this question?

In part (a), as well as baldly stating that the environment is important, you might like to say *why* each of the PEST and competition factors is significant to any company in the long term. For example, the ageing population has an impact on people's transport needs. In part (b) you can narrow the focus on to the specific short-term issues in the marketing environment (eg overcapacity in the car industry), which will affect Daewoo's decision in this case.

We have given you two sets of issues to construct your answer: time horizon (short and long term) and focus (*general* environmental factors, and their *specific* impact on Daewoo).

This topic also came up in June 1997 in the context of one of the shorter exam questions In this question, your wider commercial knowledge was tested: you had to identify an industry whose marketing environment had changed over the past five to ten years, and then show how the marketing mix of typical competitors had changed in response.

9 CONDUCTING A MARKETING AUDIT 12/97

9.1 Marketing management aims to ensure the company is pursuing effective policies to promote its products, markets and distribution channels. This involves exercising strategic control of marketing, and the means to apply strategic control is known as the **marketing audit**.

9.2 It is easy to confuse marketing planning with corporate planning. The following diagram illustrates the relation between planning at corporate level and marketing planning, and shows the position of the marketing audit.

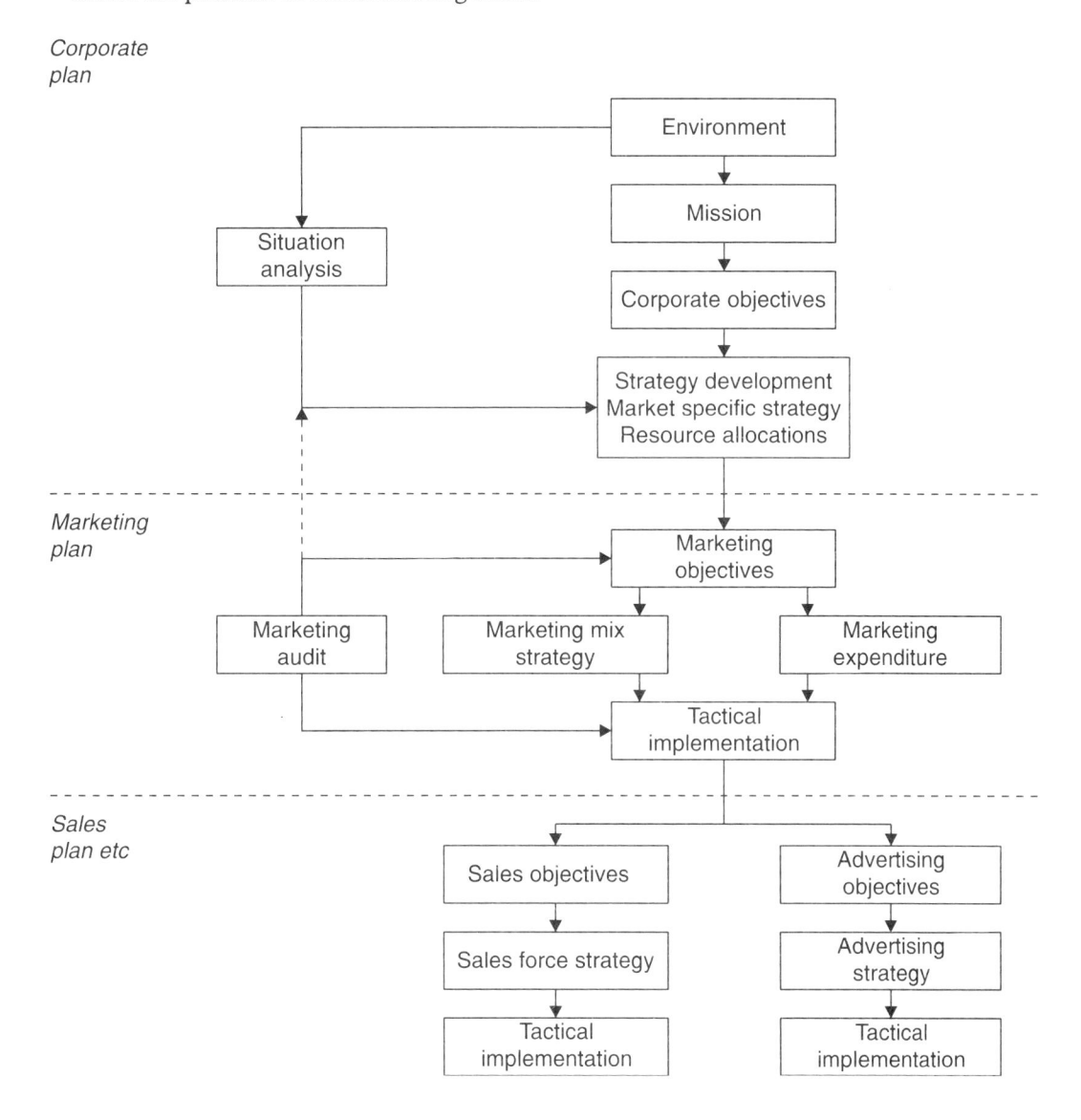

Corporate plan

```
                          Environment
                              │
                              ▼
                           Mission
       Situation              │
       analysis               ▼
                       Corporate objectives
                              │
                              ▼
                     Strategy development
                     Market specific strategy
                     Resource allocations
```

Marketing plan

```
                       Marketing
                       objectives
                           │
       Marketing    Marketing mix      Marketing
       audit        strategy           expenditure
                           │
                           ▼
                       Tactical
                       implementation
```

Sales plan etc

```
              Sales objectives           Advertising objectives
                    │                           │
                    ▼                           ▼
              Sales force strategy        Advertising strategy
                    │                           │
                    ▼                           ▼
              Tactical                    Tactical
              implementation              implementation
```

9.3 In order to exercise proper strategic control a marketing audit should satisfy four requirements.

- It should be conducted regularly.

- It should take a comprehensive look at every product, market, distribution channel and ingredient in the marketing mix.

- It should not be restricted to areas of apparent ineffectiveness such as an unprofitable product, a troublesome distribution channel, or low efficiency on direct selling.

- It should be carried out according to a set of predetermined, specified procedures.

Part A: The marketing planning process: an overview

The auditors should be independent of particular job and organisational interests.

The audit procedure

9.4 **Elements of the marketing audit**

(a) **The marketing environment**

- What are the organisation's major markets, and how are these markets segmented? How are these market segments likely to change?
- Who are our customers, what is known about their needs, intentions and behaviour?
- Who are our competitors, and what is known about them?
- Have there been any significant developments in the broader environment (eg economic or political changes, population or social changes).

(b) **Marketing objectives and plans**

- What are the organisation's marketing objectives with respect to its products or services and how do they relate to overall corporate objectives?
- Is the allocation of resources being committed to marketing sufficient to enable the objectives to be achieved? Are the costs arising between products, areas etc satisfactory?
- Is expenditure allocated to direct selling, advertising, distribution etc appropriate for the objectives being pursued?
- What procedures are in place for formulating marketing plans and exercising management control of these plans; are they satisfactory?
- Are marketing organisations (and personnel) operating efficiently?
- What lessons can be learned from the success or failure of past marketing plans?

(c) **Marketing activities and the marketing mix**

- A review of sales price levels (looking at, for example, supply, demand, customer attitudes, the use of temporary price reductions and value for money).
- A review of the state of each individual product and of the product mix as a whole including range, quality, competitive advantage, stage of the life cycle and technical reputation.
- A critical analysis of the distribution system including availability of the product, channels of distribution used, waiting lists and the availability of distribution services like credit for end users.
- A review of the size and organisation of the personal sales force.
- A review of the effectiveness of advertising and sales promotion activities including image and reputation of the organisation and various products and brands in the market place. Brand loyalty and corporate image.
- A review of aftersales service reputation for after sales customer care, provision of spare parts, servicing etc.

(d) **The marketing organisation** - marketing systems, organisation structure, degree of market orientation in the corporate philosophy and the quality of marketing information available, should all be taken into account.

1: Conducting a marketing audit

9.5 Amongst all this review procedure, the 4Ps of the marketing mix are the key controllable factors, and should be given central importance. The company's products' current market position may be mapped in terms of important variables such as price and quality.

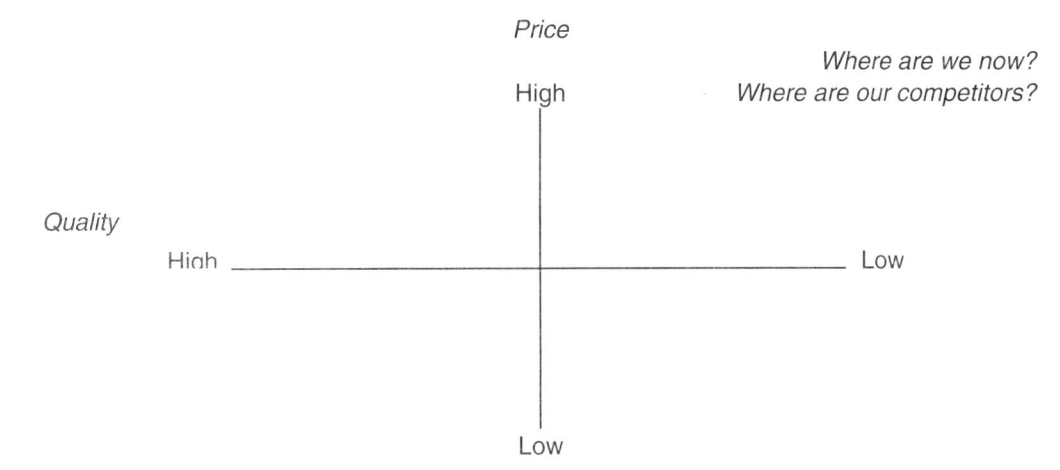

```
                    Price
                     |
                    High      Where are we now?
                     |        Where are our competitors?
                     |
   Quality           |
     High _____|_____ Low
                     |
                     |
                     |
                    Low
```

Several such maps could be constructed in order to consider the real position of a complex product. The variables used should be those recognised as having the greatest influence on purchasing decisions.

9.6 **External aspects of the marketing audit are the product/market opportunities and threats which evolve from changes in the macro environment identified at the corporate level.** For example, a demographic shift increasing the proportion of older customers for overseas holidays may have been identified in the environmental audit of a package holiday company. At marketing level this raises a number of possibilities.

- A marketing opportunity to sell existing holidays to this new target market
- A marketing opportunity to develop new products specifically developed to meet the needs of this emerging segment
- The option of diverting resources from segments showing less growth potential

9.7 The **Ansoff matrix** can provide a formulation of options and opportunities available. In relation to this example, the matrix reveals the following.

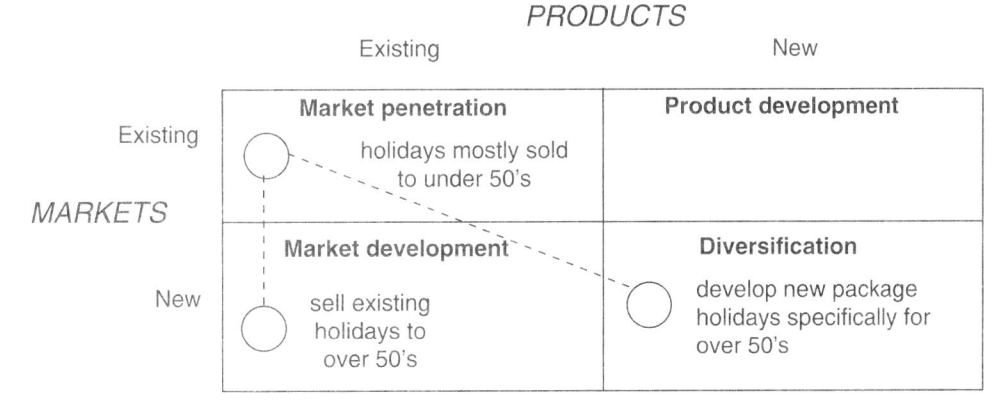

PRODUCTS

	Existing	New
Existing (MARKETS)	Market penetration — holidays mostly sold to under 50's	Product development
New	Market development — sell existing holidays to over 50's	Diversification — develop new package holidays specifically for over 50's

This is dealt with in detail later.

Action Programme 6

Now do the same exercise - identifying information required - for the *task environment* element.

Part A: The marketing planning process: an overview

> **Exam Tip**
>
> The marketing audit most recently came up in a shorter question in the June 1999 exam.
>
> It first appeared in a longer case study question in December 1994. In this question, you had to consider a marketing audit in the context of the company's wish to develop a new home entertainment system with other suppliers. The marketing audit was an input to the planning process. To answer this question successfully you had to consider the firm's marketing activities, its current marketing strategy, marketing organisation, systems, productivity and functions. Indeed, you could have used the contents of paragraph 6.3 above as a checklist.

> **Chapter Roundup**
>
> - The marketing audit is part of corporate planning and similar to the part of strategic planning which is called the situation analysis because it deals with similar information and problems. We have treated the marketing audit as part of marketing planning, that is to say, operational planning for the marketing function.
>
> - Strategic planning begins with the definition of the corporate mission. Strategic objectives are then set which support the mission. A detailed situation analysis follows. This has two main parts: the internal appraisal and the external appraisal. The latter deals with the very important forces making up the organisation's environment.
>
> - Marketing objectives will support and flow from the overall corporate strategic objectives. The marketing audit is a detailed analysis of marketing capacity and practice which enables the making of marketing plans. Marketing audits must be comprehensive and objective and should be carried out regularly.

> **Quick Quiz**
>
> 1. Define a mission statement. (3.1, Key concept)
> 2. How are typical corporate objectives expressed? (3.8)
> 3. Why is it difficult for a company to pursue long term aims effectively? (3.14, 3.15)
> 4. What are the 5 Ms? (4.2)
> 5. What is a limiting factor? (4.5)
> 6. What does SWOT stand for and what is its purpose? (5.1)
> 7. State six areas of marketing activity which would be examined during internal appraisal. (6.3)
> 8. What is the business environment? (7.1, Key concept)
> 9. State six economic influences on business. (7.9)
> 10. Summarise the effect of technological change on business. (7.23)
> 11. How did Porter analyse competitor responses? (8.6)
> 12. State a framework for a marketing audit. (9.4)
> 13. What are the axes of the Ansoff matrix? (9.7)

Action Programme Review

1. Typical examples of decisions which sacrifice longer term objectives.

    - Postponing or abandoning capital expenditure projects, which would eventually contribute to (longer term) growth and profits, in order to protect short term cash flow and profits

    - Cutting R&D expenditure to save operating costs, and so reducing the prospects for future product development

    - Reducing quality control, to save operating costs

    - Reducing the level of customer service, to save operating costs

2. Gathering this information involves obtaining answers to the following sort of questions.

1: Conducting a marketing audit

(a) *Men and women*

   (i) *Labour*. What is the size of the labour force? What are their skills? How much are they paid? What are total labour costs? What proportion of the organisation's added value or sales revenue is accounted for by labour costs? How efficient is the workforce? What is the rate of labour turnover? How good or bad are industrial relations?

   (ii) *Management*. What is the size of the management team? What are its specialist skills? What management development and career progression exists? How well has management performed in achieving targets in the past? How hierarchical is the management structure?

(b) *Money*

   (i) *Finance*. What are the company's financial resources? What are its debt and gearing ratios?

   (ii) *Working capital*. How much working capital does the organisation use? What are the average turnover periods for stocks and debtors? What is the credit policy of the organisation? What credit is taken from suppliers? What is the level of bad debts? How is spare cash utilised by the treasury department? How are foreign exchange transactions dealt with? How profitable is our product portfolio?

(c) *Materials*

   Where do they come from? Who supplies them? What percentage of the total cost of sales is accounted for by materials? What are wastage levels? Are new materials being developed for the market by suppliers?

(d) *Machines*

   Fixed assets. What fixed assets does the organisation use? What is their current value (on a going concern value and on a break-up value basis)? What is the amount of revenue and profit per £1 invested in fixed assets? How old are the assets? Are they technologically advanced or out of date? What are the organisation's repairs and replacement policies? What is the *percentage fill* in the organisation's capacity? This is particularly important for service industries, such as cinemas, football grounds and trains, where fixed costs are high and resources need to be utilised as much as possible to earn good profits. R & D experience and level of technological expertise should also be assessed.

(e) *Markets*

   Market share, reputation, level of competition, deals with distributors and the level of goodwill. Is the company customer oriented and how is the customer contact/service perceived?

3
- A *strength* may be a particular skill or distinctive competence which the organisation possesses and which will aid it in achieving its stated objectives. Examples may include experience in specific types of markets or specific skills possessed by employees, or factors such as a firm's reputation for quality or customer service.

- A *weakness* is simply any aspect of the company which may hinder the achievement of specific objectives. This may be, for example, limited experience of certain markets/technologies, or the extent of financial resources available.

- An *opportunity* is simply any feature of the external environment which creates conditions which are advantageous to the firm in relation to a particular objective or set of objectives.

- A *threat* is any environmental development which will present problems and may hinder the achievement of organisational objectives. An opportunity to some firms may constitute a threat to others.

4 Opportunities and threats may arise in the following areas.

(a) *Political:* legislation involving, for example, pollution control or a ban on certain products would be a *threat* to various industries, but also an *opportunity* for selling, eg lead-free petrol and suitable cars. Taxation incentives, rent-free factory buildings, or investment grants might be available for exploitation. Government policy may be to increase expenditure on housing, defence, schools and hospitals or roads and transport and this gives *opportunities* to private companies and the relevant government organisations alike. Political upheaval might damage market and investment prospects, especially overseas.

(b) *Economic:* unemployment, the level of wages and salaries, the expected total market behaviour for products, total customer demand, the growth and decline of industries and suppliers, general

Part A: The marketing planning process: an overview

investment levels etc. At an international level, world production and the volume of international trade, demand, recessions, import controls, exchange rates.

(c) *Social:* Social attitudes will have a significant effect on customer demand and employee attitudes. Social issues such as environmental pollution, women's roles, and the need to solve social problems offer *opportunities* for new products and services. Demographic change and population structure will provide continuing product *opportunities*. There are recognised opportunities for growth in the personal pensions market. Unemployment will strongly affect the total spending power of consumers. This has been a chronic and long term *threat* in certain parts of the UK.

(d) *Technology:* new products appearing, or cheaper means of production or distribution will clearly have profound implications in these types of analysis.

5
- Comparative growth rates, inflation rates, interest rates and wage rates in other countries
- The extent of protectionist measures against imports
- The nature and extent of exchange controls in various countries
- The development of international economic communities such as the European Union and the prospects of international trade agreements between countries
- The levels of corporate and personal taxation in different countries

6 (a) Markets. What changes are occurring in market trends - sales, profits, geographic distribution? What changes are occurring in market segments and niches?

(b) Customers. How do customers/potential customers rate us on aspects such as reputation, product quality, service, salesforce, advertising/price etc, relative to our competitors? What sorts of customers do we have? Are they changing? What is our customers' buying behaviour? Is it changing? How well do we understand our customers and their buying motives?

(c) Competitors. Who are our major competitors? What are their market shares? What are their strengths and weaknesses? Competitors' marketing strategies and likely responses to our marketing actions. Future changes in competition.

(d) Distributors. What are the major distributive channels in our markets? What are the channels' efficiency levels and growth trends?

(e) Suppliers. Outlooks for future supplies. Trends in patterns of buying/selling. Changes in power bases. Evaluations of suppliers against buying/ marketing criteria

(f) Agencies. What are the costs/availability outlooks for transportation services, for warehousing facilities, for financial resources etc? Just how effective are our advertising, PR and marketing research agencies?

(g) Publics. What publics offer particular opportunities or problems for us? What steps have we taken to deal effectively with each public?

Now try illustrative question 1 at the end of the Study Text

2 Developing Marketing Objectives and Strategies

Chapter Topic List	Syllabus reference
1　Setting the scene	-
2　Objectives and strategy	1.2
3　Marketing strategies	1.2
4　The mass market approach	1.2
5　Market segmentation	1.2
6　Segmenting consumer markets	1.2
7　Segmenting industrial markets	1.2
8　Targeting	1.2
9　Positioning	1.2

Learning Outcome

Students will be able to understand the process of marketing planning at an operational level.

Key Concepts Introduced

- Gap analysis
- Market segmentation
- Brand positioning

Examples of Marketing at Work

- Cinemas
- Market development
- Ethnic minorities

1 SETTING THE SCENE

1.1 Having dealt with the marketing audit against the background of wider corporate planning, we now look more closely with marketing objectives and strategies. Section 2 considers possible corporate strategic objectives and Section 3 goes on to discussing techniques for setting marketing objectives. Once again, be aware that some of these ideas may be relevant at both the corporate and marketing departmental levels.

Part A: The marketing planning process: an overview

1.2 Market segmentation is a vital aspect of marketing strategy and is discussed in section 5 after a brief look at the mass market approach in section 4.

1.3 Techniques for segmentation are covered in sections 6 and 7 and the complementary ideas of targeting and product positioning in sections 8 and 9.

2 OBJECTIVES AND STRATEGY

Primary objectives

2.1 Most commercial organisations will express their primary objective in financial terms. There are three main measures.

- Profitability
- Return on capital employed (ROCE) or return on investment (ROI)
- Earnings per share (EPS)

Although a company must make profits, **profit** on its own is not satisfactory as an overall long term corporate objective because it fails to allow for the size of the capital investment required to make the profit.

> **Action Programme 1**
>
> What other drawbacks can you identify to the use of profitability as a primary objective?

Return on investment or **return on capital employed** might be more appropriate objectives than profitability. They take into account the funds actually required to generate given levels of profit, though they still do not allow for long term investment.

2.2 **Earnings per share** is often used as a corporate objective. It recognises that a company is owned by its shareholders and the ultimate purpose of a company must be to provide a satisfactory return for them. When earnings and dividends are low, the market value of shares will also be depressed, unless there is a strong prospect of growth in the future.

Non-financial objectives

2.3 *Drucker* (*Theory of Business Behaviour*) suggested that the prime objective of a company is **survival**. There are five major areas in which to decide objectives for survival.

- A business must anticipate the social climate and effect of economic policy in those areas where it operates. It must organise its behaviour in such a way as to survive in both.
- A business is a human organisation and must be organised to achieve high performance by everyone in it.
- A business must provide an economic product or service.
- A business must innovate, because the economy and markets are continually changing.
- Inevitably, a business must be profitable to survive.

2.4 Some argue that a company should make **growth** its prime objective. However, this approach has its problems.

- A primary measure of growth, such as turnover or EPS must be chosen. There will be trade-offs between, for instance, growth of turnover and growth of profits.
- Growth might lead to diseconomies of scale and inefficiencies.

2: Developing market objectives and strategies

- Growth must be financed; it may be difficult to obtain the extra working capital.

Multiple objectives - the balanced scorecard

2.5 Modern thinking acknowledges that a single measure of performance may not be adequate for controlling a large business. *Kaplan and Norton* suggested a **balanced scorecard** to give a fuller picture.

2.6 The balanced scorecard they described looks at the business in four perspectives.
- The financial perspective, or 'how do we look to shareholders?'
- The customer perspective, or 'how do customers see us?'
- The internal business perspective, or 'what must we excel at?'
- The innovation and learning perspective, or 'can we continue to improve and create value?'

Performance in all must be satisfactory if the business is to prosper:

2.7 It is necessary for each business to set goals and establish performance measures for each perspective. Some will be fairly simple and traditional. For instance, **shareholders** will want to see their company survive and grow; suitable measures here would be cash generation and profits respectively. The **internal perspective** will vary widely between companies but will concentrate on efficiency goals and measures. Measuring **customer** satisfaction can be done in a variety of ways such as counting complaints or starting a programme of interviews. The innovation and learning perspective will, perhaps, be the most difficult to handle. Kaplan and Norton give the example of an electronics company with several goals in this perspective; one is technology leadership and the chosen measure is how long it takes to develop a new generation of product.

Subsidiary objectives

2.8 Whatever primary objective or objectives are set, subsidiary objectives will then be developed beneath them. The diagram below illustrates this process in outline.

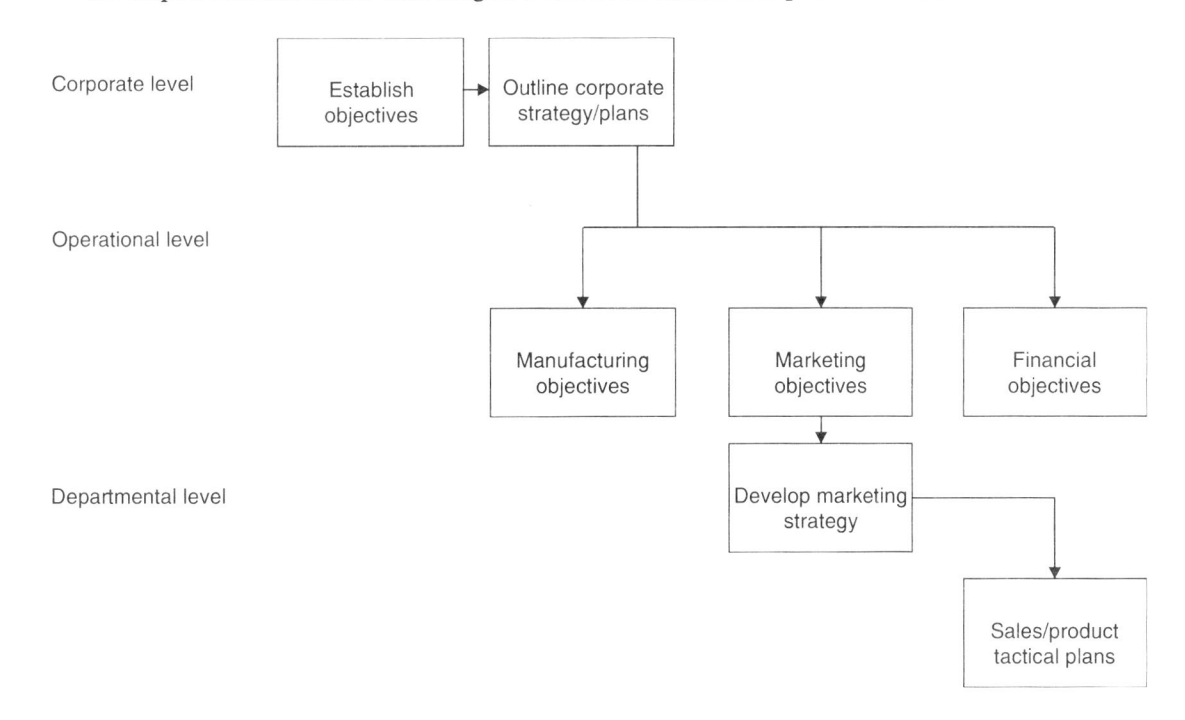

Corporate level: Establish objectives → Outline corporate strategy/plans

Operational level: Manufacturing objectives | Marketing objectives | Financial objectives

Departmental level: Develop marketing strategy → Sales/product tactical plans

Part A: The marketing planning process: an overview

2.9 Unless an organisation is so small that it is a single unit, without functional departments, the overall objectives of the organisation must indicate different requirements for different functions. While some corporate goals, such as those outlined in the balanced scorecard cannot be stated in quantifiable terms, subsidiary objectives must be very clear cut, so that performance can be **measured**. The SMART criteria are often used to ensure that objectives are adequately stated.

- **Specific**. Vague generalities must be avoided.
- **Measurable**. Desired outcomes must be quantified so that clear measures of performance can be set.
- **Attainable**. A pious hope is useless for controlling performance or motivating staff.
- **Results-orientated**. Objectives should be stated in terms of **outcomes** rather than **inputs**. Politicians are very bad at this.
- **Time-bounded**. A time by which the objective is to be achieved should be set.

Ranking objectives in order of importance

2.10 While some objectives are clearly subordinate to others (departmental objectives are subsidiary to corporate objectives) problems of ranking arise where there are multiple objectives, since resources, including time, are always limited.

2.11 *Kepner and Tregoe* rank objectives in the following way.

(a) Objectives should be divided into two categories: **must** and **want** objectives. 'Must' objectives are absolutely essential, whereas 'want' objectives are not. 'Must' objectives rank equally, since they all have to be achieved and so resources must somehow be committed to them.

(b) A minimum level of achievement should be specified for each 'must' objective.

(c) Anything beyond the minimum level of achievement for 'must' objectives are 'want' objectives, and should be ranked in order of preference. There may not be enough resources to achieve all the 'want' objectives, and management must ensure that resources are not diverted away from achieving the 'must' objectives. If commitment to 'must' objectives is threatened, then 'want' objectives are best forgotten.

The monitoring and revision of objectives

2.12 Successful planning requires a commitment to objectives, and so objectives should not be subject to frequent change. A planning review, in which objectives should be reassessed and planning horizons reviewed, should be held regularly, perhaps once a year.

Marketing objectives

2.13 Marketing objectives should be clear statements of where the organisation wants to be in marketing terms. They describe what the organisation expects to achieve as a result of its planned marketing actions. Remembering the SMART criteria, examples of marketing objectives might look like this:

'To increase market share from the current X% to Y% by 20XX.'
'To achieve a sales revenue of £X million at a cost of sales not exceeding 80% in 20X1.'

2: Developing market objectives and strategies

2.14 Objectives can be set for overall achievement as above, or for elements of the strategic plan. For example, if one of the strategies to achieve a profitable increase in sales revenue was to increase awareness of the product, then an advertising objective (a marketing sub-objective) might be: 'To increase product awareness in the target market from V% to W% in 20X1.'

2.15 When developing a strategy, a company is seeking a match with its operating environment. This may mean adjusting the company's strategy to fit into the existing market environment, although it may possibly involve attempting to change the environment to fit the company. Overall, the strategy must enable the company to meet the specific needs of its consumers and to do so more efficiently than its competitors.

2.16 As we have already seen, strategies develop at a number of levels. **Corporate strategy** is concerned with the overall development of an organisation's business activities, while **marketing strategy** is concerned with the organisation's activities in relation to the markets which it serves. Strategy takes two main forms.

- **Deliberate strategies** are conscious, planned activities.
- **Emergent strategies** are the outcome of activities which develop without clear objectives. Most strategies are part deliberate and part emergent.

3 MARKETING STRATEGIES

Gap analysis

> **Key Concept**
> **Gap analysis** is a planning technique which identifies likely shortfalls in future performance and considers how best they can be filled.

3.1 Gap analysis starts with a comparison of what the organisation **wishes to achieve** and what it is **likely to achieve if nothing changes**.

3.2 *Argenti* uses the term F_0 **forecast** to mean a forecast of future results assuming that the company continues to operate as at present. He identifies four stages in their preparation.

- The analysis of revenues by units of sale and price, and the analysis of costs into variable, fixed, and semi-variable.
- Projections into the future, based on past trends, to the end of the planning period.
- Consideration of other factors affecting profits and return, such as the likelihood of deterioration in labour relations or machine servicability and the possibility of scarcity of raw materials.
- Combination of these items into a single forecast.

When complete, F_0 forecast may be compared with the organisations objectives. Differences make up the 'gap' which has to be filled. The gap may have several elements such as a **profits gap** or a **sales gap**.

3.3 The **profit gap** is the difference between the target profits and the profits on the F_0 forecast. The options for bridging the gap need to be identified.

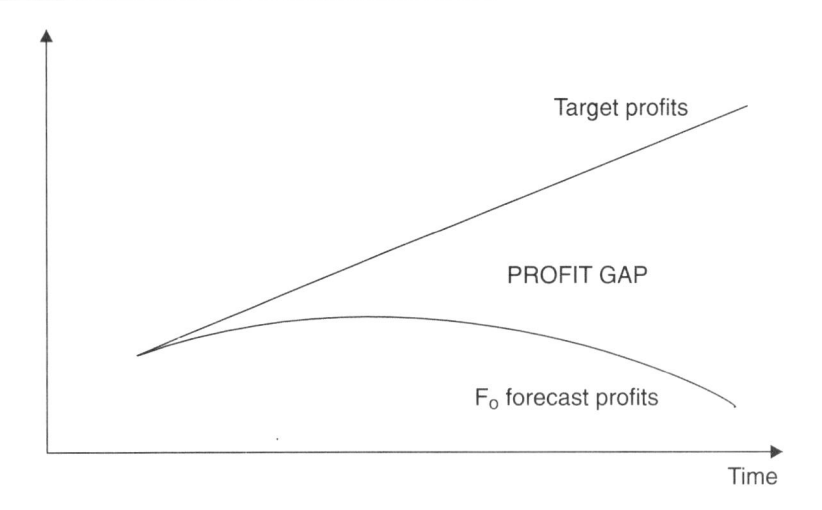

Part A: The marketing planning process: an overview

[Graph showing Target profits line increasing linearly and F₀ forecast profits curve leveling off, with PROFIT GAP between them, plotted against Time]

3.4 *Sizer* (1968) described a **sales gap** that could be filled by new product-market growth strategies as follows.

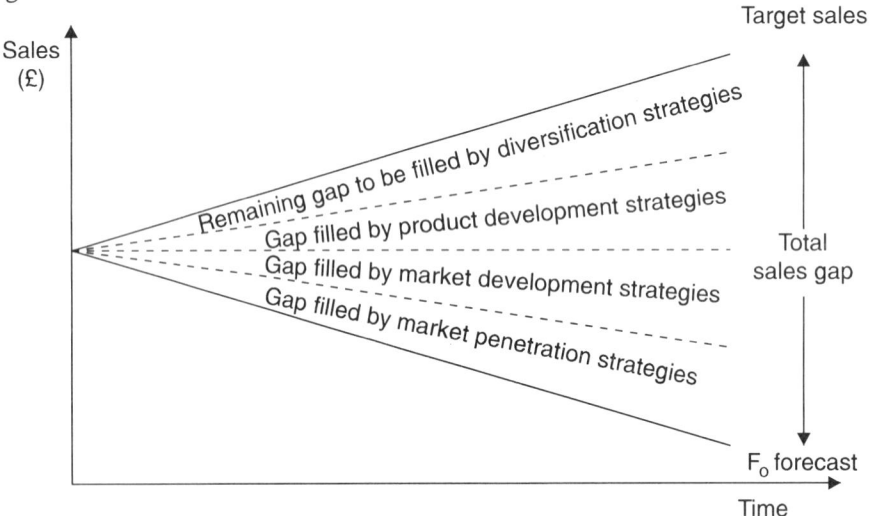

[Graph showing Sales (£) vs Time, with Target sales at top and F₀ forecast at bottom, showing the Total sales gap divided into: Remaining gap to be filled by diversification strategies, Gap filled by product development strategies, Gap filled by market development strategies, Gap filled by market penetration strategies]

3.5 The same basic technique can serve as the basis for formulating any particular strategy.

In planning for human resources, gap analysis would be used to assess the difference over time between two quantities.

- What the organisation **needs to have** in terms of staff of differing skills and seniority
- What the organisation is **likely to have,** allowing for natural wastage of staff, assuming that it does nothing to train staff or appoint new staff as vacancies arise

A strategy would then be needed to fill the gap between target and current forecasts.

Marketing at Work

Cinemas

The *cinema industry* had been booming for successive years before Virgin bought into it in 1995. Admissions had risen every year from a low in 1985 of £54 m. Last year was even better.

The main cause of the cinema's fortunes is the investment that has been made in modern multiplex cinemas with eight to twelve screens, surround sound, air conditioning, car parking and comfy seats. According to consultants Dodona, there are 600 multiplex screens planned over the next few years.

The investment, and Virgin's usual aggressive newcomer approach, is breaking down the tacit agreement that cinema chains must not compete too closely with each other.

This maturing of the market is leading the cinema chains to take a fresh look at their marketing strategies. For years the chains had no national coverage so they restricted themselves to the listings pages of local newspapers. This is being rapidly re-evaluated.

"The target market for multiplexes are 14-25 year olds with a male bias," says a source at one of the big five. "Now you do not have to be a media expert to work out that 14-25 -year-olds are not big readers of local newspapers. It is an entirely inappropriate mechanism."

UCI launched a radio promotion on BRMB last year called Movie Meltdown, where the chain's branding is mixed with film reviews and celebrity interviews.

The presence of Virgin has also caused the chains to sharpen their marketing efforts. Virgin is likely to harness all aspects of its empire to cross-promote its chain and UCI has anticipated this by signing a long-term joint promotion deal with music retailer HMV.

Marketing Week, January 31 1997

Competitive strategies

Competitive advantage

3.6 Firms constantly strive for competitive advantage. *Michael Porter* argues that strategy is essentially a method for creating and sustaining a profitable position in a particular market environment. The profit made by the firm depends first on the nature of its strategy and second on the inherent profitability of the industry in which it operates. An organisation in a basically profitable industry can perform badly with an unsuitable strategy while an organisation in an unprofitable industry may perform well with a more suitable strategy.

3.7 Porter identified **five forces** affecting the profitability of an industry generally.

- Bargaining power of suppliers
- Bargaining power of consumers
- Threat of entry of new competitors
- Competition from substitutes
- Competition between firms already in the industry

3.8 A competitive strategy is based on a thorough analysis of these factors. Porter suggests that the organisation must decide whether to compete throughout the market or only in certain segments and whether to achieve low costs or a differentiated product. Three possible strategies, as outlined below, follow from these decisions.

(a) **Cost leadership** aims to achieve high profits by driving down costs. Typically, the product is undifferentiated, and the cost savings for the consumer must compensate for the loss of product features. The very low cost base discourages competition allowing high profits at a competitive price. Any discount offered by the firm should not be so high as to offset cost advantages.

(b) **Differentiation** aims to offer products which are recognised as unique in areas which are highly valued by the consumer. It is the products' uniqueness and the associated customer loyalty that protects the firm from competition. However, the price premium received must outweigh the costs of supplying the differentiated product and the customer must feel that the extra features more than compensate for the price premium.

(c) **Focus** uses either **costs** or **differentiation** but rather than serving the entire market, the organisation looks to operate only in particularly attractive segments or niches. Differentiation focus is the most common form of focus strategy and implies producing highly customised products for very specific consumer groups.

Part A: The marketing planning process: an overview

The choice of competitive strategy

3.9 Competitive strategy may be based on product/market strategies or manufacturing strategy. As we saw above, Porter suggests that there are three broad competitive strategies. One of them is a manufacturing strategy, two of them are product/market strategies. The type of competitive strategy adopted will depend on the competitive strategies adopted by rivals and the structure of the business and type of product or service that the firm is producing.

> **Action Programme 2**
>
> A cost leadership strategy aims to be lowest-cost producer. The manufacturer can then compete on price with every other producer in the industry, and earn the highest unit profits. Explain what steps the organisation must take if it adopts this strategy.

3.10 Where there is a low **critical mass of production output** and maximum economies of scale are easily achievable, **cost leadership** would be difficult to attain, because many rival firms should be able to achieve similar low costs too. Only when the critical mass of production is high is a cost leadership strategy likely to be effective.

3.11 **Cost leadership** has implications for pricing, product quality and promotion.

  (a) **Pricing**. To achieve high volumes of sales, the firm may need to keep prices low, if the **price elasticity of demand** for a product is high.

  (b) **Product quality**. A cost leadership strategy is well suited to **search products**, where consumers compare the attributes of competing products from rival firms. With such products, firms must be able to match the product quality of rivals, otherwise they will lose customers. On the other hand, firms should not incur costs to improve quality attributes which have little, if any, impact on the consumer's purchasing decision.

  (c) **Promotion**. Advertising may be used to boost sales volume, especially where it emphasises price discounts. In the case of search products, advertising should be informative about the key attributes of the product (for example, price) and persuasive advertising is unlikely to have much effect on demand.

3.12 **Differentiation seeks to add value to the product**, and in doing so, to raise the product's cost and sales price. The improvements should be more value to the customer than the price increase, so that the customer is willing to pay more for the superior quality is a perceived added value.

3.13 A differentiation strategy assumes that competitive advantage can be gained through particular characteristics of a firm's products.

  (a) **Breakthrough products** offer either a radical performance advantage over competition, a drastically lower price, or, possibly, both.

  (b) **Improved products** are not radically different from their competition but are obviously superior in terms of better performance at a competitive price. It will usually be the result of incorporation of recent advances in technology, applied to a particular product. Examples would be the much-improved capabilities of colour televisions in the 1970s, pocket calculators in the 1980s, and personal computers in the 1990s. A problem for producers is that product improvements are quickly copied by competitors.

2: Developing market objectives and strategies

3.14 A successful differentiation strategy builds up loyalty to the firm's products and so the firm can sell its products at prices that are higher than the least-cost producer in the market. A firm which uses a strategy of differentiation is unlikely to be the market leader.

3.15 A **focus strategy is based on segmenting the market** and focusing on particular market segments. The firm will focus on a particular type of buyer or geographical area.

- A **cost-focus** strategy involves selecting a segment of the market and achieving the lowest cost **in serving that segment only**.

- A **differentiation-focus strategy** provides its chosen market segment with a product or service whose particular characteristics are particularly desirable within that segment. In consumer goods this is often achieved by emphasis on quality.

3.16 The risk is that the market segment might not be large enough to be profitable. The niche marketing of the 1980s (eg Sock Shop, Tie Rack) illustrates focus strategy, but few of the niche retailers survived the recession of the early 1990s, indicating that their market segments may have been too narrow to cover a burgeoning cost base. Body Shop, reflecting the growing appeal of its positioning as a 'caring' company as far as the environment is concerned, and its exploitation of the widespread belief that 'natural' equals 'healthy', has survived. Also, Body Shop focused on a customer segment, rather than a product.

> **Exam Tip**
> Although Porter's competitive forces have appeared, his competitive strategies have yet to be examined in any depth. Watch this space...

Growth strategies

3.17 Porter's three generic strategies do not directly address the central marketing issues of customers and products in a specific operational way. *Ansoff's* competitive strategy framework fills this gap and also relates well to the sub-strategies of the marketing mix.

Ansoff's competitive strategies

		Products Existing	New
Markets	Existing	Market Penetration 1	Product Development 4
	New	Market Development 2	Diversification 16

(a) **Market penetration** involves increasing sales of the **existing products in existing markets**. This may include persuading existing users to use more (a credit card issuer might try to increase credit card use by offering higher credit limits or gifts based on expenditure); persuading non-users to use (for example, by, offering free gifts with new credit card accounts); or attracting consumers from competitors. Market penetration will, in general, only be viable in circumstances where the market is not already saturated.

(b) **Market development** entails **expansion into new markets using existing products**. New markets may be different geographically, new market segments or new uses for

Part A: The marketing planning process: an overview

products amongst existing consumers. This strategy requires swift, effective and imaginative promotion, but can be very profitable if markets are changing rapidly.

(c) **Product development** involves the redesign or repositioning of most existing products to appeal to existing markets. Recent developments in the mortgage market, for example, illustrate product development as the traditional standardised mortgage account is rapidly being supplemented by variants which offer lower starting rates, special terms for particular types of customer and particular mixes of fixed and flexible repayment rates. This strategy relies on good service design, packaging and promotion and on company reputation to attract consumers.

(d) **Diversification** is much more risky than the other three because the organisation is moving into areas in which it has little or no experience. Instances of pure diversification are consequently rare and as a strategic option it tends to be used in cases when there are no other possible routes for growth available.

3.18 Most companies adopt, at least initially, a strategy of market penetration which carries the lowest risk. However, when market saturation is reached, a company needs to consider entering into new markets with existing products to maintain growth. Technological advance and competitive pressures will normally force companies into some degree of product development, ranging from cosmetic alterations through tangible product improvements to revolutionary new products. Diversification may involve merger or takeover, but not necessarily.

3.19 Ansoff's matrix then leads naturally into marketing operations such as research to identify new markets and new products and the deployment of the marketing mix in exploiting these product/market opportunities for growth.

Marketing at Work

Market development

General Electric yesterday further extended its reach beyond its traditional manufacturing operations with the $530 acquisition of the largest independent servicer of aircraft engines in the US.

The purchase of Greenwich Air Services extends the US group's push into services businesses, where growth rates are often higher and profit margins stronger than in its traditional manufacturing businesses.

GE already generates $2.3bn of revenue and employs 6,200 people in its existing aircraft engine servicing unit. This business derives "the vast bulk" of its business from servicing large commercial jet engines built by GE, the company said.

However, it also services engines made by other manufacturers. A facility in Wales, for instance, handles the maintenance of engines on British Airways aircraft, regardless of the maker.

The purchase of Greenwich Air, on the other hand, gives the company a presence in maintaining engines for smaller business jets. This is not a market in which the company has a manufacturing presence, and most of the engines are made by AlliedSignal and Allison.

Financial Times, 11 March 1997

Strategic planning tools

3.20 The **Boston Consulting Group's Product Portfolio Analysis** is a tool for determining marketing strategy and is based upon the premise that market share relative to competitors and market growth are important strategic choice criteria. The method uses a 2×2 diagnostic matrix. The method is based on the principle that a company should have a balanced portfolio of products. It is thus useful for product planning.

2: Developing market objectives and strategies

	High Market Share	Low
High Market growth rate	Star	Problem child
Low	Cash cow	Dog

(a) **Stars** are products with high market share and high growth, ie leaders, but often **needing a large cash investment** in order to maintain growth in face of competition.

(b) **Cash cows** are typically former stars entering a period of low growth, but still **generating large amounts of cash**. Because of high market share over a period of years, cash cows enjoy economies of scale and high profit margins.

(c) **Dogs** have low market shares in a low-growth market and **tend to generate either a loss or a relatively low profit**. They typically take up more management time than warranted and, unless they can be strategically justified, are candidates for withdrawal.

(d) **Problem children** are sometimes labelled **question marks**, because, with low share but high growth prospects, they **need considerable investment for initially low returns**. They are therefore **cash users but potential stars**. Management must choose between further speculative investment or withdrawal.

This topic is covered in more detail in Chapter 6.

3.21 **PIMS, or Profit Impact on Marketing Strategy**, is a large database covering more than 3,000 SBUs, developed largely in America but now adding a considerable number of European businesses to the portfolio. It is 'owned' by the Strategic Planning Institute which has a London office. Clients input detailed confidential data on their expenditure and returns which are then computer-analysed to determine norms for groups of like businesses (as defined in terms of data characteristics rather than type of product-markets). This diagnostic tool thus enables a business to compare its own strategic performance (outputs relative to inputs) with 'par for the course', ie the norm. The data is claimed to show in what respects the business is under-performing and how its performance might be improved.

3.22 Certain factors have been persistently revealed as the most influential determinants of profitability.

- The business' competitive position including market share and relative product quality.

- The attractiveness of its served market as indicated by growth rate and customer characteristics.

- Its production structure including operational productivity and investment intensity.

Part A: The marketing planning process: an overview

> **Exam Tip**
> Developing marketing objectives is a fundamental part of the marketing planning process and is examined fairly frequently. It appeared most recently in a 20 mark question in June 1999. This concerned options for increasing turnover at a privately owned gymnasium.
> The easiest way to answer such a question is to draw the grid, and explore each option in turn in the text underneath. For each of the four Ansoff strategies you could have identified the supposed level of risk. Diversification as a means of increasing sales revenue is generally the most risky. (Don't assume that this guide is a formula which is always true. Market penetration is most risky if, for example, its structure and characteristics are changing rapidly.)
> Having used this grid as a framework, you can then go on to explore each option in turn. For example, how do you increase market penetration? Sell more to current customers? Gain customers from competitors?

Strategy evaluation

3.23 Strategies are evaluated to decide whether they will help to achieve the organisation's objectives and so, whether they are desirable. The final list of desirable strategic opportunities, if it is not empty, will be a list for ranking in order of priority.

3.24 Individual strategies could be tested against a list of criteria for acceptance as follows.

(a) To what extent will the strategy contribute towards company's **financial objectives** in both the short and long term?

(b) Is the strategy consistent with the **social responsibilities** of the company?

(c) Does the strategy **conform** to other strategies pursued by the company, or is it a completely new direction? (for example, conglomerate diversification, or investment in pure research might be proposed strategies which are currently not pursued by the company).

(d) The element of **risk** attached to a proposed strategy should not be too high compared with the potential rewards. If the strategy can only be successful under the most favourable conditions, then the risk is probably too great.

(e) Is the strategy capable of succeeding in spite of the likely reaction by **competitors**?

(f) Will there be adequate **control**? A new strategy needs a careful check on performance to put any necessary remedial steps into effect, particularly in the early stages. The lack of an adequate control system may be serious hindrance to effective decision making.

(g) Is the strategy **preferable** to other, mutually exclusive strategies? Is there an option to combine two separate strategies into one action? Argenti used the example of one department buying a computer for £50,000 for accounting work, a second department buying a £30,000 computer for scientific work, when a £60,000 computer would have been capable of handling the workload of both departments.

3.25 *Argenti* proposes six rather different criteria for testing strategy.

- Can it be shown that the strategy gives the company an expected return with a given business risk attached, similar to the one expected by its shareholders?
- Does the company have the necessary competence to carry out the strategy?
- Does the strategy eliminate all the significant weaknesses of the company, as identified by the internal appraisal?
- Does the strategy exploit any opportunities which have been identified as possibly arising in the future?

2: Developing market objectives and strategies

- Does the strategy reduce the impact of any significant external threats?
- Does the strategy call for action by the company which is objectionable on social or moral grounds?

3.26 The selection of strategies is formulated in a **policy statement**, which describes the planned long-term strategy of the company, identifying the objectives, constraints and strategies to be pursued over the corporate planning period. This statement should be short, and restricted to identifying a few key strategies. However, to 'sell' the plan to junior managers and employees, the ideas in the statement might need to be internally marketed with explanations for presentation and communication to staff.

4 THE MASS MARKET APPROACH

4.1 The **mass** or **total market approach** does not distinguish between customers. It assumes that majority needs can be satisfied with a single marketing mix, ie the same product at the same price, promoted to everyone in the same way and using a single method of distribution. Thus, in the past, consumers brought staples such as sugar, butter, lard and milk in totally unbranded wrappings. Items such as sugar were ladled from larger sacks into thick blue paper bags by assistants at corner grocery shops.

4.2 In highly developed countries this approach becomes less effective as people's wants and needs grow in variety and sophistication. The **segmentation approach** recognises that people have different wants and needs and that some are willing to pay more or go to greater lengths to satisfy them. More opportunities are open to organisations which are willing to satisfy needs with a differentiated marketing mix.

4.3 Examples of the total market approach are still prevalent in industrial markets. In the building industry, customers buy sand, cement and timber with scant regard for brand. In the metals market copper, steel, and aluminium are bought on a commodity basis.

5 MARKET SEGMENTATION   6/96, 12/97, 12/98, 6/99

5.1 Marketing activity is more effective if groups can be identified and targeted. This is done by **market segmentation** which groups potential customers according to identifiable characteristics relevant to their purchasing behaviour.

> **Key Concept**
> **Market segmentation** is the subdividing of a market into distinct subsets of customers, where any subset may conceivably be selected as a target market to be reached with a distinct marketing mix.
> (Kotler)

5.2 The important elements of market segmentation are as follows.

(a) While the total market consists of varied groups of consumers, each group has **common needs and preferences**, and may well react to market stimuli in the same way. For example, the market for umbrellas might be segmented according to sex. Women might seem to prefer umbrellas of a particular size and weight. The men's market might further be subdivided by age or activity, for example, professionals, commuters, golfers. Each subdivision of the market will show increasingly common traits. Golfers appear to buy large multi-coloured umbrellas.

Part A: The marketing planning process: an overview

(b) **Each market segment can become a target market for a firm, requiring a unique marketing mix. Segmentation should enable a company to formulate an effective strategy for selling to a given group.**

5.3 There are many possible characteristics of buyers which could be chosen as segmentation variables and a variety of criteria which can be used to identify the most effective characteristics for use in market segmentation.

5.4 There are a number of criteria for effective market segmentation.

(a) **Measurability** refers to the degree to which information exists or is cost effectively obtainable on the characteristics of interest. Whilst a car manufacturer may have access to information about **location** of customers, **personality traits** are more difficult to obtain information about, because the required tests may be impractical to administer.

(b) **Accessibility** refers to the degree to which the company can identify and communicate with the chosen segments. Thus whilst a car dealer may be able to access potential corporate customers, by direct mail or tele-sales, identifying individual customers with family incomes in excess of £30,000 pa would not be so easy.

(c) **Substantiality** refers to the degree to which the segments are large enough to offer profitable returns. Thus, whilst a large number of people in social group DE aged over 65 could be identified, their potential profitability to a retailer is likely to be less in the long term than a smaller number of 17-18 year olds. This latter group might be worth cultivating, using a specially devised marketing approach, whereas the former might not be.

Action Programme 3

Ignoring for a moment the objective of maximising profitability, what do you think are the benefits of segmentation?

Key aspects of segmentation

5.5 Segmentation only makes sense if it brings appropriate benefits.

(a) Segmentation should increase benefits to consumers by providing product features more closely matching their needs.

(b) Segmentation enables the firm to identify those groups of customers who are most likely to buy. This ensures that resources will not be wasted, and marketing and sales activity can be highly focused. The result should be lower costs, greater sales and higher profitability.

(c) Across the industry, segmentation will provide greater customer choice by generating a variety of products within a particular class from which consumers can choose.

6 SEGMENTING CONSUMER MARKETS

6.1 There are a number of ways in which a consumer market can be segmented.

2: Developing market objectives and strategies

Geographic segmentation

6.2 Segmentation based on location may be important for retailers, who need to get to know about the different groups of customers within their catchment area. Segmentation by location can also be a feature of international marketing strategy. Needs will be influenced by a range of factors including climate, religion, culture and infrastructure.

6.3 A national chain of supermarkets will use geographic segmentation because it interacts closely with the chain's outlet strategy. Each branch or group of retail outlets could be given mutually exclusive areas to service and so make more effective use of target marketing. The obvious advantage to customers is convenience of access, which is one of the major reasons why customers choose particular stores.

Demographic segmentation

6.4 Demography is the study of population and population trends. The following demographic factors have an impact on market segmentation.

- Changes in national population and in regional distribution
- Changes in the age distribution of the population. All over the developed world populations are ageing, as a result of improved health care and falling birth rates
- The concentration of population into certain geographical areas

6.5 The total size of the population defines the total possible level of demand for a product. With the formation of the Single European Market in 1992, the market for UK companies became comparable in size to the US market.

6.6 The population is usually broken down into groups defined by demographic characteristics such as sex or age. The total size of each segment will suggest possible levels of demand for corresponding products.

Social class (socio-economics)

6.7 The social class of a person is also likely to influence buying habits and preferences. Although there are a number of factors involved in social class position, such as income, education and background the most commonly used classification, in the marketing world, is the JICNARs scale, based on the occupation of the main wage earner in the household. This involves the following classification scheme.

Social grade	Social status	Occupation
A	Upper middle class	Higher managerial, professional or administrative jobs.
B	Middle class	Middle managerial, professional or administrative jobs.
C1	Lower middle class	Supervisory or clerical jobs, junior management.
C2	Skilled working class	Skilled manual workers.
D	Working class	Unskilled and semi-skilled manual workers.
E	Those at the lowest level of subsistence	Pensioners, the unemployed, casual or low grade workers.

Part A: The marketing planning process: an overview

6.8 This scheme lacks precision as it divides the total population into just six large groups. It is very difficult to make significant distinctions between a B and a C1 class person. Also, because it is based on the occupation of the 'chief income earner' only, it does not reflect the income of the whole family unit, or the background and aspirations of members.

6.9 Computer databases using census details, market research and commercial data has over recent years made possible the use of segmentation systems based on a number of different household characteristics, from the *names* of occupants to the types of houses they occupy. By linking this to postcode data it is possible to identify very precisely the characteristics of consumers in a particular location, or to build up a *profile* of the types of people sending for goods by mail order, or completing hire purchase forms.

6.10 We will look at two more sophisticated approaches to geo-demographic segmentation, ACORN and MOSAIC, in the next section of this chapter.

Marketing at Work

Ethnic minorities

Marketing Business in March 1997 carried an article about ethnic minorities in the UK and how marketers fail to communicate with them adequately.

- Ethnic minorities spend £10 billion a year.
- In customer profile terms, they can be divided into : 'survivors' - often first generation who are inward-looking and less sophisticated, 'socially mobile' - who want to make the most of their opportunities, and 'sophisticates' - often second or third generation, who are younger and well-educated, ambitious and critical. However, all three groups are united in wanting to be part of British life.
- Marketing alienates ethnic minorities.
- They miss many nuances and references in UK advertising.
- Tokenism is rejected by ethnic minorities, who want to appear naturally within mainstream advertisements.
- The young are most attuned and comfortable with brand imagery, but they risk becoming alienated from brand images as they grow older and retreat to their own cultural identity.
- Thirty per cent of Indians between 19 and 35 are studying for a degree, compared with 13 per cent of whites.
- Indian families are most likely to own two or more cars.
- More Indian households than white households own telephones, washing machines, video recorders, microwaves and PCs.

Family characteristics

6.11 Another form of segmentation is based on the size and constitution of the family unit. As the following table illustrates, there have been changes in the characteristics of the family unit in the last few decades.

2: Developing market objectives and strategies

Percentages

	1961	1971	1981	1991	1995-6
One person households					
Under pensionable age	4	6	8	11	13
Over pensionable age	7	12	14	16	15
Two or more unrelated adults	5	4	5	3	2
One family households					
Married couple[1] with:					
No children	26	27	26	28	29
1 - 2 dependent children[2]	30	26	25	20	19
3 or more dependent children	8	9	6	5	4
Non-dependent children only	10	8	8	8	6
Lone parent[1] with:					
Dependent children[2]	2	3	5	6	7
Non-dependent children only	4	4	4	4	3
Two or more families	3	1	1	1	1
Number of households (=100%)(millions)	16.2	18.2	19.5	21.9	23.5

1 Other individuals who were not family members may also have been included.
2 May also include non-dependent children.

Action Programme 4

What factors do you think have caused the changes in trends apparent in the above table?

Family life cycle

6.12 Family circumstances may be used to segment consumer markets. The segments are based on eight categories of **family decision making units.**

- Young and single
- Young, married, no children
- Young, married, youngest child under six years old
- Young, married youngest child over six years old
- Older, married, with children
- Older, married, no children under eighteen
- Older and single
- Other

6.13 The *family life cycle* (FLC) is a summary demographic variable. It brings together factors of age, marital status, career status (income) and the presence or absence of children. As a consequence, it is able to characterise the various stages through which households progress, with each stage involving **different needs and resources**. It is analysed in the table on the next page.

Summary

6.14 Demographic segmentation methods are powerful tools especially when each of the bases is combined with other methods. The bases for demographic segmentation are clearly interdependent. Age and family life cycle stage are patently linked, as are housing and socio-economic group. Using a combination of these bases it is possible to define targets for marketing campaigns and sales activities.

Psychographic segmentation

6.15 Psychographic or **life style** segmentation seeks to classify groups according to their values, opinions, personality characteristics, interests and so on. The ability to introduce new dimensions to existing customer information, for example customers' disposition towards savings, investment and the use of credit makes it extremely flexible.

6.16 Lifestyle refers to distinctive ways of living adopted by particular communities or sub-sections of society. It involves factors such as motivation, personality and culture, and depends on accurate description. When a group has been identified and characterised, products can be tailored and promoted for this particular group. It is possible for the same person to belong to several different psychographic groups at the same time.

Lifestyle dimensions

Activities	Interests	Opinions	Demographics
Work	Family	Themselves	Age
Hobbies	Home	Social issues	Education
Social events	Job	Politics	Income
Vacation	Community	Business	Occupation
Entertainment	Recreation	Economics	Family size
Club membership	Fashion	Education	Dwelling
Community	Food	Products	Geography
Shopping	Media	Future	City size
Sports	Achievements	Culture	Stage in lifecycle

Joseph Plummer, 'The Concept and Application of Lifestyle Segmentation',
Journal of Marketing (January 1974), pp 33-37

6.17 A different scheme generalises life style in terms of four categories.

(a) **Upwardly mobile, ambitious**. People seek a better and more affluent lifestyle, principally through better paid and more interesting work, and a higher material standard of living. Persons with such a lifestyle will be prepared to try new products.

(b) **Traditional and sociable**. Compliance and conformity to group norms bring social approval and reassurance to the individual. Purchasing patterns will therefore be 'conformist'.

(c) **Security and status seeking**. 'Safety' needs and 'ego-defensive' needs are stressed. This lifestyle links status, income and security. It encourages the purchase of strong and well known products and brands, and emphasises those products and services which confer status and make life as secure and predictable as possible. These would include insurance and membership of the AA or RAC. Products that are well established and familiar inspire more confidence than new products, which will be resisted.

(d) **Hedonistic preference**. The emphasis is on 'enjoying life now' and the immediate satisfaction of wants and needs. Little consideration is given to the future.

THE FAMILY LIFE CYCLE

No	Stage	Characteristics
I	*Bachelor stage.* Young single people not living at home.	Few financial burdens. Fashion/opinion leader led. Recreation orientated. Buy: basic kitchen equipment, basic furniture, cars, equipment for the mating game, holidays. Experiment with patterns of personal financial management and control.
II	*Newly married couples.* Young, no children	Better off financially than they will be in the near future. High levels of purchase of homes and consumer durable goods. Buy: cars, fridges, cookers, life assurance, durable furniture, holidays. Establish patterns of personal financial management and control.
III	*Full nest I.* Youngest child under six	Home purchasing at peak. Liquid assets/saving low. Dissatisfied with financial position and amount of money saved. Reliance on credit finance, credit cards, overdrafts etc. Child dominated household. Buy necessities: washers, dryers, baby food and clothes, vitamins, toys, books etc.
IV	*Full nest II.* Youngest child six or over	Financial position better. Some wives return to work. Child dominated household. Buy necessities: foods, cleaning material, clothes, bicycles, sports gear, music lessons, pianos, holidays etc.
V	*Full nest III.* Older married couples with dependent children.	Financial position still better. More wives work. School and examination dominated household. Some children get first jobs; other in further/higher education. Expenditure to support children's further/higher education. Buy: new, more tasteful furniture, non-necessary appliances, boats, holidays, etc.
VI	*Empty nest I.* Older married couples, no children living with them, head of family still in labour force	Home ownership at peak. More satisfied with financial position and money saved. Interested in travel, recreation, self-education. Make financial gifts and contributions. Children gain qualifications and move to Stage I. Buy: luxuries, home improvements, eg fitted kitchens etc.
VII	*Empty nest II.* Older married couples, no children living at home, head of family retired.	Significant cut in income. Keep home. Buy: medical appliances or medical care, products which aid health, sleep and digestion. Assist children. Concern with level of savings and pension. Some expenditure on hobbies and pastimes.
VIII	*Solitary survivor I.* In labour force	Income still adequate but likely to sell family home and purchase smaller accommodation. Concern with level of savings and pension. Some expenditure on hobbies and pastimes. Worries about security and dependence.
IX	*Solitary survivor II.* Retired	Significant cut in income. Additional medical requirements. Special need for attention, affection and security. May seek sheltered accommodation. Possible dependence on others for personal financial management and control.

Benefit segmentation

6.18 This form of segmentation relates to different benefits being sought from a product or service by customer groups. Individuals are segmented directly according to their needs. In this form of segmentation, it is usual for varying customer groups to share the same benefits from the product or service. Benefit segmentation may be based on benefits sought or usage rates.

6.19 In segmenting the market in terms of **benefits sought**, there is a need to identify common characteristics which the customer requires from the product or service. Amstrad, the computer manufacturer, has developed its strategy around the principle of benefit segmentation. The requirement for basic word processing and spreadsheet packages has been synonymous with small businesses, students, home use and the professional. Amstrad has been able to meet these common needs, albeit with technology which is not necessarily at the leading edge.

Benefit segmentation of the toothpaste market

Segment name	Principal benefit sought	Demographic strengths	Special behavioural characteristics	Brands dis-proportionately favoured	Personality characteristics	Lifestyle characteristics
The sensory segment	Flavour, product appearance	Children	Users of spearmint flavoured toothpaste	Colgate, Stripe	High self-involvement	Hedonistic
The sociables	Brightness of teeth	Teens, young people	Smokers	Macleans, Ultra Brite	High sociability	Active
The worriers	Decay prevention	Large families	Heavy users	Crest	High hypo-chondriasis	Conservative
The independent segment	Price	Men	Heavy users	Brands on sale	High autonomy	Value-oriented

6.20 Individuals can be categorised by **usage patterns** - whether they are light, medium or heavy users of a product or service. The TGI (Target Group Index) helps to identify these groups for a wide range of products and services. This form of segmentation assists the marketer in developing distinct and personalised strategies aimed at specific users, based upon their existing consumption of a product or service. For example, banks and other financial institutions have introduced incentive schemes for customers when using their credit cards. This allows heavy users of the service to amass points and convert them into gifts.

Segmentation in practice

6.21 When dealing with an individual customer, care needs to be taken **to avoid stereotypes** and not jump to conclusions. Sales staff may use segmentation as a benchmark, but should act cautiously on their assumptions.

Action Programme 5

Make suggestions as to factors which might be used to segment each of the following markets.

- The market for adult education courses provided by a local authority
- The market for national magazines and periodicals
- The market for sports clubs and facilities across the UK

Fragmented industries and market segmentation

6.22 Industries begin to fragment and market segments proliferate when certain conditions prevail.

- Entry barriers are low and new firms can enter the market relatively easily;
- Economies of scale or learning curve effects are few, and so it is difficult for big firms to establish a significant overall cost leadership;
- Transport and distribution costs are high, and so the industry fragments on a geographical basis;
- Customer needs are extremely diverse;
- There are rapid product changes or style changes, which small firms might succeed in reacting to more quickly than large firms;
- There is a highly diverse product line, so that some firms are able to specialise in one part of the industry;
- There is scope for product differentiation, based on product design/quality differences or even brand images.

ACORN and MOSAIC

6.23 In this section, we continue our review of segmentation of consumer markets by looking at two well-known approaches to geo-demographic segmentation.

- ACORN (A Classification of Residential Neighbourhoods) was the first geo-demographic method of segmentation classification. It was originally based on 1971 census data and was developed by CACI Ltd.
- MOSAIC is a rival system marketed by CCN Marketing.

ACORN

6.24 ACORN divides up the entire UK population in terms of the type of housing in which they live. For each of these areas, a wide range of demographic information is generated and the system affords the opportunity to assess product usage patterns, dependent upon the research conducted within national surveys. There are 54 separate groupings.

6.25 Although the census is only conducted once every ten years, the ACORN database is updated annually to take account of latest population projections. An abbreviated version of the 1995 classification is given below.

Part A: The marketing planning process: an overview

The ACORN targeting classification

A Thriving (19.7% of population)

    A1 Wealthy Achievers, Suburban Areas (15.0%)
    A2 Affluent Greys, Rural Communities (2.3%)
    A3 Prosperous Pensioners, Retirement Areas (2.4%)

B Expanding (11.6% of population)

    B4 Affluent Executives, Family Areas (3.8%)
    B5 Well-Off Workers, Family Areas (7.8%)

C Rising (7.8% of population)

    C6 Affluent Urbanites, Town and City Areas (2.3%)
    C7 Prosperous Professionals, Metropolitan Areas (2.1%)
    C8 Better-Off Executives, Inner City Areas (3.4%)

D Settling (24.1% of population)

    D9 Comfortable Middle Agers, Mature Home Owning Areas (13.4%)
    D10 Skilled Workers, Home Owning Areas (10.7%)

E Aspiring (13.7% of population)

    E11 New Home Owners, Mature Communities (9.7%)
    E12 White Collar Workers, Better-Off Multi-Ethnic Areas (4.0%)

F Striving (22.7% of population)

    F13 Older People, Less Prosperous Areas (3.6%)
    F14 Council Estate Residents, Better-Off Homes (11.5%)
    F15 Council Estate Residents, High Unemployment (2.7%)
    F16 Council Estate Residents, Greatest Hardship (2.8%)
    F17 People in Multi-Ethnic, Low-Income Areas (2.1%)

6.26 Possible applications of the ACORN classifications.

(a) *Site Location Analysis.* Using ACORN profiles of the purchasing behaviour and socio-economic status of people living in the catchments of successful trading outlets, it is possible to identify sites with similar profiles for new stores or branches.

(d) *Market Research Sample Frames.* ACORN can help generate the most representative sample frames for market research, identifying areas with the right consumer mix.

(f) *Database Analysis.* ACORN can be used to profile both in-house customer files or bought-in lists by ACORN type, providing information which can be used to target people with similar characteristics.

(g) *Direct Mail.* Selecting from CACI's Electoral Roll database of 40 million names and addresses, according to the ACORN types relevant to particular products, can identify new prospect lists for direct mailings

(h) *Door-to-Door Leaflet Campaigns.* ACORN can segment and define target markets by postal sector for effective and customised distribution planning in door-to-door promotions.

MOSAIC

6.27 This system analyses information from a variety of sources.

2: Developing market objectives and strategies

- **the census**, used to give housing, socio-economic, household and age data
- **the electoral roll**, to give household composition and population movement data
- **post code address files** to give information on post 1981 housing and special address types such as farms and flats
- **CCN files/Lord Chancellor's office** to give credit search information and bad debt risk respectively

6.28 MOSAIC can provide information down to post code level. The current classification includes 52 separate neighbourhood types.

Other geo-demographic classifications

6.29 **Other classification systems**

(a) PORTRAIT, developed by Equifax Europe (UK) Ltd and NDL to combine geo-demographic and lifestyle data. It is not census-based, but uses a range of other data sources including county court judgements, unemployment statistics, loan applications, births and deaths registers, electoral registers and credit searches. PORTRAIT uses a four-digit classification structured on three bases.

- Gradations of income, from 'extremely affluent' to 'very low income' in ten roughly equal groups
- Gradations of age, in four roughly equal groups
- Lifestyle clusters, of which there are 175

(b) PSYCHE is based on consumer values, which are assumed to affect purchasing behaviour. It is based on a continuous rolling survey and uses **social value groups**.

- **Self-explorers**. Motivated by self-expression and self-realisation. Less materialistic than other groups, and showing high tolerance levels.
- **Social resisters**. The caring group, concerned with fairness and social values, but often appearing intolerant and moralistic.
- **Experimentalists**. Highly individualistic, motivated by fast-moving enjoyment. They are materialistic, pro-technology but anti-traditional authority.
- **Conspicuous consumers**. They are materialistic and pushy, motivated by acquisition, competition, and getting ahead. Pro-authority, law and order.
- **Belongers**. What they seek is a quiet, undisturbed family life. They are conservative, conventional rule followers.
- **Survivors**. Strongly class-conscious, and community spirited, their motivation is to 'get by'.
- **Aimless**. The young unemployed, who are often anti-authority and the old, whose motivation is day-to-day existence.

7 SEGMENTING INDUSTRIAL MARKETS

7.1 Industrial markets are usually smaller and more easily identified than consumer markets. Segmentation may still be worthwhile, however, to identify and target specified groups within the total market.

Part A: The marketing planning process: an overview

7.2 Various segmentation schemes for industrial markets exist and may be used in combination. Databases have been developed to provide additional intelligence information which allows much tighter targeting of industrial customers. Industrial markets may be segmented using a variety of bases.

- **By location**. Many business sectors are concentrated in particular locations for example, engineering in the West Midlands, computer companies along the M4 corridor. The UK Office for National Statistics divides the country into eleven standard statistical regions, eight for England, defined by country, and one each for Wales, Scotland and Northern Ireland.

- **Company size** either by turnover or employees. This can give a good indication of their possible needs for products or services.

- **Usage rates**: Heavy, medium or light. This is most relevant in raw material and parts markets, and the market for some industrial services such as telecommunications and travel.

- **Industry classification** indicates the nature of the business and may provide a useful method to classify sales leads. The UK Standard Industrial Classification is based on the European classification. It classifies businesses by their main type of economic activity. It is a hierarchical system using five levels of detail which start with 17 broad categories and work down to individual products such as soft furnishings.

- **Product use**. An industrial organisation may buy a fleet of cars for use by its salesforce, or to hire out to the public as the basis for its service. Different uses are likely to be associated with different needs.

7.3 In industrial markets, just as in consumer markets, segmenting markets enables companies to devise strategies which more closely match the identified needs of customers. These smaller subgroups allow the marketing and sales team to get to know customers much better and resources and efforts to be channelled towards the most profitable segments. Remember that to be effective, segments must display three qualities.

- Measurability
- Accessibility
- Substantiality

Exam Tip

Segmentation might come up in almost any marketing question. It featured in a 20 mark question in June 1999 and in the December 1996 case study which concerned the Red Cross. In both of these questions, you were asked to suggest how to segment both business *and* consumer markets.

You have been given several approaches to consumer segmentation in this chapter. Is benefit segmentation appropriate to the Red Cross? For the Red Cross's clients, yes – but not for its donors. Perhaps psychographic segmentation is particularly promising in this regard. Charity is a 'good' a person buys for someone else. One good way of tackling this question is to list types of segmentation and then to see how they apply in the Red Cross's situation.

For corporate donors a similarly systematic approach can be taken. Even though we have not yet covered business-to-business marketing in this Study Text, you should be able to think of ways the business-to-business markets can be segmented. How about area, for a start, size of business and type of business? A firm giving to charity will normally hope for some public relations benefit in return, in which case this is similar to sponsorship.

8 TARGETING

8.1 Limited resources, competition and large markets make it ineffective and inappropriate for companies to sell to the entire market; that is, every market segment. For the sake of efficiency they must select target markets. Marketing managers may choose one of the following policy options.

- **Undifferentiated marketing** aims to produce a single product and get as many customers as possible to buy it. Segmentation is ignored.

- **Concentrated marketing** attempts to produce the ideal product for a single segment of the market (eg Rolls Royce cars, Mothercare mother and baby shops).

- **Differentiated marketing** attempts to introduce several versions of a product, each aimed at a different market segment (for example, the manufacture of several different brands of washing powder).

Action Programme 6

Identify one disadvantage of adopting a concentrated marketing approach and one disadvantage of adopting differentiated marketing.

8.2 The choice between these three approaches will depend on three factors.

- The degree to which the product and/or the market can be considered homogeneous.

- How far the company's resources are overextended as a consequence of differentiated marketing. Small firms, for example, may perform better by concentrating on only one segment.

- How far the product is advanced in its life cycle. If it is in the early stages, segmentation and target marketing is unlikely to be profitable, because each segment would be too small.

8.3 The potential benefit of segmentation and target marketing is that the seller will have increased **awareness** of how product design and development stimulates demand in a particular section of the market. Also, the **resources** of the business will be more effectively employed, since the organisation should be more able to make products which the customer demands.

9 POSITIONING

Key Concept

Brand positioning. Brands can be positioned in relation to competitive brands on product maps in which space is defined in terms of how buyers perceive key characteristics.

9.1 Products may be positioned in the market by emphasising a variety of factors.

(a) **Positioning by specific product features.** The most common approach to positioning, especially for industrial products. Most car advertisements, for example, stress the combination of product features available and usually also stress good value for money as well.

Part A: The marketing planning process: an overview

(b) **Positioning by benefits, problems, solutions, or needs**. Benefits are emphasised. This is generally **more effective than positioning on product features independent of benefits**. Pharmaceutical companies position their products to doctors by stressing effectiveness and side effects. Other examples include Crest, which positions its toothpaste as a cavity fighter, and DHL, which uses its worldwide network of offices as a basis for its positioning.

(c) **Positioning for specific usage occasions**. Similar to benefit positioning but this uses the occasion of usage as the main basis for the positioning. Johnson's Baby Shampoo is positioned as a product to use if you shampoo your hair every day, and Hennessy Cognac is for special occasions.

(d) **Positioning for user category**. 7-Up's use of the Fido Dido character to target urban adolescents illustrates how age has been used as a basis for positioning. Many breakfast cereal producers have also positioned by age.

(e) **Positioning against another product**. Although Avis never mentions Hertz explicitly in its advertising, its positioning as Number 2 in the rent-a-car market is an example of positioning against a leader. 'Me too' products can always be related to leaders in this way.

(f) **Product class disassociation**. This is a less common basis for positioning, but effective when introducing a new product clearly distinct from standard products in an established product category. For example, lead-free petrol is positioned against leaded petrol.

(g) **Hybrid basis**. On occasion, a positioning strategy may be founded on several of these alternatives, incorporating elements from more than one positioning base. Porsche, for example, use a combination of the product benefits and user characteristics.

9.2 A basic **perceptual map** positions brands in perceived price and perceived quality terms.

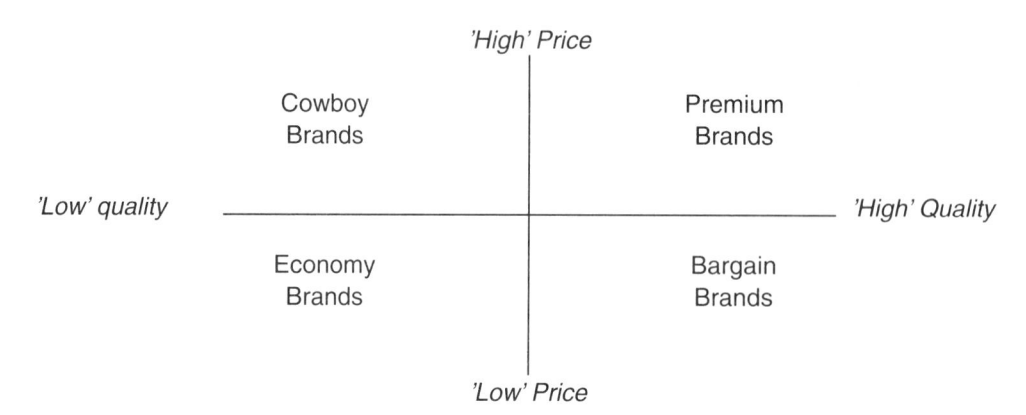

```
                        'High' Price
                             |
            Cowboy           |       Premium
            Brands           |       Brands
                             |
'Low' quality ───────────────┼─────────────── 'High' Quality
                             |
            Economy          |       Bargain
            Brands           |       Brands
                             |
                         'Low' Price
```

9.3 Price and quality are clearly important elements in every marketing mix, but, in the customer's opinion, **they cannot be considered independent variables. A 'high' price will almost always be associated with high quality and equally low price with low quality**. Everybody would like to buy a bargain brand problem to overcome is the question of belief: will customers accept that a high quality product can be offered at a low price?

9.4 MFI would claim to be in the 'bargain' quadrant. Many consumers perceive them to be at the lower end of the economy segment. Frequent sales and discounts in the store have the effect of overcoming at least some of the difficulties resulting from individuals using price as a surrogate for assessment of quality. Thus, the price label shows the higher pre-discounted price and the low sale price. **Customers appear to use the pre-sale price in order to confirm promotional claims about quality**.

9.5 Public concern about such promotional pricing has resulted in the introduction of restrictions on the use of these techniques. Promotions have to be part of a genuine 'sale', and stores must provide evidence of this fact.

Gaps in the market

9.6 Market research into consumer perceptions can determine how customers locate competitive brands on a matrix.

Restaurants in Anytown

9.7 The hypothetical model above shows a gap in the market for a moderately priced reasonable quality eating place. This is evident between clusters in the high price/high quality and the low price/low quality segments.

9.8 It would be wise to think before acting on this assumption. Why does the gap exist? Is it that no entrepreneurial restaurateur has noticed the opportunity? Or is it that, while there is sufficient demand for gourmet eating and cheap cafes, there are insufficient customers to justify a restaurant in the middle range segment? There may well be other factors, such as these, to be taken into consideration in this case. More research would be needed to determine which of these conditions apply.

Competitive positioning

9.9 Competitive positioning is concerned with 'a general idea of what kind of offer to make to the target market in relation to competitors' offers' (Kotler). Product quality and price are obviously important for competitive positioning, but Kotler identified a 3 × 3 matrix of nine different competitive positioning strategies.

Price Product quality	High	Medium	Low
High	Premium strategy	Penetration strategy	Superbargain strategy
Medium	Overpricing strategy	Average quality strategy	Bargain strategy
Low	Hit and run strategy	Shoddy goods strategy	Cheap goods strategy

9.10 Further material on brand management appears in Chapter 6.

Part A: The marketing planning process: an overview

Chapter Roundup

- Overall corporate objectives are normally expressed in financial terms. A modern trend is to use a *balanced scorecard* rather than a single financial objective. Marketing strategies flow from and support corporate objectives.

- Gap analysis quantifies the size of the profit gap, or other appropriate 'gap' between the objective/targets for the planning period and the forecast based on the extrapolation of the current situation. The organisation must then identify different actions or strategies which would help to fill the identified gap.

- The purpose of competitive strategy is to provide the organisation with a competitive advantage. A number of alternative approaches to competitive strategy exist, but Porter suggests three basic types: overall cost leadership, differentiation and focus.

- Ansoff's product/market matrix is used for the analysis and determination of growth strategies. It suggests four possible options.

- The BCG's product portfolio analysis is a tool for determining marketing strategy.

- PIMS is a diagnostic tool based on a database. It allows organisations to compare their strategic performance with that of other organisations.

- A market is rarely a mass, homogeneous group of customers, each wanting an identical product. Market segmentation is based on the recognition that every market consists of potential buyers with different needs, and different buying behaviour. These different customer attitudes may be grouped into segments and a different marketing approach will be taken by an organisation for each market segment.

- A total market may occasionally be homogenous, but this is rare. Each market segment becomes an individual target market for the organisation, and requires a unique marketing mix. The organisation can formulate a marketing strategy for each target market. Segmentation is an extremely important marketing tool.

- There are a number of ways in which a consumer market can be segmented, for example by location, by demography, by social class or by life style. Industrial markets can also be segmented.

- Limited resources and competition in large markets make it impossible for companies to sell to the entire market. For the sake of efficiency they must select target markets. There are three basic options in marketing products for target markets.

- Brands can be positioned in relation to competitors on 'product maps', on which space and positioning is defined in terms of how key characteristics of products are perceived by buyers.

Quick Quiz

1. What are the suggested balanced scorecard perspectives? (see para 2.6)
2. What does gap analysis involve? (3.1)
3. What types of products can be categorised in a differentiation strategy? (3.13)
4. What four options are suggested by Ansoff's product/market matrix? (3.17)
5. Sketch a diagram of the Boston Consulting Group's product portfolio analysis. (3.20)
6. What is Kotler's definition of market segmentation? (5.1 Key Concept)
7. What are the three requirements for effective market segmentation? (5.4)
8. What is the most commonly used classification in segmentation by social class? (6.7)
9. What is psychographics? (6.15)
10. What is ACORN? (6.23)
11. Give four examples of how industrial markets might be segmented. (7.2)
12. What is concentrated marketing? (8.1)
13. Give five examples of characteristics which may be used to position products. (9.1)
14. Draw Kotler's 3 × 3 matrix of different competitive positioning strategies, plotting price against product quality. (9.9)

2: Developing market objectives and strategies

Action Programme Review

1. (a) Capital is a scarce resource so profitability must be assessed in opportunity cost terms. The **cost of capital** is the return which would be available from the best alternative investment opportunity with the same riskiness. If we cannot beat this, we should question whether we should continue with what we are doing.

   (b) There is often a conflict between short-term and long-term profitability in that expenditure today may be rewarded only in the fairly distant future; cutting that expenditure will improve short-term profits, but may jeopardise profits in the longer term. Investment in basic research is an example.

2. This requires the following.

   - Setting up production facilities for mass production, so as to obtain economies of scale.
   - Using the latest technology.
   - In high-technology industries, and in industries depending on labour skills for product design and production methods, there will be a learning curve effect (also called a cost experience curve). By producing more items than any other competitor, a firm can benefit more from the learning curve, and achieve lower average costs.
   - Concentrating on productivity objectives, and seeking productivity improvements and cost reductions (for example by zero base budgeting, or value analysis).
   - Minimisation of overhead costs.

3. The following non-profit benefits can be identified.

   - The identification of new marketing opportunities as a result of better understanding of consumer needs in each of the segments.
   - Specialists can be developed and appointed to each of the company's major segments. Operating practices then benefit from the expertise of staff with specialist knowledge of the segment's business.
   - The total marketing budget can be allocated more effectively, according to needs and the likely return from each segment.
   - Precision marketing approaches can be used. The company can make finer adjustments to the product and service offerings and to the marketing appeals used for each segment.
   - Specialist knowledge and extra effort may enable the company to dominate particular segments and gain competitive advantage.
   - The product assortment can be more precisely defined to reflect differences between customer needs.
   - Improved segmentation allows more highly targeted marketing activity. For instance, the sales team develops an in-depth knowledge of the needs of a particular group of consumers and can get to know a network of potential buyers within the business and there is an increased likelihood of referrals and recommendations.
   - Feedback and customer problems are more effectively communicated. Producers develop an understanding in the needs of a target segment and expertise in helping to solve its problems.

4. A rising divorce rate is one of the factors underlying an increase in single-parent families and a decline in the incidence of the nuclear family of working husband, home-making wife and dependent children. Declining traditional industries and the increasing employment of women in service orientated industries, often involving part rather than full-time work, has produced more households in which the sole breadwinner is female rather than male, and households with two or more wage earners.

   Structural changes have been accompanied by a trend towards later marriage and delayed child bearing. Rising house prices plus high interest rates have meant that many newly formed households often contain partners who both work. Greater financial independence for women is also growing as a result of the economic and social changes of the 1980s and 1990s.

5. (a) The market for *adult education classes* may be segmented by several criteria.

   - Age (younger people might prefer classes in, say, yoga)
   - Sex (women might prefer self defence courses)
   - Occupation (apprentices may choose technical classes)

Part A: The marketing planning process: an overview

- Social class (middle class people might prefer art or music subjects)
- Education (poorly educated people might prefer to avoid all forms of evening class)
- Family life cycle (the interests of young single people are likely to differ from those of young married people with children)

(b) In the *magazines and periodicals* market the segmentation may be by different criteria.

- sex (Woman's Own)
- social class (Country Life)
- income (Ideal Home)
- occupation (Accountancy Age, Computer Weekly)
- leisure interests (Practical Boat Owner)
- political ideology (New Statesman)
- age ('19', Honey)
- lifestyle (Playboy)

(c) The market for *sporting facilities* could be segmented in yet another way.

- Geographical area (rugby in Wales, ski-ing in parts of Scotland, sailing in coastal towns)
- Population density (squash clubs in cities, riding in country areas)
- Occupation (gymnasia for office workers)
- Education (there may be a demand from ex-schoolboys for facilities for sports taught at certain schools, such as rowing)
- Family life cycle or age (parents may want facilities for their children; young single or married people may want facilities for themselves)

6 *Concentrated marketing* runs the risk of relying on a single segment of a single market. This can lead to problems. For example, the de Lorean sports car firm ran into irreversible financial difficulties in 1981-82 when the sports car market contracted in the USA. Specialisation, nonetheless, can enable a firm to capitalise on a profitable, although perhaps temporary, competitive edge over rivals (such as Kickers specialising in leisure footwear).

The main disadvantage of *differentiated marketing* is the additional cost of marketing and production (extra product design and development costs, the loss of economies of scale in production and storage, extra promotion and administrative costs and so on). When the costs of further differentiation of the market exceed the benefits from further segmentation and target marketing, a firm is said to have *over-differentiated*. Some firms have tried to overcome this by aiming the same product at two market segments, Johnson's baby powder, for example, is sold to adults for their own use.

Now try illustrative question 2 at the end of the Study Text

3 Implementing the Marketing Plan

Chapter Topic List	Syllabus reference
1 Setting the scene	-
2 The marketing control process	1.3
3 Measurement and evaluation of performance	1.3
4 Measuring the effectiveness of the marketing mix	1.3
5 Taking control action	1.3
6 Centralisation and decentralisation	1.3
7 Sales-led, marketing-led and product-led organisations	1.3
8 Organising marketing activities	1.3

Learning Outcome

Students will understand the need to integrate marketing mix tools to achieve effective implementation of plans.

Key Concepts Introduced

- Control
- Sales-led organisation
- Market-led organisation
- Product-led organisation

Examples of Marketing at Work

- Advertising to children
- Rentokil
- Schweppes reorganisation
- Bridon plc
- Financial services

1   SETTING THE SCENE

1.1   Having considered how objectives are arrived at both for the organisation as a whole and in specifically marketing terms, we now turn our attention to putting the plan into action.

Part A: The marketing planning process: an overview

There are two main aspects covered in this chapter. These are, first, methods which may be used to measure progress towards achieving our objectives and, second, how we might organise ourselves in order to be most effective in our work.

1.2 Section 2 looks in outline at the process of controlling marketing operations. Section 3 looks at principles and methods for measuring marketing performance generally, while section 4 considers the effectiveness of the marketing mix. Section 5 is concerned with control action and re-emphasises the need for consideration of possible trade-offs between the long and short term.

1.3 Section 6 begins the discussion of organising the marketing function by considering centralisation and decentralisation and Section 7 looks at the extent to which companies achieve a marketing outlook; this is reflected in their marketing structure. Section 8 looks in detail at ways a marketing department could be organised and, finally, Section 9 considers the roles of the key members of the marketing function.

2 THE MARKETING CONTROL PROCESS 12/98

> **Exam Tip**
> Control and evaluation has not been examined very often so far. It was last dealt with as a specific issue in December 1998.
> So, should you ignore this topic? No, of course not, for at least these reasons.
> (a) Don't assume that because a topic has not been examined recently it won't be examined in future.
> (b) You might earn yourself the odd extra mark by mentioning the need for adequate controls to go with your marketing plans.
> (c) The marketing audit is a control device which can be used as an input to the planning process – so any question about the marketing audit can mention the fact that it is a control over the marketing activity.

2.1 The marketing control process is vital to the achievement of marketing objectives and the successful completion of marketing plans. Control is every bit as important a feature of the role of the marketing manager as new product development or promotional creativity.

> **Key Concept**
> To **control** is to measure results against targets and take any action necessary to adjust performance.

2.2 Because marketing is essentially concerned with people, who can be both unpredictable and awkward, **controlling marketing activities is particularly problematic**. Difficulties arise with information, timing and the cost aspects of marketing plans.

2.3 The marketing control process is **iterative** and can be broken down into four stages.

- Development of objectives and strategies
- Establishment of standards
- Evaluation of performance
- Corrective action

2.4 Part of the corrective action stage may well be to adjust objectives and strategies in the light of experience.

3: Implementing the marketing plan

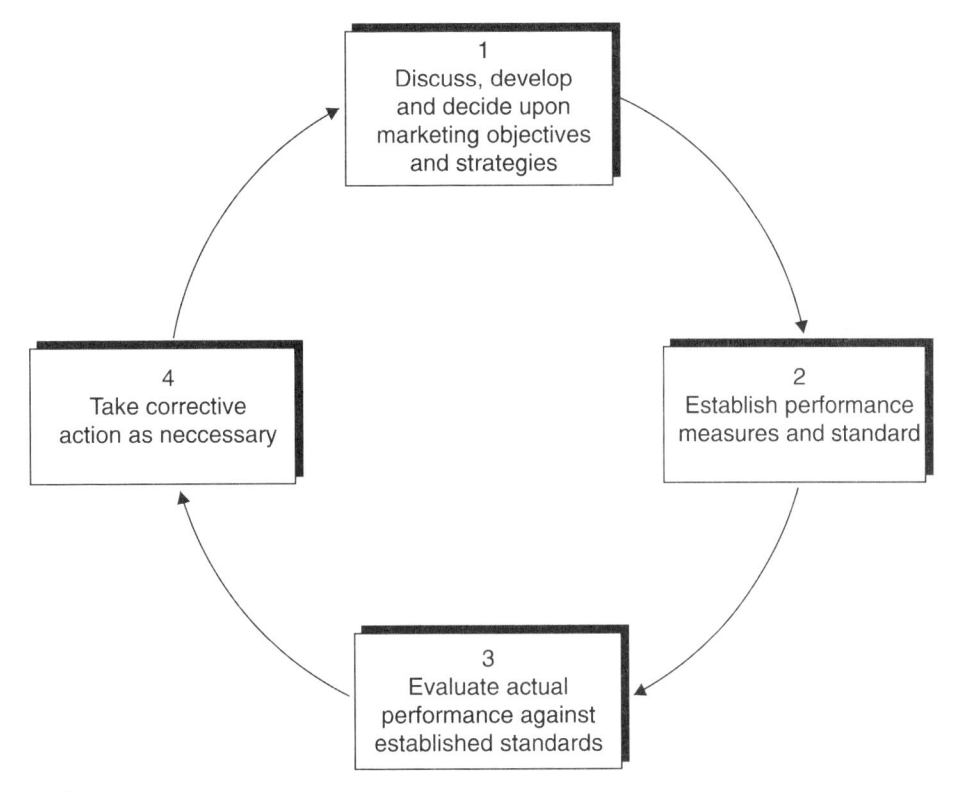

```
        ┌─────────────────┐
        │        1        │
        │ Discuss, develop│
        │  and decide upon│
        │ marketing       │
        │ objectives      │
        │ and strategies  │
        └─────────────────┘
       ↗                    ↘
┌──────────────┐      ┌──────────────────┐
│      4       │      │        2         │
│Take corrective│      │Establish         │
│action as     │      │performance       │
│neccessary    │      │measures and      │
│              │      │standard          │
└──────────────┘      └──────────────────┘
       ↖                    ↙
        ┌─────────────────┐
        │        3        │
        │ Evaluate actual │
        │ performance     │
        │ against         │
        │ established     │
        │ standards       │
        └─────────────────┘
```

The marketing control process

Development of objectives and strategies

2.5 Setting objectives and developing strategies has been covered in Chapters 1 and 2 of this manual and will not be discussed further here.

Efficiency and effectiveness

2.6 Efficiency and effectiveness are two fundamental aspects of performance. Drucker wrote:

> 'Efficiency is concerned with doing things right. Effectiveness is doing the right thing ... Even the healthiest business, the business with the greatest effectiveness, can die of poor efficiency. But even the most efficient business cannot survive, let alone succeed, if it is efficient in doing the wrong things, ie if it lacks effectiveness. No amount of efficiency would have enabled the manufacturer of buggy whips to survive.'

Efficiency

2.7 The fact that most organisations try to achieve certain objectives with limited resources gives rise to the concept of **efficiency** or **productivity**.

2.8 Efficiency can be defined as the ratio of output quantities to input resources. Efficiency and inefficiency are measures along the same scale, with 'efficiency' referring to a higher ratio of output to input than the norm or standard and 'inefficiency' referring to a lower ratio.

2.9 Inputs comprise *all* those factors which contribute to the production of organisational outputs. Drucker points out that efficiency or productivity is now less related to the productivity of manual labour or machinery, and more related to the increasing role of knowledge workers such as managers, researchers, planners, designers and innovators. Many managers today believe that the only opportunity left for competitive advantage lies in their human resources.

Effectiveness

2.10 Effectiveness can be defined as success in producing a desired result. Generally, an organisation is effective **if it meets the needs of its chosen client group(s)** and deploys its resources in the best possible way.

2.11 Effectiveness can be measured internally by establishing whether or not an organisation has achieved the targets set for itself in its planning processes. However, one organisation might set itself easier targets than another and so it might be effective in terms of its *own* targets but not effective when compared with other organisations.

2.12 In addition, there are several more general problems of measuring effectiveness.

(a) **Effectiveness over time**. Effectiveness has to be measured over time as the organisation and its environment change. The problem is essentially one of how best to balance short-term considerations against long-term interest.

(b) **Measurements of effectiveness which relate to the organisation as a whole** are not entirely satisfactory because they ignore the vital role played by individual sub-units of the organisation.

(c) **Different organisations have different characteristics and goals** and this fact suggests that different criteria of effectiveness ought to apply to different types of organisation. Furthermore, even with similar types of organisation, the appropriate measure of effectiveness may vary according to the stage of development that an organisation has reached or even to the nature of the ownership (for example, a public company or a state-owned business).

2.13 Performance should be measured and judged by obtaining data about actual results for a direct comparison with the targets or standards set. Performance measures must therefore have two characteristics.

- They must be measurable.
- They must relate directly to the targets or standards set in the plan.

2.14 Targets or standards may be for the long term or short term. Long-term targets for achievement will relate to the organisation's **objectives and strategic plans**. Short-term targets and standards will be for operational planning and control at a junior management level, and for medium-term planning and budgeting, and budgetary control by middle management.

Quantitative and qualitative targets

2.15 Performance can be measured in quantitative or qualitative terms.

- **Quantitative measurements are expressed in figures**, such as cost levels, units produced per week, delay in delivery time and market penetration per product.

- **Qualitative targets**, although not directly measurable in quantitative terms, may still be **verified by judgement and observation**.

2.16 **Where possible, performance should be measured in quantitative terms because these are less subjective** and liable to bias. Qualitative factors such as employee welfare and motivation, protection of the environment against pollution, and product quality might all be gauged by quantitative measures (such as employee pay levels, labour turnover rates, the level of toxicity in industrial waste, reject and scrap rates).

3: Implementing the marketing plan

Financial control information

2.17 Management control information is often expressed in **monetary** terms because this serves as a measurable and readily understandable measure of performance. Money is a useful measure.

(a) It allows direct performance comparisons between completely different functions and activities: the relative costs and profit contributions of, say, a purchasing manager and a sales manager cannot readily be compared except on a monetary basis.

(b) It facilitates the processing of technical information by non-technical personnel because monetary terms can be understood.

(c) Profitability is the main measure of corporate performance.

Action Programme 1

What are the disadvantages of using money as a measure when collecting management control information?

Marketing performance standards

2.18 Performance standards are set for two reasons.

- To tell managers what they are required to accomplish, given the authority to make appropriate decisions
- To indicate to managers how well their actual results measure against their targets, so that control action can be taken where it is needed

2.19 **It follows that in setting standards for performance, it is important to distinguish between controllable items and uncontrollable ones**. Any matters which cannot be controlled by an individual manager should be excluded from his or her standards for performance.

2.20 The most common measures by which marketing performance is judged are sales levels, costs and market shares. However, responsible companies will also have ethical and social responsibility standards. The most marketing-orientated organisations will be likely to pursue **relationship marketing** which entails a high degree of customer care. Thus, in addition to sales measures, many companies will seek to measure **customer satisfaction**.

2.21 Performance standards could thus be set at sales of £X for the period, Y% market share and Z% profit, all set against a maximum number of customer complaints.

Evaluation of performance

2.22 The organisation monitors performance at given time intervals **by comparing actual results with the standards set** to determine whether it is on, above or below these targets.

Corrective action

2.23 Where performance against standard is below a tolerable level then remedial action needs to be taken. This may mean invoking **contingency plans** previously drawn up for this purpose

Part A: The marketing planning process: an overview

or taking *ad hoc* actions such as initiating sales promotions. On reflection, it may be decided that the original target was, in fact, unattainable.

Problems in controlling marketing activities

2.24 A number of problems can occur. Information may not be available at the right time or indeed at an affordable cost. Competitors can take retaliatory action, for example, aimed at sabotaging a new product launch. Unforeseen changes may occur in the environment: new laws may be passed, for example, regarding Sunday trading; economies can grow or decline and fashions can change. In the internal environment, there may be inadequate support from staff both inside and outside the marketing field. Some may actively resist the performance standards set. Finally, there is the element of creativity. Many organisations are in the hands of their advertising agencies in seeking the image breakthrough that makes the difference between success and failure.

Marketing at Work

Advertising to children

When first advertising Children's' World, Boots found that child viewers did not identify themselves with children of similar age on television - they liked to see themselves as older. If child viewers then thought themselves too old for Children's' World, catastrophe could have resulted. However, Boots were conducting tracking studies during the TV campaign and were able to adjust accordingly.

Action Programme 2

Give examples of measures by which performance could be judged.

Marketing at Work

Rentokil

Thompson's formula for success is simple and very clear. Rentokil is a diversified services group, with a defined core competence being the ability to carry out high-quality services (from pest control through healthcare to manned guarding) on other people's premises through well recruited, well trained and well-motivated people. Exposure to cyclical business is minimal, and it has expanded into all the major developed economies.

Head office is lean and mean and there are no functional hierarchies. Rentokil is run through a branch structure whereby every manager has their own budget and profit centre and is incentivised according to their own success. There are no big ad budgets: marketing is embedded in the way everyone does their job, and decision making is influenced by a true 'customer needs first' orientation. Market intelligence is facilitated by the fact that most employees have daily contact with their customers. Not only is profit responsibility devolved as far as possible down the organisation, but the businesses are run geographically rather than by business stream. What's more, all Rentokil's services are presented and marketed in the same way in every country where they operate.

A habitual challenger of received wisdom, Thompson makes no apologies for wanting to know exactly what is going on in his business. 'I go around with a view that things are going as budgeted or forecast unless I know to the contrary. If that's control that's control and I believe enormously in control.'

He believes in clear communication and monitoring progress, and adheres to the adage 'don't expect, inspect' in the belief that much management failure is to do with lack of attention to detail.

Marketing Business, July/August 1996

3 MEASUREMENT AND EVALUATION OF PERFORMANCE

3.1 Performance can be measured by formal reporting systems, or by personal observation. The latter is usually the most convenient method for a *qualitative* evaluation of human performance. Conversely, it is easy for the eye to be deceived and for qualitative judgement to be wrong. Formal reporting systems, such as management accounting systems, provide a much more objective *quantitative* assessment than the human observer and, once systems are set up, can be much less time-consuming.

3.2 When performance objectives are not being achieved, the reason will not necessarily be obvious and due consideration must be given before corrective action is taken. For example, if sales in a particular region are low, increasing the sales supervision or sending the representative on additional sales training programmes will be of little effect if the cause of the poor sales is a product which is not suited to local tastes.

Evaluation of marketing activities

3.3 **The three major ways in which marketing activities may be evaluated are sales analysis, market share analysis and cost analysis.** However, there are other analyses which could be almost as important in particular product-market situations. For example, when launching a major new FMCG product, it would be crucial to evaluate awareness, trial and re-purchase during the test market phase.

Sales analysis

3.4 The table below is a sales analysis for the first quarter of the year.

Month	Actual sales £'000	Budgeted sales £'000	Variance ± £'000	Cumulative variance £'000
1	90	100	− 10	− 10
2	115	120	− 5	− 15★
3	150	140	+ 10	− 5

3.5 At the start of the period, sales were well below the performance standard. At the point asterisked (★) remedial action was taken which boosted sales above budget for month 3, so that at the end of the quarter the cumulative adverse variance has been greatly reduced.

Market share analysis

3.6 This table shows a comparison of brands over a two year period.

Brand	Sales 1996 £m (est)	Market share % 1996	Position 1996	Market share % 1995	Position 1995
Ours	12	20	3	15	3
Brand X	20	33	1	30	2
Brand Y	18	30	2	32	1
Others	10	17	-	23	-
Total	60	100		100	

3.7 This table shows that our position in 1996 is unchanged from 1995 but that we have increased our market share by 5% over 1995, largely at the expense of the minor players. (Care should be taken with interpretation: it is possible, for example, that in fact we have taken 5% from Brand Y and that Brands X and Y have each taken 3% from 'others'.)

3.8 We can also see that Brand Y has lost its brand leadership to Brand X (1996 versus 1995).

Part A: The marketing planning process: an overview

3.9 In order to make this analysis more meaningful we should want to know what our market share objective was for 1996. It would also help to know sales for 1995 so that we can establish whether the total market has risen, fallen or remained the same.

Marketing cost analysis

3.10 The next table illustrates some of the difficulties in controlling marketing costs.

Period	Cost item	Actual expenditure £'000	Budgeted expenditure £'000	Variance ± £'000
Quarter 2	Advertising	100	110	−10
	Exhibitions	50	40	+10
	Literature	40	80	−40
	Marketing research	20	5	+15
	Other prom	15	10	+5
	Salesforce	400	440	−40
	Totals	625	685	−60

3.11 At first sight it appears that the performance standards have been poorly set but it should be noted these are only one quarter's figures. Some of the variances might well disappear over the year and some might be easily explained, for example, the salesforce may be temporarily below establishment, literature may be underspent because a new catalogue is late in delivery and so on.

3.12 Also, it is good practice to have a contingency reserve, which would normally be added to the year's total at, say, 10% of the total budget.

Special analyses: major new product launch

3.13 Finally we look at an example of a special analysis. This table shows research results for the launch of product X. (*Note.* All figures are percentages of a total target market of 15 million.)

	Awareness		Trial purchase		Purchase	
	Target	Actual	Target	Actual	Target	Actual
Pre-launch period Weeks 7 and 8	40	30	-	-	-	-
Launch period Weeks 9 and 10	75	60	50	55	-	-
Post-launch period Weeks 11 to 20	80	70	-	-	40	40

3.14 The table shows that the awareness level achieved is less than that targeted. This could indicate a fault in media reach which needs investigation with the media research department of the advertising agency.

3.15 However, despite having reached a smaller target audience than planned, trial purchase was higher than targeted, indicating highly effective advertising content. Due to this and a repurchase rate which is about on target, we have achieved our total sales objective. Nevertheless, it seems clear that if we can improve awareness then we should be able to achieve repurchase sales above target.

3: Implementing the marketing plan

Other aspects of performance

Market share performance

3.16 Changes in market share have to be considered against the change in the market as a whole. A product might be increasing share when the market is declining, because the competition is losing sales even more quickly. The reverse may also be true. The market could be expanding, and a declining market share might not represent a decline in absolute sales volume, but a failure to take more of the growing market.

3.17 It may well be difficult initially to define the market and market share of the organisation's products but these are important pieces of information.

Monitoring competitor performance

3.18 Budgetary control comparisons will tell the management of an organisation whether the established targets are being achieved, but this sort of comparison can tend to be very inward looking. When an organisation operates in a competitive environment, it should try to obtain information about the financial performance of competitors, to make a comparison with the organisation's own results.

3.19 Financial information about competitors is available from published financial statements.

- Total profits, sales and capital employed
- ROCE, profit/sales ratio, cost/sales ratios and asset turnover ratios
- The increase in profits and sales over the course of the past twelve months and prospects for the future
- Sales and profits in each major business segment that the competitor operates in
- Dividend per share and earnings per share
- Gearing and interest rates on debt
- Share price, and P/E ratio (stock exchange information)

3.20 A more detailed comparison of financial performance might be obtainable when there is a scheme of interfirm comparison for the industry.

Monitoring customers

3.21 In some industrial markets or reseller markets, **a producer might sell exclusively to a small number of key customers**. The performance of these customers would therefore be of some importance to the producer: if the customer prospers, he will probably buy more and if he does badly, he will probably buy less. It may also be worthwhile monitoring the level of profitability of selling to each customer.

3.22 **Key customer analysis calls for seven main areas of investigation.**

(a) **Key customer identity**
- Name of each key customer
- Location
- Status in market
- Products
- Size of firm (capital employed, turnover, number of employees)

Part A: The marketing planning process: an overview

(b) **Customer history**

- First purchase date.
- What is the average order size, by product?
- What is the regularity/ periodicity of the order, by product?
- What is the trend in size of orders?
- What is the extent of the customer's knowledge of the firm's products?
- What is the extent of the customer's knowledge of competitors' products?
- Were there any lost or cancelled orders? For what reason?

(c) **Relationship of customer to product**

- Are the products purchased to be resold? If not, why are they bought?
- Do the products form part of the customer's service/product?

(d) **Relationship of customer to potential market**

- What is the size of the customer in relation to the total end-market?
- Is the customer likely to expand, or not? Diversify? Integrate?

(e) **Customer attitudes and behaviour**

- What interpersonal factors exist which could affect sales by the firm?
- Does the customer also buy competitors' products?
- To what extent may purchases be postponed?
- What emotional factors exist in buying decisions?

(f) **The financial performance of the customer**

How successful is the customer in his own markets? Analysis similar to that conducted on competitors can be carried out.

(g) **The profitability of selling to the customer**

- What profit is the organisation making on sales to the customer?
- What would be the financial consequences of losing the customer?
- Is the customer buying in order sizes that are unprofitable to supply?
- What is the level of inventory required specifically to supply these customers?
- Are there any other specific costs involved in supplying this customer, for example, technical and test facilities, R & D facilities, special design staff?

This analysis might be extended to other categories of customer by companies with larger customer bases.

Market performance ratios

3.23 An organisation should study information not only about its share of a particular market, but also the performance of the market as a whole.

(a) Some markets are more profitable than others. The reasons why this might be so (rivalry among existing firms, the threat of new entrants, the bargaining power of buyers, the bargaining power of suppliers and the threat from substitute products or services) were discussed in an earlier chapter.

(b) Some markets will be new, others growing, some mature and others declining. The stage in the **product's life cycle** might be relevant to performance analysis.

3.24 Information about market performance is needed to enable an organisation to plan and control its product-market strategy.

3: Implementing the marketing plan

4 MEASURING THE EFFECTIVENESS OF THE MARKETING MIX

4.1 Marketing managers are responsible for monitoring their progress towards the agreed targets and standards. To do this it is necessary to evaluate the effectiveness of the marketing mix.

4.2 This section will consider ways of assessing the effectiveness of four of the mix elements.

- Price
- Promotion (in particular, advertising)
- Place
- Personal selling (which you will encounter as an element of the 'extended marketing mix' later, when we look at services marketing).

Price

4.3 There are several aspects to pricing which should be reviewed. These include discount policy, sales volume and positioning strategy.

4.4 **Discount policy** should be directed towards one of two aims.

(a) Encouraging a greater volume of sales. This is a marketing policy.

(b) Obtaining the financial benefits of earlier payments from customers, which ought to exceed the costs of the discounts allowed. This is a financial management policy and therefore, principally, the responsibility of the finance staff.

4.5 Sales prices are set with a view to the **total volume of sales** they should attract.

(a) **New product pricing policy** might be to set high **skimming** prices or low '**penetration**' prices. The effectiveness of such pricing policies should be judged in the light of the following.

(i) For **skimming prices**, whether they have been too high, because the market has grown faster than anticipated, leaving the organisation with a low market share because of its high prices

(ii) For **penetration prices**, whether the price level has succeeded in helping the organisation to achieve its target share of the market

(b) Decisions to raise prices or lower prices will be based on assumptions about the **elasticity of demand**. Did actual increases or decreases in demand exceed or fall short of expectation?

4.6 An aspect of **product-market strategy** is the mixture of product quality and price which gives the product a *position* in relation to competing products. An organisation might opt for **a high price and high quality** strategy, or a **low price and average quality** strategy for instance. Actual price performance can be judged in two years

- By comparing the organisation's prices with those of competitors, to establish whether prices were comparatively low, average or high, as planned

- By judging whether the mix of product quality and price appears to have been effective

Part A: The marketing planning process: an overview

Promotion

4.7 It is difficult, if not impossible, to measure the success of an individual advertising campaign, although volume of sales may be a short-term guide.

4.8 A campaign to launch a new product, however, may have to be judged over a longer period of time to see how well the product establishes itself in the market. A comparison of the relative efficiency of sales promotion methods is also difficult to make, since a combination of methods is necessary for any successful sales promotion campaign. Shop window displays, for example, may be an important reminder to consumers who have seen a television advertisement.

4.9 The effectiveness of advertising is therefore usually measured by marketing researchers in terms of customer attitudes or psychological response. Kotler, writing in an American context, commented that:

> 'most of the measurement of advertising effectiveness is of an applied nature, dealing with specific advertisements and campaigns. Of the applied part, most of the money is spent by agencies on *pre-testing* the given advertisement or campaign before launching it into national circulation. Relatively less tends to be spent on *post-testing* the effect of given advertisements and campaigns.'

4.10 Post-testing involves finding out how well people can recall an advertisement and the product it advertises, and whether (on the basis of a sample of respondents) attitudes to the product have changed since the advertising campaign. Post-testing can be conducted over a long period of time, to establish how customer attitudes change over time in response to advertising. This might be particularly relevant in the case of advertising a corporate image: post-testing would help to establish whether an organisation is succeeding in getting the corporate image it is trying to build up in the public mind.

4.11 It would seem sensible too, to try to consider the effectiveness of advertising in terms of cost, sales and profit, but only if the aim of an advertising campaign was directed towards boosting sales. If there is a noticeable increase in sales volume as a result of an advertising campaign, it should be possible to estimate the extent to which advertising might have been responsible for the extra sales and contribution, and the extra net profit per £1 of advertising could be measured.

Action Programme 3

Give examples of types of sales promotions to which the consumer sales response is easily measurable.

Place

4.12 Some organisations might use channels of distribution for their goods which are unprofitable to use, and which should either be abandoned in favour of more profitable channels, or made profitable by giving some attention to cutting costs or increasing minimum order sizes.

4.13 It might well be the case that an organisation gives close scrutiny to the profitability of its products, and the profitability of its market segments, but does not have a costing system which measures the costs of distributing the products to their markets via different distribution channels.

Personal selling

4.14 The effectiveness of personal selling can be measured in three different ways.

- For the sales force as a whole
- For each group of the sales force (for example, each regional sales team, or the 'special accounts' sales staff etc)
- For each individual salesperson

If there is a telephone sales staff, their performance should be measured separately from the travelling sales staff.

Action Programme 4

Give examples of possible measures of performance which might be used to measure results of personal selling against target or standard.

4.15 Actual performance is measured in order to compare it against a standard, and it is not an easy task to decide what the standards should be. How would an individual's sales quota be set, for example? The standards or budget might be strict or lax. One person might be given an easy quota and another a difficult one to achieve. There is rarely an objectively correct standard or target which seems fair to everyone concerned. It is important not to assume that the efficient sales person who makes ten calls a day is doing a better job by the colleague who makes fewer calls but wins more orders.

4.16 The costs of selling and distribution can be a very large proportion of an organisation's total costs, and so the performance of a sales force should be based on productivity and profitability, rather than sales alone.

> 'In recent years the cost of fielding a sales force has increased dramatically ... Faced with such large and continually rising costs, many firms set expense goals all the way down to the territory level. Moreover, although representatives and sales managers tend to focus on the 'top line' (net sales), more and more firms are using profitability and productivity goals (the 'bottom line') to help evaluate the performance of their sales force.'

(P Bennett, Marketing)

5 TAKING CONTROL ACTION

Tolerance limits for variances

5.1 No corporate plan has the detail or accuracy that a budget has. Consequently, the tolerance limits giving 'early warning' or deviations from the plan should be wider. For example, if tolerance limits in budgetary control are variance ± 5% from standard, then corporate planning tolerance limits might be set at ± 10% or more from targets.

5.2 Whatever the tolerance limits are, the reporting of results which go outside the limits must be prompt. If sales have dropped well below target, the reasons must be established quickly and possible solutions thought about. Tolerance limits should be set on both the favourable and the adverse side of the planning targets. For example, if a company's products unexpectedly gain second highest market share, the questions that should be asked are as follows.

- How did it happen?

Part A: The marketing planning process: an overview

- Can profitability targets be maintained or exceeded at the sales volumes supporting that market share?
- Can second place be maintained, and if so, what needs to be done to secure the position?
- Can the market leader be toppled? (And if so, is this profitable?)

The trade-off between the short term and the long term for control action

5.3 We have already introduced the idea of the trade-off between short and long term goals in the context of developing marketing objectives. This trade-off is also relevant to control action.

5.4 It is often the case that in order to rectify short-term results, control action will be at the expense of long-term targets. Similarly, controls over longer-term achievements might call for short-term sacrifices. *Bhattacharya* argues that there are times when the long-term targets **must** be adversely affected by the need for short-term controls, but there should be a control mechanism to ensure that the trade off is properly judged and well balanced. He recommends the following.

(a) An organisation should recognise whether or not trade-offs in control action could be a serious problem for it.

(b) Managers should be aware that trade-offs take place.

(c) Controls should exist to prevent or minimise the possibility that short term controls can be taken which damage long-term targets, without an appraisal of the situation by senior management.

(d) Senior management must be given adequate control information for long-term as well as short term consequences.

(e) The planning and review system should motivate managers to keep long-term goals in view.

(f) Short-term goals should be **realistic**. Very often, the pressure on managers to sacrifice long term interests for short-term results is caused by the imposition of stringent and unrealistic short term targets on those managers in the first place.

(g) Performance measures should reflect both long-term and short-term targets. There might be, say, quarterly performance reviews on the achievement of strategic goals.

Revising forecasts

5.5 Real life data can be used to revise forecasts. Managers need information about whether actual results so far show that short term targets have been met. They also need to know whether longer-term targets are likely to be met.

5.6 Control at a strategic level, and the review of strategic plans, should be an iterative process, with revised forecasts for the future serving as an important part of the control information.

Corrective action

5.7 When performance does not meet target, managers have two options.

- Take steps to improve actual performance

3: Implementing the marketing plan

- Change the performance standard. A combination of these two control actions is also possible

5.8 Improving actual performance can be achieved by a range of methods, depending on the analysis of the reasons for the adverse variance. The marketing manager might, for example, need to find new ways of motivating marketing personnel or develop better techniques for successful co-ordination of marketing activities.

5.9 Changes to the performance standard are sometimes necessary., The standard might have been unrealistic when it was prepared, or subsequent changes to the marketing environment might have invalidated some of the assumptions made in its preparation.

6 CENTRALISATION AND DECENTRALISATION 6/99

6.1 Part of the process of marketing planning might be to consider the organisation of the marketing function. This section and the next two are about different approaches to marketing organisation structure.

Centralisation

6.2 In a **centralised organisation** all major decisions are made by top management and passed downwards for implementation by lower management. The result is consistency of approach and control to centralisation. It can slow down decision making and limit the information available before decisions are taken.

6.3 There are disadvantages, however. It can also destroy initiative and de-motivate lower management who might otherwise make a significant contribution to the decision-taking process.

Marketing at Work

Schweppes reorganisation

Schweppes Europe has embarked on a major management reorganisation designed to give more power to the company's headquarters and increase its focus on Schweppes, Dr Pepper and Crush brands.

The plans leave a question mark over future marketing spend for brands such as Sunkist, Canada Dry, Gini and Oasis.

According to sources the shake-up which will also affect the African, Indian and the Middle-East markets has been instigated by the division's new president, Doug Tough, in an attempt to recover lost markets and volume share.

He wants to reduce the influence of local national management to put an end to conflict between the regions and the Watford head office.

There was no one available at Cadbury Schweppes to comment. But Marketing Week understands that Dominic Lowe, vice president of marketing, will assume more control within the new structure, with regional marketing teams and their heads reporting directing to him.

Marketing Week, 14 February 1997

Decentralisation

6.4 In a **decentralised organisation** decision-taking authority is delegated outwards and downwards from top management to middle management. Such an approach encourages initiative and allows decisions to be taken where the action is taking place, which may reduce response times and lead to better decisions.

Part A: The marketing planning process: an overview

> **Action Programme 5**
>
> What do you think are the main disadvantages of too much decentralisation?

6.5 Most organisations seek to achieve a balance between centralised and decentralised decision-taking so as to gain the benefits of both. This may mean clearly identifying and communicating the types of decisions which may be taken at the various levels and giving guidance in the attempt to avoid contradictions between one region and another.

6.6 For example, in a large retail organisation, major product/brand decisions may be made centrally, but individual branch managers may be allowed some discretion with regard to stocking and pricing decisions according to local conditions.

7 SALES-LED, MARKETING-LED AND PRODUCT-LED ORGANISATIONS
6/97

> **Key Concept**
>
> A **sales-led organisation** is one where the selling function is dominant. It is typically found where capacity exceeds demand and where the organisational aim is to sell what it makes rather than make what it can sell.

7.1 A sales-led orientation tends to follow a period when the organisation concentrated on increasing its production capacity without necessarily improving its products. When the decline stage of the product life cycle begins, the organisation finds itself 'over-planted' and emphasis switches to selling. Unfortunately, some organisations adopt the hard-sell approach where products or services are pushed onto prospects irrespective of their real needs thus building up considerable bad will (as occurred in the holiday market with timeshares and, it is claimed, in the insurance market with PEPs).

> **Key Concept**
>
> A **market-led organisation** is one which first of all determines what customers want and then sets about providing goods or services which meet customers' wants and needs, at the right price, at the right time, at the right place and communicates effectively with these customers. The organisation will do this in a way consistent with achieving its own objectives.

7.2 The market-led organisation is therefore characterised by an emphasis on marketing research so that decisions on the marketing mix are based upon a continual flow of information from customers and potential customers.

7.3 When a company becomes marketing oriented, a number of changes take place.

(a) Long-term orientation changes to market-led.

(b) Planning emphasises the market.
- The right products
- The right channels
- The right level of service
- The right marketing strategy to meet the customer's long-term needs

7.4 The marketing approach, according to Lancaster and Massingham:

3: Implementing the marketing plan

'challenges every member of a company, whatever his or her specialist function, to relate his or her work to the needs of the marketplace, and to balance it against the firm's own profit needs. Nowhere is this more important than in the area of product design, where customers' views, rather than the views of production, should be the starting point'.

Marketing-led and sales-led organisations compared

7.5 Clearly, some kinds of conflicts are likely to arise where marketing staff attempt to make a positive impact on a sales-led organisation. In a marketing oriented company, however, senior personnel are much more likely to come from a marketing background. The marketing manager is usually given a position of authority which is equal to that of production or financial directors.

7.6 The respective emphases within sales and marketing oriented companies can be depicted as follows.

Department	Sales emphasis	Marketing emphasis
Sales	Short-term sales Sales most important One department	Long-term profits Customer satisfaction most important Whole organisation
Purchasing	Narrow product line Standard parts	Broad product line Non-standard parts
Finance	Hard and fast budgets Price to cover costs	Flexible budgets Market-oriented pricing
Accounting	Standard transactions	Special terms and discounts
Manufacturing	Long runs Few models Standard orders Long production lead times	Short runs Many models Custom orders Short production lead times

Product-led organisations

7.7 There is also a third type of organisation: the **product-led organisation**.

> **Key Concept**
> A **product-led organisation** is one which concentrates on the product itself and tends to de-emphasise other elements of the marketing mix. It tends to take the view that if the product is right it will sell itself and the world will beat a path to its doorstep.

7.8 The product-led approach is typically adopted by companies in high technology, or small companies set up to exploit a new invention. Product-led organisations can develop 'marketing myopia' to the extent that they forget the need. As *Levitt* says 'people who buy ¼' drills want ¼' holes'. If someone comes along with a better way of making ¼' holes, such as a laser beam, the drill becomes redundant. Design tends to be decided by the technicians rather than the customers.

Part A: The marketing planning process: an overview

Marketing at Work

Bridon plc

A new chief executive joined Bridon plc in September 1993. The recession was seriously denting its core wire and rope manufacturing businesses, raw material prices were soaring and his predecessor but one had taken early retirement.

Due to serious deficiencies in marketing and too many organisational overlaps, the new chief executive believed that Bridon was missing out on many opportunities in its core markets.

In response to these inadequacies, reports *Marketing Business (September 1995)*, he launched Project 360 early in 1994. So named because it involved taking a 360 degree view of the business, Project 360 aimed to transform Bridon from a production-driven dinosaur into a more nimble marketing-led company capable of responding to customers' needs on a worldwide basis.

The development of marketing departments

7.9 Although every organisation is different, common patterns appear in the structure of all organisations. The position occupied currently by departments of marketing evolved from the existence of sales departments. Traditionally, all dealings with a market would have been the responsibility of a sales director. As a marketing oriented approach developed a marketing director might appear in parallel to the sales director, but with two distinct departments. As fuller recognition of the marketing approach to business was granted, sales and marketing would become a single functional department, with sales as a sub group within marketing.

7.10 Marketing affects all of a company's activities. This means, in service industries, that the structure of operations is increasingly being designed, not so much around administrative convenience, but around the customer. For example, a British Telecom advertisement showed one member of staff dealing with a variety of queries from one caller, as opposed those enquiries being re-routed to several different departments.

7.11 The adoption of a marketing philosophy by a business leads inevitably to involvement of the marketing function in other business activities. Our section on 'internal markets' later deals with this issue in more detail.

Exam Tip

Few questions have been set so far about the position of the marketing department within the organisation as a whole, but bear in mind these points.

(a) The structure of an organisation can suggest whether or not it is genuinely marketing-led. For example, if there is no marketing director on the Board but marketing staff are responsible to a sales director, then the organisation might be product-led, or sales-led.

(b) There is a relationship between marketing and corporate planning and in such questions you can briefly mention the organisational implications of this.

In June 1997, you were asked about the role of marketing in sales-, product-, and marketing-led organisations. Answers to this should have been illustrated by diagrams showing the different organisation structure in each type of organisation.

8 ORGANISING MARKETING ACTIVITIES

8.1 There is no single best way to organise a department. The format chosen will depend on the nature of the existing organisational structure, patterns of management and the spread of the firm's product and geographical interests, among other things. However it is organised, every marketing department must take responsibility for four key areas.

3: Implementing the marketing plan

- Functions (promotion, pricing)
- Geographical areas (domestic, EU, International)
- Products (current accounts, deposits accounts, personal loans)
- Markets (personal, corporate)

Functional organisation

8.2 The department organised by function is typically headed by a marketing director who is responsible for the overall co-ordination of the marketing effort. A number of functional specialists such as a market research manager and a sales manager will be found in the second tier of management and they take responsibility for all activities in their functional specialism across all products and markets. This is a very simple format and is relatively straightforward in administrative terms. It also allows individuals to develop their particular specialisms, at the same time imposing a burden on the marketing director who will be required to perform co-ordinating and arbitrating activities to ensure the development of a coherent marketing mix for elements of the product range.

Functional organisation

```
                    Marketing
                    Director
        ┌──────────────┼──────────────┬──────────────┐
  Communications   Market Research   Product        Sales
    Manager          Manager         Manager        Manager
```

8.3 For a limited range of products, the burden on the marketing director is unlikely to be severe. As the organisation's range of products and markets expands, however, this arrangement will tend to be less efficient. Then there is always the danger that a particular product or market may be neglected because it is only one of a great variety being handled by a specific functional manager.

Geographical organisation

8.4 A simple geographical organisation for a marketing department is an extension of the functional organisation in which responsibility for some or all functional activities is devolved to a regional level, through a national manager. There will often be a similar regional devolution in other parts of the organisation, such as finance and personnel, with the establishment of multi-functional regional offices. This type of organisation would probably be more common in firms operating internationally where the various functional activities would be required for each national market or group of national markets.

8.5 The structure tends to be adopted by larger companies with too many people to be managed nationally and where there are perceived regional differences. An FMCG manufacturing company, for example, may supply multiple grocery chains that are organised regionally and therefore develop regional sales/sales promotions managers to link up with customers and regional store managers. Where sales promotion activities are needed quickly in response to competition, there may be a case for regional promotions managers to decide and implement these in conjunction with regional sales managers.

Part A: The marketing planning process: an overview

Geographical organisation

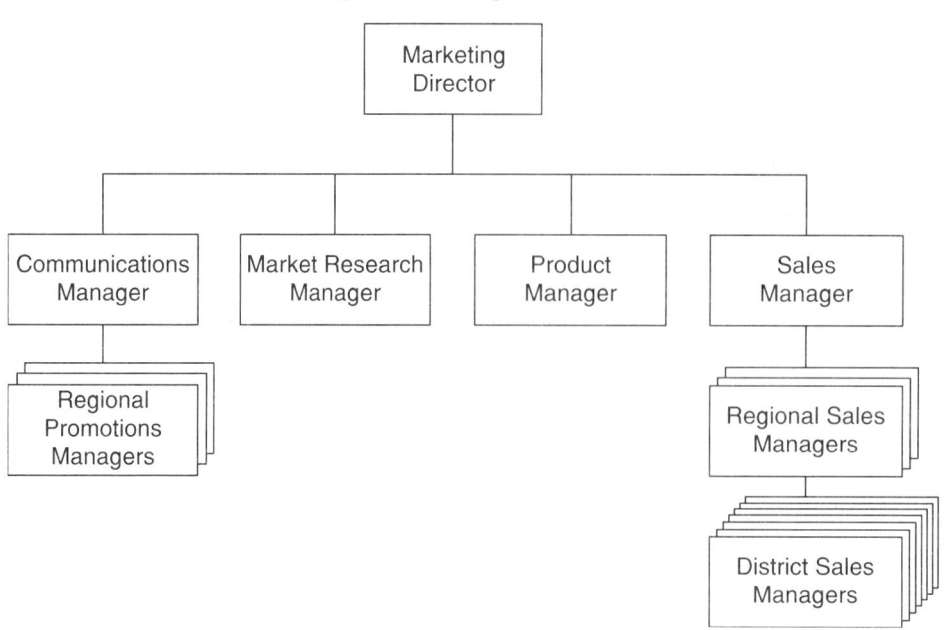

```
                        Marketing
                        Director
        ┌──────────────┬──────────┬──────────────┐
   Communications  Market Research  Product     Sales
     Manager         Manager       Manager     Manager
        │                                        │
   Regional                                  Regional Sales
   Promotions                                 Managers
   Managers                                       │
                                             District Sales
                                               Managers
```

Product-based organisation

8.6 This involves adding an additional tier of management which supplements the activities of functional managers. **Product managers take responsibility for specific products or groups of products**. This type of approach is likely to be particularly appropriate for organisations with either very diverse products or with a large range of products.

Product management

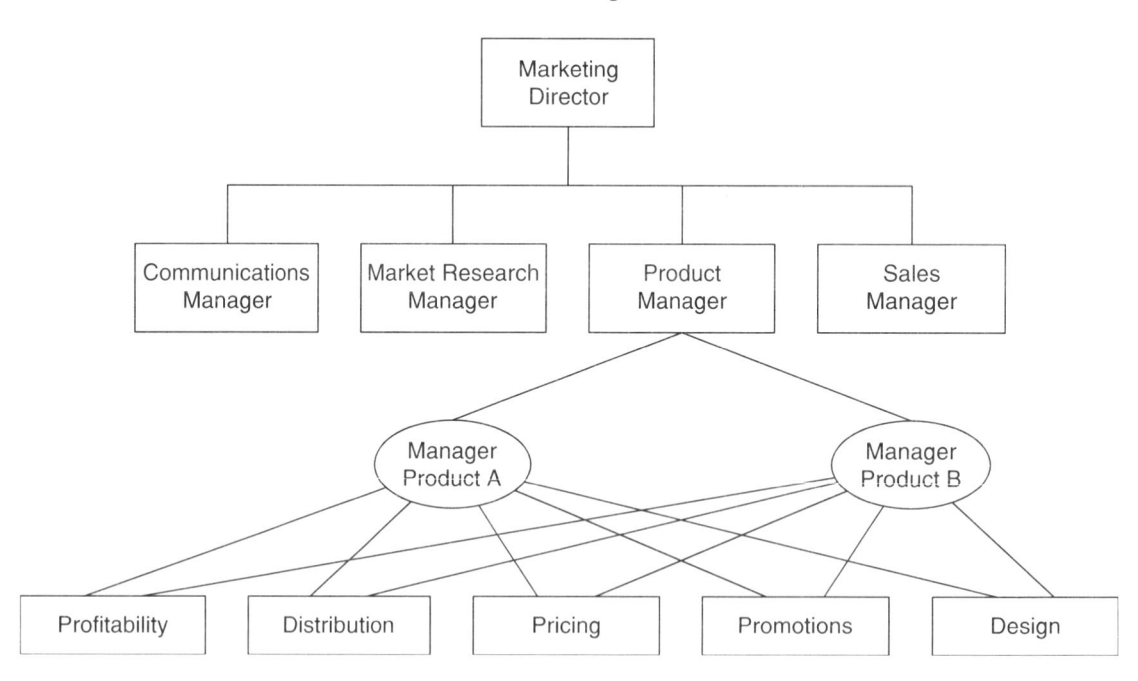

```
                        Marketing
                        Director
        ┌──────────────┬──────────┬──────────────┐
   Communications  Market Research  Product     Sales
     Manager         Manager       Manager     Manager

                   Manager              Manager
                   Product A            Product B

   Profitability | Distribution | Pricing | Promotions | Design
```

8.7 The individual product manager is responsible for developing plans to suit specific products and ensures that products remain competitive, drawing on the experience and guidance of functional managers. This allows the individual product managers to build up considerable experience and understanding of particular product groups, which is invaluable within a rapidly changing competitive environment. Very often the title **brand manager** rather than product manager will be used.

3: Implementing the marketing plan

8.8 It would be rare that a salesforce would be dedicated to a particular product, so that product manager A would have to compete with other product managers for the attention and support of the salesforce.

8.9 The product-based approach is becoming increasingly important, because the benefits of managers with particular responsibility and experience for specific product groups outweighs the costs associated with a loss of functional specialisation. Where the product group is large enough, the product manager may draw on the assistance provided by a product team, with individuals in that team concentrating on relevant functional specialisms.

Organisation by customer type (market management)

8.10 In a variant on the product management structure, instead of individual managers taking responsibility for particular products, **they instead take responsibility for particular markets**. The advantage of this approach lies in an organisation offering a variety of different products into particular markets. The understanding of the product here is perceived to be slightly less important than the understanding of the market.

8.11 In the case of **services**, market management would be consistent with the need to develop relationships with customers, since the individual marketing manager would be in a position to understand fully the range of needs displayed by particular groups and to draw on the organisation's product range to meet those needs in a systematic fashion. Individual market managers would also be able to draw on the skills and experiences of functional specialists as and when required. In contrast with the product management approach, market managers are likely to be well versed in the needs of their specific markets but may be short on knowledge of a large product range, particularly when that range is highly varied and technical.

8.12 **Where the buying motives and the buying behaviour of groups of customers differ radically from those of other groups, there is a case for organising marketing by customer type** - often to the extent that each type will have its own dedicated marketing mix, its own dedicated marketing team and sometimes even a dedicated salesforce.

8.13 EXAMPLE

A large pharmaceutical product manufacturing company could be organised in this way. There might, for example, be separate marketing teams for hospitals and GPs, farmers, retail outlets and veterinary surgeons respectively. If there were many hospitals, GPs or retail outlets, each of these markets or customer groups could be serviced by a salesforce organised regionally. Conversely, there may be relatively few farmers and veterinary surgeons and so salesforces for each of these types of customers might be organised nationally.

Clearly, buying motives and hence selling approach would be different in each of the markets. The organisation would promote drugs to GPs as being effective with minimal side effects; in store promotions could be used with chemists while farmers buying commodity chemicals in bulk would be mostly interested in price.

8.14 Companies with diverse groups of customers will often be organised alternatively by division. This is examined further below.

Part A: The marketing planning process: an overview

> **Action Programme 6**
>
> What would be the characteristics of a market based approach to organising marketing departments in a banking environment?

Matrix management

8.15 Market management is a simple form of **matrix management** in which the responsibility of the market manager can cut across the authority of other departments, particularly production. Another form of matrix management can be applied within the marketing function. This is an integration of the product and customer type approaches. In an organisation dealing with a variety of products in a variety of markets the product based approach will require managers to be familiar with a wide variety of different markets while the market based approach will require managers to be familiar with a wide variety of products. Nonetheless, expertise may not be fully or efficiently utilised. The matrix based system combines the two. A group of managers deals with markets and a further group with products. The market managers will take responsibility for the development and maintenance of profitable markets while the product manager will focus on product performance and profitability. The system is interlinked with each product manager dealing with a variety of market managers and each market manager dealing with a variety of product managers.

Matrix management

Market Managers

	Corporate	Personal	International
Insurance			
Investment			
Lending			

Product managers (row labels)

> **Action Programme 7**
>
> What are the advantages of adopting a matrix structure?

8.16 While this system may seem the ideal approach to resolving the dilemma about the most appropriate form of organisation for a marketing department, it presents certain problems. Cost is likely to be significant because of the extension of the range of management. There are also possible sources of conflict between product and market managers to consider and, particularly, the issue of who should take responsibility for certain activities. Rigidity and status concerns may make a matrix structure and the culture of participation, shared authority and ambiguity that it fosters, difficult to accept.

Divisional marketing organisation

8.17 So far we have considered marketing within a unitary organisation, but within many organisations, larger product groups have developed into separate divisions. This is a multi-divisional or 'M' form organisation). These have a high degree of autonomy, but ultimately are responsible to head office. **Marketing activity here will often be devolved to**

divisional level. Some marketing activities will be the responsibility of corporate headquarters, but the extent of corporate involvement can vary a great deal. No particular level of corporate involvement is desirable although it is often suggested that corporate involvement will tend to be more extensive in the early stages of the organisation's development when the divisions are individually quite weak. As divisions increase their strength, the extent of corporate involvement in marketing declines.

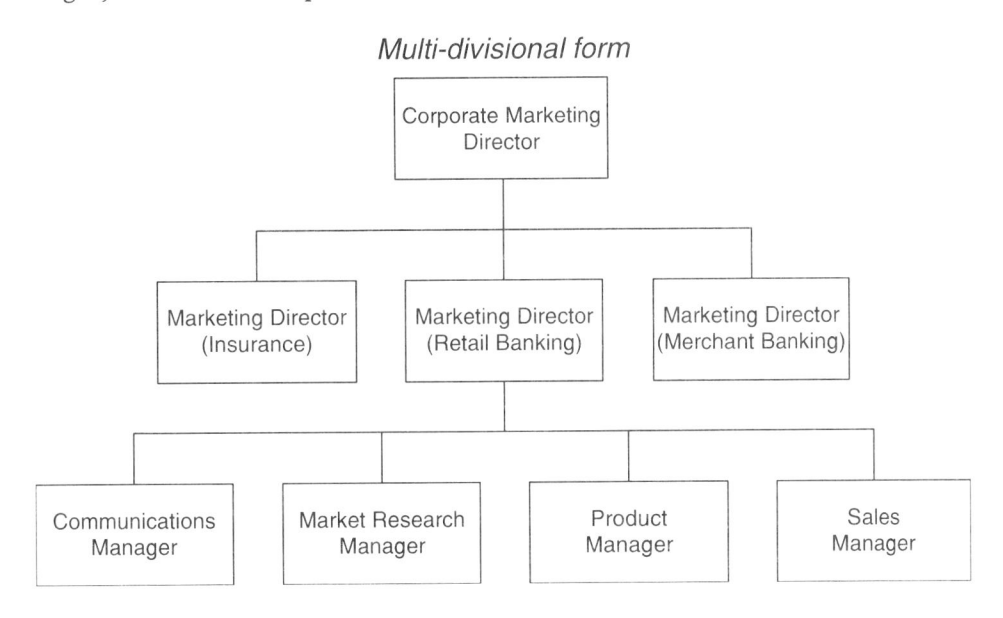

Multi-divisional form

```
                    Corporate Marketing
                         Director
                            |
        ┌───────────────────┼───────────────────┐
        │                   │                   │
  Marketing Director   Marketing Director   Marketing Director
    (Insurance)        (Retail Banking)     (Merchant Banking)
                            |
        ┌───────────┬───────┴───────┬───────────┐
        │           │               │           │
  Communications  Market Research  Product     Sales
    Manager         Manager        Manager    Manager
```

Marketing at Work

Financial Services

The organisation of marketing within financial services institutions varies considerably and is still at a relatively early stage of development when compared with many other large business organisations. In the UK clearing banks, the major marketing activities tend to be located centrally in a marketing services department (marketing as a staff management function).

The manager responsible for the marketing department will essentially be responsible for providing marketing services and support to lower tiers of management with specific responsibility for a variety of line management functions. While many of the functional activities associated with marketing such as advertising, new product development and public relations tend to be managed centrally but, in the case of the banks, many of the line management functions, particularly those relating to sales, are the responsibility of general, regional or branch managers.

The pace of change in the market environment facing banks and the general increase in competition has forced them to develop an increasingly market oriented approach to their business. This may create a need to shift from a functional based organisation structure to a flexible one which focuses on products or markets.

With regard to *retail banking*, the traditional head office/branch relationship may need to be changed radically to reflect the need to market different products in different ways. Some banks have developed a 'hub and spoke' form of organisation, with the hub being a larger branch offering a full service including responsibility for generating corporate business. The hub may control up to fifteen spoke or satellite branches offering a limited or even automated service concentrating on individuals and small businesses.

Part A: The marketing planning process: an overview

Chapter Roundup

- Control is vital if management is to ensure that planning targets are achieved. The control process involves three underlying components.
  - Setting standards or targets
  - Measuring and evaluating actual performance
  - Taking corrective action.

- In setting standards, a distinction can be made between controllable and uncontrollable variables.

- Performance should be measured by obtaining data about actual results for a direct comparison with the targets or standards set. In performance evaluation, two terms recur. These are efficiency and effectiveness. Measurement should be in qualitative terms wherever possible.

- Monitoring for control purposes should include monitoring of competitor performance, monitoring of customers and monitoring of market performance as a whole.

- Marketing managers should monitor their own progress by evaluating the effectiveness of the marketing mix, in particular personal selling, advertising and sales promotions, pricing and channels of distribution.

- Corrective action should only be taken if variances are outside tolerance levels. It can take two broad forms, involving either steps to improve actual performance or a change to the performance standard.

- An organisation may be sales oriented, product oriented or marketing oriented. All the key functional departments will have a different emphasis, depending on which orientation is present.

- There is a range of possible organisation structures. The position and prominence of marketing will, to some extent, depend on the structure. Generally speaking, marketing departments must take responsibility for the four key areas of functions, regions, products and markets.

- The concept of matrix management is now widely adopted. There are attendant advantages and disadvantages.

Quick Quiz

1. What are the four stages in the marketing control process? (see para 2.3)
2. Distinguish between efficiency and effectiveness. (2.6)
3. What are the necessary characteristics of performance measures? (2.13)
4. Why are monetary measurements of performance popular? (2.17)
5. What are the three main methods of evaluating marketing activities? (3.3)
6. What financial information about competitors is publicly available? (3.19)
7. What is post-testing? (4.10)
8. How should managers address the trade off between the short term and the long term? (5.4)
9. What two options are available for taking corrective action? (5.7)
10. What are the characteristics of a centralised organisation? (6.2)
11. What are the characteristics of a marketing oriented company? (7.2, 7.3)
12. What are the key distinctions between a sales oriented and a marketing oriented company? (7.6)

Action Programme Review

1. Disadvantages of using monetary information

   (a) If absorption costing techniques are used, the process of apportioning and absorbing overhead costs is arbitrary and meaningless and hampers decision making.

   (b) The common assumption that all costs charged to a product or department are controllable by the manager is actually incorrect. A manager of a production department, for example, cannot control the prices of raw materials, nor the amount of production overhead charged to the department.

   (c) Costs and profits may not be the best way of comparing the results of different parts of a business.

   (d) Some managers may prefer to quantify information in non-monetary terms.

3: Implementing the marketing plan

- The sales manager may look at sales volume in units, size of market share, speed of delivery, volume of sales per sales representative or per call and so on.
- A stores manager might look at stock turnover periods for each item, volume of demand, the speed of materials handling, breakages, obsolescence and so on.

(e) Where qualitative factors (notably human behaviour and attitudes) are important, monetary information is less relevant. This is one reason why strategic planning information, which relies more heavily on both external and qualitative factors, is generally more imprecise and not necessarily expressed in money terms.

2 Possible performance measures
- Sales levels
- Market share
- Marketing costs
- Profitability
- Customer satisfaction

3 The consumer sales response to the following is readily measurable.
- Price reductions as sales promotions (for example, introductory offers).
- Coupon 'money-off' offers.
- Free sendaway gifts.
- On-pack free gift offers.
- Combination pack offers.

4 Measures of performance in personal selling
- Sales, in total, by customer, and by product
- Contribution, in total, by customer and by product
- Selling expenses (budget versus actual). If selling expenses exceeded budget, did actual net sales exceed budgeted sales by a corresponding amount?
- Customer call frequency
- Average sales value per call
- Average contribution per call
- Average cost per call
- Average trade discount
- Number of new customers obtained
- Percentage increase in sales compared with previous period
- Average number of repeat calls per sale
- Average mileage travelled per £1 sales

5 In a decentralised organisation there is the danger of overlap and contradictory decisions as well as the possibility of confusion. Senior management may also have to accept a reduced degree of control.

6 In the case of banking, a market based approach would be characterised by managers with responsibility for personal markets, large corporates, small corporates and so on.

7 Advantages of a matrix structure
- Greater flexibility of people. Employees and departments are geared to change.
- Greater flexibility of tasks and structure. The matrix structure may be short term (as with project teams) or readily amended.
- Re-orientation. Responsiveness to customer needs is closer to pure market-orientation.
- Responsibility is directly placed on individual managers.
- Interdisciplinary co-operation and a mixing of skills and expertise.
- Arguably, motivation of employees by providing them with greater participation in planning and control decisions.

Now try illustrative questions 3, 4 and 5 at the end of the Study Text

Part B
The marketing mix

4: The Background to Promotional Operations

Chapter topic list	Syllabus reference
1 Setting the scene	-
2 A simple communication model	2.1
3 Consumer buying behaviour	2.1
4 The process of consumer buying behaviour	2.1
5 Factors influencing consumer buying behaviour	2.1
6 Models of consumer buying behaviour	2.1
7 Promotional tools	2.1

Learning Outcome

Students will be able to select and justify the use of one or more promotional techniques for a particular marketing context.

Key Concepts Introduced

- Consumer buying behaviour
- Culture
- Reference groups
- Motivation

Examples of Marketing at Work

- Virgin and the grim reaper
- Fragrances for men
- Apple Tango

1 SETTING THE SCENE

1.1 This is the first of two chapters on promotional operations. In the next chapter we examine the various techniques in practice.

1.2 In this chapter we discuss the process of communication (section 2) and the theory of consumer buying behaviour. This behaviour occurs in several forms and these are outlined

Part B: The marketing mix

in section 3. Section 4 looks at the mental processes involved in more complex buying behaviour, while section 5 considers the factors which influence it.

1.3 Section 6 is concerned with some theoretical models and section 7 introduces the process of choosing promotional tools.

2 A SIMPLE COMMUNICATION MODEL

2.1 The prime aim of marketing communications is to influence consumer's buying behaviour. Because of this marketers need to know how communication works. The simplest model starts with a **sender** who creates a **message** and sends it to a **receiver**. The next step in analysis is to recognise that most communication is a two-way process and involves an element of **feedback**. If you think about this you will realise that you rarely speak without expecting a reply and even writing a letter would usually elicit some kind of response. Feedback might not be in the same form as the message, though; it might take the form of some other kind of behaviour such as paying an overdue account, but whatever it is, it will indicate that the original message was at least received.

Kotler's model

2.2 *Kotler* has put forward a more complex model of the communication process. This is shown in the diagram below.

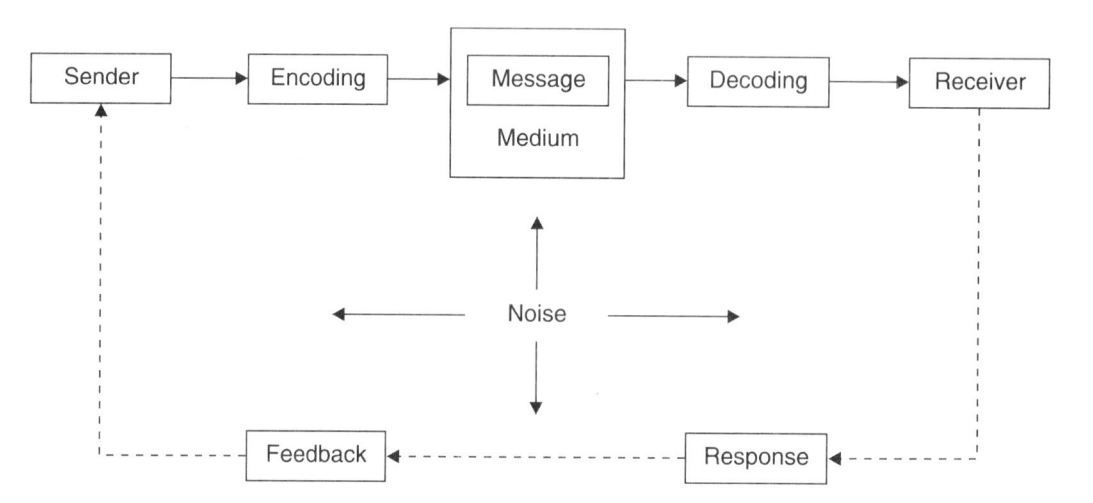

```
Sender → Encoding → Message/Medium → Decoding → Receiver
  ↑                        ↑                          ↓
  |                      Noise                        |
  |                        ↓                          |
  └─── Feedback ← ──────────────── Response ← ────────┘
```

2.3 **Noise** can be defined as all those factors which prevent the decoding of a message by the receiver in the way intended by the sender.

2.4 The **sender** is the party sending the message, and may also be referred to as the communicator or the source. The **receiver** is the party who receives the message, and who may also be known as the audience or the destination.

2.5 The **encoding** process encompasses the means by which a meaning is placed into symbolic form such as words, signs, images and sound.

2.6 The **medium** is the communication channel or channels through which the message moves from sender to receiver.

2.7 The **decoding** process is carried out by the receiver who converts the symbolic forms transmitted by the sender into a form that makes sense to him. It is how the receiver interprets the message sent.

2.8 When the message has been decoded the receiver will react to it - this is the **response**.

2.9 **Feedback** is the part of the receiver's response that the receiver communicates back to the sender.

2.10 This model underscores many of the factors in effective communication. Senders need to understand the motivation of their audiences in order to structure messages that the audience will interpret correctly through the decoding process. The sender also has to ascertain the most effective communication media through which to reach the audience and also establish effective feedback channels in order to find out the receiver's response to the message.

Action Programme 1

(a) Find some adverts - watch TV for half an hour or flick through a newspaper or a magazine. (This should not be too hard!)

(b) Analyse each ad in the above terms. Consider who are the parties involved (*you* may not be the intended receiver), what communication tools are used, what sort of codes are used and how they will be decoded (for example by people in different income brackets or with different tastes), what form feedback will take, and so on.

Noise and selectivity

2.11 This communication process is not carried out in isolation. There are many senders competing with their messages for the attention of the receiver. As a result there is considerable noise in the environment and an individual may be bombarded by several hundred commercial messages each day. The task of the sender is to get his message to the receiver but, as Kotler states, there are a number of reasons why the target audience may not receive the message.

Selective attention

2.12 A receiver will not notice all the commercial messages that he comes into contact with, so the sender must design the message in such a way so as to win attention in spite of the surrounding noise.

Selective distortion

2.13 In many cases receivers may distort or change the information received if that information does not fit in with their existing attitudes, beliefs and opinions. In other words, people hear what they want to hear.

Selective recall

2.14 A receiver will retain in his permanent memory only a small fraction of the messages that reach him.

Part B: The marketing mix

3 CONSUMER BUYING BEHAVIOUR

> **Key Concept**
> **Consumer buying behaviour** can be defined as 'the decision processes and acts of individuals involved in buying and using products or services.' (*Dibb et al, Marketing: Concepts and Strategies*).

The purchase decision

3.1 Not all consumers behave in the same way. The decision processes involved in a major purchase, such as a car, are very different from the decision processes involved in the purchase of chocolate confectionery. *Assael* presents a typology of consumer decision making based on two main dimensions.

- The extent of decision making
- The degree of involvement in the purchase.

This is represented diagrammatically below.

	High involvement	*Low involvement*
Decision making (information search, consideration of brand alternatives)	Complex decision making	Limited decision making
Habit (little or no information search, consideration of only one brand)	Brand loyalty	Inertia

3.2 The vertical axis represents a continuum from **decision making** to **habit**, based on the extent that the customer goes through the **cognitive process of information search and evaluation**.

3.3 The horizontal axis represents a continuum from **high to low involvement purchases. High involvement purchases are those that are important to the customer** in some way; for example, they may be closely tied to the customer's ego and self image. Such purchases involve risk. **Low involvement purchases are not as important to the customer** and therefore the level of risk is lessened. With such purchases it may not be worth the customer's while to engage in information search and evaluation and therefore a limited process of decision making usually occurs.

3.4 Assael's typology comprises four types of decision making.

(a) **Complex decision making occurs when involvement is high and the consumer searches and considers alternatives,** such as in the purchase of major items like cars, brown goods and white goods.

(b) However, complex decision making will not occur every time and if the brand choice is repetitive the consumer learns from experience and **brand loyalty** is built up.

(c) **Low involvement decision making.**

   (i) Customers sometimes go through a decision making process even if not highly involved in the purchase because they have little experience of the product area. this is called **limited decision making**.

(ii) Limited decision making may also occur when the customer seeks variety. The brand switch is unlikely to be preplanned and may occur at the place of purchase.

(d) The fourth option identified by Assael is **inertia**, comprising low involvement with the product and no decision making.

4 THE PROCESS OF CONSUMER BUYING BEHAVIOUR

4.1 The general stages in the buying process have been identified by Kotler.

- Need recognition
- Information search
- Evaluation of alternatives
- Purchase decision
- Post purchase evaluation

Referring back to the previous section, we may say that these stages will only be fully developed in the case of **complex decision making**.

Each stage will be considered in turn.

Need recognition

4.2 The process begins when the buyer recognises a need or problem. This can be triggered by internal stimuli, such as hunger or thirst, or external stimuli, such as lack of social esteem. If the need rises to a threshold level it will become a drive. The task for the marketer is to identify the circumstances and stimuli that trigger a particular need and use this knowledge to trigger consumer interest.

Information search

4.3 Once aroused, the customer will search for more information about the products that will satisfy the need. The information search stage can be divided into two levels. The first is 'heightened attention', where the customer simply becomes more receptive to information about the particular product category. The second stage is 'active information search'.

4.4 According to Kotler consumer information sources fall into four groups.

- **Personal sources**: family, friends, neighbours, work colleagues
- **Commercial sources**: advertising, salespeople, packaging, displays
- **Public sources**: mass media, consumer rating organisations
- **Experiential sources**: handling, examining, using the product

A consumer will generally receive the most information exposure from commercial sources, but the most **effective** information exposure comes from personal sources.

4.5 Kotler states that, as the consumer is trying to satisfy some need with the buying process, he will be looking for certain benefits from the product chosen and each product will be seen as a 'bundle of attributes' with varying capabilities of delivering the benefits sought and hence satisfying the need. The consumer is likely to build up a set of brand beliefs about the position of each brand with regard to each attribute. The sum of these brand beliefs will make up the brand image.

4.6 In order to ensure that the brand has the best chance of being chosen by the consumer, the marketer has a range of options for action including the following.

Part B: The marketing mix

(a) **Modifying the brand.** Redesigning the product so that it offers more of the attributes that the buyer desires. Kotler calls this 'real repositioning'.

(b) **Altering beliefs about the brand.** Kotler recommends that this course of action be pursued if the consumer **underestimates** the qualities of the brand, and calls it 'psychological repositioning'.

(c) **Altering beliefs about competitors' brands.** This course of action would be appropriate if the consumer mistakenly believes that a competitor's brand has more quality than it actually has, and can be referred to as 'competitive repositioning'.

Purchase decision

4.7 Having evaluated the range of brand choices the consumer may have formed a purchase intention to buy the most preferred brand. However, some factors could intervene between the purchase intention and the purchase decision. The first factor is the attitude of others. A strong negative opinion regarding the brand choice may influence the consumer to change his or her mind. Other factors could include a change in financial circumstances such as redundancy, or circumstances in which some other purchase becomes more urgent.

Post purchase evaluation

4.8 Having purchased the brand the consumer will experience some level of satisfaction or dissatisfaction, depending on the closeness between the consumer's product expectations and the product's perceived performance. These feelings will influence whether the consumer buys the brand again and also whether the consumer talks favourably or unfavourably about the brand to others.

5 FACTORS INFLUENCING CONSUMER BUYING BEHAVIOUR 6/96

5.1 The 'core' process of consumer buying behaviour described above will be influenced by a number of outside variables. These variables have been classified by *Wilson et al*, as follows, with the focus progressively narrowing.

- Cultural
- Social
- Personal
- Psychological

These various factors interact and they influence buyer behaviour both separately and in their totality.

Cultural factors

5.2 These are the most fundamental of the influencing factors, and include culture, subculture and social class.

> **Key Concept**
> **Culture** comprises 'the values, attitudes, beliefs, ideas, artefacts and other meaningful symbols represented in the pattern of life adopted by people that help them interpret, evaluate and communicate as members of society'
> *Rice.*

5.3 Culture is largely the result of a learning process.

5.4 This broad set of values is then influenced by the **subcultures** in which we develop. Subcultural groups can be defined in terms of religion, ethnic characteristics, racial characteristics and geographical areas, all of which further influence attitudes, tastes, taboos and lifestyle.

5.5 A third cultural influence is **social class**. The key characteristics of social class have been highlighted as follows by *Wilson et al*.

- People within a particular social class are more similar than those from different social classes
- Social class is determined by a series of variables such as occupation, income, education, and values rather than by a single variable
- Individuals can move from one social class to another.

Social factors

> **Key Concept**
> **Reference groups** have been defined as groups 'with which an individual identifies so much that he or she takes on many of the values, attitudes or behaviours of group members' (*Dibb et al*).

5.6 Four types of reference group have been identified.

- **Primary membership groups**, which are generally informal and to which individuals belong and within which they interact
- **Secondary membership groups**, which tend to be more formal than primary groups and within which less interaction takes place. Trade unions, religious groups and professional societies are examples
- **Aspirational groups**, to which an individual would like to belong
- **Dissociative groups**, whose values and behaviour the individual rejects

> **Action Programme 2**
> The CIM is, presumably, one of your own aspirational groups. What other reference groups do you have? Divide them according to the above classifications.

Opinion leaders

5.7 Opinion leaders are 'those individuals who reinforce the marketing messages sent and to whom other receivers look for information, advice and opinion' (Rice). In addition, opinion leaders may communicate a marketing message to those members of the group who may have missed the original message. A person may be an opinion leader in certain circumstances but an opinion follower in others.

The family

5.8 Another major social influence is the family, particularly with regard to the roles and relative influence exerted by different family members. Research has indicated three

Part B: The marketing mix

patterns of decision making within the family and identified the sorts of product categories with which each is typically associated.

- **Husband dominated:** life insurance, cars and television
- **Wife dominated:** washing machines, carpets, kitchenware and non living-room furniture
- **Equal:** living-room furniture, holidays, housing, furnishings and entertainment.

Personal factors

5.9 Influencing factors that can be classified as personal include such things as **age and life cycle, occupation, economic circumstances and lifestyle**.

5.10 **Age** is particularly relevant to such products as clothes, furniture and recreation. However, consumption may also be shaped by the stage of the **family life cycle** within which an individual falls. The stages of the **family life cycle** were discussed in Chapter 2 of this text.

5.11 **Occupation** will influence consumption and the task for marketers is to identify the occupational groups that have an above average interest in their products and services.

5.12 Kotler discerns four main facets to an individual's **economic circumstances**.

- spendable income, its level, stability and time pattern
- savings and assets, including the percentage that is liquid
- borrowing power
- attitude toward spending versus saving

5.13 People from the same subculture, social class and occupation may have completely different **lifestyles**. A lifestyle is 'an individual's mode of living as identified by his or her activities, interests and opinions' (Assael). Marketers will search for relationships between their products and lifestyle groups.

Psychological factors

5.14 The process of buyer behaviour is also influenced by four major psychological factors: **motivation, perception, learning and beliefs and attitudes**.

Motivation

> **Key Concept**
> **Motivation** has been defined as, 'an inner state that energises, activates, or moves, that directs or channels behaviour towards goals'.
> *Assael*

5.15 **Motivation arises from perceived needs**. These needs can be of two main types - biogenic and psychogenic. **Biogenic needs** arise from physiological states of tension such as hunger, thirst and discomfort, whereas **psychogenic needs** arise from psychological states of tension such as the need for recognition, esteem or belonging.

5.16 **Freud's theory of motivation assumes that the real psychological forces influencing people's behaviour are unconscious**. From a marketing perspective, Freud's theory implies that a person buys a product, not only for the rational reasons that he or she may state

4: The background to promotional operations

overtly, but also for a hidden set of underlying unconscious motives (such as the need for social esteem or belonging), that the person may not articulate. The marketer, therefore, should be aware of the impact of all aspects of the product that could trigger consumer emotions that stimulate or inhibit purchase.

5.17 **Maslow's theory of motivation seeks to explain why people are driven by particular needs at particular times.** Maslow argues that human needs are arranged in a hierarchy, comprising, in their order of importance: physiological needs, safety needs, social needs, esteem needs and self-actualisation needs.

```
              /\
             /  \
            /Self\     - Fulfilment of personal potential
           /actual-\
          /isation  \
         /------------\
        / Esteem needs \  - For independence, recognition, status,
       /                \   respect from others
      /------------------\
     /   Social needs     \  - For relationships, affection, belonging
    /----------------------\
   /    Safety needs        \  - For security, order, predictability,
  /                          \   freedom from threat
 /----------------------------\
/    Physiological needs       \  - Food, shelter
--------------------------------
```

5.18 Maslow states that a person will attempt to satisfy the most important need first. When that need is satisfied it ceases to be a motivator and the person will attempt to satisfy the next most important need. For example, if you are hungry (a physiological need) you will venture out from the relative warmth and safety of your desk to get a sandwich.

5.19 *Herzberg* developed a 'two factor theory' of motivation that distinguishes between factors that cause **dissatisfaction** and factors that cause **satisfaction**. The task for the marketer is, therefore, to avoid 'dissatisfiers' such as, for example, poor after-sales service, as these things will not sell the product but may well *unsell* it. In addition, the marketer should identify the major satisfiers or motivators of purchase and make sure that they are supplied to the customer.

Marketing at Work

Virgin and the grim reaper

To coincide with Richard Branson's first attempt to circumnavigate the world in a balloon, Virgin Atlantic ran an ad that was an emotional appeal to viewers to live life to the full.

The Grim Reaper appears next to an unsuspecting man at a bus stop. A huge piece of masonry is about to fall on the man's head. His life flashes before his eyes, but he has done so much travelling that this takes an unexpectedly long time. The Grim Reaper gets bored and dials for a pizza while more and more of the man's exploits are revealed. Eventually it gets dark, the Reaper is curled up asleep and the man sneaks away (the masonry still hovering in mid-air) to the voice-over: 'When your life flashes before your eyes, make sure you've got plenty to watch'.

'Standard airline advertising goes something like this: 'We fly 50 times a day and have a fleet that can do synchronised flying'. Branson's ad eschews such an approach. Instead it talks about emotions. The ad says everything there is to say about the Virgin brand.'

Financial Times, 20 January 1997

Part B: The marketing mix

Perception

5.20 **Perception** is defined by Assael as 'the process by which people select, organise and interpret sensory stimuli into a meaningful and coherent picture. The way consumers view an object (for example their mental picture of a brand or the traits they attribute to a brand)'. Possible difference in perception can be explained by the three perceptual processes described in the last chapter: selective attention, selective distortion and selection retention.

Learning

5.21 'Learning describes changes in an individual's behaviour arising from experience' (Kotler). Theories about learning state that learning is the result of the interplay of five factors: **drives, stimuli, cues, responses and reinforcement**.

5.22 A **drive** is a strong internal force impelling action, which will become a motive when it is directed to a particular drive-reducing **stimulus** object (the product). **Cues** are minor stimuli (such as seeing the product in action) that determine when, where and how the person responds. Once the product is bought, if the experience is rewarding then the **response** to the product will be reinforced, making a repeat purchase more likely. Marketers must, therefore, build up demand for a product by associating it with strong drives, using motivating cues, and by providing positive **reinforcement**.

Beliefs and attitudes

5.23 A **belief** is 'a descriptive thought that a person holds about something' (Kotler). Beliefs are important to marketers as the beliefs that people have about products make up the brand images of those products.

5.24 An **attitude** describes a person's 'enduring favourable or unfavourable cognitive evaluations, emotional feelings, and action tendencies toward some object or idea' (Kotler). Attitudes lead people to behave in a fairly consistent way towards similar objects. by ensuring that they do not have to interpret and react to every object in a fresh way. Attitudes settle into a consistent pattern and to change one attitude may entail major changes to other attitudes. Marketers should ensure that their product fits into people's existing attitudes rather than try to change attitudes.

Marketing at Work

Fragrances for men

Marketing Week runs regular 'Brandtrack' surveys looking at the market for different products and including an analysis of reasons for purchase.

In February 1996 the product was fragrances for young men. The reasons for purchase illustrate many of the points above.

'Women were twice as likely as men to select a brand because of an accompanying free gift or money-off promotion, or because it was cheaper than other brands. This seems to imply that economics intrude more into a purchase where the person buying is not the ultimate wearer.

Women were also more likely than men to take advice from a consultant, and to have tried the fragrance in the shop, perhaps reflecting the relative time spent, and their enjoyment in, browsing at sales counters. Nearly three-quarters of all CK One buyers [a Calvin Klein fragrance], both men and women, attributed their choice of fragrance to trial at point of purchase.

A third of men, compared with a quarter of women, had chosen a fragrance as a result of 'smelling it on someone else'. This would therefore seem to be one of the main male routes for discovering a suitable scent.

4: The background to promotional operations

Advertising has a similar influence on both sexes, although men are more likely to be persuaded by television, and women by press advertising.'

6 MODELS OF CONSUMER BUYING BEHAVIOUR

Response hierarchy models

6.1 Response hierarchy (or hierarchy of effects) models attempt to **predict the sequence of mental stages that the consumer passes through on the way to a purchase**. Some major response hierarchy models are regularly used in marketing.

- The AIDA model
- The adoption model
- DAGMAR (Defining Advertising Goals for Measured Advertising Response)
- Lavidge and Steiner's model

These are shown in the diagram below.

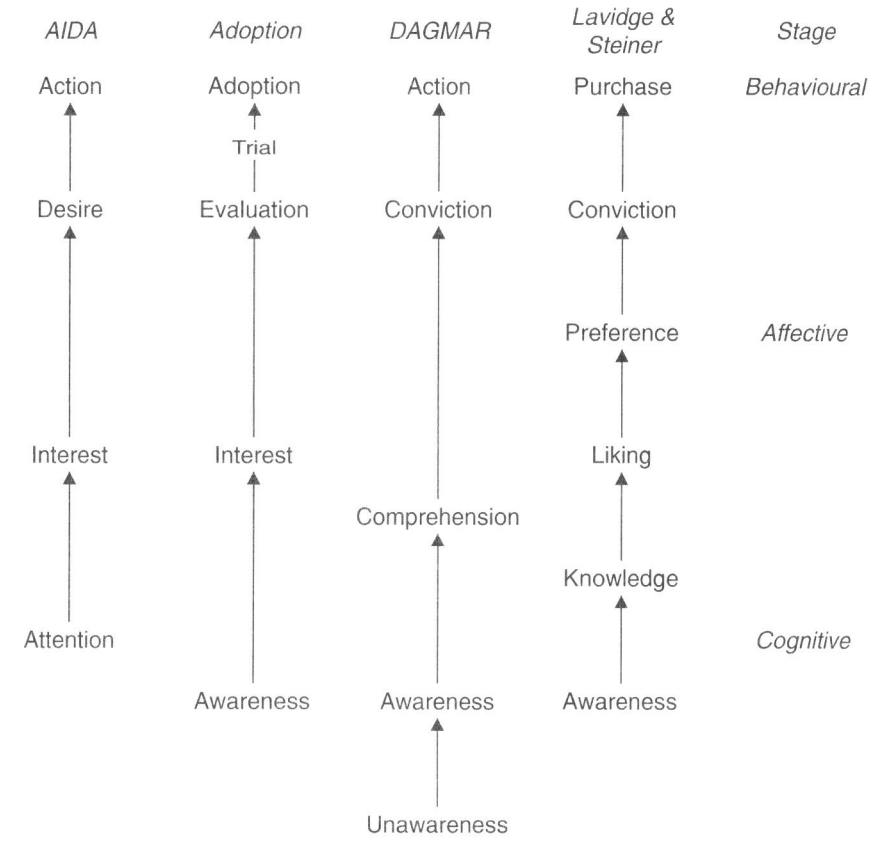

AIDA	Adoption	DAGMAR	Lavidge & Steiner	Stage
Action	Adoption	Action	Purchase	*Behavioural*
↑	↑	↑	↑	
	Trial			
Desire	Evaluation	Conviction	Conviction	
↑	↑	↑	↑	
			Preference	*Affective*
			↑	
Interest	Interest		Liking	
↑	↑		↑	
		Comprehension	Knowledge	
		↑	↑	
Attention				*Cognitive*
	Awareness	Awareness	Awareness	
		↑		
		Unawareness		

Source: *Adapted from PR Smith, Marketing Communications (1993)*

Adapted from PR Smith, Marketing communications (1998)

Evaluation

6.2 These models attempt to **prioritise the communication objectives at various stages of the buying process**. These objectives can be classified into three main areas - cognitive, affective or behavioural. **Cognitive objectives** are concerned with creating knowledge or awareness in the mind of the consumer. **Affective objectives** are concerned with changing the consumer's attitude to the product as a whole or a specific aspect of the product. **Behavioural objectives** are concerned with getting the consumer to act in some way (buy the product).

Part B: The marketing mix

6.3 However, the core model of buying behaviour is most applicable to **complex buying behaviour**. In other situations the consumer may not go through the staged process of information search and evaluation of objectives before the purchase decision. Indeed, some of the stages might occur simultaneously, as in the case of an impulse purchase. Buyers may also bypass the hierarchy of stages. For example, during the evaluation stage a buyer may go back to the information search stage in order to obtain more information before making the decision to buy.

7 PROMOTIONAL TOOLS

7.1 The diagram below shows a complete range of tools that can be used to influence a customer or potential customer.

Promotional influences on the customer

A wheel diagram with "The Customer" at the centre, surrounded by the following promotional tools: Personal selling, Branding, Word of mouth, Sales promotion, Public relations, Merchandising, Direct marketing, Exhibitions, Internal marketing, Corporate image, Packaging, Sponsorship, Advertising.

These tools represent the deployment of deliberate and intentional methods calculated to bring about a favourable response in the customer's behaviour. The diagram represents the most obvious promotion methods, though other parts of the marketing mix, including the product itself, pricing, policy and distribution channels, will also have decisive effects.

7.2 Choosing the correct tools for a particular promotions task is not easy. The process is still very much an art, though it is becoming more scientific because of the access to consumer and media databases. Matching consumer characteristics with media databases can be carried out very rapidly by computer and promotional budgets can be evaluated for a variety of different mixes.

7.3 At its most basic the choice of promotional tools should be exercised within the following top-down hierarchy of objectives.

4: The background to promotional operations

```
Business mission
      ↓
Business objectives
      ↓
Marketing objectives
      ↓
Promotion objectives
      ↓
Choice of correct tool
```

7.4 At a more detailed level the choice of the correct promotion tools can be tackled like any other management problem. The following is a useful sequence of events.

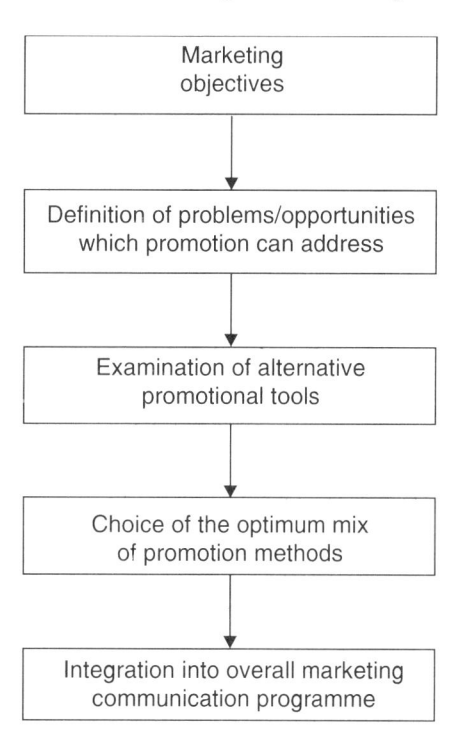

```
Marketing objectives
      ↓
Definition of problems/opportunities which promotion can address
      ↓
Examination of alternative promotional tools
      ↓
Choice of the optimum mix of promotion methods
      ↓
Integration into overall marketing communication programme
```

In reality, an experienced marketing manager is able to reach sensible conclusions almost intuitively, based on what has been successful in the past and on his intimate knowledge of both customers and competitors.

Consumer and business-to-business markets

7.5 The comment above about experience of a particular market can be generalised in the case of the two broad categories of consumer and business-to-business markets. Consumer

Part B: The marketing mix

markets are categorised as consisting of mass audiences which are cost-effectively accessible by television or national newspaper advertising. Supermarkets allow customers to serve themselves and there is little or no personal selling. The business-to-business markets, by contrast, involve a great deal of personal selling at different levels in the organisation. The needs of individual companies are different and therefore mass advertising would be most wasteful. Building on these generalised comments it is possible to present the mix of appropriate tools in the following diagram.

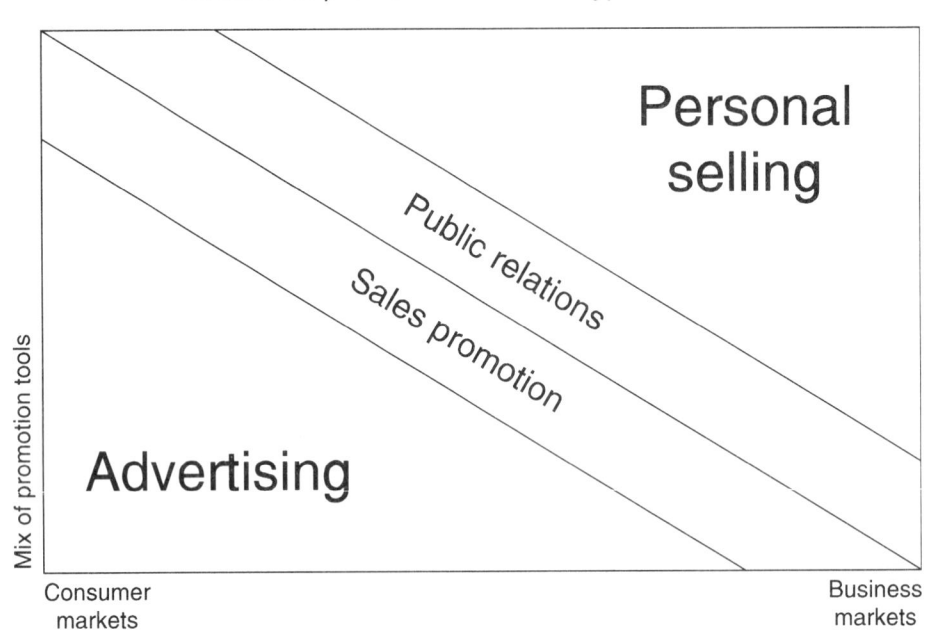

Variation of promotion tools with type of market

Integrated marketing communications

7.6 It is necessary to integrate all the promotional elements to achieve the maximum influence on the customer. **Integrated marketing communications** represents all the elements of an organisation's marketing mix that favourably influence its customers or clients. It goes beyond the right choice of promotion tools to the correct choice of the marketing mix. This is illustrated in the diagram below.

4: The background to promotional operations

The integrated marketing communication process

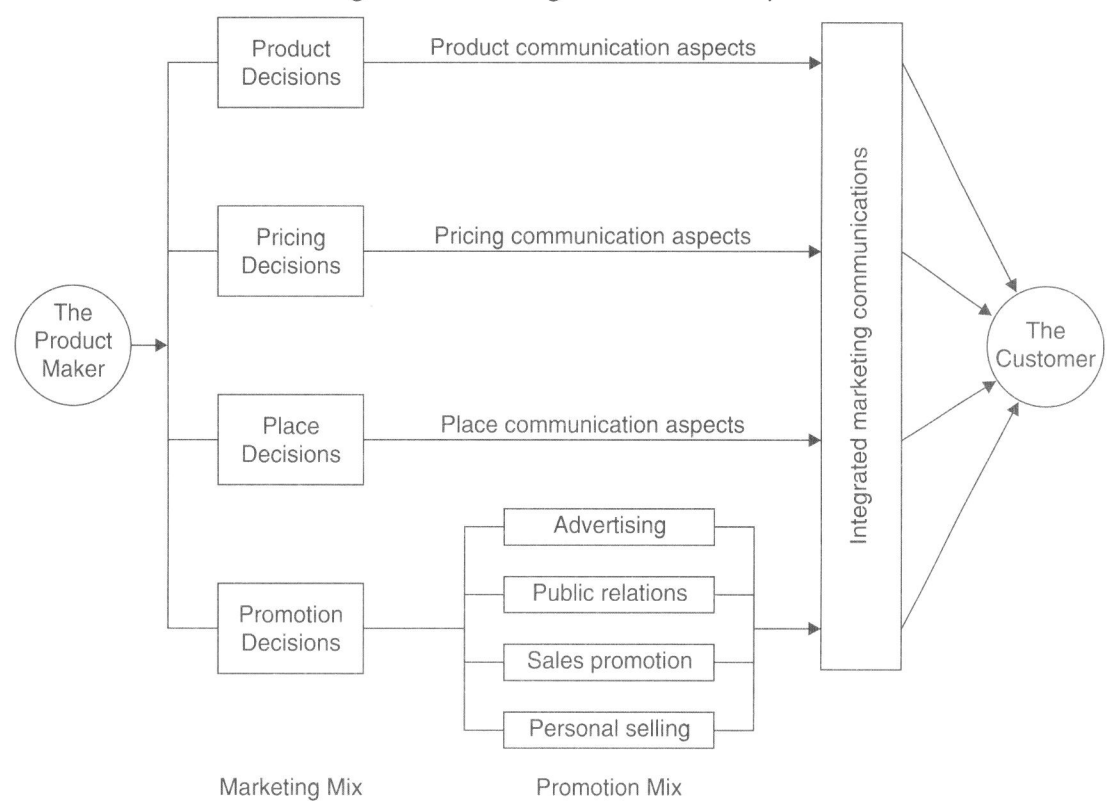

```
The Product Maker
  ├── Product Decisions ──── Product communication aspects ────┐
  ├── Pricing Decisions ──── Pricing communication aspects ────┤
  ├── Place Decisions ────── Place communication aspects ──────┤── Integrated marketing communications ──→ The Customer
  └── Promotion Decisions ──┬── Advertising ──────┐            │
                            ├── Public relations ─┤            │
                            ├── Sales promotion ──┼────────────┘
                            └── Personal selling ─┘

   Marketing Mix              Promotion Mix
```

Marketing at Work

Apple Tango

Apple Tango won the Integrated Consumer Campaign award in the 1995 Direct Marketing Association/ Royal Mail awards.

'The Apple Tango campaign began with TV advertising which invited viewers to phone in if they were having problems with the seductive properties of Apple Tango. Subsequently, the campaign was extended to radio and cinema, followed by a return to TV to coincide with an on-pack promotion.

The promotion invited consumers to take a photograph of themselves out on a date with a can of Apple Tango and offered a prize of £500 and the chance to appear on millions of Apple Tango cans.

Half a million calls have been logged since the campaign began and more than 1,000 competition entries have been received. Apple Tango's volume share, it is claimed, has increased by 22%.'

Marketing: The 1995 DMA/Royal Mail Direct Marketing Awards

Exam Tip

Promotional practice used to be a separate examination, but it is included in this paper in the new syllabus. Questions on the theoretical background were rare in the old exam but you should not ignore it. The background of theory can be used to explain, illustrate and justify chosen promotional techniques.

Part B: The marketing mix

Chapter Roundup

- Kotler's model of the communication process underscores many of the factors in effective communication. In particular, it discusses the importance of selectivity; selective attention, selective distortion and selective recall all tend to limit the success which is attainable in commercial communications.

- Purchase decisions are of several types. Complex decision making may occur in high involvement purchases, which are the ones that are very important to the consumer. Simpler decision making occurs when the purchase is not seen as particularly important or if it is repetitive. In these cases limited decision making or brand loyalty take over.

- The process of decision making begins with information search which leads to the evaluation of alternatives. The marketer can aim to influence both of these processes. After making the purchase, the consumer experiences satisfaction or dissatisfaction, either of which influence the possibility of repeat purchases.

- Consumer buying behaviour is influenced by cultural, social, personal and psychological factors. Social class is a cultural factor; social factors include reference groups, opinion leaders and the family. Age, occupation, economic circumstances and lifestyle are all examples of personal factors. Psychological factors include motivation, perception, learning, beliefs and attitudes.

- Models of consumer behaviour help to prioritise the communication objectives at various stages of the buying process and thus assists with the selection of promotional tools. The process of promotion and the tools used should be integrated within the marketing communications process which, in turn, should support overall marketing objectives.

Quick Quiz

1. Sketch Kotler's model of the communication process. (see para 2.2)
2. Why may a target audience not receive the message sent? (2.11-2.14)
3. When does complex decision making take place? (3.4)
4. What are the two stages of information search? (4.3)
5. What can the marketer do to influence the consumer's evaluation of brands. (4.6)
6. What are the key characteristics of social class? (5.5)
7. What are 'opinion leaders'? (5.7)
8. What determines a person's economic circumstances? (5.12)
9. Explain Maslow's theory of motivation. (5.17,5.18)
10. What 5 factors influence learning? (5.21)
11. What are the stages of the AIDA model of consumer buying behaviour? (6.1)
12. What is the classification of communication objectives during the buying process? (6.2)

Now try illustrative question 6 at the end of the Study Text

5 Promotional Operations in Practice

Chapter Topic List	Syllabus reference
1 Setting the scene	-
2 Advertising	2.1
3 Advertising media	2.1
4 Personal selling	2.1
5 Sales promotion	2.1
6 Public relations	2.1
7 Sponsorship	2.1
8 Direct marketing	2.1
9 The Internet	2.1

Learning Outcome

Students will be able to select and justify the use of one or more promotional techniques for a particular marketing context.

Key Concepts Introduced

- Advertising
- Sales promotion
- Public relations
- Public
- Sponsorship
- Direct marketing
- Telemarketing

Examples of Marketing at Work

- Advertising and taboos
- Tesco
- Instant coupon machine
- Pogs and Tazos
- Greyhound racing
- Equitable Life
- Coca Cola
- Glaxo and the arts
- Customer loyalty
- Database applications
- St James Norland Parish Church
- Golden Wonder
- P&G and Excite

Part B: The marketing mix

1 SETTING THE SCENE

1.1 Having looked at some of the theoretical background relating to consumer buying behaviour, it is time to consider the techniques available to the marketer to influence that behaviour.

1.2 Advertising and media are covered in sections 2 and 3. Advertising can be used for a variety of purposes and its use must be carefully planned and briefed. It is difficult to measure the effectiveness of advertising, but this must be attempted.

1.3 Section 4 describes personal selling, which is the oldest form of promotion and includes a wide range of sales tasks. The front line sales person can be effectively supported with information of various kinds which help to maximise customer contact time.

1.4 Sales promotion, which is dealt with in section 5, includes a range of tactical techniques effective in both consumer and industrial markets. The success of these techniques can be quantified with some accuracy in terms of take-up.

1.5 Section 6 looks at public relations and section 7 at the related subject of sponsorship. PR should be seen as a strategic activity with a long term effect on success, though it may have to deal with short-term problems. There is a wide range of image-building techniques available to the PR specialist.

1.6 Direct marketing, which is examined in section 8, is about developing direct relationships with customers who might otherwise be reached only through mass marketing techniques. It makes extensive use of telephone contact and computer database technology.

1.7 The Internet has been the focus of much attention in recent years. Huge amounts of money have been invested in attempts to exploit it for commercial purposes. Section 9 looks at some of the ways the internet is used.

2 ADVERTISING 12/98

Key Concept
Advertising may be defined as non-personal paid-for communications targeted through mass media with the purpose of achieving set objectives. It is an impersonal communications tool.

2.1 Advertising is a means of reaching large audiences in a cost-effective manner. Personalised feedback from an advertising message is not usually obtained. It is normally undertaken by specialist agencies.

Advertising objectives

2.2 **Examples of broad advertising objectives**

- To support sales increases
- To encourage trial
- To create awareness
- To inform about a feature or benefit
- To remind
- To reassure
- To create an image

- To modify attitudes
- To gain trade and sales staff support

Campaign planning

Campaign briefing

2.3 A good brief should include, as minimum, the following elements.

(a) The **background to the proposed campaign** including comments about the internal and external environment, how it has shaped the need for the current advertising, and how the advertising and communications strategy fit into the overall strategy for the brand.

(b) Advertising **objectives** should be stated, alongside the marketing objectives which they support.

(c) **Target markets** should be specified.

(d) The client should provide **as much detail as possible about the physical product or service** to be featured. The agency should understand about the processes involved in product/service delivery, alongside features, benefits and how the product/service is differentiated from competitive offerings.

(e) The **budget** must be clear.

(f) The **timescale** must be specified. The advertising may need to be timed to coincide with a particular calendar date such as Easter, Christmas or Valentine's Day.

Creative briefing

2.4 The creative brief will include a summary of the points outlined above as well as several other elements.

Background/ introduction	This would be taken from the campaign brief.
Target market(s)	This might include more than a simple listing of the target audience characteristics. It could also include an assessment of what audiences currently think about the product or service.
Advertising objectives	Again, these would be as given in the campaign briefing, together with the marketing objectives.
Advertising proposition	The proposition should be summed up in a short sentence or two, stating in laymen's terms the response that is desired from the audience on seeing the advertising. Some agencies call this the **brand promise**.
Support	This is the backup for the advertising proposition. It would include the information or attributes that might help to produce the desired response. Support might take the form of factual benefits that a product possesses which differentiate it from the competition, or it might include findings from research.
Tone of voice	Should the advertising be authoritative, serious, friendly, modern in approach?
Mandatory inclusions	Typical examples of these would be 'pack shot must be included', or 'parent company logo must be easily identifiable in end freeze frame.'

Part B: The marketing mix

Creative ideas

2.5 It is enormously tempting for the client to interfere in the creative process, but as far as possible this should be left to the agency. The agency should be changed if its creative work is unacceptable to the client: this is in fact the commonest reason for taking advertising business elsewhere.

Marketing at Work

Advertising and taboos

There is an argument that many advertisements are created as much for the agency trophy cupboard as for client sales, but the real issues run deeper. Taking risks may be the only way for agencies to hold on to business.

Agencies have broken practically every taboo possible. Teenage suicide was adopted as a theme by Pepe, Tarantino-style murder by Don't Tell It magazine, AIDS by Benetton and transvestites by Levi's and MAC cosmetics.

Breaking taboos may not be the only way of making an impact, but agencies say *clients* are often convinced that this is the case.

'Clients come and say, 'I'm after a controversial script, I want a Tango ad',' says Viv Walsh, art director for Saatchi and part of the team behind the controversial Great Frog jewellery store and Don't Tell It ads.

Marketing Week, 28 July 1995

Execution

2.6 Advertising messages can be presented in many different advertisement execution styles.

Slice-of-life	This style shows one or more people using the product in a normal setting. A family seated at the dinner table might talk about a new biscuit brand.
Life style	This style shows how a product fits in with a life style. For example, cereal ads might show a person exercising and talk about how the cereal adds to a healthy, active life style.
Fantasy	This style creates a fantasy around the product or its use.
Mood or image	This style builds a mood or image around the product.
Musical	This style shows one or more people or cartoon characters singing a song about the product.
Personality symbol	This style creates a character that represents the product, e.g. the 'Marlboro-man'.
Technical expertise	This style shows the company's expertise in making the product.
Scientific evidence	This style presents survey or scientific evidence that the brand is better or better liked than most other brands.
Testimonial evidence	This style features a highly believable or likeable source endorsing the product. It could be a celebrity saying how much they like a given product.

Advertising effectiveness

2.7 Advertising may be judged to have been effective if it has met the objectives or tasks previously set for it. The following table gives some examples.

Advertising task/objectives	Example of measure of effect
Support increase in sales For example, a local plumber's advert in a regional newspaper	Orders; levels of enquiries
Inform consumers For example, an Amnesty International advert about political prisoners	Donations Number of new members clipping appeal coupon
Remind For example, a Yellow Pages television commercial	Awareness levels
Create/re-inforce image For example, the Halifax Building Society 'people' commercials	Awareness levels Image created
Change attitude For example, British Nuclear Fuel Ltd's Sellafield open door poster campaign	Attitude

2.8 Although there may well be a number of short-term effects resulting fairly soon after an advertising campaign has appeared, it is likely that a brand will reap positive long-term effects from advertising effort stretching over a number of years. All advertising, (whatever the objectives for any individual campaign), will contribute to the overall perception of that brand by the consumer.

2.9 Advertisers and their agencies go to some lengths to try to ensure that advertising campaigns are well designed and executed and are meeting objectives. Different types of advertising research can be used at different stages of a campaign's life, in order to gauge whether the advertising is fulfilling its roles.

Creative development research

2.10 This is research carried out early in the advertising process, using qualitative techniques to guide and help develop the advertising for a product or service. It can be used to help feed into initial creative ideas or alternatively, to check whether a rough idea is understood by consumers.

Pre-testing

2.11 Advertising pre-testing is research for predictive and evaluative purposes. Advertisements are tested quantitatively, at a much more highly finished stage than in creative development research, against set criteria. As advertising budgets are made to work harder, advertisers have felt the need to build in more checks to ensure that their advertising is on target. Quantitative testing can be administered via hall or studio tests. Specialist research agencies can cater for all kinds of media executions. Respondents are shown clusters of TV commercials either on their own or within television programmes; print executions are shown in folders amongst other adverts; poster executions may be shown in a simulated road drive scene via 35mm slides.

2.12 Adverts are measured against specific criteria.

Part B: The marketing mix

- **Impact**. Does the advert stand out against others?
- **Persuasion**. Does the advert create favourable predisposition towards the brand?
- **Message delivery**. Does the advert deliver the message in terms of understanding and credibility?
- **Liking**. This attribute is deemed to mean not only that the advert is enjoyable and interesting, but also covers the notion of an advert being personally meaningful to the consumer, relevant and believable. Thus, an RSPCA advert depicting a maltreated animal might not be likeable in the conventional sense, but may be rated highly by a respondent on this attribute because it draws attention to an important issue that is relevant to the consumer.

2.13 Criticisms have been levelled against quantitative pre-testing on the basis that it destroys creativity. A very new or radical creative treatment is likely to research badly, so the tendency may be to go with blander, but safe executions.

Tracking studies

2.14 Advertising effects may be measured over time via tracking studies which monitor pre- and post-advertising variables. Clients will normally buy into a series of **omnibus surveys** to monitor a variety of variables.

- Brand/product awareness (unprompted vs prompted recall)
- Attitudinal change
- Imagery associations

2.15 **Panel research** is another form of tracking study. For instance, Taylor Nelson's Superpanel monitors changes in the grocery shopping behaviour of 8,500 households. The research company have placed portable bar code scanners in homes, and families undertake to use the device to record purchases made. The data is collated every week and gives diagnostic information. For instance, if the panel buy less of a particular brand, it is possible to identify what brand they have switched to instead.

2.16 With tracking studies, it is important to try to examine all possible reasons for any changes in audience behaviour. An increase in the level of sales as tracked over time by panel-based research may be ascribed in part to the effect of the advertising. However, sales increases are equally likely to have come about due to changes in price levels, seasonality, competitive activity or a change in product quality levels.

3 ADVERTISING MEDIA

3.1 Media planning and buying is a specialised activity. The selection of media for a campaign depends on a number of factors.

3.2 The UK is a media rich country. The UK media spectrum includes the following.

- Television.
- Newspapers
- Magazines
- Radio
- Cinema
- Posters

5: Promotional operations in practice

3.3 New opportunities are offered by interactive advertising through the media of digital TV and, especially, the Internet.

Market background

3.4 Market size, shares and trends must all be taken into account. If a client is trying to break into a highly competitive marketplace, such as washing powder, perfumes or confectionery, then heavyweight multi-media advertising may be the only way of making a presence felt. On the other hand, if a small advertiser is trying to establish himself in the market for a highly specialised service (for example, genealogical research services for the family historian), a tightly targeted campaign through a specialist medium will probably suffice.

Target market

3.5 Obviously, media must be able to deliver the target market required. Some audiences are more difficult to deliver than others, due to their media viewing habits. Young adults tend to be light television viewers and may be best targeted with cinema advertising. Mass media will rarely deliver niche audiences, special interest magazines being a more appropriate media vehicle.

Budget

3.6 Budget can prove to be a media constraint. Clients should always specify the amount of money which is intended to be spent on *media* as opposed to the production budget for a campaign. A budget of £100,000 would tend to dictate a campaign that ran on a local basis only, or a national campaign which utilised only one medium. A budget of £1m would allow for a national campaign across a mix of media.

Media characteristics

3.7 Media choice is also governed by a number of factors arising from the different **properties** of the various media options.

3.8 The **nature of the medium** in its own right is an important consideration. Editorial stance, style, language and personality, will tend to rub off onto the advertising and particular magazines will be chosen for their compatibility with the products and services being promoted.

Marketing at Work

Tesco

In the run-up to the 1997 General Election in the UK, Tesco ran some very clever spoof election ads in the *Spectator* and the *New Statesman* with lines such as 'IT'S TIME FOR CHANGE' (beneath, a picture of some coins, and then 'TESCO ☒ UNBEATABLE VALUE'!) and 'DEMON PIES' (a rather jolly looking man with reddish fruit pies in place of eyes, along the lines of the satanic Tony Blair posters that won the Conservatives the 'Best campaign of 1996' award).

However, the bulk of Tesco shoppers are not generally readers of either publication. Many in the industry felt that the ads did far more good for the creative reputation of the ad agency responsible for them than they did for Tesco.

3.9 Similarly, the **positioning** of adverts within television, radio or cinema contexts can make a difference to how they are perceived. An advert scheduled in the middle of a TV game show

Part B: The marketing mix

will deliver an audience with a different mind set from one scheduled in the centre break of a documentary.

3.10 Another consideration is **the way in which people use media**. For instance, many popular radio stations are used as a background to other activities. By contrast, reading a newspaper is a main activity in its own right. Whether the medium is used as sole activity or minor activity will affect the ability of that medium to deliver the advertising it contains.

3.11 The amount of **time spent with the medium** can be a factor. Daily newspapers are a relatively quick read in the busy environment of the working week. Saturday and Sunday papers are a more leisurely read in the relaxed environment of the weekend.

3.12 Some media options lend themselves to particular **creative opportunities**. A full page Lufthansa advert ran in the daily press during the first week of Wimbledon 1994, following the elimination of two of the top German seeds, Graf and Stich. The advert thanked the opponents of the two players for providing the airline with some unexpected business. Such topicality can also be achieved by local radio and the Internet.

3.13 Television and cinema allow advertisers to use **the power of sound and vision together to create an impression**. Special effects originally created for film or pop video production can be used to give adverts an up to the minute feel.

3.14 Other characteristics must be considered when judging a medium on its **creative scope**.

- Potential for colour advertising
- Potential for movement and sound
- Space and time limitations
- Reprographic standards

3.15 **Booking and production lead times** may rule out the use of certain media. Magazine space is generally booked months in advance. Television and cinema commercials with high production values will take months to prepare, film and edit. As well as taking into account the inherent features of each medium, media channels must be **evaluated quantitatively** for their ability to deliver against criteria such as coverage, frequency and cost.

Media scheduling

3.16 As the media planner works through the available choices, a media schedule begins to evolve. This is the formal listing of which adverts are to appear where. Media schedules can be constructed for short-term campaigns, or for a whole year's advertising cycle.

3.17 **Burst v drip scheduling**. A large budget which allows for year round advertising is usually allocated in one of two ways.

- A **burst** campaign concentrates expenditure into promotional bursts of three or four weeks in length.
- A **drip** campaign allows for a continuous but more spread-out presence. Clearly in some markets there will be a burst of marketing communications at particular seasons, for example, at Christmas for toys, at Easter for garden products, or in January for holiday booking.

3.18 Other scheduling questions which need to be addressed include the following.

- When is media value at its greatest?
- How fast is advertising decay?

- Will over exposure to advertising be counter productive?
- Does advertising timing need to link into other communications events such as PR, sales promotion or salesforce cycles?

4 PERSONAL SELLING

4.1 **Personal selling has been defined as 'the presentation of products and associated persuasive communication to potential clients, employed by the supplying organisation.** It is the most direct and longest established means of promotion within the promotional mix' (Baron *et al*, *Macmillan Dictionary of Retailing* 1991).

Sales tasks

4.2 McMurray offered the following classification of **sales positions**.

Position	Salesperson's role
Deliverer	Predominantly to deliver the product.
Order taker	Passively takes orders from the customer. The customer has already been persuaded to use the product, or has been using the product in the past.
Missionary	Not expected or permitted to take an order but is expected to build goodwill or educate the customer in the use of the product. Medical representatives from pharmaceutical companies may fall into this category.
Technician	The application of technical knowledge relating to the product. The salesperson acts primarily as a consultant to the customer.
Demand creator	To stimulate demand and creatively sell tangible or intangible products.

4.3 Kotler states that a salesperson could perform as many as **six different activities**, as follows.

Activity	Detail
Prospecting	Gathering additional prospective customers in addition to sales leads generated by the company on his behalf.
Communicating	Communicating information to existing and potential customers about the company's products and services can take up a major proportion of the salespersons time.
Selling	'The art of salesmanship', encompassing approaching the customer, presenting, answering objections and closing the sale.
Servicing	Providing various services to the customer, such as rendering technical assistance and arranging finance and expediting delivery.
Information gathering	Source of marketing intelligence due to the links with the end customer.
Allocating	The allocation of products to customers in times of product shortages.

4.4 Salesforce activity must be undertaken within the context of the organisation's overall marketing strategy. For example, if the organisation pursues a 'pull' strategy, relying on massive consumer advertising to draw customers to ask for the brands, then the role of the salesforce may primarily be **servicing**, ensuring that retailers carry sufficient stock, allocate adequate shelf space for display and co-operate in sales promotion programmes. Conversely, with a 'push' strategy, the organisation will rely primarily on the salesforce to sell the brands to the marketing intermediaries.

Part B: The marketing mix

4.5 The mix of a salesperson's tasks may vary with the prevailing economic conditions. For example, in times of product shortage the art of selling may not be as important and one could argue that the salesforce are redundant. However, such a view neglects the other roles of the salesperson that will be of greater importance in such circumstances, such as allocating, counselling customers, communicating company policy to customers and perhaps selling other products that are not in short supply.

The mechanics of the selling process

4.6 *Lancaster and Jobber* identify six phases in the selling process:

- The opening
- Need and problem identification
- Presentation and demonstration
- Dealing with objections
- Negotiation
- Closing the sale

4.7 However, it must be remembered that the stages need not occur in this order. Objections may occur during the presentation and if the salesperson perceives that the process of selling is going well, an attempt to close the sale may be attempted at any stage. Also, the salesperson's job begins before meeting the buyer. Preparation could include finding out about the buyer's personal characteristics, the history of the trading relationship, and the specific requirements of the buyer and how the product being sold meets those requirements. In this way the salesperson can frame his sales presentations and answers to objections in the most effective way.

4.8 At the other end, the selling process does not finish when the sale is made. Indeed, the sale itself may only be the start of a long-term relationship between buyer and seller.

The opening

4.9 First impressions are important so it is essential for the salesperson to open the sales meeting in a professional way. First, the salesperson is expected to be businesslike in personal appearance and behaviour. Second, the opening remarks set the tone of the whole interview. Normally these remarks should be business-related so as not to show the buyer that his time is being wasted, although if the buyer wishes to talk of more social matters then the salesperson should oblige. However, these social pleasantries should not get in the way of the main business of the interview.

Need and problem identification

4.10 The first objective is to ascertain the circumstances of the customer. The salesperson will then be in a position to sell the product that best meets the needs of the buyer. As most salespeople now sell a range of products this initial information-gathering is of great importance. The salesperson should use 'open' rather than 'closed' questions to get the buyer to discuss his needs and problems.

The presentation and demonstration

4.11 This stage should follow on naturally from need identification which should have enabled the salesperson to select the most appropriate product to meet the customer requirements. In addition, need identification should have given the salesperson an indication of the specific benefits to stress. Buyers are only interested in product features in as much as they provide **the required benefits**. *McDonald and Leppard* classify benefits into three categories: standard benefits, company benefits and differential benefits.

(a) **Standard benefits** are those which arise from the features of the product.

(b) **Company benefits** arise from the links between the buyer and seller. Whenever a customer buys a product or service, he is simultaneously buying into a relationship with the seller on a number of levels. The buyer needs to have confidence in the selling company and will be concerned about the company's reputation, quality of staff, and its willingness and ability to provide what it promises. An example of such a benefit may be the fact that a company is a multi-national organisation meaning that it can provide a uniform level of service anywhere in the world.

(c) **Differential benefits** relate to competing product offerings. If a seller can identify a benefit that cannot be matched by competitors then this clearly gives an advantage. Examples could include the ability to provide a superior level of after-sales service.

Not all benefits are equally attractive to the customer so the salesperson has to frame the offer around those benefits with the highest appeal.

4.12 **Sales aids** in the form of brochures, presentation kits and demonstration models have a number of advantages.

- They add tangibility to a service or product not available for demonstration at the point of sale.
- They add interest and variety to the sales presentation.
- They make it easier to explain key selling points or complex products.
- They show the products in use and customers benefiting from them.

4.13 Lancaster and Jobber state that many selling situations involve **risk** for the buyer which may make him reluctant to buy even if the salesperson has put forward a very persuasive case. The salesperson has some weapons in his armoury to **enable risk to be reduced**. These include reference selling, demonstrations, guarantees and trial orders.

- **Reference selling** involves the use of satisfied customers in order to convince the buyer of the effectiveness of the salesman's product.
- **Demonstrations** show that the product actually functions.
- **Guarantees** can build confidence and lessen the cost to the buyer should something go wrong.
- **Trial orders** allow sellers to demonstrate their capability to satisfy requirements at minimal risk. Such tactics may be uneconomic in terms of finance and time in the short term, but may secure a higher proportion of that customer's business in the long term.

Dealing with objections

4.14 During the course of the sales interview there will be **objections raised by the buyer**, irrespective of the quality of the sales presentation. Objections should, however, be regarded by the salesperson in a positive manner. By raising objections the potential buyer is asking for further information.

4.15 McDonald and Leppard classify objections into two main types. **Fundamental** objections occur when the buyer fails to see the need for the product or service on offer. **Standard**

Part B: The marketing mix

objections occur when the buyer recognises the need for the product but wishes to delay making a positive decision. Standard objections may be classified according to what motivates them.

(a) **Feature objections** occur if a buyer is unhappy about a particular feature of a product.

(b) **Information-seeking objections** are similar to feature objections but the motivation behind them is rooted in the buyer's lack of knowledge or understanding about the product. These objections imply that the buyer is interested in the product offered.

(c) **Delay objections** can be motivated by three factors; first, that the buyer is not really convinced by the salesperson's case, second, that the buyer genuinely needs time to consult and/or reflect on the purchase decision, or, third, that there is some other reason for avoiding the decision (a hidden objection).

(d) **Hidden objections**. If the buyer has been given all the information needed to make the decision but still procrastinates, it can only be assumed that there is a further objection that is hidden from the salesperson.

(e) **Price objections**. Price features prominently in many sales negotiations. Often the price objection is not merely about cost to the buyer but about **value for money**. The price objection should, therefore, be answered by benefits which emphasise value.

Negotiation

4.16 **Negotiation has been defined as, 'conferring with another with the view to compromise or agree on some issue'** (Gillam). In many selling situations both buyer and seller will have a degree of discretion regarding the terms of the sale, and therefore, negotiation will enter into the selling process as each party tries to get the best deal within the constraints under which they operate. The final deal that is struck will largely depend on **two main factors: the negotiating skills** of the participants **and the balance of power** between the participants (Lancaster and Jobber).

4.17 Four key factors determine the **balance of power**.

(a) **The number of options available to each party**. If a seller is a unique source of supply of a product he will be in a powerful position, whereas if a buyer has many potential sources of supply the position will be reversed. Indeed, many buyers will deliberately contact a number of potential suppliers to strengthen their bargaining position.

(b) **The quality and quantity of information held by each party**. The more information held about the other party to the negotiation, the better.

(c) **Need recognition and satisfaction**. The greater the salesperson's understanding of the needs of the buyers and the more capable he is or satisfying those needs, the stronger will be his bargaining position.

(d) **The pressures on the parties**. These will vary depending on circumstances. For example, if a seller needs an order to make up his sales quota for a period, then the buyer may be able to extract very favourable terms.

Closing the sale

4.18 The sale is closed only when the buyer makes a firm commitment to place an order and the whole sales interview should be regarded as a process leading to a close. The sale can be closed at any stage in the process. The right time can be ascertained by looking for buying signals from the buyer. Buying signals can take many forms, including body language, committing statements or questions, which are asked based on the assumption that the product will be bought.

4.19 In some circumstances it may not be appropriate to close the sale, particularly where the selling process is a protracted one. The best that the salesperson can hope for is an **action agreement** whereby the salesperson and buyer agree to do something for the next meeting, thereby allowing the relationship to continue and develop.

Sales support

4.20 The role of sales support activities.

- To maximise the proportion of sales time spent in face to face client contact
- To provide direction, and to ensure sales resources are targeted at the market segments and leads offering the greatest potential
- To provide the necessary backup to help the sales person ensure a continuing relationship with a satisfied customer

Sales research

4.21 Good information can both reduce sales costs and help to increase sales revenues.

(a) Profiling the 20% of customers who generate 80% of the business, provides segmentation information, which means more customers of the same type can be identified and targeted.

(b) Analysis of the sales effort reveals important management information.

- The most profitable balance of new to old calls
- The most effective call rate per day
- The best use of presentations and demonstrations etc in a sales call
- The most effective frequency of sales calls

4.22 The average sales person often spends less than 10% of his or her time in direct customer contact. Any improvements either in the amount of effective selling time or the effectiveness of the selling process, can generate significant improvement in performance. Information provides the clues which enable managers to facilitate these incremental improvements.

Customer and competitor intelligence

4.23 Good salespeople are ones who know their customer's business. This means not only knowing who they are competing with for the contract, but also who their customers are competing with. This knowledge of a market is built up over a considerable period. It is one of the reasons why organising sales forces by industry or sector can be very effective.

4.24 New technology provides the systems to both store and retrieve rapidly such information. Sales teams should be able to access an up to date record on a company immediately before a sales visit. This should record four main categories of information.

- Sales contacts made, including those made by other sales teams from the company
- Orders received, value, frequency and so on
- Current financial standing, including overdue accounts

Part B: The marketing mix

- Any intelligence on changing personnel in the company, new business won, contracts signed or plans announced

4.25 Information should also be gathered on competitors. Providing the sales team with early information about proposed special offers, or new products being launched by competitors, helps the salesperson be better prepared when negotiating with a customer.

Measuring sales potential

4.26 Both specific sales information about calls and sales actually made, and market intelligence about customers and competitors provide managers with an insight into sales potential. The sales resource is both valuable and scare, and it must be used with care. Maximising its value to the organisation means using it in areas where the sales potential is perceived to be greatest. Whilst it is possible to identify a number of factors likely to influence sales potential, it should be remembered that sometimes the greatest opportunities are not the most obvious and the customer who seems to offer the least potential may in fact offer the greatest. Too narrow an approach, prescribed by managers, may hinder the salespersons ability to identify new sales opportunities.

4.27 Sales potential can be affected by a number of issues.

(a) **Competition**. It can be more profitable to concentrate activities on a part of the market with a lower total potential because there is less competition.

(b) **Future forecasts**. Sales potential should not be judged only on a short-term basis, but should also be assessed on a forecast of the longer-term future. A company in a mature industry wishing to place a very large order now, may offer a lower potential in the long term than a smaller company operating in a growth market, which today only requires a small order.

(c) **External factors**. All business is influenced by its external environment. Suppliers should assess the both factors which affect their business, but also those which affect their customers.

Providing leads

4.28 A role of sales support is to provide a flow of qualified leads. These should represent potential customers who are aware of the company and/or product, are already interested in it and who have, or have begun to have, a positive attitude to its purchase. The conversion rate of contacts already this far down the decision-making process is likely to be higher than if the buyer has to be introduced to the produce or company by the salesperson. Leads may come from unsolicited enquiries, mail-in responses to advertising, the identification of cross-selling opportunities or database mining.

The advantages and disadvantages of personal selling

4.29 *Shimp* identifies a number of advantages that can accrue from using personal selling compared to other promotional tools.

- Personal selling contributes to a **relatively high level of customer attention** since, in face-to-face situations, it is difficult for a potential buyer to avoid a salesperson's message.

- Personal selling enables the salesperson to **customise the message** to the customer's specific interests and needs.

5: Promotional operations in practice

- The two-way communication nature of personal selling allows **immediate feedback** from the customer so that the effectiveness of the message can be ascertained.

- Personal selling **communicates a larger amount of technical and complex information** than would be possible using other promotional methods.

- In personal selling there is a greater ability to **demonstrate a product's functioning and performance characteristics**.

- Frequent interaction with the customer gives great scope for the **development of long-term relations** between buyer and seller, making the process of purchase more of a team effort.

4.30 The primary **disadvantage of personal selling is, of course, the cost inherent in maintaining a salesforce**. In addition, a salesperson can only interact with one buyer at a time. However, the message is generally communicated more effectively in the one-to-one sales interview, so the organisation must make a value judgement between the effectiveness of getting the message across against the relative inefficiency of personal selling in cost terms.

5 SALES PROMOTION

> **Key Concept**
> The Institute of Sales Promotion (ISP) defines **sales promotion** as 'a range of tactical marketing techniques, designed within a strategic marketing framework, to add value to a product or service, in order to achieve a specific sales and marketing objective.'

Sales promotion objectives

5.1 The following are examples of consumer sales promotion objectives stated in broad terms.

  (a) To increase awareness and interest amongst target audiences.
  (b) To achieve a switch in buying behaviour from competitor brands.
  (c) To smooth seasonal dips in demand.

5.2 Sales promotion objectives will link into overarching marketing and marketing communications objectives.

Marketing objective	To increase brand X market share by 2 percentage points in the period January to December 1997
Marketing communications objective	To contribute to brandshare gain of 2% in 1997 by increasing awareness of X from 50% to 70% amongst target consumers.
Sales promotion objective	To encourage trial of brand X amongst target consumers by offering a guaranteed incentive to purchase.

Part B: The marketing mix

> **Action Programme 1**
>
> Tesco, Safeway and Sainsbury all now issue a card which shoppers present when they reach the check-out. Points are awarded for sums spent over a minimum amount and these are added up each quarter. Money-off vouchers to be used against future grocery bills are sent to the shopper's home.
>
> What is the purpose of this?

Consumer sales promotion techniques

Reduced price

5.3 **Price promotions** may take the form of a discount to the normal selling price of a product, or alternatively, offer the consumer more product at the normal price. This form of promotion does not usually require the assistance of a specialist agency, as it can be administered in-house. Increased sales gained from this form of promotion must be balanced against loss in profit from the discounting activity.

5.4 **Cross-brand promotions** may be regarded as a form of reduced price promotion as they offer the opportunity for the customer to sample the promoted product plus the complementary product at a discount (shampoo and styling mousse, or teabags and biscuits are typical examples).

Coupons

5.5 Coupons are often used as a way of offering a discount. This is a highly versatile form of sales promotion, as coupons may be used in a variety of ways.

- On pack to encourage the consumer to repeat purchase
- In coupon books or inserts distributed with regional or national newspapers
- As part of a media advertisement
- In coupon machines on shelf edges

> **Marketing at Work**
>
> *Instant coupon machine*
>
> Money-off coupons, long dismissed as tacky and downmarket, are to be given a new lease of life. J Sainsbury's, Budgens and Iceland are testing an in-store coupon dispenser at 400 supermarkets in the UK.
>
> Initial results suggest that this new form of 'instant redemption' is attractive to shoppers of all socio-economic backgrounds.
>
> The Instant Coupon Machine is placed at eye level next to the brand being discounted, with a flashing red light to attract attention.
>
> The introduction of an ICM - either on a single brand or on a collection of grocery and household lines - can have a remarkable effect on sales. Kelloggs, Cadbury's, Unilever's Van den Bergh Foods and Danone, all taking part in the trails, report sales increases of more than 60 per cent.
>
> Sales of Bic razors have increased by 257 per cent, while the sales boost for Shredded Wheat has been 207 per cent.
>
> *Financial Times, 30 April 1999*

5.6 Redemption rates are highest with in-pack, or on-pack coupons and lowest with coupons distributed via newspapers and magazines.

Gift with purchase

5.7 '**Gift with purchase**' promotions are often referred to as **premium** promotions, as the consumer receives a bonus when he purchases. This promotion tends to be used with higher ticket goods and services, A slight variation to the method is the gift with purchase **mail-in**, where consumers have to send in proofs of purchase or collect tokens in order to be eligible for the incentive.

Marketing at Work

Pogs and Tazos

'Pogs' or 'Tazos' are little tiddly-wink like tokens bearing colourful designs. They were introduced in Britain in 1995 and quickly became a playground craze that swept the country. They were named the toy of the year by the British Association of Toy Retailers. They form a sort of currency amongst children. Like marbles, they are won and lost in playground competitions.

Early in 1996 UK snack producers jumped on the bandwagon.

'Starting in a few weeks Golden Wonder will be distributing 45 million Pogs in its crisp packets. Not to be outdone, Walkers will begin placing 250 million Tazos (its own version of Pogs) in packets of Walkers crisps, Doritos, Quavers and Monster Munch. This represents a magic figure of 25 for every person under the age of 15. ... While the original Pog is cardboard, Tazos are plastic. Tazos also have a notch in them that allows children to stick them together.

Walkers ... expects its Tazos promotion to generate huge sales increases. Pepsico Food International [Walkers parent company] decided to 'go global' with Tazos promotions after initial tests produced sales increases of 50 per cent and more. In Holland, more Tazos collectors' albums have been purchased than the country has children. If Walkers achieves half of that sort of uptake in the UK, it will be close to overtaking Coca-Cola to become the country's biggest supermarket brand.

The Times, February 1996

Competitions and prizes

5.8 This term covers any form of prize promotion and is popular with all types of organisations. There are some standard types.

- Complete the sentence
- Answer a series of questions
- Spot the something
- Rank a series of attributes in order
- Estimate a quantity

5.9 There are also **lucky dip** type competitions where you win a prize if you happen to buy the lucky toilet roll, or whatever. Most prize promotions are subject to legal restrictions and expert legal advice is a must.

Action Programme 2

Over the next few weeks, identify and note the different forms of sales promotion you encounter as you shop.

- Categorise the types of sales promotion into groups. Are certain types of promotion a characteristic of certain product categories?
- Are all the promotions appropriate to the products? Why?
- Try to distinguish objectives of the different promotions. What are they and, in your opinion, are they being achieved?

Part B: The marketing mix

Trade promotions

5.10 This category of promotion acts to **encourage the distributor to stock or sell more of a product or service**. In addition to the examples listed below, discounts and special terms may be used as part of the trade promotional armoury.

Baker's dozen

5.11 This is a popular form of price promotion, where 13 items/cases/crates are offered for the price of 12.

Tailor-made promotion

5.12 Any of the standard consumer promotional techniques can be offered to a retailer as a tailor-made promotion exclusively for his store or group of stores. The offer of a tailor-made promotion can help a sales person negotiating with a buying group. Often, a tailor-made promotion will include promotional aspects for the retailer's sales staff to motivate them to push the promoted product at point of sale.

Mystery shoppers

5.13 **Mystery shoppers are sometimes used as a trade motivator** alongside a consumer promotion that has gained national distribution. All retail outlets are forewarned (as part of the promotion) that a mystery shopping team will be touring the country, checking that the consumer promotion is properly displayed and accurately described by sales assistants dealing with queries. Outlets satisfying the mystery shopper's judging criteria are rewarded. Be careful not to confuse mystery shopping that is used as a sales promotional tool with mystery shopping used as a research technique to gauge customer satisfaction.

> **Exam Tip**
> The December 1999 exam included a question in Part B which required a report on sales promotion techniques. This was the first exam under the new syllabus and the question was fairly simple. Expect something a little more complex at some point in the future.

Promotional evaluation

5.14 The results of a promotion should always be measured against objectives. All sales promotions can be measured in terms of promotional take-up, for example, number of vouchers redeemed, or number of competition entries. The absolute redemption figure should be expressed as a percentage of all possible redemptions in order to give a benchmark for future promotions.

5.15 Electronic household panel information, which tracks shopping day by day, can give information about the overall level of promotional activity for a market or brand and show how this breaks down between different types of promotion. The table below was generated by Nielsen's Homescan panel and gives an example of how consumers spent their money by type of promotion in the grocery market.

Consumer expenditure by promotion type

	%
Store price promotion	35.8
Additional quality	12.6
Quantity purchase	12.1
Send away offer	9.4
Manufacturer price reduction	7.3
Branded pack	4.9
Free item	4.1
Coupon used	2.8
On pack coupon	2.7
Other	8.3

Nielsen Homescan: 12 weeks ending 5th September 1992

5.16 *Ad hoc* research can be undertaken into the effects of specific promotions. For example, Heinz have used research to monitor promotional effort. Five thousand reply-paid questionnaires are supplied to the handling house to be mailed off alongside purchase vouchers to a random selection of promotion applicants. Questionnaire content is tailored to the specific needs of the promotion, but core questions are retained for comparability.

6 PUBLIC RELATIONS

> **Key Concept**
> The Institute of Public Relations has defined **public relations** as 'the planned and sustained effort to establish and maintain goodwill and mutual understanding between an organisation and its publics'.

6.2 PR activities

- **Establishing and maintaining two-way communication** based on truth and full information
- **Preventing conflict and misunderstandings**
- **Promoting mutual respect** and social responsibility
- **Promoting goodwill** with staff, suppliers and customers
- **Attracting good personnel** and reducing labour turnover
- **Promoting** products and services

Four models of PR

6.3 *Grunig and Hunt* suggest that there are four models of public relations practice.

Press agentry/publicity

6.4 In this model the role of PR is primarily one of **propaganda**, spreading the faith of the organisation, often through incomplete, half-true or distorted information. Communication is **one-way** from the organisation to its publics.

Public information

6.5 In this model the role of PR is the **dissemination of information, not necessarily with a persuasive intent**. This type of communication is one-way, but it presents a complete picture of the organisation.

Part B: The marketing mix

Two-way asymmetric

6.6 The main function of the two-way asymmetric model is scientific persuasion, using social science theory and research about attitudes and behaviour. The aim is to achieve the maximum change in attitudes and behaviour. There is a flow of information back to the organisation from the publics, but communication is asymmetric because the response to this feedback from the publics is to improve the effectiveness of the outgoing communication.

Two-way symmetric

6.7 In the two-way symmetric model, the PR practitioner serves as a **mediator between the organisation and its publics with the aim of facilitating mutual understanding between the two**. The communication is therefore more of a dialogue than a monologue. If persuasion occurs it is as likely to persuade the organisation's management to change its attitude as it is to persuade the publics to change theirs.

6.8 Grunig and Hunt suggest that the model used varies depending on the type of organisation concerned.

PR model	*Area of practice*
Press agentry/publicity	Sports, theatre, product promotion
Public information	Government and non-profit organisations
Two-way asymmetric	Competitive business and PR agencies
Two-way symmetric	Regulated business agencies (water, electricity)

6.9 The organisation can be either reactive or proactive in its management of relationships.

(a) **Reactive** PR is primarily concerned with the communication of what has happened and responding to factors affecting the organisation. It is primarily defensive.

(b) In contrast, **proactive** public relations practitioners have a much wider role and thus have a far greater influence on overall organisational strategy. The scope of the PR function is much wider, encompassing communications activities in their entirety, counselling and strategic planning.

6.10 Traditionally, marketing texts have portrayed public relations as one element of the communication mix, with the prime objectives of all the communication tools being to increase sales of the products or services provided. However, a distinction must be made between public relations *techniques* and the public relations *function*. **Whilst public relations techniques can contribute to the maximisation of sales objectives as part of the marketing communications mix, the broader public relations function has roles to play with other non-customer publics**. These other roles entail building relationships with a wide range of publics. They may well contribute to the achievement of the organisation's marketing objectives, but they will do so indirectly, through their impact on the organisation's wider environment.

Publics

> **Key Concept**
> In the context of public relations, a **public** is a group of people united by a common interest that is specific to them or their situation.

5: Promotional operations in practice

6.11 An organisation may have a wide range of publics with whom it wishes to communicate. *Black* gives an indication of this range.

- Customers - existing, past and potential
- Members of the public in general
- The trade and distributors
- Financial publics - shareholders, the City, banks, institutions and stockbrokers
- Pressure groups
- Opinion leaders
- The media - as a special type of public as well as a channel of communication
- Overseas governments, EU bodies and International bodies
- Central and local government bodies, MPs and members of the House of Lords
- Research bodies and policy-forming units
- The local community
- Trades Unions
- Employees

6.12 The different types of publics have been classified by Grunig and Hunt, who identified three categories.

- **Active publics** - groups which organise themselves to discuss and do something about a problem.
- **Aware publics** - groups which have recognised that a problem exists
- **Latent publics** - groups that face a particular problem as a result of an organisation's actions but fail to recognise that there is a problem.

Grunig states that a public relations problem could arise when an organisation or its publics behave in a way that has consequences for the other. Grunig looks at the identification of relevant publics from two perspectives.

- The publics can be defined by considering who is **likely to be affected by the actions of the organisation.**
- PR practitioners can identify those groups or organisations whose opinions and behaviour are **likely to affect the activities of the organisation**.

6.13 **Subsequent research** by Grunig led him to identity four broad types of publics, as follows.

- **All-issue publics** - who are active on all issues
- **Apathetic publics** - who are apathetic on all issues
- **Hot-issue publics** - who are active only on issues involving a majority of the population
- **Single-issue publics** - who are only active on a small subset of issues.

Action Programme 3

How would you classify the following groups, using the above scheme?
(a) An organisation's shareholders
(b) An organisation's employees
(c) An organisation's suppliers

Part B: The marketing mix

> **Exam Tip**
> The June 1998 Promotional Practice examination included a question about the publics a tourism director might have to identify. This is a good illustration of putting theory in a specific context. You could use the analysis given above as a starting point, perhaps identifying a hot-issue public relating to beach cleanliness. However, you would need to use your general awareness to suggest other publics such as low paid workers (in catering) and local residents.

Public opinion

6.14 Once publics have been identified, the aim of public relations practitioners will be to influence the opinions of those publics.

- To reinforce favourable opinions
- To transform latent attitudes into positive beliefs
- To modify and neutralise hostile or critical opinions

6.15 An important aspect of public opinion is the influence of **opinion leaders**. Black classifies opinion leaders into two groups.

- **Formal opinion leaders**, who are opinion leaders by virtue of their rank or position, such as Members of Parliament, newspaper editors, teachers or the clergy.

- **Informal opinion leaders**, who are opinion leaders by virtue of charisma, personality or background and exert a strong influence on their peers, friends or acquaintances.

In attempting to modify public opinion it seems sensible to concentrate on trying to influence opinion leaders who, in turn, are likely to spread understanding to ever widening circles of the general public. This is often termed the '**multiplier effect**'.

Public relations techniques

6.16 Public relations programmes may be subdivided into **contact** and **convince** programmes.

- First, it is necessary to **identify and contact** the relevant target publics.
- Then PR must **convince** them of the merit of particular arguments, or to behave in a particular manner.

The resulting communication process may be broken down into a number of stages.

- People are made aware of an idea or argument.
- Their interest in it is aroused.
- They are persuaded of its merits (and the potential benefits for themselves).
- They are shown how to respond and are encouraged to do so.

The range of PR techniques

6.17 The choice of the specific techniques in a PR programme is a value judgement involving the balance of the expected impact of the chosen techniques against their relative costs. The range of appropriate techniques from which the PR practitioner can choose will be determined by the nature of the problem, the publics involved and the budget available. Black and Moss use the analogy of a menu to indicate the range of PR techniques that can be used. A point to remember is that this 'media menu' is dynamic, with the number of potential techniques available continuing to expand.

> **Media Menu**
>
> *Corporate Advertising*
>
> *Exhibitions*
>
> *Conferences and tele-conferences*
>
> *Community involvement programmes*
>
> *Internal newsletters/house journals*
>
> *Special events*
>
> *Audio-visual material*
>
> *Direct mail (also for news releases distribution)*
>
> *Sponsorship (sports, art etc)*
>
> *Networking*
>
> *Lobbying activities*
>
> *Counselling management on issues and policies*
>
> *Research*
> to assist with issues monitoring
> as the basis for news stories
> to assist in the development of strategies
> to monitor results and provide the basis for counselling
>
> *Corporate identity programmes, involving the design of*
> corporate logos
> literature
> corporate livery
> facilities/premises
> operating policies etc
>
> *Design of*
> literature
> brochures
> stationery
> annual reports
>
> *Media relations for print and broadcast media*
> press releases
> articles
> features
> background material
> film
> photographs

6.18 Inevitably some techniques will be more appropriate in certain circumstances with certain types of publics than others. It is possible, therefore, to classify the different types of techniques or media according to the type of project areas in which they appear to be most effective. Some frequently used techniques are as follows.

(a) **Consumer marketing support area techniques**

- Consumer and trade press releases

- Product/service literature

- Promotional videos

- Special events (in-store competitions, celebrity store openings, product launch events, celebrity endorsements etc)

Part B: The marketing mix

(b) **Business to business communication area techniques**

- Corporate identity design
- Corporate and product videos
- Direct mailings
- Trade exhibitions

(c) **Internal/employee communications area techniques**

- In-house magazines and employee newsletters
- Recruitment exhibitions/conferences
- Company notice boards

(d) **Corporate, external and public affairs area techniques**

- Corporate literature
- Corporate social responsibility programmes and community involvement programmes
- Trade, local, national and possibly international media relations
- Local or central government lobbying

(e) **Financial public relations area techniques**

- Financial media relations on both a national and international basis
- Design of annual and interim reports
- Facility visits for analysts, brokers, fund managers etc
- Organising shareholder meetings

Marketing at Work

Greyhound Racing

With the advent of the National Lottery in 1994, horse racing and greyhound racing were quick to feel the pinch. Greyhound racing was particularly concerned, as many tracks were soon seeing their numbers fall and the amount staked each week reduced.

Charles Barker, acting for the British Greyhound Racing Board (BGRB) for over ten years, recommended that a campaign be mounted to protect this popular sport from falling into decline. The objective of the strategy was to obtain a cut in betting duty.

A campaign was devised, focusing on the Treasury - with constituency MPs acting as the foot soldiers and further ammunition provided by a Henley Centre study into the lottery's impact on greyhound racing. Common cause was also made with other sectors of the racing world. A combination of debates and questions in the House of Commons, bolstered by direct follow-up with key MPs and a meeting with the Paymaster General paid the desired dividends. In his Budget Statement of 29 November 1995, the Chancellor announced a 1% cut on betting duty.

Considering that campaigns to reduce taxation normally start at odds of at least 100-1, this win was viewed as a spectacular achievement.

Charles Barker website

Choosing PR techniques

Suitability criteria

6.19 Suitability criteria are concerned with assessing the **extent to which the chosen techniques are suited to the situation, the publics, the messages and the wider objectives of the organisation.**

5: Promotional operations in practice

- The extent to which particular techniques or media are suited to the content, tone and creative requirements of the message;
- The compatibility of techniques with other elements of the organisation's strategy;
- The extent to which techniques allow an organisation to exploit its particular strengths and opportunities;
- The influence and credibility which different techniques are likely to have with the particular publics being targeted.

Feasibility criteria

6.20 These criteria are concerned with assessing the **extent to which the techniques chosen are capable of being successfully implemented** given constraints such as time, cost and resources.

- Whether the **available budget** will permit a particular form of media or a particular type of activity to be used effectively
- Whether an organisation has access to the **technology** needed to implement a particular type of technique
- Whether an organisation possesses, or can afford to hire, the **skilled personnel** needed to exploit a particular form of media
- Whether it is possible for the techniques under consideration to be carried out within the **timescale** available
- Whether the media or techniques being considered offer a **realistic means** of achieving the objectives set by management

Acceptability criteria

6.21 These assess the extent to which the chosen techniques and their expected outcomes are **acceptable to the organisation**.

- The extent to which different techniques or media can achieve an acceptable level of **coverage** of target publics;
- The extent to which the expected degree of **impact** which different techniques or media are likely to have meets with the programme's objectives;
- The extent to which different techniques or media allow an acceptable degree of **control** over the message;
- The degree of **risk of failure** associated with the use of different techniques.

Action Programme 4

British Gas withdrew from the Charter Mark scheme in November 1995 but came under fire because it continued to use the Charter Mark logo on its bills for some time prior to renaming its domestic supply division 'British Gas Trading'.

How might PR have helped to avoid the criticism?

Part B: The marketing mix

Control

6.22 Without adequate mechanisms for monitoring and control it is impossible to know whether the objectives of the PR activity have been met. The evaluation of PR activities often concentrates on the measurement of the effectiveness of the process of communications rather than on the **impact of the communications programmes on the target publics**. *Moss* identifies a number of **typical measures of PR activity**.

- The monitoring of any **media coverage received**, which may include an assessment of the number of column inches/minutes of broadcast coverage, the position of articles, the accuracy of the content and the use of key words or phrases
- **Attendance at exhibitions** together with the **number of orders and enquiries** received
- **Replies to response coupons** included in advertorials
- **Telephone enquiries** following the appearance of an article or broadcast programme

However, such methods only provide a measure of the effectiveness of the implementation of the programme, not of its ultimate impact. In order to do this, it is necessary to carry out more detailed research into the attitudes and behaviour of the target publics.

7 SPONSORSHIP

> **Key Concept**
> **Sponsorship** entails supporting an event or an activity by providing money (or something else of value to the event-organiser), usually in return for advertising space at the event and as part of any publicity for the event.

7.1 Some sponsorship is undertaken for altruistic reasons.

Programme sponsorship

7.2 Programme sponsorship is a relatively new promotional technique in the UK, though it has been common in other countries such as the USA for many years. The 1990 Broadcasting Act released the majority of programmes broadcast on the independent media for sponsorship (the only exceptions are news and current affairs programming).

Fragmentation of the media with the advent of satellite TV and the proliferation of commercial radio stations means that **there is now a greater variety of channels to choose from and a more price-competitive environment. There are far greater opportunities for closer and tighter targeting of the prospective audience**. Sponsored programmes can have both front and end credits for the sponsor and 'bumpers and trailers' at the beginning and end of commercial breaks. In the case of a feature length film this could equate to up to six separate opportunities to view.

Marketing at Work

Equitable Life

Equitable Life is to sponsor television sitcom Frasier in a deal worth £4m a year.

This means Equitable sponsorship credits will appear around episodes of Frasier shown on Channel 4, the Paramount Comedy Channel and British airway's inflight TV service. It includes a merchandising arrangement with Paramount Pictures – Comedy Channel parent and owner of the Frasier TV rights

5: Promotional operations in practice

New PHD is working on both elements of the deal, which will run initially for six months and is expected to continue for at least a year.

Mark Boyd, account manager for Equitable at New PHD, says 'Final details of the merchandising element are to be confirmed, but we are likely to see Equitable policy holders given merchandise such as Frasier videos, as well as the Equitable logo appearing on Frasier videos and T-shirts in stores selling Paramount products.'

'Frasier is fair, intelligent, professional and upmarket just like Equitable's customer base.' adds Boyd.

Paramount will include some Equitable material on its Website.

The first sponsorship credits will be broadcast on C4 tomorrow (Friday) and feature a redesigned corporate identity, created by Euro RSCG Direct Marketing.

Equitable recently won a High court case that allows it to renege on its pension income guarantees. It had lost a lot of credibility when it decided not to honour the guaranteed annuity rates it promised on some of its pensions. These offered policy holders a guaranteed income from the pot of money they had built up during the course of their policy.

Marketing Week, 6 January 2000

Benefits

7.3 Benefits of programme sponsorship

(a) **Standout**. The sponsorship of *Inspector Morse* by Beamish generated 50% consumer awareness of the sponsorship activity and 92% of those who were aware named Beamish as the sponsor.

(b) **Association value**. Beamish has come to be seen as a premium brand by association with a quality TV programme. Programme sponsorship is particularly appropriate for organisations that wish to augment their brand profile rather than convey a specific message.

(c) **Cost effectiveness**. Television advertising can be extremely expensive, with slots costing up to £30,000 for 30 seconds in the larger regions. Sponsorship could provide a substantially more cost-effective promotional tool.

(d) **Precision targeting**. There are few programme exceptions and few sponsor exceptions, in other words most advertisers can sponsor most programmes.

(e) **Blocking competition**. Under the ITC sponsorship guidelines, most sponsored programmes may not contain promotional reference to more than one product.

Weaknesses

7.4 The techniques does of course have a number of weaknesses.

(a) Programme sponsorship can only communicate a **restricted amount of information**.

(b) A **considerable amount of time** may be required to establish a sponsorship agreement.

(c) The ITC **guidelines may be regarded as prohibitive**.

- The sponsor is not permitted any influence on either the content or the scheduling of the programme.
- No promotional reference to the sponsor, or to his product or service, is permitted *within* the programme he has sponsored.
- Product placement is prohibited.

7.5 The key considerations in picking specific programmes are **time and compatibility**. For example, for a swimwear company it would probably be more appropriate to sponsor

Part B: The marketing mix

programmes that are broadcast during the summer or (if a very sexy image is wanted) in the later evening. It would, of course, be highly inappropriate to sponsor programmes that have no suggestion of swimming (*Coronation Street*, say) or make the idea of swimming seem unattractive (such as programmes featuring real life accidents).

Sports sponsorship

7.6 Major sporting events and competitions have the advantage of being attended by large numbers of people in person and watched by millions more on TV. They also attract many column inches of coverage in the sports pages of newspapers and allow access to the best seats, for corporate hospitality purposes. It is possible to sponsor:

Marketing at Work

Coca Cola

In an *average* year about 20% of Coca-Cola's annual consumer marketing budget (of £960m) is used to 'support' sports. Spending in 1996 is likely to have been much higher than this which the company spent nearly £30m alone on buying the rights to be an Olympic sponsor, and more than £60m on TV commercials during the Games.

7.7 Many of the points made about programme sponsorship apply to sports sponsorship too. For example, 'the Carling Premiership' conveys a certain image, and football is a highly appropriate choice for a lager brewer, but it does not tell us anything specific about the brand. Drink-related violence at a football match could easily damage the brand.

Arts sponsorship

7.8 Arts events are not as high profile as sports events but are generally regarded as more 'worthy'. **The associations of arts events may be more in keeping with the images of some businesses** and the opportunities for corporate hospitality more appealing.

Marketing at Work

Glaxo and the arts

'Glaxo is currently sponsoring *Spanish Still Life* at the National Gallery. Still life - fruit, flowers, tableware and food - enjoys some general appreciation.

But it is only thanks to this exhibition, with pictures from the Prado and private collections worldwide, that the Spanish contribution to the art form, more extreme in its range of subject matter, colour and spiritual significance, has been fully appreciated. *Spanish Still Life* has arguably been the exhibition hit of the season. Critical assessment has been unanimously praising. Critics and audiences who came for the Goyas and Velazquezs have left marvelling also at the revelatory works of Cotan, Zurbaran and 'El Labrador'. During the first month alone, 45,000 people saw the exhibition. Quality and prestige are evident. The youth element is met by an associated education programme directed at schools. Added value comes with the Spanish-internationalist dimension, which allowed the company to emphasise its international compass, and to involve Glaxo Spain in producing a Spanish edition of the catalogue for VIP distribution in its own territory.'

ABSA Bulletin, Spring 1995

Educational sponsorship

7.9 Educational sponsorship may take a variety of forms.

5: Promotional operations in practice

(a) One example is Tesco's Computers for Schools scheme. Although technically this is a form of sales promotion (since Tesco customers receive a free computer voucher with every £10 spent) it enhances Tesco's image as an organisation that cares about the community.

(b) Many companies sponsor individuals through college in the hope of recruiting promising graduates when they leave college.

(c) Some organisations sponsor University chairs and departments not only to gain research and development facilities and the benefits of any successful research, but also to gain publicity, because scientific breakthroughs tend to be widely reported.

Developing a sponsorship programme

7.10 Smith (1993) suggests the following approach to developing and managing a sponsorship program.

(a) **Analyse the current situation,** looking especially at who else is a present or previous sponsor in the chosen field, and what else competitors are sponsoring.

(b) **Define sponsorship objectives**. There may be many of these, such as raising awareness; building an image; or getting round advertising bans (tobacco companies).

(c) **Clarify the strategy**: how does the sponsorship programme contribute to the overall corporate, marketing and communication objectives and how can it be integrated with other promotions?

(d) **Develop the tactical details** of the programme.

(e) **Define target audiences**. Sport in particular may reach a number of very different audiences.

(f) **Consider what resources are needed** to run the programme.

(g) Establish a **method of measuring the effectiveness** of the sponsorship.

8 DIRECT MARKETING

Definitions

8.1 (a) The Institute of Direct Marketing in the UK defines direct marketing as 'The planned recording, analysis and tracking of customer behaviour to develop relational marketing strategies'.

(b) The Direct Marketing Association in the US defines direct marketing as 'An interactive system of marketing which uses one or more advertising media to effect a measurable response and/or transaction at any location'.

8.2 It is worth studying these definitions and noting some key words and phases.

- **Response.** Direct marketing is about getting people to respond by post or telephone to invitations and offers.

- **Interactive.** The process is two-way involving the supplier and the customer.

- **Relationship.** Direct marketing is in many instances an on-going process of selling again and again to the same customer.

- **Recording and analysis.** Response data are collected and analysed so that the most cost-effective procedures may be arrived at.

Part B: The marketing mix

- **Strategy.** Direct marketing should be seen as a part of a comprehensive plan stemming from clearly formulated objectives.

> **Key Concept**
> **Direct marketing** creates and develops a direct relationship between the consumer and the company on an individual basis.

8.3 Because direct marketing **removes all channel intermediaries** apart from the advertising medium and the delivery medium, there are no resellers, therefore avoiding loss of control and loss of revenue.

Components of direct marketing

8.4 Direct marketing encompasses a wide range of media and distribution opportunities.

- Television
- Radio
- Direct mail
- Telemarketing
- Inserts
- Take-ones
- Mail order
- Computerised home shopping

The growth of direct marketing

8.5 Since the late 1980s there has been a major increase in the amount spent on direct marketing activities. A number of factors have contributed to this growth.

8.6 The **nuclear family** is no longer the dominant group within the population. Single parent families and co-habitants now form over 35% of the households in the UK. This trend will lead to the **emergence of new customer groups** with a diverse range of needs, which will require a more **individualistic marketing strategy**.

8.7 **Retailers** have acquired much information about consumers through the use of loyalty cards and bar-coded goods. This gives them the ability to launch and target new goods and services more effectively.

8.8 The continued growth in acceptance and use of **credit cards** has provided financial institutions, multiple retailers and mail order companies with a plethora of personal information which, when merged with other data sources, transforms the art of marketing into a scientific skill. The ability to target tightly-defined customer groups has never been greater.

> **Action Programme 5**
> In the light of these comments, how effective do you think your bank is at targeting you and your personal financial needs?

8.9 There has been a significant rise in the **real cost of television advertising**. The advent of satellite and cable television will fragment further the potential audience, and unless advertising rates adequately reflect the changing structure of the market, then advertisers will seek to pursue other more cost effective forms of advertising.

8.10 Consumers are becoming more **educated** in terms of what they are purchasing and, as a consequence, are much more likely to try out alternatives. The shift away from habitual **brand loyalty** coupled with a constant array of **new products** in the market place means that customers have to be more precisely segmented and targeted.

8.11 Over 90% of UK households now own a **telephone**, which has improved accessibility for the direct marketers. Direct Line, the insurance company, have turned the motor insurance industry on its head through their ability to by-pass the traditional brokers and offer the average consumer not only a cheaper form of insurance but a high degree of service direct.

8.12 Above all, the power of the **computer** has transformed the processes by which marketers relate to their customers. Improvements in database software and reductions in the cost of computer systems, now provide the opportunity for the smallest of operations to develop and benefit from the information era.

Marketing at Work

Customer loyalty

' ... more consumer goods companies are realising that the old, unsegmented markets of the 1960s and 1970s have disappeared. Pushing brands and numerous extensions out of the door does not work, particularly because of the increasingly vice-like grip of retailers.

Companies also recognise that loyalty is what counts. It has been estimated that recruiting a new customer can cost six times as much as retaining an existing one. Moreover, the cost of above-the-line advertising has soared, whereas database technology is becoming more powerful, cheaper and accessible to the average marketer.

A good example is Helena Rubenstein. According to Fran Longford, board director at Helena Rubenstein's agency, Triangle, its database initiative is part of a long-term marketing strategy: 'It wants to plan over the next two to three years and beyond, rather than on a year-to-year basis. Its key marketing objectives for 1995 are to convert new customers into regular customers, and regular customers into more loyal customers.'

The more you know about someone, the easier it is to keep them happy, she says: 'When I talk to clients about database marketing I usually start by asking what they would rather have - a one-night stand or a long-term relationship?"
Marketing Business, July/August 1995

Direct mail and direct response media

8.13 **Direct mail has been the third largest and fastest growing advertising medium during the past 10 years**. Between 1981 and 1991, the number of mailings received per head of household increased from 18 to 31. Direct mail tends to be the main medium of **direct response advertising**. The reasons for this is that other major media, newspapers and magazines, are familiar to people in advertising in other contexts. Newspaper ads can include coupons to fill out and return, and radio and TV can give a phone number to ring (DRTV is now very common). However, direct mail has a number of strengths as a direct response medium.

(a) **The advertiser can target down to individual level** and the communication can be personalised. Known data about the individual can be used, whilst modern printing techniques mean that parts of a letter can be altered to accommodate this.

(b) **Testing potential is sophisticated**: a limited number of items can be sent out to a 'test' cell and the results can be evaluated. As success is achieved, so the mailing campaign can be rolled out.

(c) What you do is **less visible to your competitors** than other forms of media.

Part B: The marketing mix

8.14 There are, however, a **number of weaknesses** with direct mail.

(a) It **does not offer sound or movement**, although it is possible for advertisers to send out audio or video tapes, and even working models or samples.

(b) There is obvious concern over the **negative associations of junk mail** and the need for individuals to exercise their right to privacy,

(c) **Lead times may be considerable** when taking into consideration the creative organisation, finished artwork, printing, proofing, inserting material into envelopes where necessary and, finally, the mailing.

(d) The most important barrier to direct mail is that **it can be very expensive on a *per capita* basis**. A delivered insert can be 24 to 32 times more expensive than a full page colour advert in a magazine. It therefore follows that the mailshot must be very powerful and, above all, well targeted to overcome such a cost penalty.

8.15 The cornerstone upon which the direct mailing is based is the **mailing list**. It is far and away the most important element in the list of variables, which also include the offer, timing and creative content.

Building the database

8.16 **A database is a collection of available information on past and current customers together with future prospects, structured to allow for the implementation of effective marketing strategies.** Database marketing is a customer oriented approach; it is only possible if modern computer database systems are used. It enables the company to do three things.

- To extend help to a company's target audience
- To stimulate further demand
- To stay close to them. Recording and keeping a record of customers and prospects and of all communications and commercial contacts helps to improve all future contacts.

8.17 The database may be used to meet a variety of objectives with numerous advantages over traditional marketing methods.

- Focusing on prime prospects
- Evaluating new prospects
- Cross-selling related products
- Launching new products to potential prospects
- Identifying new distribution channels

8.18 An effective database can provide important management information.

- **Usage patterns**, for example, reasons for account closures
- **Evaluation** of marketing activities, for example response rates
- **Segmentation** analysis to ensure accurate targeting
- **Account analysis**, for example value, duration, product type
- Updated **market research** information

Marketing at Work

Database applications

There are many examples of companies which are already employing or experimenting with (database applications). In the US, Levi Strauss, the jeans company, is taking measurements and preferences from female customers to produce exact-fitting garments. The customisation is currently limited to one line of jeans but ... the approach 'offers the company tremendous opportunities for building learning relationships'.

The Ritz-Carlton hotel chain has trained staff throughout the organisation to jot down customer details at every opportunity on a 'guest preference pad'.

The result, he says, could be the following: 'You stay at the Ritz-Carlton in Cancun, Mexico, call room service for dinner, and request an ice cube in your glass of white wine. Months later, when you stay at the Ritz-Carlton in Naples, Florida, and order a glass of white wine from room service, you will almost certainly be asked if you would like an ice cube in it.'

Financial Times

8.19 The database should not be seen as a tool simply to generate the one-off sale, requiring the marketing effort to be re-engaged time and time again. The reason for this is simple: it is four times more expensive to win a new customer than it is to retain an existing one.

Obtaining information

8.20 The type of information required for a database marketing to operate can easily be obtained from both internal and external sources. This will typically include customer, market and competitor information. A large amount of this data is often already collected for invoicing or control purposes, but is frequently not in a format suitable for use by the marketing department.

8.21 Information on the firm's existing customers will form the core of the database, with the sales invoice being perhaps the most valuable input. Whilst the invoice is created for financial purposes, it contains a considerable amount of customer data which can be made immediately available to marketers. A typical selection of data recorded on a sales invoice is shown below.

Information	*Marketing use*
Customer title	Sex, job description identification
Customer first name	Sex coding, discriminates households
Customer surname	Ethnic coding
Customer address	Geodemographic profiling and census data
Date of sale	Tracking of purchase rates, repurchase identification
Items ordered	Benefit/need analysis, product clusters
Quantities ordered	Heavy/light/medium use
Price	Life time value of customer

Marketing at Work

St James Norland Parish Church

The database award in the 1995 Direct Marketing Association/ Royal Mail awards went to The Friends of St James Norland Parish Church.

The church was threatened with closure and so a campaign was launched to raise awareness of its plight and the plans to make it self-supporting. Simultaneously, the objective was to raise half the £300,000 needed to implement the rescue plan.

The strategy was to find out as much as possible about the population of the parish and who used the church and send them simple, emotive and relevant letters, based on each group's greatest point of leverage.

A database was compiled from a range of sources and segmented by wealth (house value), location and by each individual's use of the church. A manual search identified celebrities.

Part B: The marketing mix

Key segments included extremely wealthy people who lived on the church square, patrons, previous donors, celebrities in the parish – including Elton John – couples married in the church, parents of children baptised in it, well-off people in the parish and church attendees.

'It was the most imaginative and effective use of data' said the judges. 'The database was segmented to such an extent that the data was almost driving the creative. The personalisation of the letters was superb.'

Marketing: The 1995 DMA/Royal Mail Direct Marketing Awards

Buying lists from elsewhere

8.22 The sources of data available to an organisation from its own database are finite and will ultimately diminish as customers cease to trade with the organisation. Therefore, it is necessary to go outside to other sources.

- **List owners and managers** may rent direct, through a broker or not at all. They may also swap lists.
- **List brokers** are independent of both compiler and user.
- **List compilers**, who manage and rent their lists directly.
- **Directories** (telephone and commercial)
- **Exhibition organisers**
- **Publishers**
- **Associations and clubs**
- **Professional organisations**.

Some of the best lists will be those which are noted as **mail responsive**. It is a proven fact that people who have responded by mail or telephone to anything in the past will be more likely to do so again.

8.23 In the process of evaluating lists, the following are some of the questions to which answers will be needed.

- What is the source?
- Who is the owner?
- Are there names as well as addresses?
- Is it mail responsive or compiled from other sources?
- How active are the names?
- How up-to-date are the addresses?
- Are they buyers or enquirers?
- How frequently do they buy?
- How much do they spend?
- How did they pay?

Possibly the major problem with any list, is the task of keeping it up to date. Industry sources quote a 35% rate of atrophy for occupational lists over a period of years. Therefore, a list bought in from outside may have to be checked to ensure that it is up-to-date and accurate.

Budgeting

8.24 One of the methods in determining the direct marketing budget is to ask how much can the business afford in recruiting an extra customer. One of the oldest methods available is to calculate the **allowable cost-per-order**. This is calculated by constructing a mini profit and

5: Promotional operations in practice

loss statement for an average sale, including the desired profit level, but **excluding the promotional costs**.

	£	£
Selling price		60
Less returns		5
Net order Value		55
Costs		
Cost of goods	18	
Fulfilment (see below)	6	
Bad debts	4	
		28
Contribution to break even		27
Desired profit		8
Allowable costs per order		19

By undertaking such a calculation, the amount which can be budgeted for the direct marketing effort is precisely determined.

8.25 The next step is to calculate the required response rate which is needed, by building in the costs of the promotion and the quantity to be mailed.

Using the data from the above example, suppose the promotional cost is £38,000. How many sales do we need to achieve if the allowable cost per order is £19?

$$\text{Number of orders} = \frac{£38,000}{£19} = 2,000 \text{ orders}$$

If we are to carry out a mailing of 60,000 potential customers, then the required response rate is as follows.

$$\text{Response rate} = \frac{2,000}{60,000} \times 100 = 3.33\%$$

8.26 In building up the costs of a direct marketing campaign, the following costs need to be considered.

- Press advertising
- Agency artwork
- List preparation
- Printing
- Mailing
- Response handling
- Fulfilment costs
- Bad debts/returns

Action Programme 6

The selling price of an item is £75 with returns estimated at £5. The cost of goods sold is £20 and bad debts £3. The desired level of profit is £15 per unit. The total promotional costs are budgeted at £45,000 and the total number of customers to be mailed is 150,000.

Calculate:

- The allowable cost-per-order
- The number of orders required
- The response per thousand

Part B: The marketing mix

Fulfilment

8.27 Perhaps the most important element, and the vital link in the direct marketing plan is the extent to which the promise to the customer is kept. Direct marketing by definition requires a response, and **fulfilment is the act of servicing the customer's response**. The act of fulfilment may take on a number of different activities including handling customer complaints, taking orders, offering advice and providing service and despatching goods. In all of these cases, it is safe to assume that the customer requires a prompt, courteous and effective response.

8.28 **Typical activities carried out within the fulfilment stage**

- Processing requests
- Picking, packaging and despatch
- Credit card validation and processing
- Analysing and reporting response data

8.29 Whether carried out within the company or handled by an external agency, **the area of fulfilment is a potential disaster area**, where even the most professional of organisations can come unstuck.

(a) **Inaccurate forecasting** by the organisation in the take-up of a particular offer may lead to items being out-of-stock, resulting in unhappy customers.

(b) Fulfilment operations can lead to extensive demands upon the organisation in terms of **human resources**, and **work space**. Organisations need to consider the trade-off between the costs of setting up the fulfilment service and the volume of business that will be generated by direct marketing activity. A decision has to be made whether to set up in-house or utilise an outside fulfilment house.

(c) **Delays** in stock delivery and pilferage of stock can lead to frustrated customers.

(d) **Human error** when inputting data can result in the wrong items being despatched to the wrong address. Errors of this type require careful handling when the complaints arise.

Telemarketing

> **Key Concept**
> **Telemarketing** is the planned and controlled use of the telephone for sales and marketing opportunities.

8.30 Unlike all other forms of direct marketing, telemarketing allows for **immediate two-way communication**.

8.31 Telemarketing is a quick, accurate and flexible tool for gathering, maintaining and helping to exploit relevant up-to-date information about customers and prospects. It can be utilised at all stages, from the point of building highly targeted mailing lists through to screening respondents to determine the best type to follow up, and thenceforward to supporting the salesforce in maximising customers' value throughout their lifetime.

8.32 **Characteristics of telemarketing**

- **Targeted**. The message is appropriately tailored to the recipient

5: Promotional operations in practice

- **Personal**. Telemarketers can determine and respond immediately to the specific needs of individuals, building long-term personal and profitable relationships

- **Interactive**. Since the dialogue is live, the conversation can be guided to achieve the desired results; the representative is in control

- **Immediate**. Every outbound call achieves an immediate result, even if it is a wrong number or 'not interested'. Customers and prospects can be given 24 hour constant access to the company

- **High quality**. Minimum amounts of information can be gathered accurately, kept up-to-date and used to select and prioritise leads for follow up calls

- **Flexible**. Conversations can be tailored spontaneously as the representative responds to the contact's needs. There are no geographical constraints on calls and they can be timed to suit the contact

- **Accountable**. Results and effectiveness can be checked continuously

- **Experimental**. Campaign variables can be tested quickly, and changes made whilst the campaign is in progress

Problems with telemarketing

8.33 Telemarketing can be costly. There are few economies of scale, and techniques such as direct mail and media advertising can work out to be cheaper. Labour overheads are potentially high, although this can be counterbalanced by operating the business from a central point.

8.34 A telemarketer can only contact around 30 to 40 customers in a day, whereas media advertising can reach a mass audience in a single strike. However, media advertising married with a telephone contact number can be a very powerful combination.

8.35 If poorly handled, telemarketing may be interpreted as intrusive. This may alienate the customer and lead to lost sales opportunities.

Telemarketing as an integrated marketing activity

8.36 Telemarketing has several important ancillary functions.

- **Building, maintaining, cleaning and updating databases**.

- **Market evaluation and test marketing**. Almost any feature of a market can be measured and tested by telephone. Feedback is immediate so response can be targeted quickly to exploit market knowledge.

- **Dealer support**. Leads can be passed on to the nearest dealer.

- **Traffic generation**. The telephone, combined with postal invitations, is the most cost effective way of screening leads and encouraging attendance at promotional events.

- **Direct sales and account servicing**. The telephone can be used at all stages of the relationship with the prospects and customers. This includes lead generation, establishing buying potential and defining the decision-making process.

- **Customer care and loyalty building**. Every telephone contact opportunity can demonstrate to customers that they are valued.

- **Crisis management**. If, for example, there is a consumer scare, immediate action is essential to minimise commercial damage. A dedicated hotline number can be advertised to provide information and advice.

Part B: The marketing mix

Marketing at Work

Golden Wonder

Golden Wonder won first place in the Business to Business Telemarketing category of the 1995 Direct marketing Association/Royal Mail awards.

In June 1995 Golden Wonder ran an integrated promotion 'How Long is your Wotsit', which included telemarketing to the trade in two TV regions.

It had two aims – to test the effectiveness of telemarketing support and to persuade retailers to take a Long Wotsits promotional display bin.

'Results were excellent,' the judges noted. 'we also liked the way that, as the promotion progressed, the telephone was used to research how well it was working.'

It is hard to quarrel with that verdict. An eight-fold increase was recorded in Long Wotsits being stocked in the areas where telemarketing was used – substantially more than in the non-telemarketing regions.

More than 2,300 displays were ordered through telemarketing, compared with only 94 through direct mail or trade press advertising.

And 74% of retailers contacted by telephone completed questionnaires on the effectiveness of Golden Wonder marketing, which both provided useful feedback and help to build customer loyalty.

9 THE INTERNET

Web strategies

9.1 The Internet is widely seen as likely to revolutionise many aspects of business. It certainly has huge potential wherever data and communication are important and is currently used for business in several different ways.

9.2 It can enhance **customer service** and thus promote stronger marketing relationships. Two good example of this are software fixes that can be downloaded from IT manufacturers' web sites and the publication of flight schedules.

9.3 Manufacturers' web sites can be used to provide information on new uses for old products; this very simple type of **market development** can mean increased sales. They are also very useful as an ancillary to advertisements in other media: 'See our web site for full catalogue'.

9.4 Web sites can be used for **direct sales**. Sometimes this amounts to little more than a modern version of catalogue selling, but the 'Add to shopping cart' approach can help the customer by making it unnecessary to complete and add up an order form. There are a number of useful techniques.

- Give something away, charge for something else. For example, give the abstract, sell the book; give a fuzzy picture, sell a clear one.

- Precede the free download with a commercial for something else.

- Use 'today only' offers; a web site can be changed extremely quickly. Only local radio and daily papers are as good for short availability offers.

9.5 As always, where material goods are involved, **fulfilment** is crucial to the success of the venture. No problem exists where the goods can themselves be delivered over the Internet, as is the case with software, music and images.

9.6 Media companies can use their web sites to provide a new dimension of information and entertainment, which leads to increased product involvement and hence enhanced perceived value. Examples are newspaper web editions and home pages for movies.

9.7 **Information** can be obtained from site visits since the Internet is interactive and visitors can be asked questions. One popular approach is to run competitions; filling in the entry form can glean significant information. Such information is invaluable for database marketing purposes.

Marketing at Work

P&G and Excite

Proctor and Gamble is teaming up with Excite UK to develop a youth-oriented Website to promote P&G goods to UK teenagers.

The site, as yet unnamed, will provide community, chat and other interactive services alongside content secured through third-party deals. It will have a budget of several million pounds.

James Eadie, P&G brand manager for interactive marketing Europe, says: 'This site is a great opportunity for P&G to increase the relevance of our brands to the teenage audience.'

Among P&G's youth-focused brands are Clearasil, Sunny Delight and Pringles. The company also owns a large number of personal care products – such as Max Factor, Secret, Pantene, Tampax and Always – which could be targeted at a young female online audience.

The company ranks as a major online advertiser and Website content sponsor in the US, and has already established an extensive portfolio of consumer Websites which could be exploited in overseas markets.

P&G, which has followed a strategy of 'taking ownership' of health and personal care issues on the Net, has developed online information sites such as the Pampers Parent Institute (www.pampers.com) in the US, and registered generic domain names such as www.badbreath.com, which lead surfers through to P&G online content.

The UK teenage site is expected to launch later this year.

Excite Europe managing director Evan Rudowski says: 'P&G's decision to partner us confirms Excite's position as Europe's most sophisticated portal player.'

Marketing Week, 27 January 2000

Rules for Internet success

9.8 Surfers are quick on the move; if a site is to succeed it **must seize the attention immediately**.

- It is important to use a fast computer and connection.
- Attention grabbers should appear early in the text, based on the chosen web strategy. For instance, a media company might offer free browsing of back issues.
- Anything new about the site should be emphasised early.
- There should be early interactivity in the text.

9.9 **Long download times** may produce beautiful graphics and video, but few people will wait for them.

9.10 Selling must offer **price savings** over normal shopping; surfers know that Internet selling costs are much reduced.

9.11 It is important to **cross-promote** a site. The Internet is unlike traditional direct mail methods in that it does not intrude into the potential customer's life: the customer must come looking for the website. It is therefore essential to register with major web indexes such as Yahoo! Using the right key words will help customers find a site.

Part B: The marketing mix

Page design

9.12 Unfortunately, the web site designer does not have total control over page layout or use of colour because of the nature of the system. Presentation and colour palette depend on browser in use. Many colour palettes used. The surfer can control font size and sometimes font itself.

Action Programme 7

Assuming you have Internet access, when you are surfing, look critically at commercial web sites and assess them against the ideas outlined above.

Exam Tip

It is unlikely that a complete mini-case study would be set on promotion, but it could very easily form part of a mini case. If you are asked for a promotional plan, think about what you see every day in the real world.

Chapter Roundup

- Advertising is paid-for mass communication. Campaigns must be properly briefed to the agency, including creative briefing. Advertising effectiveness can be tested by creative development research, pre-testing and tracking studies.

- The selection of media for a campaign depends on matching the target market and budget to the characteristics of the media themselves. Burst and drip campaigns are the two common ways of scheduling the campaign.

- Personal selling encompasses a wide variety of tasks including prospecting, information gathering and communicating as well as actually selling. The classic selling process is built around the identification and satisfaction of the prospect's needs. Sales support maximises the time the sales person spends selling, targets the best customers and enhances customer satisfaction.

- Sales promotion techniques add value to a product in order to achieve a specific marketing objective. Consumer promotion techniques include reduced price; coupons; gift with purchase; and competitions and prizes. Trade promotion techniques include baker's dozen, tailor made promotion and mystery shoppers.

- Public relations aims to enhance goodwill towards an organisation from its publics. Models of PR range from dissemination of propaganda to a two-way dialogue of mutual understanding. Organisations will have to deal with more than one public; they may be active or apathetic. PR techniques may be selected from a wide 'media menu' according to their suitability, feasibility and acceptability.

- Sponsorship entails providing money for an event or activity in return for publicity and prestige. Programme sponsorship can be more cost-effective than TV advertising and can block the competition. Sports sponsorship can provide wide coverage and promotes a very clear image. Arts and educational sponsorship may be seen as worthy activities.

- Direct marketing involves both direct selling and the use of IT to develop customer databases. A wide variety of media are used to communicate with the target market; a well developed database allows individually targeted mail shots and telephone selling. Lists may be developed in-house or purchased. Fulfilment is the keeping of the promise to the customer and is a vital part of the direct marketing process.

- The Internet is already in use for commercial purposes. It is most productively used for giving and receiving information. Web-surfers need to know a site is there, so indexes and key words are important. Sites must be carefully designed if they are to be useful.

Quick Quiz

1. Give five examples of advertisement styles. (see para 2.6)
2. What are the main advertising media used in the UK? (3.2)
3. Which media allow highly topical advertising? (3.12)
4. State six tasks for the sales person. (4.3)
5. What are the six phases of the selling process? (4.6)
6. How can the sales person reduce the amount of risk the prospect perceives? (4.13)
7. How may coupons be distributed? (5.6)
8. How can the effectiveness of sales promotion be measured? (5.14-5.16)
9. State five types of PR activity. (6.2)
10. How do Grunig and Hunt analyse PR practice? (6.8)
11. What is a public? (6.11, key concept)
12. What benefits does programme sponsorship offer? (7.3)
13. What is the main medium of direct response advertising? (8.13)
14. Give five types of information which could be obtained from an effective database. (8.18)
15. Give eight characteristics of telemarketing. (8.32)
16. What are the rules for successful selling on the Internet? (9.8-9.11)

Action Programme Review

1. On the launch of its 'Clubcard' Tesco said that it was a way of saying thank you to customers and that it wanted to 'recreate the kind of relationship that existed between consumers and local shops half a century ago'.

    In practice, however, the schemes give supermarkets the chance to build up a massive database containing customers' names, addresses and intimate details of individual shopping habits.

3. In very general terms, the first two are likely to be single issue publics (concerned with profits and conditions of work respectively). Suppliers may well be apathetic. The situation is far more complicated than this in reality, however. The question can only be answered in very broad terms. Why, for example, might shareholders become concerned about conditions of work for employees?

4. British Gas argued that there was not enough lead time to change the bills before it shed its old corporate identity in March 1996.

    'It's not in the customer's interest for us to trash all the bills and bring something else in,' it said last night.

    'We are not trying to mislead the customer. Everything is going to change totally on March 1, and there can be few people who do not know that we withdrew from the Charter Mark scheme last November.'

    Are you convinced? Could British Gas at least have included some explanation of its approach with its bills? What separate PR problems might this approach have caused? This is worthy of class discussion, though you may well end up going round in circles: there is not an easy answer that we can see.

5. One way of measuring is to see how much of what your bank sends you ends up in the bin! Arguably, the UK High Street banks are better at *collecting* information than at *using* it intelligently, though this is gradually changing.

6. (a) £32
    (b) 1407 (round up)
    (c) 10 in every thousand need to respond. The precise answer is 9.375, but what is 0.375 of a response?

Now try illustrative question 7 at the end of the Study Text

6 Product, Price and Place Operations

Chapter Topic List	Syllabus reference
1 Setting the scene	-
2 The product life cycle and portfolio analysis	2.3
3 New product development	2.3
4 Brands and packaging	2.3
5 Price	2.2
6 Pricing policy	2.2
7 Cost accounting and breakeven analysis	2.2
8 Place	2.4
9 Logistics management and Just-in-Time	2.4

Learning Outcomes

- Students will be able to understand the need to integrate marketing mix tools to achieve effective implementation of plans.
- Students will be able to select an appropriate integrated mix for a particular marketing context.

Key Concepts Introduced

- The product life cycle
- Brand
- Equilibrium price
- Price elasticity of demand
- Direct costs and overheads
- Contribution

Examples of Marketing at Work

- Ipana toothpaste
- Product choice
- Innovators and survivors
- Packaging innovations
- Low-cost air carriers
- Luxury hi-fi
- Supermarkets
- Real-life pricing
- Downstream drift
- Safeway's logistics
- Thornton's chocolates
- Avon cosmetics
- OTC medicines
- The paper industry

1 SETTING THE SCENE

1.1 This chapter draws together the remaining elements of the marketing mix: product, price and place. The product life cycle is an important concept and can offer guidance on marketing activity. Portfolio analysis addresses how an organisation's products interrelate and affect one another. Both of these concepts are discussed in Section 2.

1.2 Section 3 deals with a related topic, new product development, which is essential for any market oriented company. The final elements of product input are dealt with in section 4: brands and packaging.

1.3 Setting price is commonly seen as a particularly important and difficult process and is often controlled at the highest level. Section 5 covers both the economic theory of pricing and the methods used in practice. Price elasticity of demand is a theoretical concept of great importance for market segmentation. Pricing policy and strategies are dealt with in Section 6.

1.4 Section 7 introduces some cost accounting background and considers breakeven analysis and the associated computations.

1.5 Place, or distribution, is the final element of the mix to be considered. Section 8 looks at the nature of various distribution structures and discusses some of the influences which affect choice of channel. Finally, section 9 looks at the important practical area of logistics management and just-in-time systems.

> **Exam Tip**
> The topics covered in this chapter used to be in the Marketing Fundamentals syllabus at Certificate level. If you took that paper, be aware that you will need more knowledge and deeper insight at Advanced Certificate level.

2 THE PRODUCT LIFE CYCLE AND PORTFOLIO ANALYSIS

The product

2.1 A product may be said to satisfy needs by possessing the following attributes.

(a) **Tangible attributes**
- Availability and delivery
- Performance
- Price
- Design

(b) **Intangible attributes**
- Image
- Perceived value

2.2 These features are interlinked. A product has a tangible **price**, for example, but for your money you obtain the **value** that you perceive the product to have. You may get satisfaction from paying a very high price for your wine glasses, because this says something about your status in life: the glasses become part of your self-image.

Part B: The marketing mix

Product classification

2.3 The term consumer goods is used to distinguish goods that are sold directly to the person who will ultimately use them from goods that are sold to people that want them to make other products. The latter are known as industrial goods.

2.4 **Classification of consumer goods**

(a) **Convenience goods**. The weekly groceries are a typical example. There is a further distinction between **staple goods** like bread and potatoes, and **impulse buys**, like the unexpected bar of chocolate that you find at the supermarket checkout. Brand awareness is extremely important in this sector.

(b) **Shopping goods**. These are more durable items, like furniture or washing machines. This sort of purchase is usually only made after a good deal of **advance planning and shopping around**

(c) **Speciality goods**. These are items like jewellery or the more expensive items of clothing.

(d) **Unsought goods**. These are goods that you did not realise you needed! Typical examples would be the sort of items that are found in catalogues that arrive in the post.

Action Programme 1

Think of three products that you have bought recently, one low-priced, one medium priced, and one expensive item. Identify the product attributes that made you buy each of these items and categorise them according to the classifications shown above.

2.5 **Classification of industrial goods**

- **Installations**, for example, major items of plant and machinery like a factory assembly line

- **Accessories**, such as PCs

- **Raw materials:** plastic, metal, wood, foodstuffs chemicals and so on

- **Components**, for example, the Lucas headlights in Ford cars or the Intel microchip in most PCs

- **Supplies:** office stationery, cleaning materials and the like

2.6 There are very few **pure products** or **pure services**. Most products have some service attributes and many services are in some way attached to products. However, we shall consider some of the features that characterise service marketing later on in this chapter.

The product life cycle

Key Concept
The product life cycle concept asserts that products are born (or introduced), grow to reach maturity and then enter old age and decline.

6: Product, price and place operations

2.7 Despite criticisms, the product life cycle (PLC) has proved to be a useful control device for monitoring the progress of new products after introduction. As Professor Robin Wensley of Warwick University puts it:

> 'The value of the product life cycle depends on its use, ie *it has greater value as one goes down the scale* from a predictive or forecasting tool, through a planning tool to a control tool.'

2.8 The profitability and sales position of a product can be expected to change over time. The product life cycle is an attempt to recognise distinct stages in a product's sales history. Here is the classic representation of the PLC.

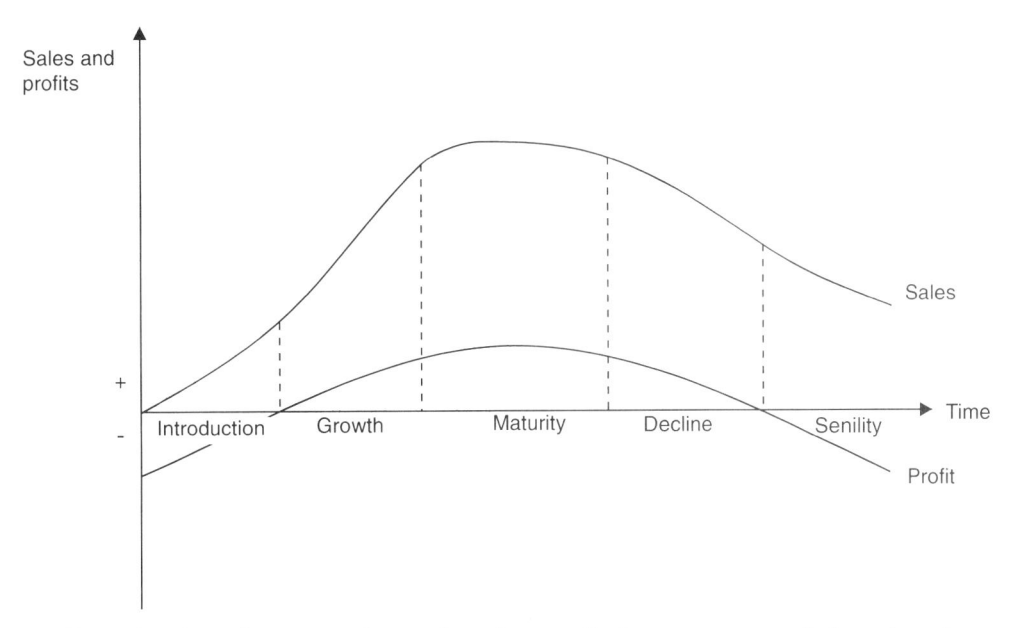

(a) **Introduction**. A new product takes time to find acceptance and there is a slow growth in sales. Unit costs are high because of low output; there may be early teething troubles with production technology and prices may be high to cover production and sales promotion costs. Pocket calculators, video cassette recorders and mobile telephones were all very expensive when launched. The product, for the time being, is a **loss maker**.

(b) **Growth**. Sales will eventually rise more sharply and the product starts to make profits. As production rises, unit costs fall. Since demand is strong, prices tend to remain fairly static for a time. However, the prospect of cheap mass production and a strong market will attract competitors so that the number of producers is increasing. With the increase of competition, manufacturers must spend a lot of money on product improvement, sales promotion and distribution to obtain a dominant or strong position in the market.

(c) **Maturity**. The rate of sales growth slows down and the product reaches a period of maturity which is probably the longest period of a successful product's life. Most products on the market will be at the mature stage of their life. Eventually sales will begin to decline so that there is **overcapacity of production in the industry**. Severe competition occurs, profits fall and some producers leave the market. The remaining producers seek means of prolonging the product life by modifying it and searching for new market segments.

(d) **Decline**. Many producers are reluctant to leave the market, although some inevitably do because of falling profits. If a product remains on the market too long, it will become unprofitable and the decline stage in its life cycle then gives way to a 'senility' stage.

Part B: The marketing mix

> **Action Programme 2**
>
> Can you think of any products that have disappeared in your lifetime or are currently in decline?

Buying participants through PLC stages

2.9 The introductory stage represents the highest risk in terms of purchasing a new and, as yet, untested product. Buyers reflect this: they typically consist of the relatively wealthy, to whom the risk of a loss is relatively small, and the young, who are more likely to make risky purchases.

2.10 In the growth and mature stages the mass market needs to be attracted. By the time decline sets in the product is well tested with all its faults ironed out. At this stage enter the most risk-averse buyers, termed **laggards**. These are the mirror image of those who participated in the introductory stage, being the poorer and older sections of the community.

Comparing products at different PLC stages

2.11 The above display of products, at various stages through the PLC, represents the USA in the late 1960s and early 1970s. Studies were conducted to establish whether or not there were significant differences in the purchasers of refrigerators in the mature stage and compacters (waste disposal units) in the introductory stage.

2.12 The high income group with a family income of $10,000 or more made up some 90% of those purchasing compactors. There was also a noticeable lack of 65+ year olds. In contrast, the mature refrigerator market appeared to reflect the complete population range.

How are life cycles assessed?

2.13 It is plausible to suggest that products have a life cycle, but it is not so easy to sort out how far through its life a product is, and what its expected future life might be. To identify these stages, the following should be carried out.

6: Product, price and place operations

- There ought to be a **regular review** of existing products.
- The future of each product should be estimated in terms of both **sales revenue and profits**.
- **Estimates of future life and profitability should be discussed with any experts available** to give advice, for example, R & D staff about product life, management accountants about costs, and marketing staff about prices and demand.

2.14 Once the assessments have been made, decisions must be taken about what to do with each product. There are three possibilities.

- **To continue selling** the product, with no foreseeable intention of stopping production
- To initiate action **to prolong a product's life**, perhaps by advertising more, by trying to cut costs or raise prices, by improving distribution, or packaging or sales promotion methods, or by putting in more direct selling effort
- To plan **to stop producing the product** and either to replace it with new ones in the same line or to diversify into new product-market areas

2.15 Costs might be cut by improving productivity of the workforce, or by redesigning the product slightly, perhaps as a result of a value analysis study.

Strategic and marketing mix decisions are considered in Part C of this Study Text.

Action Programme 3

Where do you consider the following products or services to be in their product life cycle?

- Mobile telephones
- Baked beans
- Satellite television
- Cigarettes
- Carbon paper
- Mortgages
- Writing implements
- Car alarms
- Organically grown fruit and vegetables

Criticisms of the product life cycle

2.16 Although it is widely used, the PLC remains controversial. There have been contradictory papers directed at establishing or refuting the validity of the product life cycle by empirical tests. *Polli and Cook* concluded that the PLC is most likely to be relevant for products where consumer demand is high. From these results, Polli and Cook concluded that 'for given categories of goods the product life cycle can be a useful model for marketing planning'.

2.17 *Dhalla and Yuspeh* attempt to expose what they term the myth of the PLC. They point out that:

'in the absence of the technological breakthroughs *many product classes appear to be almost impervious to normal life cycle pressures, provided they satisfy some basic need*, be it transportation, entertainment, health, nourishment or the desire to be attractive.'

Whilst accepting the possibility of the existence of a **product** life cycle, the paper denies the existence of **brand** life cycles. The authors assert that any underlying PLC is a *dependent*

Part B: The marketing mix

variable which is **determined by marketing actions**; rather than an *independent* variable to which **companies should adapt**. In other words, **if a brand appears to be in decline, this is not happening as a result of market changes, but because of either reduced or inappropriate marketing by the producer, or better marketing by competitors.**

Marketing at Work

Ipana toothpaste

Dhalla and Yuspeh consider that this notion of the PLC as a binding constraint has led to many marketing errors. They cite the example of Ipana, an American toothpaste, that was marketed by a leading packaged goods company until 1968 when it was abandoned after entering 'decline'. Two Minnesota businessmen who acquired the brand name, with hardly any promotion, generated 250,000 dollars sales in the first seven months of operations. Intelligent marketing, they point out, has kept such brands as Budweiser Beer, Colgate toothpaste and Maxwell House around long after competitive brands have disappeared.

2.18 The Marketing Science Institute examined over 100 product categories and concluded

'.... Our results suggest strongly that the life cycle concept, when used without careful formulation and testing as an explicit model, is more likely to be misleading than useful.'

2.19 Dhalla and Yuspeh come to the general conclusion that managers adhering to the sequences of marketing strategies recommended for succeeding stages of the cycle are likely to do more harm than good. In particular, they cite the potential neglect of existing brands and wasteful expenditures on replacement 'me-too' products.

2.20 **Criticisms of the practical value of the PLC.**

(a) Stages cannot easily be defined.

(b) Some products have no maturity phase, and go straight from growth to decline. Others have a second growth period after an initial decline. Some have virtually no introductory period and go straight into a rapid growth phase.

(c) **Strategic decisions can change a product's life cycle**: for example, by repositioning a product in the market, its life can be extended. If strategic planners decide what a product's life is going to be, opportunities to extend the life cycle might be ignored.

(d) Competition varies in different industries, and the strategic implications of the product life cycle will vary according to the nature of the competition. The traditional life cycle presupposes increasing competition and falling prices during the growth phase of the market and also the gradual elimination of competitors in the decline phase. This pattern of events is not always found in financial markets, where there is a tendency for competitors to follow-my-leader very quickly. Competition may build up well ahead of demand. The rapid development of various banking services is an example of this: for example, with bank cash dispenser cards, when one bank developed the product all the other major banks followed immediately.

Action Programme 4

There must be many products that have been around for as long as you can remember. Companies like Cadbury's have argued that they spend so much on brand maintenance that they should be able to show a value for their brands as an asset in their accounts (though accountants find this hard to swallow).

Think of some examples of products that go on and on from your own experience and try to identify what it is about them that makes them so enduring.

6: Product, price and place operations

The strategic implications of the product life cycle

2.21 Having made these reservations about product life cycle planning, the strategic implications of the product life cycle might be as follows.

	Phase			
	Introduction	*Growth*	*Maturity*	*Decline*
Product	Initially, poor quality Product design and development are a key to success No standard product and frequent design changes (eg microcomputers in the early 1980s)	Competitor's products have marked quality differences and technical differences Quality improves Product reliability may be important	Products become more standardised and differences between competing products less distinct	Products even less differentiated. Quality becomes more variable
Customers	Initial customers willing to pay high prices Customers need to be convinced about buying	Customers increase in number	Mass market Market saturation Repeat-buying Markets become segmented	Customers are sophisticated buyers of a product they understand well
Marketing issues	High advertising and sales promotion costs High prices possible Distribution problematic	High advertising costs still, but as a % of sales, costs are falling Prices falling More distributors	Segment specific Choose best distribution Brand image	Less money spent on advertising and sales promotion
Competition	Few or no competitors	More competitors enter the market Barriers to entry can be important	Competition at its keenest: on prices, branding, servicing customers, packaging etc	Competitors gradually exit from the market Exit barriers can be important
Profit margins	High prices but losses due to high fixed costs	High prices. High contribution margins, and increasing profit margins High P/E ratios for quoted companies in the growth market	Falling prices but good profit margins due to high sales volume High prices in some market segments	Still low prices but falling profits as sales volume falls, since total contribution falls towards the level of fixed costs Some increases in prices may occur in the late decline stage

Part B: The marketing mix

	Phase			
	Introduction	Growth	Maturity	Decline
Manufacturing and distribution	Overcapacity High production costs Few distribution channels High labour skill content in manufacture	Undercapacity Move towards mass production and less reliance on skilled labour Distribution channels flourish and getting adequate distribution is a key to marketing success	Optimum capacity Low labour skills Distribution channels fully developed, but less successful channels might be cut	Overcapacity because mass production techniques still used Distribution channels dwindling

Product portfolio planning

2.22 A company's product mix (or product assortment or portfolio) is all the product lines and items that the company offers for sale.

Product mix	Characteristics of company's product line
Width	Number of product lines
Depth	Average number of items per product line
Consistency	Closeness of items in product range in terms of marketing or production characteristics.

2.23 The product mix can be extended in a number of ways.

- Introducing **variations** in models or style
- Changing the **quality** of products offered at different price levels
- Developing **associated items**, such as a paint manufacturer introducing paint brushes
- Developing **new products** that have little technical or marketing relationships to the existing range

2.24 **Managing the product portfolio** involves broad issues such as what role should a product play in the portfolio, how should resources be allocated between products and what should be expected from each product. Maintaining balance between well-established and new products, between cash-generative and cash-using products and between growing and declining products is very important. If products are not suitable for the market or not profitable, then corporate objectives will be jeopardised. Equally, if potentially profitable products are ignored or not given sufficient support then crucial marketing opportunities will be lost.

2.25 It follows that **there are benefits to be gained from using a systematic approach to the management of the product range**. Marketing is not an exact science and there is no definitive approach or technique which can determine which products should remain, which should be pruned and how resources should be shared across the current product range. There are, however, techniques which can aid decision making.

Product-market matrices

2.26 The product-market matrix is used to classify a product or even a business **according to the features of the market and the features of the product**. It is often used at the level of corporate strategy to determine the relative positions of businesses and select strategies for resource allocation between them. The same techniques are **equally valuable when considering products and the management of the product portfolio**. The two most widely used approaches are the **Boston Consulting Group (BCG) growth-share matrix and the General Electric (GE) Business Screen**.

The BCG matrix

2.27 The BCG matrix was introduced in Chapter 2. Here we discuss it in more detail. The matrix, illustrated below, classifies products (or businesses) on the basis of their market share relative to that of their competitors and according to the rate of growth in the market as a whole. The split on the horizontal axis is based on a market share identical to that of the firm's **nearest competitor**, while the precise location of the split on the vertical axis will depend on the rate of growth in the market. Products are positioned in the matrix as circles with a diameter proportional to their sales revenue. The underlying assumption in the growth-share matrix is that a larger market share will enable the business to benefit from economies of scale, lower per unit costs and thus higher margins.

	High Market share	Low Market share
High Market growth rate	Star	Problem child
Low Market growth rate	Cash cow	Dog

2.28 On the basis of this classification, each product or 'strategic business unit' will then fall into one of four broad categories.

(a) **Problem child**: a small market share but in a high growth industry. The generic product is clearly popular, but customer support for the company brand is limited. A small market share implies that competitors are in a strong position and that if the product is to be successful it will **require substantial funds**, and a new marketing mix. If the market looks good and the product is viable, then the company should consider a **build** strategy to increase market share. This would require the commitment of funds to permit more active marketing. If the future looks less promising then the company should consider the possibility of withdrawing the product. The problem child is sometimes referred to as the **question mark**.

(b) **Star**: this is a product with a high market share in a high growth industry. By implication, **the star has potential for generating significant earnings** currently and in the future. However, at this stage it may still require substantial marketing

Part B: The marketing mix

expenditures to maintain this position, but would probably be regarded as **a good investment for the future**.

(c) **Cash cow:** a high market share but in a mature slow growth market. Typically, a well established product with a high degree of consumer loyalty. Product development costs are typically low and the marketing campaign is well established. **The cash cow will normally make a substantial contribution to overall profitability**. The appropriate strategy will vary according to the precise position of the cash cow. If market growth is reasonably strong then a **holding** strategy will be appropriate, but if growth and/or share are weakening, then a **harvesting** strategy may be more sensible: cut back on marketing expenditure and maximise short-term cash flow.

(d) **Dog:** a product characterised by low market share and low growth. Again, typically a well established product, but one which is apparently losing consumer support and may have cost disadvantages. The usual strategy would be to consider **divestment** unless cash flow position is strong, in which case the product would be **harvested** in the short term prior to deletion from the product range.

2.29 **Implicit in the matrix is the notion that markets are dynamic**. The typical new product is likely to appear in the problem child category to begin with; if it looks promising and with effective marketing it might be expected to become a star, then, as markets mature, a cash cow and finally a dog. The suggestion that most products will move through these stages does not weaken the role played by marketing. On the contrary, it strengthens it, since poor marketing may mean that a product moves from being a problem child to a dog without making any substantial contribution to profitability. Equally, of course, good marketing may enable the firm to prolong the star and cash cow phases, thus maximising cash flow from the product.

2.30 The framework provided by the matrix can offer guidance in terms of developing **appropriate strategies** for products and in maintaining a **balanced product portfolio**, ensuring that there are enough cash-generating products to match the cash-using products.

2.31 However, there are a number of **criticisms**.

(a) The BCG matrix **oversimplifies product analysis**. It concentrates only on two dimensions of product markets, size and market share, and therefore may encourage marketing management to pay too little attention to other market features.

(b) It is not always clear what is meant by the terms 'relative market share' and 'rate of market growth'. **Not all companies or products will be designed for market leadership**, in which case describing performance in terms of relative market share may be of limited relevance. Many firms undertaking this approach have found that all their products were technically dogs and yet were still very profitable, so they saw no need to divest. Firms following a 'niche' strategy will commonly find their markets are (intentionally) small.

(c) The matrix **assumes a relationship between profitability and market share**. There is empirical evidence for this in many but not all industries, particularly where there is demand for more customised products.

(d) The basic approach **may oversimplify the nature of products** in large diversified firms with many divisions. In these cases, each division may contain products which fit into several of the categories.

Despite these criticisms, the BCG matrix can offer guidance in achieving a balanced portfolio. However, given the difficulty of generalising such an approach to deal with all product and market situations, its recommendations should be interpreted with care.

The General Electric Business Screen

2.32 The basic approach of the GE Business Screen is similar to that of the BCG matrix but it tries to avoid the criticism levelled against that technique of using a highly restrictive classification system by including a broader range of company and market factors in assessing the position of a particular product or product group. A typical example of the GE matrix is provided below. This matrix classifies products (or businesses) according to industry attractiveness and company strengths. Typical examples of the factors which determine industry attractiveness and company strength are the following.

(a) **Industry attractiveness:** market size, market growth, competitive climate, stability of demand, ease of market entry, industry capacity, levels of investment, nature of regulation, profitability.

(b) **Company strengths:** relative market share, company image, production capacity, production costs, financial strengths, product quality, distribution systems, control over prices/margins, benefits of patent protection.

2.33 Although a broader range of factors are used in the classification of products, this is a highly subjective assessment. Products are positioned on the grid with circles representing market size and segments representing market shares. The strategy for an individual product is then suggested on the basis of that position. It is interesting to note the apparent similarity in recommendations between the BCG matrix and the GE matrix; the basic difference arises from the method of classification.

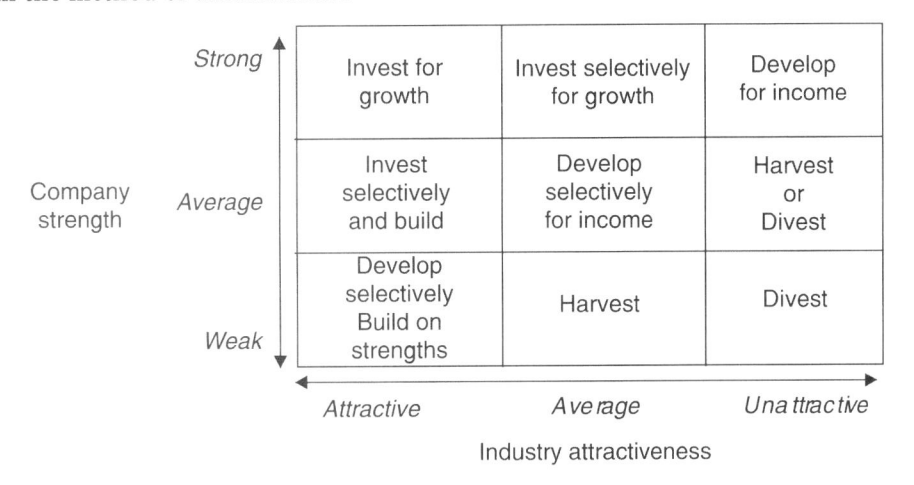

Company strength	Attractive	Average	Unattractive
Strong	Invest for growth	Invest selectively for growth	Develop for income
Average	Invest selectively and build	Develop selectively for income	Harvest or Divest
Weak	Develop selectively Build on strengths	Harvest	Divest

Industry attractiveness

2.34 The broader approach of the GE matrix emphasises the attempt to match distinctive competences within the company to conditions within the market place. Difficulties associated with measurement and classification mean that again the results of such an exercise must be interpreted with great care and not seen as a prescription for strategic decisions.

'New' and 'old' products

2.35 The energy and effort placed into adding new products and brands to the portfolio is seldom mirrored by a similar effort in identifying and weeding out the weak or declining. One of the benefits of effective marketing strategy is to ensure the organisation's resources are directed to the most suitable market segments; this can easily be thrown away by a **proliferation of products**.

Part B: The marketing mix

Marketing at Work

Product choice

At one time, Procter & Gamble was selling 35 variations of Crest toothpaste and different nappies for girls and boys. The average supermarket in America devotes 20 ft of shelving to medicine for coughs and colds. Most of this choice is trumpery. New York-based Market Intelligence Service found that only 7% of the 25,500 new packaged products launched in America in 1996 really offered new or added benefits.

In fact, more choice does not translate into more sales. Ravi Dhar, of Yale University, examined how students decided what to buy, based on the number of versions of each product-category on offer. As the choice increased, so did the likelihood that students would not buy anything at all. John Gourville at Harvard Business School believes that some types of choice are more trouble than others. His – as yet incomplete – research suggests that consumers like to be offered choices in a single dimension: different sizes of cereal packet, say. If they are asked to make many trade-offs, such as whether to buy a computer with a modem or speakers, consumers start to feel anxious or even irritated.

The Economist, 14 March 1998

3 NEW PRODUCT DEVELOPMENT 12/99

3.1 Innovation is the life blood of a successful organisation and the management of innovation is central to this success.

(a) **New products** may be developed as a result of a technical breakthrough, or as a consequence of changes in society, or simply to copy and capitalise on the success of existing products.

(b) Management, however, can adopt a **proactive approach to product development** by establishing research and development departments to look into ideas for new products, although they do not have to come through this formal departmentalised system. Management, sales people, customers and competitors can all generate new product ideas.

3.2 **What is a new product?**

- One that opens up an entirely new market
- One that replaces an existing product
- One that broadens significantly the market for an existing product

An old product can be new

- If it is introduced to a new market
- If it is packaged in a different way
- If a different marketing approach is used
- If a mix variable is changed

Any new product must be perceived in terms of customer needs and wants.

Action Programme 5

Can you think of examples of new products and 'new' old products to fit into each of the above categories?

3.3 There are several degrees of newness.

(a) **The unquestionably new product.** Marks which distinguish such a new product include technical innovation, high price, performance problems and patchy distribution. An example is the MP3 music player.

6: Product, price and place operations

(b) **The partially new product**, such as the cassette tape recorder. The mark distinguishing such a product is that it performs better than the old ones did. An example would be the Pentium microchip.

(c) **Major product change**, such as the transistor radio. The mark distinguishing this product is the radical technological change which alters the accepted concept of the order of things.

(d) **Minor product change**, such as styling changes. It is these extras which give a boost to a product.

3.4 Sources for new products

- Licensing (eg Formica, Monopoly)
- Acquisition (buy the organisation making it)
- Internal product development
- Customers (listen to and observe them, analyse and research - this is how the Walkman developed)
- External inventors (Kodak and IBM rejected Xerox)
- Competition (Kodak instant cameras, following the Polaroid concept)
- Patent agents
- Academic institutions (for example, the pharmaceutical industry funds higher education department research)

Screening new product ideas

3.5 The mortality rate of new products is very high.

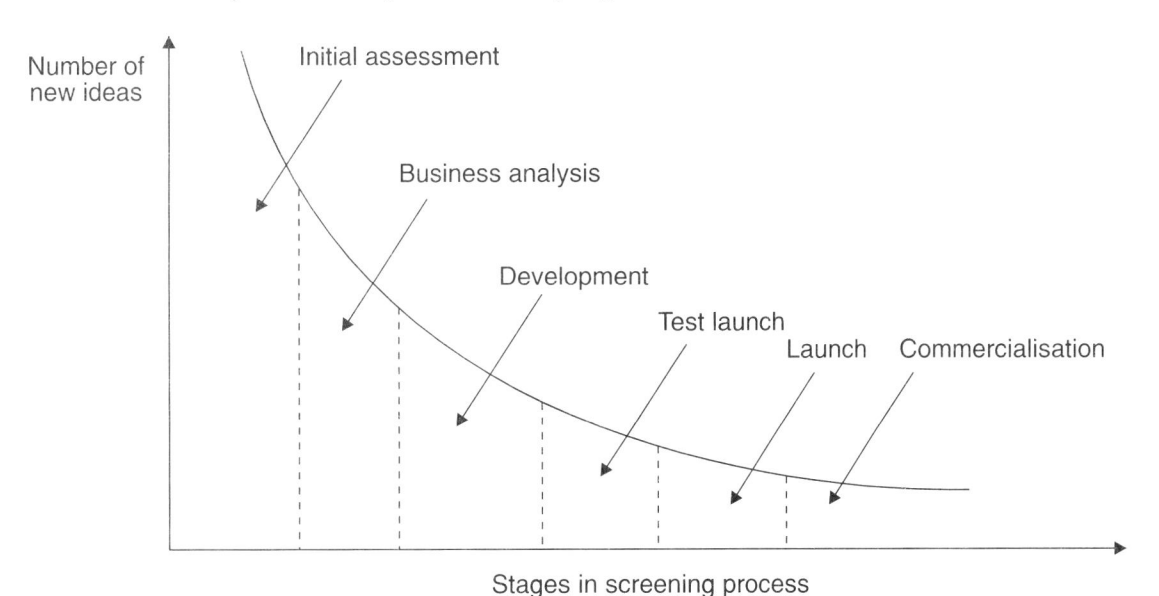

Stages in screening process

3.6 To reduce the risk of failure new product ideas should always be **screened**. There is some evidence that the product screening process is becoming more effective. A study by *Booz, Allen and Hamilton* in 1968 concluded that it took fifty-eight ideas to yield one successful product that achieved commercial success. A repeat study in 1981 showed a dramatic improvement; on average only **seven ideas were needed for every successful product**.

Part B: The marketing mix

New product development plan

3.7 New products should only be taken to advanced development if they satisfy three conditions.

- Adequate **demand**
- Compatibility with existing **marketing** ability
- Compatibility with existing **production** ability

Initial concept testing

3.8 At a preliminary stage the concept for the new product should be tested on potential customers to obtain their reactions. It is common to use the company staff as guinea pigs for a new product idea although their reaction is unlikely to be typical. But it is difficult to get sensible reactions from customers. Consider the following examples.

(a) **New designs for wallpaper.** When innovative new designs are tested on potential customers it is often found that they are conditioned by traditional designs and are dismissive of new design ideas.

(b) **New ideas for chocolate confectionery** have the opposite problem. Potential customers typically say they like the new concept (because everyone likes chocolate bars) but when the new product is launched it is not successful because people continue to buy old favourites.

Nevertheless, the concept testing may also permit useful refinements to be made to the concept, if it is not totally rejected.

Product testing

3.9 A working prototype of the product, which can be tried by customers, is constructed. This stage is also very useful for making preliminary explorations of whether the product could be produced in sufficient quantities at the right price were it to be launched. The form the product test takes will depend on the type of product concerned. To get realistic responses the **test should replicate reality as clearly as possible**.

- If the product is used in the home, a sample of respondents should be given the product to use **at home**

- If the product is chosen from amongst competitors in a retail outlet (as with chocolate bars) then the product test needs to rate response against **competing products**

- If inherent **product quality** is an important attribute of the product, then a 'blind' test could be used in which customers are not told who is producing the new product;

- An industrial product could be used for a **trial period** by a customer in a realistic setting.

Quality policy

3.10 Different market segments will require products of different price and quality. When a market is dominated by established brand names, one entry strategy is to tap potential demand for a cheaper, lower quality 'me-too' item.

3.11 **Customers often judge the quality of an article by its price.** Quality policy may well involve fixing a price and then manufacturing a product to the best quality standard that can be achieved within these constraints, rather than making a product of a certain quality and then deciding what its price should be.

3.12 Quality should also be related to the expected physical, technological and social life of the product.

(a) There is no value in making one part of a product good enough to have a physical life of five years, when the rest of the product will wear out and be irreplaceable within two years (unless the part with the longer life has an emotional or symbolic appeal to customers; for example, a leather covering may be preferred to plastic).

(b) If technological advances are likely to make a product obsolescent within a certain number of years, it is wasteful and uneconomic to produce an article which will last for a longer time.

(c) If fashion determines the life of a product, the quality required need only be sufficient to cover the period of demand; the quality of fashion clothes, for example, is usually governed by their fashion life. Fashion items are only intended to be worn a relatively small number of times, while non-fashion items are more durable.

3.13 Quality policy must be carefully integrated with sales promotion. If a product is branded and advertised as having a certain quality, and customers then find this is not true, the product will fail. The quality of a product must be established and maintained before a promotion campaign can use it as a selling feature.

Test marketing

3.14 The purpose of test marketing is to obtain information about **how consumers react to the product** in selected areas thought to be representative of the total market. This avoids a blind commitment to the costs of a full scale launch while permitting the collection of market data. The firm will use the sales outlets it plans to use in the full market launch, and the same advertising and promotion plans it will use in the full market. It helps to forecast sales, and can also be used to identify flaws in the product or promotional plans which can be dealt with before the national launch.

The diffusion of innovation

3.15 The **diffusion** of the new product refers to the **spread of information about the product** in the market place. **Adoption** is the process by which consumers incorporate the product into their buying patterns. The diffusion process is assumed to follow a similar shape to the PLC curve. Adoption is thought to follow a normal bell shaped distribution curve. The classification of adopters is shown below.

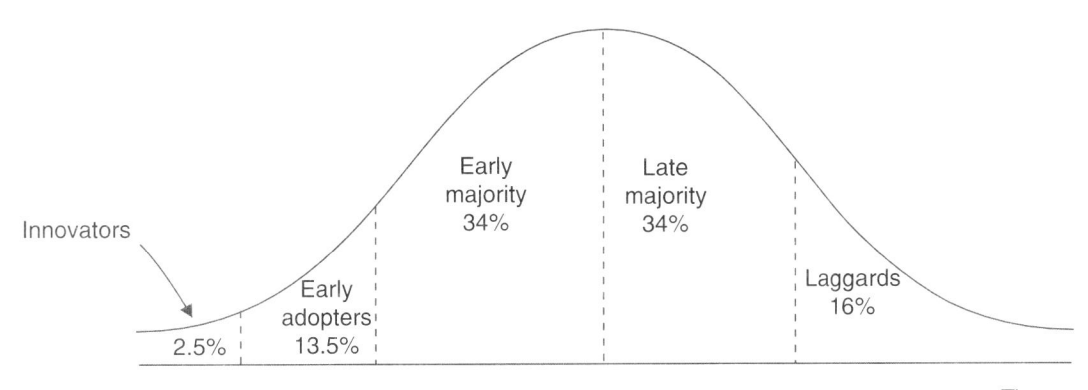

Part B: The marketing mix

3.16 Early adopters and innovators are thought to operate as 'opinion leaders' and are therefore targeted by companies in order to influence the adoption of a product by their friends.

Marketing at Work

Innovators and survivors

The marketing *orthodoxy*, backed up by *some* research studies, has suggested that 'first movers' are more likely to become market leaders and dominate the market. Research by Prahalad and Hamel argues this position. First movers, they argue, can reap benefits in lots of ways.

- By establishing a monopoly if only for a short time (Sony and the Walkman)
- By setting standards (Microsoft and DOS)
- By dictating the rules of the game (Wal-mart and the hypermarkets)

Tellis and Golder, in a recent paper, have argued the converse. Previous research, they say, has surveyed surviving companies, and so excludes innovators who have failed. This enables some companies to look like pioneers when actually they are not.

Tellis and Golder have studied 50 different markets using product categories familiar to consumers, and carefully avoided using hindsight to identify pioneers. This revealed a very different picture.

(a) The failure rate for pioneers turned out to be very high; almost half did not survive.
(b) In only 11% of the markets surveyed were today's leaders true pioneers.
(c) The average market share of survivors is only 10%.

The real success goes to *early leaders* - firms that entered the market an average of 13 years after the pioneers, and now have a market share three times the size of the pioneers. The reasons for this success are pioneers often fail to conjure up a mass market. Quality is often low, prices high and applications limited at this stage.

Examples of this would include the personal computer and the video recorder. The VCR market was pioneered by Ampex in 1956, when it charged $50,000 for its early models and sold only a few, making little effort to cut costs and expand the market. Sony, JVC and Matsushita, in contrast, saw the potential for mass market sales and set out to make a video recorder that would cost $500 - which took them 20 years to achieve.

Many first movers, such as Ampex, were content to have pioneered the technology, believing the breakthrough was enough to bring market leadership. Micro Instrumentation and Telemetry Systems invented the PC in the mid-1970s but ceded market leadership to latecomers (such as Apple Computers and IBM) who invested heavily to turn the PC into a mass-market product. Other examples include *alcopops*: 'Two Dogs' was first in the market but was beaten by 'Hoopers' Hooch', which was more extensively marketed.

The Economist, 16 March 1996

4 BRANDS AND PACKAGING

> **Key Concept**
> A **brand** is a name, term, sign, symbol or design intended to identify the product of a seller and to differentiate it from those of competitors. It amounts to a promise of consistent quality and value.

4.1 Not long ago most products were sold unbranded from barrels and bins. Today in developed countries hardly anything goes unbranded. Even salt, oranges, nuts and screws are branded. There has however been a limited return recently to *generics*. These are cheap, unbranded products, packaged plainly and not heavily advertised.

4.2 **Branding** is a very general term covering brand names, designs, trademarks, symbols, jingles and the like. A **brand name** refers strictly to letters, words or groups of words which can be spoken. A **brand image** distinguishes a company's product from competing products in the eyes of the user. **Brand positioning** was dealt with in Chapter 2.

6: Product, price and place operations

4.3 A **brand identity** may begin with a name, such as 'Kleenex', 'Ariel', but extends to a range of visual features which should assist in stimulating demand for the particular product. The additional features include typography, colour, package design and slogans.

4.4 Often brand names suggest desired product characteristics. For example, 'Fairy' gives impressions of gentleness and, hence, mildness.

Action Programme 6

What characteristics do the following brand names suggest to you?

Brillo (scouring pads)
Pampers (baby nappies)
Cussons Imperial Leather (soap)
Kerrygold (butter)
Hush Puppies (shoes)

4.5 Branding is a form of **product differentiation**.

(a) **Brand identity** conveys a lot of information very quickly and concisely. This helps customers readily to identify and select the goods or services and so helps to create a **customer loyalty** to the brand. It is, therefore, a means of increasing or maintaining sales.

(b) Advertising needs a brand name to sell to customers, and advertising and branding are very closely related aspects of promotion; the more similar a product (whether an industrial good or consumer good) is to competing goods, the more branding is necessary to **create a separate product identity**.

(c) Branding leads to a readier acceptance of a manufacturer's goods by **wholesalers and retailers**.

(d) It **facilitates self-selection** of goods in self-service stores and also makes it easier for a manufacturer to obtain display space in shops and stores.

(e) It reduces the importance of **price differentials** between goods.

(f) Brand loyalty in customers gives a manufacturer more **control over marketing strategy** and his choice of channels of distribution.

(g) Other products can be introduced into a brand range to 'piggy back' on the articles already known to the customer (but ill-will as well as goodwill for one product in a branded range will be transferred to all other products in the range). Adding products to an existing brand range is known as **brand extension strategy**.

(h) It eases the task of **personal selling**.

(i) **Branding makes market segmentation easier**. Different brands of similar products may be developed to meet specific needs of categories of users.

4.6 The relevance of branding does not apply equally to all products. The cost of intensive brand advertising to project a brand image nationally may be prohibitively high. Goods which are sold in large numbers, on the other hand, promote a brand name by their existence and circulation.

4.7 Where a brand image promotes an idea of quality, a customer will be disappointed if his experience of a product fails to live up to his expectations. **Quality control is therefore an important element in branding policy. It is especially a problem for service industries**

Part B: The marketing mix

such as hotels, airlines and retail stores, where there is less possibility than in a manufacturing industry of detecting and rejecting the work of an operator before it reaches the customer. Bad behaviour by an employee in a face-to-face encounter with a customer will reflect on the entire company and possibly deter the customer from using any of the company's services again.

4.8 The decision as to whether a brand name should be given to a range of products or whether products should be branded individually depends on quality factors.

(a) If the brand name is associated with **quality**, all goods in the range **must** be of that standard. An example of a successful promotion of a brand name to a wide product range is Virgin.

(b) If a company produces different quality (and price) goods for different market segments, it would be unwise to give the same brand name to the higher and the lower quality goods because this would deter buyers in the high quality/price market segment.

Branding strategies

4.9

Branding strategy	Description	Implies
Family branding	The power of the family name to help products	Image of family brand applicable across a range of goods
Brand extension	Adding new products to the brand range	High consumer loyalty to existing brand
Multi-branding	Different names for similar goods serving similar consumer tastes	Consumers make random purchases across brands

4.10 **Family branding:** the power of the 'family' name to assist all products is being used more and more by large companies, such as Heinz. In part, this is a response to retailers own-label goods. It is also an attempt to consolidate highly expensive television advertising behind just one message rather than fragmenting it across the promotion of numerous individual items. Individual lines can be promoted more cheaply and effectively by other means such as direct marketing and sales promotions.

4.11 **Brand extension:** new additions to the product range are beneficial for two main reasons.

(a) They require a **lower level of marketing investment** (part of the image already being created).

(b) The extension of the brand presents **less risk to consumers** who might be worried about trying something new. This is particularly important in consumer durables with relatively large 'investment' such as a car. Recent examples of brand extension include the introduction of Persil washing up liquid and Mars ice cream.

4.12 **Multi-branding:** the introduction of a number of brands that all satisfy very similar product characteristics.

(a) This can be used where little or no brand loyalty is noted, the rationale being to run a large number of brands and so pick up buyers who are constantly changing brands.

(b) The best example is washing detergents. The two majors, Lever Brothers and Proctor & Gamble, have created a barrier to fresh competition as a new company would have to launch several brands at once in order to compete.

4.13 A manufacturer might supply large retailers with goods under their own brand names, (own label or dealer brands). The major examples are the own brands of supermarkets and major chain stores (eg Tesco, Sainsburys, St Michael for Marks & Spencer and Winfield for Woolworths). This industrial structure has developed for several reasons.

(a) A high level of sales may be necessary to cover **fixed costs of production**; supplying dealer branded goods may be a way of achieving a profitable sales level. New market segments can be covered profitably at less risk and outlay to the producer.

(b) Large retailers with a high sales turnover and considerable control over the retail trade may **insist on having their own brand**, and supplying dealer branded goods may be essential to retain their business.

(c) A manufacturer may wish **to concentrate on production only**, leaving the problem of design, quality and distribution to a multiple retailer.

4.14 **Advantages of dealer brands to dealers**

- The use of a brand helps to create **customer loyalty** to the store
- The buying-in price is lower and cost of sales promotion negligible, therefore the price of dealer branded goods to customers can be lower
- 'Me-too' products may benefit from the **generic promotion effect** of the market leader's success, but enjoy a price advantage

Brand management

4.15 It is usual to appoint a marketing professional to manage a brand, or group of brands. This **brand manager** is responsible for the long-term integration of the corporate effort that goes into making the brand a success. A matrix style of management is indicated here, since the brand manager is unlikely to have direct authority over the resources needed by the brand. Inputs will be needed from all departments and top management is likely to take a close interest. The primary role of the brand manager is therefore co-ordination. The job may require a small team of marketing people for each major brand.

4.16 The most important aspect of this co-ordination is the promotion of customer orientation. The brand manager must be the focus for all communication to and from the customer. In particular, complaints should be dealt with by the brand management team.

4.17 A secondary role for the brand manager is to act as the brand's advocate in the internal contest for organisational resources.

Brand values

4.18 In the Key Concept box at the start of this section we remark that a brand amounts to a promise of consistent quality and value. The overall object of branding is that the customer should perceive greater value in the branded good than in the unbranded equivalent. There may be some objective basis for this perception, but much brand value in fact exists exclusively in the mind of the purchaser. The customer places a subjective valuation on such brand messages as style, quality, masculinity, sophistication and reliability.

Part B: The marketing mix

4.19 Clearly, such customer perceptions are extremely valuable and can lead to higher than average returns. They must also be protected from erosion or dilution of brand values by neglect or the hostile action of competitors. Manufacturers of exclusive brands will therefore go to great lengths to ensure that they are distributed only through up-market outlets, for instance.

4.20 Brands can be valued in money terms; when mergers and acquisitions take place, some part of the purchase price may represent brand value. However, current accounting practice does not allow brands to be shown as assets on the balance sheet. This is because a brand's value can be extremely volatile, depending on both good management and market conditions.

Threats to the brand

4.21 There are three main threats to a brand.

(a) **Competition**. Brands must be protected against competition. The principle way of doing this is by promotion aimed at establishing the brand's unique identity and values.

(b) **Infringement of intellectual property rights**. Trademarks, designs and text are all forms of intellectual property and can be granted legal protection against unlicensed use.

(c) **Generic names**. A brand can be too successful. If a brand name comes into common, everyday use as the generic name of a particular type of product, its owners may forfeit their rights over it. It is for this reason that Rolls-Royce take action against claims that such-and-such a product is the 'Rolls-Royce' of its market. It is important that 'Rolls-Royce' does not become established in everyday speech as a synonym for 'best'. Nylon and aspirin were once brand names.

Packaging

4.22 Packaging has four functions.

- **Protection of contents** during distribution
- **Selling,** as the design and labelling serve promotional objectives of providing information and conveying an image
- **User convenience**, as an aid to storage and carrying, such as aerosol cans and handy packs
- Compliance with **government regulations** for example, by providing a list of ingredients and contents by weight, as in food packaging

Remember that goods are usually packaged in more than one *layer*. Consumer goods might be packaged for sale to individual customers, but delivered to resellers in cartons or some similar bulk package.

The qualities required of a pack

4.23 The qualities required of a pack are as follows.

(a) The **range of size and variety should be minimised** in order to keep down purchasing, production and distribution costs, but it should succeed in making the product attractive and distinctive to the target consumer.

6: Product, price and place operations

(b) In industries where **distribution** is a large part of total costs, packaging is an important issue. Packs should:

- protect, preserve and convey the product to its destination in the desired condition
- fit into the practices of mechanised handling and storage systems and use vehicle space cost effectively
- be space efficient, but also attractive display items
- convey product information to shoppers effectively

(c) Packaging is an **important aid to selling**. Where a product cannot be differentiated by design techniques, the pack takes over the design selling function. This is crucial where there are no real product differences between rival brands, or in the case of commodities such as flour, which are basic goods.

- A pack should help to **promote the advertising/brand image**. In addition, a **logo** should be clearly identifiable on the package, to apply customer brand loyalty to a range of products.
- Shape, colour and size should relate to **customer motivation** (for 'value' or 'quantity').
- It should be the **appropriate size** for the expected user of the product (for example, family size packets of food).
- Some may be designed to **promote impulse buying,** such as snack foods.
- A **convenience pack** (tubes, aerosols) should be provided where this is an important attribute.
- Packaging should maintain product **quality standards**.
- It should **attract attention** of potential customers, where appropriate.

4.24 Packaging must appeal not only to consumers, **but also to resellers**. A reseller wants a package design that will help to sell the product, but also one which minimises the likelihood of breakage, or which extends the product's shelf life, or makes more economic use of shelf space.

4.25 The **packaging of industrial goods** is primarily a matter of maintaining good condition to the point of use. This is a selling aid in itself in future dealings with the customer. Large, expensive and/or fragile pieces of equipment *must* be well packaged.

Marketing at Work

Packaging innovations

No one could accuse the packaging industry of running short of ideas. The past few years have brought such user-friendly designs as baby bottle-style closures on water bottles; recloseable, plastic pour devices on milk cartons and large-opening ends of beer and soft drinks cans. Even petfood is available in single-serve squeezable pouches.

Packaging is no longer designed just to protect the contents, but has become a sophisticated marketing tool that consumers expect to meet certain performance standards.

Consumers' attitudes have changed too. Packaging was seen as a 'necessary evil' in the late 1980s and early 1990s and was heavily criticised for creating excessive waste.

Environmental concerns have not gone away, but many consumers have tired of - or at least got used to - the waste issues.

Part B: The marketing mix

Convenient, easy to use containers and a wide choice of options now seem to be the top priorities for consumers. Changing lifestyles, virtually worldwide, are causing a sharp rise in snacking and eating 'on the hoof', de-skilling of cookery practices in the home and a breakdown of the structured family meal time.

Much innovation has focused on the plastics industry. One important trend, which began to move away from glass to PET (polyethylene terephthalate) jars for foods such as premium soup, pasta sauce, apple sauce, jams and jellies. These jars are safe and non-breakable and incorporate moulded side grips for easy handling.

Also big news in plastic at present are oxygen-scavenging materials inside the walls and closures of containers. These 'eat' excess oxygen inside a container, thereby lengthening the product's shelf-life.

Hilary Schrafft, Financial Times

> **Exam Tip**
> Product policy is a particularly important aspect of marketing management. There is a significant body of theory associated with it which you should master in detail.

5 PRICE

5.1 Price can be defined as a measure of the value exchanged by the buyer for the value offered by the seller. It might be expected, therefore, that the price would reflect the costs to the seller of producing the product and the benefit to the buyer of consuming it.

5.2 Pricing is the only element of the mix which generates revenue rather than creating costs. It also has an important role as a competitive tool to **differentiate** a product and an organisation and thereby exploit market opportunities. Pricing must also be **consistent** with other elements of the marketing mix since it contributes to the overall image created for the product. No organisation can hope to offer an exclusive high quality product to the market with a low price - the price must be consistent with the overall **product offer**.

> **Action Programme 7**
> In what circumstances would you expect price to be the main factor influencing a consumer's choice?

5.3 Although pricing can be thought of as fulfilling a number of roles, in overall terms a price aims to produce the desired level of sales in order to meet the objectives of the business strategy. Pricing must be systematic and at the same time take into account the internal needs and the external constraints of the organisation.

5.4 The ultimate objective of pricing, as with other elements of the marketing mix, is to produce the required level of sales so that the organisation can achieve its specified objectives. **Two broad categories of objectives may be specified for pricing decisions**; not mutually exclusive, but different nonetheless.

   (a) **Maximising profits** is concerned with maximising the returns on assets or investments. This may be realised even with a comparatively small market share depending on the patterns of cost and demand.

   (b) **Maintaining or increasing market share** involves increasing or maintaining the customer base which may require a different, more competitive approach to pricing, while the company with the largest market share may not necessarily earn the best profits.

6: Product, price and place operations

5.5 Either approach may be used in specifying pricing objectives, and they may appear in some combination, based on a specified rate of return and a specified market share. It is important that stated objectives are consistent with overall corporate objectives and corporate strategies.

Marketing at Work

Low cost air carriers

The air market in Europe is currently being deregulated. In response to this, a number of low-cost no-frills carriers have set up in business. A good example is *easyJet*. This airline flies from Luton and Liverpool as opposed to London. Another example is *Virgin Express*, operating from Brussels.

BA is keen to protect its market from this low-cost no-frills approach and has launched its own low-cost no-frills airline to compete in precisely this segment. Virgin and EasyJet were concerned that BA would subsidise its low cost service *from profits elsewhere*.

The Economist, 10 February 1996

Price setting in theory

Key Concept
Economic theory suggests that price for any good is set by market forces. Under conditions of perfect competition, an **equilibrium price** will exist such that demand and supply are perfectly matched and there is neither surplus or shortage of the good in question.

5.6 Market pricing is illustrated in the diagram below. The upward sloping supply curve shows the natural tendency of manufacturers to enter a market if prices are high and to leave it if they are low. The downward sloping demand curve reflects the unwillingness of consumers to buy at a high price and their willingness to buy at a low one. The vertical co-ordinate of the point where the two curves cross is the prevailing equilibrium price; the horizontal co-ordinate shows the amount of the good in question bought and sold in the market. The equilibrium price is also called the **clearing price**, because it 'clears the market'; there is neither unsatisfied demand nor unsold goods.

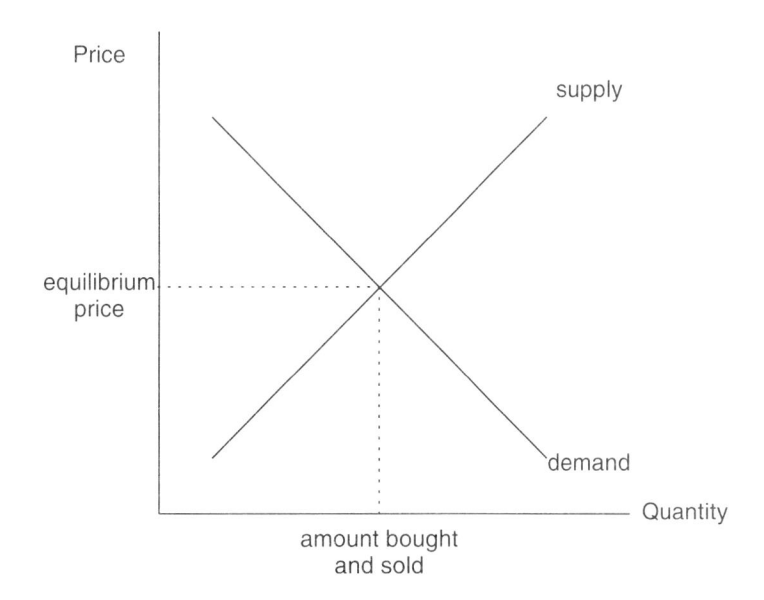

5.7 This simple mechanism gives a reasonable picture of **commodity markets**, in which there are many buyers and sellers and none has significant **market power**; that is, the ability to

Part B: The marketing mix

influence price **other than by buying and selling** relatively small quantities. More complex models are used to describe markets in which a supplier or group of suppliers has market power.

(a) A **monopolist** is the sole supplier in a market and is able to prevent other suppliers from entering. Monopolists are in a strong position to exploit the consumer and are frowned upon by government.

(b) **Oligopolists** are members of a small group who between them control supply in a market. Oligopoly is characterised by price 'stickiness'. That is to say, oligopolists typically compete with one another but only in matters **other than price**.

(c) Suppliers under **monopolistic competition** attempt to obtain some of the monopolist's market power by supplying a **differentiated** product. The success of this depends on the willingness of the consumer to accept that the product is, in fact, different. Clearly, this is a very important area for the marketer.

> **Key Concept**
> **Price elasticity of demand** is a measure of the degree of change in demand for a good when its price changes. If the change in demand is large in proportion to the change in price, demand is said to be **elastic**. If the change in demand is small in proportion to the change in price, demand is said to be **inelastic**.

> **Action Programme 8**
> What are the limitations of price elasticity as a factor in determining prices?

Price elasticity of demand

5.8 Price elasticity of demand is measured as:

$$\frac{\text{The change in quantity demanded, as a \% of demand}}{\text{The change in price, as a \% of the price}}$$

Since the demand goes up when the price falls, and goes down when the price rises, the elasticity has a negative value, but it is usual to ignore the minus sign. Values greater than 1 indicate elastic demand, while values less than 1 indicate inelastic demand.

5.9 **EXAMPLE**

The price of a product is £1.20 per unit and annual demand is 800,000 units. Market research indicates that an increase in price of 10 pence per unit will result in a fall in annual demand of 75,000 units. What is the price elasticity of demand?

5.10 **SOLUTION**

Annual demand at £1.20 per unit is 800,000 units.

Annual demand at £1.30 per unit is 725,000 units.

% change in demand $\quad \dfrac{75,000}{800,000} \times 100\% = 9.375\%$

% change in price $\quad\quad\quad\quad\quad \dfrac{10p}{120p} \times 100\% = 8.333\%$

Price elasticity of demand $= \dfrac{-9.375}{8.333} = -1.125$

Ignoring the minus sign, price elasticity is 1.125.

The demand for this product, at a price of £1.20 per unit, would be referred to as *elastic* because the price elasticity of demand is greater than 1. Now try the following exercise yourself.

Action Programme 9

If the price per unit of X rises from £1.40 to £1.60, it is expected that monthly demand will fall from 220,000 units to 200,000 units.

What is the price elasticity of demand?

Elastic and inelastic demand

5.11 **The value of demand elasticity may be anything from zero to infinity. Where demand is inelastic, the quantity demanded falls by a smaller percentage than price, and where demand is elastic, demand falls by a larger percentage than the percentage rise in price.**

5.12 There are three special values of price elasticity of demand; 0, 1 and infinity.

  (a) **Demand is perfectly inelastic.** There is no change in quantity demanded, regardless of the change in price. The demand curve is a vertical straight line. Demand for tobacco is almost perfectly inelastic in the short term, for any reasonable increase in duty, as Chancellors of the Exchequer know.

  (b) **Perfectly elastic demand** (infinitely elastic). Consumers will want to buy an infinite amount, but only up to a particular price level. Any price increase above this level will reduce demand to zero. The demand curve is a horizontal straight line. This is illustrated by a market price in a commodity market.

  (c) **Unit elasticity of demand. Total revenue for supplies** (which is the same as total spending on the product by households) **is the same whatever the price.**

The significance of price elasticity of demand

5.13 The price elasticity of demand is relevant to **total spending** on a good or service. When demand is **elastic**, an increase in price will result in a fall in the quantity demanded, and **total expenditure will fall**. When demand is **inelastic**, an increase in price will still result in a fall in quantity demanded, but **total expenditure will rise**.

5.14 Information on price elasticity of demand indicates how consumers can be expected to respond to different prices. Business people can make use of information on how consumers will react to pricing decisions as it is possible to trace the effect of different prices on total revenue and profits. Information on price elasticities of demand will be useful to a business which needs to know the price decrease necessary to clear a surplus (excess supply) or the price increase necessary to eliminate a shortage (excess demand).

Part B: The marketing mix

Factors influencing price elasticity of demand for a good

5.15 The main factors affecting price elasticity of demand are as follows.

(a) **The availability of close substitutes.** The more substitute goods there are, especially close substitutes, the more elastic will be the price elasticity of demand for a good. The elasticity of demand for a particular brand of breakfast cereal is much greater than the elasticity of demand for breakfast cereals as a whole, because the former have much closer substitutes. **This factor is probably the most important influence on price elasticity of demand.**

(b) **The time period.** Over time, consumers' demand patterns are likely to change, and so, if the price of a good is increased, the initial response might be very little change in demand (inelastic demand). As consumers adjust their buying habits in response to the price increase, demand might fall substantially. The time horizon influences elasticity largely because the longer the period of time which we consider, the greater the knowledge of **substitution possibilities** by consumers and the provision of substitutes by producers.

(c) **Competitors' pricing.** In an **oligopoly**, firms are very sensitive to price changes by their competitors. If the response of competitors to a price increase by one firm is to keep their prices unchanged, the firm raising its prices is likely to face elastic demand for its goods and lose business. If the response of competitors to a reduction in price by one firm is to match the price reduction themselves, the firm is likely to face inelastic demand but at lower prices. That is, all the firms in the market are likely to retain their market share, but at a lower price. The price 'stickiness' mentioned above tends to result and oligopolists tend to compete other than by price reductions. The diagram below illustrate the **kinked demand curve** perceived by the individual oligopolist.

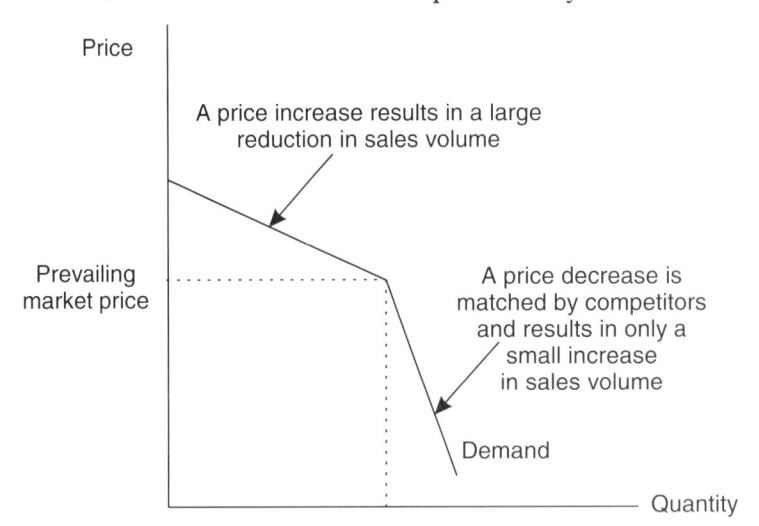

Price setting in practice

5.16 There are three main types of influence on price setting in practice: **costs, competition and demand.**

Costs

5.17 In practice, cost is the most important influence on price. Many firms base price on simple **cost-plus** rules: in other words, costs are estimated and then a profit margin is added in order to set the price. This method is fairly easy to apply and ensures that costs are covered. Costs are usually available from accounting records, sometimes in great detail.

5.18 The price may be based on **direct costs** or **full costs**, the difference being that full cost includes overheads whereas direct cost does not. In either case, a suitable margin is added to cost; under the direct cost method this has to cover overheads as well as profit. Under the full cost method, the margin represents profit only. While appearing to ignore demand, this method can take account of market conditions by adjusting the margin applied.

5.19 A common example occurs with the use of **mark-up** pricing. This is used by retailers and involves a fixed margin being added to the buying-in price of goods for resale. This fixed margin tends to be conventional within product classes. In the UK, for example: fast moving items, such as cigarettes, carry a low 5-8% margin (also because of tax factors); fast moving but perishable items, such as newspapers, carry a 25% margin; while slow moving items which involve retailers in high stockholding costs, such as furniture or books, carry 33%, 50% or even higher mark up margins. If all the firms in the industry use the same pricing basis, prices will reflect efficiency; the lowest price firm will be the most efficient.

5.20 The problems with cost-plus pricing arise out of difficulties in defining direct costs and allocating overheads, and with over or underestimation of attainable production levels. Because the cost-plus approach leads to price stability, with price changing only being used to reflect cost changes, it can lead to a marketing strategy which is **reactive** rather then **proactive**. In addition, there is very limited consideration of **demand** in cost-based pricing strategies. From a marketing perspective, cost-based pricing may lead to **missed opportunities** as little or no account is taken, particularly in the short run, of the price consumers are **willing** to pay for the brand, which may actually be higher than the cost-based price.

5.21 Particular problems may be caused by the use of cost-based pricing for a **new brand** as **initial low production levels** in the introduction stage may lead to a **very high average unit cost and consequently a high price**. A longer term perspective may thus be necessary, accepting short-term losses until full production levels are attained. Finally, if the firm is using a product line promotion strategy then there is likely to be added complexity in the pricing process.

Competition

5.22 We have already looked at price behaviour under oligopoly. In reality, the kinked demand curve theory would produce **going rate pricing** in which some form of average level of price becomes the norm, perhaps, in the case of a high level of branding in the market, including standard price differentials between brands.

5.23 In some market structures **price competition may be avoided by tacit agreement** leading to concentration on non-price competition; the markets for cigarettes and petrol are examples of this. Note that explicit agreement to fix prices is illegal. Price-setting here is influenced by the need to **avoid retaliatory responses by competitors** resulting in a breakdown of the tacit agreement and so to price competition. Price changes based on real cost changes are led in many instances by a 'representative' firm in the industry and followed by other firms. From time to time tacit agreements break down leading to a period of price competition. This may then be followed by a resumption of the tacit agreement. Often such actions are the result of external factors at work on the industry. Industry level agreements do not necessarily preclude short-term price competition for specific brands, especially where sales promotion devices, such as special offers, are used.

Part B: The marketing mix

> **Action Programme 10**
>
> There is at least one service industry in which this practice is the norm and which is regularly reported in the headlines. Can you think of it?

5.24 **Competitive bidding** is a special case of competition-based pricing. Many supply contracts, especially concerning local and national government purchases, involve would be suppliers submitting a **sealed bid tender**. In this case, the firm's submitted price needs to take account of *expected* competitor bid prices. Often the firms involved will not even know the identity of their rivals but successful past bids are published by purchasers and, if this is so, it is possible to use this data to formulate a current bid price.

5.25 If the firm has the particular problem of bidding for a number of contracts before the result of any one bid is known, the **production (or supply) capacity may be important**. The firm may need only to win *some* contracts: not too few nor too many.

5.26 If past bid data is not published, then there is very little data on which to base bid price setting. The firm may have to rely on trade gossip, on conjecture or on an estimate of likely competitors' cost and profit requirements in price-setting.

5.27 **If the contract is not awarded purely on price** (that is, if the lowest bid is not automatically accepted) **the problem is more acute**. In the case of the supply of branded goods, the relative value of each brand must be considered on a **'value for money' basis by the purchaser**. The bidder may have to rely on subjective 'feel of the market' analysis in arriving at bid prices. There are, of course, numerous instances where cases of actual and attempted bribery of officials have been uncovered as firms employ underhand means in the attempt to win contracts.

Demand

5.28 Rather than cost or competition as the prime determinants of price, **a firm may base pricing strategy on the intensity of demand**. Cost and competition factors, of course, remain influences or constraints on its freedom to set price. **A strong demand may lead to a high price, and a weak demand to a low price**: much depends on the ability of the firm to segment the market price in terms of elasticity.

5.29 Whenever there is a single price for a good, some consumers enjoy a **consumer surplus**. This is because of the downward slope of the demand curve. **If price were to rise, there would be some purchasers who would pay the higher price**. The difference between the market price and the higher price a purchaser is prepared to pay is the consumer surplus enjoyed by that purchaser. In elasticity terms, the demand of that purchaser is price inelastic. If such consumers can be identified and a higher price charged to them, the supplier obviously benefits. This is called **price discrimination** or **differential pricing**.

5.30 In practice, measurement of price elasticity and, implementing differential pricing can be very difficult. There are a number of bases on which discriminating prices can be set.

   (a) **By market segment.** A cross-channel ferry company would market its services at different prices in England, Belgium and France, for example. Services such as cinemas and hairdressers are often available at lower prices to old age pensioners and/or juveniles.

(b) **By product version.** Many car models have 'add on' extras which enable one brand to appeal to a wider cross-section of customers. Final price need not reflect the cost price of the add on extras directly: usually the top of the range model would carry a price much in excess of the cost of provision of the extras, as a prestige appeal.

(c) **By place.** Theatre seats are usually sold according to their location so that patrons pay different prices for the same performance according to the seat type they occupy.

(d) **By time.** This is perhaps **the most popular type of price discrimination**. Off-peak travel bargains, hotel prices, telephone and electricity charges are all attempts to increase sales revenue by covering variable but not necessarily average cost of provision. British rail operators are successful price discriminators, charging more to rush hour rail commuters whose demand is inelastic at certain times of the day.

5.31 Price discrimination can only be effective if a number of conditions hold.

(a) The market must be **segmentable in price terms**, and different sectors must show different intensities of demand. Each of the sectors must be identifiable, distinct and separate from the others, and be accessible to the firm's marketing communications.

(b) There must be little or no chance of a **black market** developing so that those in the lower priced segment can resell to those in the higher priced segment.

(c) There must be little chance that competitors will **undercut** the firm's prices in the higher priced market segments.

(d) The cost of segmenting and administering the arrangements should not exceed the extra revenue derived from the price discrimination strategy.

5.32 The firm could use a **market test** to estimate the effect on demand of a price change. This would involve a change of price in one region and a comparison of demand for the brand with past sales in that region and with sales in similar regions at the old prices. **This is a high risk strategy**: special circumstances (confounding factors) may affect the test area (such as a competitor's advertising campaign) which could affect the results. Also customers may switch from the test brand if a price rise is being considered and become loyal to a competitive brand; they may not switch back even if the price is subsequently lowered.

5.33 Alternately, a **direct attitude survey** may be used with respondents. **Pricing research is notoriously difficult**, especially if respondents try to appear rational to the interviewer or do not wish to offend him or her. **Usually there is a lack of realism in such research**; the respondent is not in an actual 'choice' situation faced with having to pay out hard earned income and therefore may give a hypothetical answer which is not going to be translated into actual purchasing behaviour. Nevertheless, pricing research is increasingly common as firms struggle to assess the perceived value customers attribute to a brand to provide an input to their pricing decisions.

6 PRICING POLICY

6.1 Price sensitivity will vary amongst purchasers. **Those who can pass on the cost of purchases will be least sensitive** and will respond more to other elements of the marketing mix.

(a) Provided that it fits the corporate budget, **the business traveller** will be more concerned about the level of service and quality of food in looking for an hotel than price. In contrast, a family on holiday are likely to be very price sensitive when choosing an overnight stay.

Part B: The marketing mix

(b) In industrial marketing, the **purchasing manager is likely to be more price sensitive than the engineer** who might be the actual user of new equipment that is being sourced. The engineer and purchasing manager are using different criteria in making the choice. The engineer places product characteristics as first priority, the purchasing manager is more price oriented.

Finding out about price sensitivity

6.2 Research on price sensitivity has had some interesting results.

- Customers have a good concept of a 'just price' - **a feel for what is about the right price** to pay for a commodity.

- Unless a regular purchase is involved, **customers search for price information before buying,** becoming price aware when wanting to buy but forgetting soon afterwards.

- Customers will buy at what they consider to be a bargain price without full regard for need and actual price.

- For consumer durables it is the **down payment** and **instalment price** rather than total price which is important to the buyer.

- In times of rising prices the **price image tends to lag** behind the current price, which indicates a resentment of the price increase.

Marketing at Work

Luxury hi-fi

The luxury end of the hi-fi market caters for an elite band prepared to pay huge prices for audio systems. It accounts for $1 billion in sales, compared to $70 billion for US consumer electronics alone. But this market often pioneers features and products which later become standard in the mass market, for example, noise reduction systems and CDs. The latest craze, however, is raising some eyebrows, because it threatens to turn the clock back - it is for valve (vacuum tube) powered amplifiers, which were assumed to have died out when they were replaced by transistors in the 50s and 60s.

Why should this be happening? Transistors are smaller, cheaper and more reliable. By 1990, the sales of valve amplifiers had fallen to almost zero. But enthusiasts maintain that the tubes reproduce musical notes more accurately, that the sound is better. By 1996, half of all up-market hi-fi amplifiers in the US were powered by valves.

Further, the most sought after amplifiers use the most antediluvian technology, single end amplifiers using a single 'triode', the design which in 1906 first made amplification possible. Since they produce only a few watts of power, they must be used with ancient but efficient 'horn' loudspeakers - which are consequently, also making a comeback.

This is the equivalent of going back to the Ford Model T when modern cars are on the market. Manufacturers are being tempted in by the lure of fat margins. Audio Note, a pioneer of the single ended market in Japan, sells amplifiers that range from $1,700 to $252,500 for the Gaku-On. Speakers cost around $40,000 per pair. Philips subsidiary Marantz, a mass market organisation, has just launched a tube amplifier for $50,000 while also reissuing a tube amplifier it last made in the 1950s for $8,400. Westrex, a small Atlanta firm, has resumed production of the 300B Triode, and hopes to sell 30,000 per year, giving it 40% of a market currently dominated by the Chinese and East European tube makers.

What effect will this have on the mass market? No-one really knows, but it seems likely that this will become an important segment within the audio market, although no-one can predict the potential size or profitability.

The Economist, 4 May 1996

Factors affecting price decisions

Intermediaries' objectives

6.3 If an organisation distributes products or services to the market through independent intermediaries, **the objectives of these intermediaries have an effect on the pricing decision**. Such intermediaries are likely to deal with a range of suppliers and **their aims concern their own profits rather than those of suppliers**. Also, the intermediary will take into account the needs of its customers. Thus conflict over price can arise between suppliers and intermediaries which may be difficult to resolve.

6.4 **Many industries have traditional margins for intermediaries**; to deviate from these might well cause problems for suppliers. In some industries, notably grocery retailing (as we have seen), the power of intermediaries allows them to dictate terms to suppliers. The relationship between intermediaries and suppliers is therefore complex, and price and the price discount structure is an important element.

Competitors' actions and reactions

6.5 An organisation, in setting prices, **sends out signals to rivals. These rivals are likely to react** in some way. In some industries (such as petrol retailing) pricing moves in unison; in others, price changes by one supplier may initiate a price war, with each supplier undercutting the others.

Suppliers

6.6 **If an organisation's suppliers notice that the prices for an organisation's products are rising, they may seek a rise in the price for their supplies** to the organisation, arguing that it is now more able to pay a higher price. This argument is especially likely to be used by the trade unions in the organisation when negotiating the 'price' for the supply for labour.

Inflation

6.7 In periods of inflation the organisation's prices may need to change in order to **reflect increases in the prices of supplies**, labour, rent and so on. Such changes may be needed to keep relative (real) prices unchanged (this is the process of prices being adjusted for the rate of inflation).

Quality connotations

6.8 **In the absence of other information, customers tend to judge quality by price**. Thus a price change may send signals to customers concerning the quality of the product. A rise may be taken to indicate improvements, a reduction may signal reduced quality, for example, through the use of inferior components or a poorer quality of raw material. Thus any change in price needs to take such factors into account.

New product pricing

6.9 Most pricing decisions for existing products relate to price changes. Such changes have a **reference point** from which to move (the existing price). But **when a new product is introduced for the first time there may be no such reference points**; pricing decisions are most difficult to make in such circumstances. It may be possible to seek alternative reference points, such as the price in another market where the new product has already

Part B: The marketing mix

been launched, or the price set by a competitor. Also, see below on penetration and skimming.

Income effects

6.10 In times of rising incomes, price may become a less important marketing variable than, for instance, product quality or convenience of access (distribution). When income levels are falling and/or unemployment levels rising, price will become a much more important marketing variable.

Marketing at Work

Supermarkets

In the recession of the early 1990s, the major grocery multiples such as Tesco, Sainsbury, Safeway and Waitrose, who steadily moved up-market in the 1980s with great success leaving the 'pile it high, sell it cheap' philosophy behind, suddenly found bargain stores such as 'Foodgiant' and 'Netto' a more serious threat.

This led the supermarkets to set up 'own label' product ranges which undercut prices for branded products.

Multiple products

6.11 **Most organisations market not just one product but a range of products. These products are commonly interrelated, perhaps being complements or substitutes. The management of the pricing function is likely to focus on the profit from the whole range rather than that on each single product**. Take, for example, the use of **loss leaders**: a very low price for one product is intended to make consumers buy other products in the range which carry higher profit margins. Another example is selling razors at very low prices whilst selling the blades for them at a higher profit margin. People will buy many of the high profit items but only one of the low profit items - yet they are 'locked in' to the former by the latter. Loss leaders also attract customers into retail stores where they will usually buy normally priced products as well as the loss leaders.

Sensitivity

6.12 **Price decisions are often seen as highly sensitive and as such may involve top management more clearly than other marketing decisions**. As already noted, price has a very obvious and direct relationship with profit. Ethical considerations are a further factor; whether or not to exploit short-term shortages through higher prices: illustrative of this dilemma is the outcry surrounding the series of petrol price rises following the outbreak of the Gulf crisis in 1990.

Price setting strategies

6.13 **Market penetration objective**: here the organisation sets a **relatively low price** for the product or service in order to **stimulate growth of the market and/or to obtain a large share** of it. This strategy was used by Japanese motor cycle manufacturers to enter the UK market. It worked famously: UK productive capacity was virtually eliminated and the imported Japanese machines could then be sold at a much higher price and still dominate the market.

6.14 Such sales maximisation is appropriate under three conditions.

- Unit costs will fall with increased output (economies of scale).
- The market is price sensitive and relatively low prices will attract additional sales.
- Low prices will discourage new competitors.

6.15 **Market skimming objective:** Skimming involves **setting a high initial price for a new product in order to take advantage of those buyers who are ready to pay a much higher price for a product.** A typical strategy would be initially to set a premium price and then gradually to reduce the price to attract more price sensitive segments of the market. This strategy is really an example of **price discrimination over time**. It may encourage competition, and growth will initially be slow.

6.16 This strategy is appropriate under three conditions.

- There is insufficient production capacity and competitors cannot increase capacity.
- Some buyers are relatively insensitive to high prices.
- High price is perceived as high quality.

6.17 **Early cash recovery objective:** an alternative pricing objective is to recover the investment in a new product or service as quickly as possible, to achieve a minimum payback period. The price is set to facilitate this objective. This objective would tend to be used in three circumstances.

- The business is high risk.
- Rapid changes in fashion or technology are expected.
- The innovator is short of cash.

6.18 **Product line promotion objective:** here, management of the pricing function is likely to focus on **profit from the range of products** which the organisation produces **rather than to treat each product as a separate entity.** The product line promotion objective will look at the whole range from two points of view.

- The interaction of the marketing mix
- Monitoring returns to ensure that net contribution is worthwhile

6.19 **Intermediate customers.** Some companies set a price to distributors and allow them to set whatever final price they wish. A variant involves publishing an inflated **recommended retail price** so that retailers can offer large promotional discounts.

6.20 **Cost-plus pricing.** A firm may set its initial price by marking up its unit costs by a certain percentage or fixed amount, as already discussed.

6.21 **Target pricing.** A variant on cost-plus where the company tries to determine the price that gives a specified rate of return for a given output. This is widely used by large American manufacturers, such as General Motors and Boeing.

6.22 **Price discrimination (or differential pricing).** The danger is that price cuts to one buyer may be used as a **negotiating lever** by another buyer. This can be countered in three ways.

- Buyers can be split into clearly defined segments, such as overseas and home (Rover cars are cheaper in the USA), or students' concessionary fares.
- Own branding, where packaging is changed for that of a supermarket, is a variation on this.
- Bulk buying discounts and aggregated rebate schemes can favour large buyers.

6.23 **Going rate pricing.** Try to keep in line with industry norm for prices, as discussed earlier.

Part B: The marketing mix

6.24 **Quantum price:** in retail selling the concept of a 'quantum point' is often referred to. When the price of an item is increased from, say, £9.65 to £9.95, sales may not be affected because the consumers do not notice the price change. However, if the price is increased from £9.95 to £10.05 a major fall in sales may occur, £10 acting as a **quantum point** which can be approached but not passed if the price is not to deter would be purchasers.

6.25 **Odd number pricing:** sometimes referred to as 'psychological pricing', in fact the odd number pricing syndrome (pricing at £1.99, say, rather than £2) is said to have originated not as a marketing concept but in department stores in order **to ensure the honesty of sales assistants**. The customer has to wait for change from £1.95 when, as is usual, they offer £2 in payment, so the assistant has to use the till. If the price was £2 and the customer need not wait for the change, there was thought to be a greater temptation to shop assistants to pocket the money and not to enter it into the till.

6.26 **One coin purchase:** confectionery firms have used another **psychologically based concept** of a one coin purchase. Rather than change price to reflect cost changes, such firms often alter the quantity in the unit of the product and keep the same price. This is a case of 'price-minus' pricing. The firm determines what the market will bear and works backwards, planning to produce and market a brand which will be profitable to them, selling at the nominated retail price.

6.27 **Gift purchases:** gift purchasing is often founded on the idea of price which is taken to reflect quality. Thus if a gift is to be purchased in an unfamiliar product category, a price level is often fixed by the buyer and a choice made from the brands available at that price. Cosmetics are often priced at £4.99 and £9.99 to appeal to gift purchasers at the £5 and £10 price level. Importantly, **packaging is a major part of the appeal** and must reflect a quality brand image, an important part of the psychology of gift choice.

Product line pricing

6.28 When a firm sells a range of related products, or a product line, its theoretical pricing policy should be to set prices for each product in order to maximise the profitability of the line as a whole. A firm may therefore have a **pricing policy for an entire product line**.

(a) There may be a **brand name** which the manufacturer wishes to associate with high quality and high price, or reasonable quality and low price and so forth. All items in the line will be priced accordingly. For example, all major supermarket chains have an 'own brand' label which is used to sell goods at a slightly lower price than the major named brands.

(b) If two or more products in the line are **complementary**, one may be priced as a **loss leader** in order to attract more demand for all of the related products.

(c) If two or more products in the line share joint production costs (**joint products**), prices of the products will be considered as a single decision. For example, if a common production process makes one unit of joint product A for each one unit of joint product B, a price for A which achieves a demand of, say, 17,000 units, will be inappropriate if associated with a price for product B which would only sell, say, 10,000 units. 7,000 units of B would be unsold and wasted.

Price changes caused by cost changes in the firm

6.29 During the prolonged period of inflation dating back to the 1970s, price increases generated by **increased costs to the manufacturer** were a common experience. The effect of inflation on price decisions was very noticeable and different organisations reacted in different ways.

- Some firms raised their prices regularly.

- Other firms gave advance warning of price rises, especially in an industrial market. Customers might then be persuaded to buy early in order to avoid paying the higher price at a later date.

- A firm which did not raise its prices was in effect reducing its prices in real terms.

Pricing under oligopoly

6.30 As discussed earlier under **oligopoly**, in established industries dominated by a few major firms, however, it is generally accepted that a **price initiative by one firm** will be countered by a **price reaction** by competitors. Here, prices tend to be fairly stable, unless pushed upwards by inflation or strong growth in demand. Consequently, in industries such as breakfast cereals (dominated in Britain by Kelloggs, Nabisco and Quaker) or canned soups (Heinz, Crosse & Blackwell and Campbells) a certain **price stability might be expected** without too many competitive price initiatives, except when cost inflation pushes up the price of one firm's products with other firms soon following.

6.31 In the event that a **rival cuts prices** expecting to increase market share, a firm has several options.

- It will **maintain its existing prices** if the expectation is that only a small market share would be lost, so that it is more profitable to keep prices at their existing level. Eventually, the rival firm may drop out of the market or be forced to raise its prices.

- It may **maintain its prices** but respond with a **non-price counter-attack**. This is a more positive response, because the firm will be securing or justifying its current prices.

- It may **reduce its prices**. This should protect the firm's market share at the expense of profitability. The main beneficiary from the price reduction will be the consumer.

- It may **raise its prices** and respond with a **non-price counter-attack**. The extra revenue from the higher prices might be used to finance promotion on product changes. A price increase would be based on a campaign to emphasise the quality difference between the firm's own product and the rival's product.

Price leadership

6.32 Given that price competition can have disastrous consequences for all suppliers in conditions of oligopoly, it is not unusual to find that large corporations emerge as **price leaders**. A price leader will dominate price levels for a class of products; **increases or decreases by the price leader provide a direction to market price patterns**. The price dominant firm may lead without moving at all. This would be the case if other firms sought to raise prices and the leader did not follow, then the upward move in prices will be halted. The price leader generally has a large, if not necessarily the largest, market share. The company will usually be an efficient low-cost producer with a reputation for technical competence.

6.33 **The role of price leader is based on a track record of having initiated price moves that have been accepted by both competitors and customers.** Often, this is associated with a mature well established management group. Any dramatic changes in industry competition, (a new entrant, or changes in the board room) may endanger the price leadership role.

Part B: The marketing mix

> **Exam Tip**
> There has not been a question specifically about price in recent years. However, it is a vital part of the marketing mix and a focus of much management effort in the real world. It is overdue for an airing in the examination.

7 COST ACCOUNTING AND BREAKEVEN ANALYSIS

7.1 We looked briefly at the two main approaches to accounting for costs when we considered cost-plus pricing methods. The approaches are usually known as **absorption costing** and **direct costing**.

Classification of costs

> **Key Concept**
> We may regard costs of production as being divided into two main categories. These are **direct costs** and **overheads**.

7.2 **Direct costs** are also called **variable costs** or, very frequently, **marginal costs**. They are the **costs which can be identified as directly associated with the process of producing an item of a good or service**: in a manufacturing context they would include the material which goes into the product, the labour used to produce it and any expenses traceable to it, such as power for the machine which was used to make it. The point about these costs is that **they do not arise until a unit of product is made**. They are called variable costs because they **vary with the volume of production. Overheads, on the other hand, are incurred whether production takes place or not**. This category of cost includes such items as rent, heat and insurance and will probably be far larger than the direct costs. Cost accounting schemes in large organisations usually only concern themselves with **manufacturing overheads**, marketing and administrative overheads being dealt with separately – though some organisations will absorb them into product cost as well.

7.3 **Absorption costing** calculates a cost for a product **including overheads**. This method is widely used.

- It is **required by law** for valuation of stock in the published accounts of limited companies and plcs.
- It allows a very **simple cost-plus approach to price**. This is frequently used for one-off, special orders. Cost plus pricing should ensure that the company makes a profit.
- It draws management attention to the **control of overheads**.

7.4 However, absorption costing has several disadvantages. We need to consider two in the context of pricing.

- The process of **allocating overheads to products is extremely arbitrary**; two cost accountants working separately might arrive at quite different results.
- Since overheads are fixed in the short term, they are **irrelevant for decision making in the short term**; no short term decision can affect them and so they should be ignored. Pricing is a short-term decision.

6: Product, price and place operations

As a result, the direct cost of a product should be used when making decisions about prices or comparing the financial performance of different products. This requires the use of **contribution**.

> **Key Concept**
> **Contribution** is defined as sales value less all variable costs of sale. These will include direct manufacturing costs and any direct selling costs such as a sales promotion or distribution cost per item. Contribution is an abbreviation of 'contribution to fixed costs and profit' and is widely used in product management. The **contribution/sales (c/s) ratio** is calculated as contribution divided by selling price. Contribution can be calculated per item or in total.

Breakeven analysis

7.5 Breakeven analysis is a useful application of marginal costing. Before a company starts to make a profit during a trading period, it must first earn **enough contribution to cover its fixed costs**. The volume of sales at which this occurs is known as the **breakeven point** and may be expressed in units or value. At this volume of sales, revenue just covers fixed costs plus variable costs and this implies that **contribution at this point equals fixed costs**. As total contribution equals contribution per unit times number of units sold, **the number of units of sales required to breakeven** is equal to:

$$\frac{\text{Total fixed costs}}{\text{Contribution per unit}}$$

7.6 EXAMPLE

Expected sales	10,000 units at £8 = £80,000
Variable cost	£5 per unit
Fixed costs	£21,000

Required

Compute the breakeven point.

7.7 SOLUTION

The contribution per unit is £(8 – 5)	=	£3
Contribution required to break even	=	fixed costs = £21,000
Breakeven point (BEP)	=	£21,000 ÷ £3 = 7,000 units
In revenue, BEP	=	(7,000 × £8) = £56,000

Sales above £56,000 will result in profit of £3 per unit of additional sales, and sales below £56,000 will mean a loss of £3 per unit for each unit by which sales fall short of 7,000 units. In other words, profit will improve or worsen by the amount of contribution per unit.

	7,000 units	7,001 units
	£	£
Revenue	56,000	56,008
Less variable costs	35,000	35,005
Contribution	21,000	21,003
Less fixed costs	21,000	21,000
Profit	0 (= breakeven)	3

7.8 **The sales revenue required to break even** can be calculated by dividing fixed costs by the c/s ratio.

Part B: The marketing mix

7.9 EXAMPLE

In the example in paragraph 7.6 the C/S ratio is $\dfrac{£3}{£8} = 37.5\%$

Breakeven is where sales revenue = $\dfrac{£21,000}{37.5\%} = £56,000$

At a price of £8 per unit, this represents 7,000 units of sales.

The contribution/sales ratio is a measure of how much contribution is earned from each £1 of sales. The C/S ratio of 37.5% in the above example means that for every £1 of sales, a contribution of 37.5p is earned. Thus, in order to earn a total contribution of £21,000, and if contribution increases by 37.5p per £1 of sales, sales must be:

$\dfrac{£1}{37.5p} \times £21,000 = £56,000$

7.10 An important application of breakeven analysis is the determination of **margin of safety**. This is simply the extent to which budgeted sales exceed break even. Knowledge of the magnitude of the margin of safety enables a reasoned response when sales do not reach budget. A small incursion into the margin of safety can probably be dealt with by a policy of 'wait and see', but if sales fall, more drastic action may be needed. Any adjustment of price will, of course, require a re-computation of the breakeven point and must be made in the light of what is known about price elasticity of demand.

7.11 These topics are dealt with in greater detail at Diploma level.

Marketing at Work

Real-life pricing

Before you get too worried about or carried away with the pricing methods and their technicalities described in this chapter, you should read the following extracts from an article by Vanessa Holder in the *Financial Times* (29 April 1996).

'*Pricing is guesswork. It is usually assumed that marketers use scientific methods to determine the price of their products. Nothing could be further from the truth.*'

David Ogilvy
Ogilvy on Advertising

This view of pricing is widely held. 'There is very little we know about pricing and pricing research,' admitted one international company renowned for its premium pricing recently.

'Pricing is managers' biggest marketing headache,' noted Robert Dolan of the Harvard Business School in last September's Harvard Business Review. 'It's where they feel the most pressure to perform and the least certain that they are doing a good job.'

Yet managers are only too aware of the rewards of a better pricing strategy. It offers the seductive promise of an immediate - and possibly substantial - increase in profits, without heavy upfront costs. It is an attractive lever for companies that want to put a renewed emphasis on expanding revenues after years of cost cutting.

Yet the problem is not usually a lack of familiarity with pricing options, according to Kalchas. Rather, the problem is the under-exploitation of these options as a result of roadblocks within the organisation. Many companies have a poor mechanism for setting prices; in addition, they make insufficient use of available data.

The article goes on to look at how this problem can be tackled, and indeed how some companies are already dealing with it. This is an article which is well worth reading in full (it is too long to reproduce here), so see if you can find it (perhaps in a good technical library).

8 PLACE

Marketing at Work

Downstream drift

Companies are drifting downstream. That is, they are gradually losing interest in how they make their products, and focusing more on how those goods and services reach their ultimate customer.

The car industry's new obsession with what happens to its products once they leave the factory arises in part because it has already cut the costs of production substantially. So it is planning to take an axe to distribution costs, too. Ford is the company that is reshaping itself most radically. It is handing over more of the responsibility for manufacturing to sub-contractors. But at the same time it is acquiring automotive servicing companies, such as the UK's Kwik-Fit and a Florida-based car recycling business.

The trend is visible in other industries, too. Personal computer manufacturers have delegated most of the important technical decisions that shape their products to component suppliers such as Intel and Microsoft. They increasingly delegate the mundane task of making their products to third-party manufacturers.

But they are following Dell Computer in seizing back customer relationships from distributors and dealers. Indeed, by offering customers free internet access or free online training, they seek to infiltrate themselves into the customer's life.

Peter Martin, Financial Times, 14 September 1999

Distribution channels

8.1 Independently owned and operated distributors may well have their own objectives, strategies and plans. In their decision-making processes, these are likely to take precedence over those of the manufacturer or supplier with whom they are dealing. This can lead to conflict. Suppliers may solve the problem by buying their own distribution route or by distributing direct to their customers.

8.2 In order for a product to be distributed a number of basic functions usually need to be fulfilled.

Transport	This function may be provided by the supplier, the distributor or may be sub-contracted to a specialist. For some products, such as perishable goods, transport planning is vital.
Stock holding and storage	For production planning purposes, an uninterrupted flow of production is often essential, so stocks of finished goods accumulate and need to be stored, incurring significant costs and risks.
	For consumer goods, holding stock at the point of sale is very costly; the overheads for city centre retail locations are prohibitive. A good stock control system is essential, designed to avoid stockouts whilst keeping stockholding costs low.
Local knowledge	As production has tended to become centralised in pursuit of economies of scale, the need to understand local markets has grown, particularly when international marketing takes place. The intricacies and idiosyncrasies of local markets are key marketing information.
Promotion	Whilst major promotional campaigns for national products are likely to be carried out by the supplier, the translation of the campaign to local level is usually the responsibility of the local distributor, often as a joint venture.
Display	Presentation of the product at the local level is often a function of the local distributor. Specialist help from merchandisers can be bought in but decisions on layout and display need to be taken by local distributors, often following patterns produced centrally.

Part B: The marketing mix

> **Action Programme 11**
>
> For many goods, producers use retailers as middlemen in getting the product to the customer. Try to think of some of the disadvantages of doing this, from the producer's point of view

Points in the chain of distribution

8.3 **Distributors**

(a) **Retailers**. These are traders operating outlets which sell directly to households. They may be classified in a number of ways.

- Type of goods sold (eg hardware, furniture)
- Type of service (self-service, counter service)
- Size
- Location (rural, city-centre, suburban shopping mall, out-of-town shopping centre)
- **Independent retailers** (including the local corner shop, although independents are not always as small as this)
- **Multiple chains**, some of which are associated with one class of product while others are 'variety' chains, holding a wide range of different stocks
- Still others are **voluntary groups** of independents, usually grocers.

(b) **Wholesalers**. These are intermediaries who stock a range of products from competing manufacturers to sell on to other organisations such as retailers. Many wholesalers specialise in particular products. Most deal in consumer goods, but some specialise in industrial goods, such as steel stockholders and builders' merchants.

(c) **Distributors and dealers**. These are organisations which contract to buy a manufacturer's goods and sell them to customers. Their function is similar to that of wholesalers, but they usually offer a narrower product range, sometimes (as in the case of most car dealers) the products of a single manufacturer. In addition to selling on the manufacturer's product, distributors often promote the products and provide after-sales service.

(d) **Agents**. Agents differ from distributors

- Distributors **buy** the manufacturer's goods and **re-sell** them at a profit.
- Agents do not purchase the manufacturer's goods, but earn a commission on whatever sales they make.

(e) **Franchisees**. These are independent organisations which, in exchange for an initial fee and (usually) a share of sales revenue, are allowed to trade under the name of a parent organisation. Most fast food outlets are franchises.

(f) **Multiple stores** (eg **supermarkets**) buy goods for retailing direct from the producer, many of them under their 'own label' brand name.

Marketing at Work

Safeway's logistics

Safeway has introduced a satellite tracking system in order to improve its distribution system. The company is to employ the system to track the movements of 600 trucks around the country and computers to check on

6: Product, price and place operations

drivers' techniques. It hopes to save at least £1m per year in fuel costs as well as improving the efficiency of its distribution system serving 420 supermarkets. The system could be used to tell, for example, whether a driver was overrevving in third gear, and using more fuel as a consequence; drivers could also be routed around traffic congestion, and stores warned of late deliveries. Safeway expect to recoup the costs (£1.5m installation and £350,000 per year operational) within the first year. Satellite tracking has already cut 10% off the full costs of one of the group's largest distribution depots at Warrington, and the savings could potentially be far greater in delay reduction and reduced labour costs. Streamlining the system is felt to be an essential element in improving service to customers. According to a spokesman: 'By changing the warehouse process, we can add one day's life to fresh produce'.

The computer software involved will be integrated with Safeway's bar coding system for products, allowing managers to track the whereabouts of individual items as they move from depot to store. This control is felt to be essential in developing an effective marketing system.

Financial Times, 24 February 1997

Types of distribution channel

8.4 Choosing distribution channels is important for any organisation, because once a set of channels has been established, subsequent changes are likely to be costly and slow to implement. Distribution channels fall into one of two categories: **direct** and **indirect channels**.

8.5 **Direct distribution** means the product going directly from producer to consumer without the use of a specific intermediary. These methods are often described as **active** since they typically involve the **supplier** making the first approach to a potential customer. Direct distribution methods generally fall into two categories: those using **media** such as the press, leaflets and telephones to invite response and purchase by the consumer and those using a **sales force** to contact consumers face to face.

8.6 **Indirect distribution** is a system of distribution, common among manufactured goods, which makes use of intermediaries; wholesalers, retailers or perhaps both. In contrast to direct distribution, these methods are often thought of as being **passive** in the sense that they rely on consumers to make the first approach by entering the relevant retail outlet.

Marketing at Work

Thornton's chocolates

The importance of place in marketing was borne out by the success of Thorntons in gaining a 13% rise in like-for-like sales, lifting interim profits by 30%. Roger Paffard, newly appointed chief executive, has seen his strategy of paying attention to the stores in which the company sells its chocolates pay off handsomely - in refitted stores, like-for-like sales were up by 22.5% he claimed. Pre-tax profits increased from £7.63m to £9.94m in the 28 weeks to 11 January. Christmas sales were up by 25%.

Financial Times, 3 April 1997

8.7 In building up efficient channels of distribution, a manufacturer must consider several factors.

(a) How many **intermediate stages** should be used and how many dealers at each stage?

(b) What **support** should the manufacturer give to the dealers? It may be necessary to provide an after-sales and repair service, and regular visits to retailers' stores. The manufacturer might need to consider advertising or sales promotion support, including merchandising.

Part B: The marketing mix

(c) To what extent does the manufacturer wish to **dominate a channel of distribution**? A market leader might wish to ensure that its market share is maintained, so that it could, for example, offer **exclusive distribution contracts** to major retailers.

(d) To what extent does the manufacturer wish to **integrate its marketing effort** up to the point of sale with the consumer? Combined promotions with retailers, for example, would only be possible if the manufacturer dealt directly with the retailer (rather than through a wholesaler).

Channel design decisions

8.8 In setting up a channel of distribution, the supplier must consider five things.

- Customers
- Product characteristics
- Distributor characteristics
- The channel chosen by competitors
- The supplier's own characteristics

Customers

8.9 The number of potential customers, their buying habits and their geographical locations are key influences. The use of mail order for those with limited mobility (rural location, illness) is an example of the influence of customers on channel design. Marketing industrial components to the car industry needs to take account of the geographic distribution of the car industry in the UK.

Product characteristics

8.10 Some product characteristics have an important effect on the design of the channel of distribution.

(a) **Perishability**

Fresh fruit and newspapers must be distributed very quickly or they become worthless. Speed of delivery is therefore a key factor.

(b) **Customisation**

Customised products tend to be distributed direct. When a wide range of options is available, sales may be made using demonstration units, with customised delivery to follow.

(c) **After sales service/technical advice**

Extent and cost must be carefully considered, staff training given and quality control systems set up. Training programmes are often provided for distributors by suppliers.

(d) **Franchising**

Franchising has become a popular means of growth both for suppliers and for franchisees who carry the set-up costs and licence fees. The supplier gains additional outlets quickly and exerts more control than is usual in distribution.

Distributor characteristics

8.11 The capability of the distributor to take on the distributive functions already discussed above is obviously an important influence on the supplier's choice.

6: Product, price and place operations

Competitors' channel choice

8.12 For many consumer goods, a supplier's brand will sit alongside its competitors' products and there is little the supplier can do about it. For other products, distributors may stock one name brand only (for example, in car distribution) and in return be given an exclusive area. In this case, new suppliers may face difficulties in breaking into a market if all the best distribution outlets have been taken up.

Supplier characteristics

8.13 A strong financial base gives the supplier the option of buying and operating their own distribution channel. Boots the Chemist is a prime example. The market position of the supplier is also important: distributors are keen to be associated with the market leader but the third, fourth or fifth brand in a market is likely to find more distribution problems.

8.14 **Factors favouring the use of direct selling**

(a) An expert sales force will be needed to demonstrate products, explain product characteristics and provide after sales service.

(b) Intermediaries may be unwilling or unable to sell the product. For example, the ill-fated Sinclair C5 eventually had to be sold by direct mail.

(c) Existing channels may be linked to other producers, reluctant to carry new product lines.

(d) The intermediaries willing to sell the product may be too costly, or they may not be maximising potential sales. This problem caused Nissan to terminate its contract with its sole UK distributor in 1991: Nissan believed that the distributor's pricing strategy was inappropriate.

(e) If specialised transport requirements are involved, intermediaries may not be able to deliver goods to the final customer.

(f) Where potential buyers are geographically concentrated the supplier's own sales force can easily reach them (typically an industrial market). One example is the financial services market centred on the City of London.

8.15 **Factors favouring the use of intermediaries**

(a) There may be insufficient resources to finance a large sales force.

(b) A policy decision to invest in increased productive capacity rather than extra marketing effort may be taken.

(c) The supplier may have insufficient in-house marketing 'know-how' in selling to retail stores.

(d) The assortment of products may be insufficient for a sales force to carry. A wholesaler can complement a limited range and make more efficient use of his sales force.

(e) Intermediaries can market small lots as part of a range of goods. The supplier would incur a heavy sales overhead if its own sales force took small individual orders.

(f) The existence of large numbers of potential buyers spread over a wide geographical area. This is typical of consumer markets.

Making the channel decision

8.16 Producers have a number of decisions to make.

Part B: The marketing mix

(a) What types of distributor are to be used (wholesalers, retailers, agents)?

(b) How many of each type will be used? The answer to this depends on what degree of market exposure will be sought.

- **Intensive** - blanket coverage
- **Exclusive** - appointed agents for exclusive areas
- **Selective** - some but not all in each area

(c) Who will carry out specific marketing tasks.

- Credit provision
- Delivery
- After sales service
- Sales and product training
- Display

(d) How will the performance of distributors be evaluated?

- In terms of cost?
- In terms of sales levels?
- According to the degree of control achieved?
- By the amount of conflict that arises?

8.17 To develop an integrated system of distribution, the supplier must consider all the factors influencing distribution combined with a knowledge of the relative merits of the different types of channel available.

Marketing at Work

Avon cosmetics

Nine out of ten women in the USA have bought products made by Avon, and the company is still immensely profitable ($257m profit in 1996). Yet it seems to be ageing and its marketing seems to belong to a previous age.

- The direct marketing force of 445,000 in the US looks misplaced. Many customers and potential salespeople are now working in full time jobs.
- Younger customer prefer 'hipper' products such as Body Shop, L'Oreal and Estee Lauder which can be found in stores.
- The image of the product is ageing.

Avon is trying to improve its marketing in the developed world as sales begin to fall, but this seems likely to be slow and difficult. The real profits, however, are to be made in what CEO James Preston refers to as 'Avon Heaven', the developing countries which in 1995 accounted for 38% of total sales and 49% of pre-tax profit. This has been an area of dramatic growth in the 1990s, with Avon going into 14 new markets. The main advantages for the company are:

- Underdeveloped retailing structure, which makes the traditional 'direct selling' method ideal
- Local products which are generally of poor quality and offer little competition
- Women in underdeveloped countries who are eager to work in order to supplement the family income, and make an extremely effective and active sales force, calling on three or four times as many clients as western counterparts
- Minimal investment generates huge profits. For less than $500,000 investment in the Russian market, 16,000 representatives have sold $30 million of products in 1996, from zero in 1993. Avon will obtain an operating profit margin of 30%

Because Avon's representative is often the only shop in town, the firm has been able to introduce a secondary catalogue, including the products of around 30 other companies, which account for 15% of sales in some of these markets.

6: Product, price and place operations

In trying to tie these brands together, Avon's strategy is to focus on a number of global brands it can sell worldwide. Six lines were launched in 1996. By 2000 the company expects sales from these markets to constitute 60% of cosmetics, toiletries and fragrance revenues (from 27% in 1996).

The consolidation of these brands has enabled Avon to improve quality and reduce the number of suppliers, cutting costs by 35%. Clearly the use of this old fashioned 'human distribution system' is presently more successful in developing markets, but no-one is really sure how it will develop in the traditional markets of the developed world.

The Economist, 13 July 1996

Multi-channel decisions

8.18 A producer serving both industrial and consumer markets may decide to use intermediaries for his consumer division and direct selling for his industrial division. For example, a detergent manufacturer might employ salesmen to sell to wholesalers and large retail groups in their consumer division. It would not be efficient for the sales force to approach small retailers directly. The distribution channels appropriate for industrial markets may not be suitable for consumer markets.

Industrial and consumer distribution channels

8.19 **Industrial markets** may be characterised as having fewer, larger customers purchasing expensive products which may be custom built. It is due to these characteristics that industrial distribution channels tend to be more direct and shorter than for consumer markets. It has to be remembered, however, that the most appropriate distribution channels will depend specifically on the objectives of the company regarding market exposure. There are specialist distributors in the industrial sector, which may be used as well as, or instead of, selling directly to the companies within this sector.

8.20 There are fewer direct distribution channels, from the manufacturer to the consumer in the **consumer market**. Examples may be found in small 'cottage' industries or mail order companies. It is more usual for companies in consumer markets to use wholesalers and retailers to move their product to the final consumer.

(a) **Wholesalers** break down the bulk from manufacturers and pass products on to retailers. They take on some of the supplier's risks by funding stock. Recently in the UK there has been a reduction in importance of this type of intermediary.

(b) **Retailers** sell to the final consumers. They may give consumers added benefits by providing services such as credit, delivery and a wide variety of goods. In the UK, retailers have increased in power whilst wholesalers have declined. Retailing has also become more concentrated with increased dominance of large multiples.

Distribution strategy

8.21 There are three main strategies.

(a) **Intensive distribution** involves concentrating on a segment of the total market, such as choosing limited geographical distribution rather than national distribution.

(b) Using **selective distribution**, the producer selects a group of retail outlets from amongst all retail outlets on grounds of the brand image ('quality' outlets), or related to the retailers' capacity to provide after sales service. Rolls Royce's image is safe in the hands of H R Owen but would be damaged if sold by an 'Arthur Daley'.

Part B: The marketing mix

(c) **Exclusive distribution** is an extension of selective distribution. Particular outlets are granted exclusive handling rights within a prescribed geographical area. Sometimes exclusive distribution, or franchise rights, are coupled with making special financial arrangements for land, buildings or equipment, such as petrol station agreements.

Channel dynamics

8.22 Channels are subject to conflicts between members. This need not be destructive as long as it remains manageable. Manufacturers may have little influence on how their product is presented to the public. Conflicts are usually resolved by arbitration rather than judicial means.

(a) A distribution system with a central core organising marketing throughout the channel is termed a **vertical marketing system**. Vertical marketing systems provide channel role specification and co-ordination between members.

(b) In **corporate marketing systems** the stages in production and distribution are owned by a single corporation. This common ownership permits close integration and therefore the corporation controls activities along the distribution chain. For example, Laura Ashley shops sell goods produced in Laura Ashley factories.

(c) **Contractual marketing systems** involve agreement over aspects of distribution marketing. One example of a contractual marketing system that has become popular over the last decade is franchising.

(d) If a plan is drawn up between channel members to help reduce conflict this is often termed an **administered marketing system**.

8.23 Channel leadership gives power to the member of the channel with whom it lies. In industrial markets where channel lengths are generally short, power often lies with manufacturers of products rather than 'middlemen'.

Action Programme 12

One of the fastest growing forms of selling in the US over the past decade has been the *factory outlet centres*. Discount factory shops, often situated on factory premises, from which manufacturers sell off overmakes, slight seconds, or retailers' returns are already well-established in the UK, but in the US developers have grouped such outlets together in purpose-built malls.

What would you suggest are the advantages of this method of distribution for customers and manufacturers?

Marketing at Work

OTC medicines

The supply chain is often a crucial element in the success or failure of a product. In the case of over-the-counter (OTC) medicines, because of the unique features of the product, the situation and the constraints on marketers, the supply chain plays a key role in consumer choice making.

Medicines satisfy a powerful and basic need - relief from pain. As a consequence, products tend to be evaluated in terms of their strict efficacy, and the functions of branding or advertising are far less prominent than usual. According to Mellors Reay and Partners, who work on the marketing of OTC medicines, this is compounded by regulations and restrictions on the advertising and retail promotion of products. These include:

(a) strict regulation of claims and impact of advertising;

(b) non-display of items on retailers shelves;

(c) restrictions on merchandising, discounting, the use of personality endorsement, loyalty schemes, cross promotions and free trials;

(d) huge price rises when products transfer from prescription to OTC;

(e) similarity between brand names because of reference to ingredients (for instance, paracetomol based analgesics include Panadeine, Panadol, Panaleve, Panerel, Paracets, and so on); and

(f) the influence of the pharmacist who can overcome or counter any promotional effect.

The role of the pharmacist is crucial, and is becoming more ambivalent, as the old semi-medical professional role is combined with one as an employee of commercial and market oriented enterprises. The increasing availability of OTC medicines previously only available on prescription only increases this power. Marketing OTC medicines directly to consumers must involve, to some extent, countering the respect and trust of consumers for pharmacists.

Yet brands can become established in spite of these problems. Nurofen, for example, an ibuprofen based analgesic, has established a powerful presence by building a brand which is distinctive by using advertising which suggests both power and empathy, and also by visualising and emphasising in an imaginative way the experience and relief of pain.

Admap, November 1996

International channels

8.24 As markets open to international trade, channel decisions become more complex. A company can export using host country middlemen or domestic middlemen. These may or may not take title to the goods. Implications of channel management in the case of exporters include a loss of control over product policies like price, image, packaging and service. A producer may undertake a joint venture or licensing agreement or even manufacture abroad. All will have implications for the power structure and control over the product.

9 LOGISTICS MANAGEMENT AND JUST-IN-TIME

9.1 Logistics management involves physical distribution and materials management encompassing the inflow of raw materials and goods and the outflow of finished products. Logistics management has developed because of an increased awareness of:

(a) customer benefits that can be incorporated into the overall product offering because of efficient logistics management;

(b) the cost savings that can be made when a logistics approach is undertaken;

(c) trends in industrial purchasing that necessarily mean closer links between buyers and sellers, for example, Just-in-Time purchasing and computerised purchasing.

9.2 Logistics managers organise inventories, warehouses, purchasing and packaging. There are benefits to consumers of products that are produced by companies with good logistic management. There is less likelihood of goods being out of stock, delivery should be efficient and overall service quality should be higher.

Marketing at Work

The paper industry

Distribution is now a critical factor in Europe's paper industry. Logistics is seen as a means of reducing costs and increasing efficiency, to counteract declining demand and 'dumping' of cut-price products from overseas. The *buyer* dominates the market and manufacturers therefore expect their distribution specialists to develop supply systems that result in zero damage and allow customers to minimise stockholding costs. One of the

Part B: The marketing mix

leading UK producers of paper for packaging has customers in the Benelux countries and northern France who expect orders to be delivered within 24 hours. The supplier is therefore having to set up warehouses to hold stock closer to the customers and speed up the delivery reaction time.

Just-in-Time: a creative competitive tool

9.3 **Just-in-Time (JIT) is a management philosophy covering far more than logistics.** It is an approach which has implications for all aspects of manufacturing including, for instance, labour relations, quality assurance methods and factory layout. Here we are concerned mainly with logistics, but you should be aware that JIT logistics cannot exist in isolation; the JIT approach must be applied throughout the business if it is to succeed.

9.4 JIT logistics has been described as:

> 'an inventory control system which delivers input to its production or distribution site only at the rate and time it is needed. Thus it reduces inventories whether it is used within the firm or as a mechanism regulating the flow of products between adjacent firms in the distribution system channel. It is a *pull system* which replaces buffer inventories with *channel member co-operation*.' (our italics)

JIT aims to:

> 'produce *instantaneously*, with perfect quality and minimum waste.'

Graham argues that JIT:

> 'completely tailors a manufacturing strategy to the needs of a market and produces mixes of products in exactly the order required.'

Traditional vs 'new' thinking

Issue	Just-in-Case	Just-in-Time
Official goal	Maximum efficiency	Maximum efficiency
Stocks	Integral part of system - a necessary evil	Wasteful - to be eliminated
Lead times	Taken as given and built into production planning routines	Reduced to render small batches economical
Batch sizes	Taken as given and *economic order quantity* is calculated	Lot size of *one* is the target – because of flexible system
Production planning and control	Variety of means - MRP models existing system and optimises within it. Information 'pull' for hot orders	Centralised forecasts in conjunction with local pull control
Trigger to production	Algorithmically derived schedules. Hot lists. Maintenance of sub-unit efficiencies	Imminent needs of downstream unit via *kanban*
Quality	Acceptable quality level. Emphasis on error detection	Zero defects. Error prevention
Performance focus	Sub-unit efficiency	System/organisation efficiency
Organisational design	Input-based. Functional	Output based. Product
Suppliers	Multiple; distant; independent	Single or dual sourcing. Supplier as extension

N Oliver, JIT: Issues and Items for the Research Agenda, 1991

9.5 **Synchronisation** is an essential component of JIT logistics. A successful channel will require precise synchronisation between suppliers, through the production units to retailers and finally suppliers. This depends crucially on **information being freely passed back and forth between channel members**; suppliers need to be informed about raw material deliveries, and also the components delivered to manufacturers. For their part, manufacturers must be confident that their deliveries will arrive on time. This implies **cooperation rather than confrontation** between the stages of the logistics chain. JIT means the end of aggressive buying or selling and the building of long-term cooperative relationships between organisations. A partnership approach is necessary and is often enhanced by cross-share holdings.

9.6 Information is exchanged throughout the production process by 'kanban'. Kanban is the Japanese word for **pull**. A kanban is a signal to an upstream department or supplier that goods are needed; more are provided or supplied until the kanban is received. Within a manufacturing organisation a kanban might be produced by a complex IT system or may be as simple as an empty container placed at a workstation so that it can be filled.

Market pressures encouraging a JIT approach

9.7 Customers need to be treated in a new way; loyalty is no longer to be taken for granted. Indeed, as consumers increasingly realise the power they wield, and become more sophisticated in the criteria they apply when evaluating and choosing products, manufacturers find that they must become responsive to these needs and also be able to adjust themselves rapidly in order to satisfy them. The keyword of the modern marketplace is **flexibility**, and this is coupled with **profitability**.

9.8 Manufacturing and marketing systems need to be programmable; they must be able to re-tool and re-formulate systems rapidly so that new requirements can be identified, formulated into new products, and those products constructed and made available rapidly. New production processes which aim to meet these requirements have been called **lean production**, and combine efficiency, quality and flexibility with a capacity to innovate.

9.9 Qualities of the **lean firm's** products.

(a) **Profitability,** with an emphasis on productivity and cost effectiveness

(b) **High quality** deriving from the need to compete not just on price, but standards

(c) **Match with market needs** - which requires the firm to employ flexible production processes, involving teams of multiskilled workers producing small batches of varied, diversified products

(d) **Responsiveness to change** - the firm must be customer-orientated, and able to produce products which match rapidly changing and highly individual customer requirements.

9.10 **Time lags are critical in these processes**. Reducing times taken for the product to get from the design stage to the market place is critical for success. This is one of the crucial differences between the Japanese and European or American car manufacturers. Japanese manufactures can get a concept into the marketplace in about 46 months - at least 13 months quicker than the Europeans and 14 months quicker than the Americans.

JIT at work

9.11 The need to be aware of customer needs and respond to them has been recognised as the difference between success and survival, and failure, and as a consequence have been

Part B: The marketing mix

propagated throughout the modern organisation. One of the key areas in to which this philosophy has reached is the distribution process.

9.12 **Lower investment in goods** within this process and **faster response to customer needs** means reduced costs, better value for customers, and increased benefits for other channel members within the distributive process, enabling everyone within the channel to compete more effectively.

9.13 Information about consumer demand is supplied by retailers, in the form of firm and tentative orders. The effectiveness of this for providing control on distribution costs is demonstrated in the volume car market in Japan. Nearly all cars are made to order and consequently, lead times can be as short as ten days!

9.14 If this synchronisation is effectively organised, a JIT system can meet consumer demand while at the same time profits may be maintained or enhanced, because stockpiles and inventory levels - and consequently, the costs of capital tied up unproductively in materials or products which are not being used - are cut dramatically.

9.15 **The supplier/manufacturer interface is crucial to the success of these changes, and a close relationship must be built up**. The changes mean that increasing numbers of component parts will be bought from outside the organisation, rather than being manufactured internally. When this system is instituted suppliers become important to the planning process in manufacturing and may well be brought into production forecasts, schedules and even the design stage. When decisions related to these are being made, the capacities and constraints faced by suppliers is obviously critical. In fact, liaison becomes an important function; their salespersons may well spend less time selling and become intermediaries, conveying information and mediating between buyer, engineering and their own production management. Finding new customers becomes less important than sustaining and improving relations with existing patrons.

9.16 JIT, it can be argued, **also improves product quality**. If suppliers are being provided with minimum resources and required to focus on using it to maximum effect, then it becomes even more important to get it right first time, since there is very little leeway in the amounts available to do it again. Right-first-time and just in time go together very well indeed!

9.17 However, problems with JIT have been identified, according to some commentators. These include the following.

(a) **The catastrophic effect of disruption**. If an external stress, such as the Kobe earthquake, holds up supply, there are no buffers to allow manufacturing to continue.

(b) **Conflicts with the workforce**. Excellent industrial relations are vital to the success of this system, as are flexible, sometimes multiskilled, workforces with a willingness to accept flexible work routines and hours, so that management can vary manning arrangements. Single union deals, famously, are a *sine qua non* when Japanese companies establish UK operations, and this is a major reason.

(c) **Problems over timescales**. These systems take a very long time to develop. Toyota took twenty years to develop theirs!

9.18 JIT, then, is expanding as lean production becomes more important. Focusing as it does on consumer choice, company profit and strong company-supplier relations, this concept fits comfortably alongside other managerial developments such as TQM and accelerating change in product markets.

Chapter Roundup

- The *product life cycle* model describes the progress of a product from introduction to discontinuation in terms of sales and profitability. It can offer some guidance in the management of marketing and production.

- Product portfolio planning aims to achieve a portfolio of products which fit well together in financial, marketing and production terms. *The GE screen* uses a more complex analysis than the *BCG matrix*. New product development is another aspect of product portfolio management and is about bringing innovation successfully to market.

- *Branding* is a form of product differentiation and can help to create customer loyalty. Brand strategies include brand extension, multi-branding and family branding. *Packaging* has a number of practical functions such as protecting the product and assisting the shopper, as well as contributing to promotional objectives.

- *Price* is the only element of the mix which generates revenue rather than creating cost. It must be consistent with the other elements of the marketing mix and is particularly associated with *perceptions of quality*. Economic theory deals with price in terms of market forces; its most useful aspect for the marketer is the idea of *price elasticity of demand*, which measures the extent to which a change in *price* is reflected by a proportionate change in *demand*.

- *Cost-plus pricing* is widely used because it is fairly easy to do and should lead to profitable prices. It can take account of demand by adjusting the margin added for profit. Competitor action, whether actual or expected, influences real-world price setting, especially under conditions of oligopoly and competitive bidding. Some customers enjoy a *consumer surplus* because they are prepared to pay a higher price. *Differential pricing* enables the supplier to exploit this willingness.

- Pricing policy is determined in the light of the customers' sensitivity to price, the objectives and actions of suppliers, competitors and intermediaries and the interplay of forces like inflation and income levels. Price strategies include penetration, skimming, cash recovery and product line promotion.

- Pricing decisions should be based on detailed information including knowledge of costs. Cost accountants use two main approaches: *absorption costing* and *direct costing*. Because overheads are unaffected by pricing decisions, direct costs and *contribution* should always be used for making decisions about prices and assessing profitability. Contribution is also used in *breakeven analysis*. The extent by which budgeted sales exceed the breakeven point is called the *margin of safety*.

- *Distribution channels* provide transport, stockholding and storage, local knowledge, promotion and display. *Direct distribution* occurs when the product goes direct from producer to consumer.

- Channels are designed bearing in mind the characteristics of customers, the product, the available distributors and the methods used by competitors. There are factors encouraging both direct distribution and the use of intermediaries.

- *Just-in-Time* is a management philosophy covering far more than logistics. It aims to eliminate all forms of waste. Synchronisation throughout the supply chain is achieved by the *kanban* system. Close cooperation is necessary with suppliers and distribution channels.

Part B: The marketing mix

> **Quick Quiz**
> 1 What are the stages of the product life cycle (PLC) and how do they affect profitability? (see para 2.8)
> 2 What are the criticisms of the PLC concept? (2.20)
> 3 What are the marketing implications of the PLC? (2.21)
> 4 What are the axes of the BCG matrix? (2.27)
> 5 What are the axes of the GE Business Screen? (2.33)
> 6 Why is branding used? (4.5)
> 7 How can packaging help selling? (4.16(c))
> 8 What is price elasticity of demand? (5.7 Key Concept)
> 9 How does a seller exploit consumer surplus? (5.29)
> 10 What is the difference between market penetration and market skimming? (6.13-6.16)
> 11 What is price leadership? (6.32)
> 12 What is the formula for breakeven point in units? (7.5)
> 13 Differentiate between wholesalers, distributors and agents. (8.3)
> 14 How do product characteristics influence distribution? (8.10)
> 15 How does Just-in-Time (JIT) affect the relationship between supplier and customer in industrial markets? (9.5)
> 16 What problems have been identified with JIT? (9.17)

Action Programme Review

2 Some ideas to start you off are manual typewriters, unleaded petrol and vinyl records. Also, almost anything subject to fads or fashions.

3 You could perhaps pin down some of these items, but most are open to discussion, especially if you take an international perspective. For many you may consider that the PLC is not valid, and you will not be alone.

5 You should try to think of your own examples, but these suggestions may help.

New product
Entirely new market — Web 'browsers', National Lottery
Replacing an existing product — Faster PCs
Broadening the market — Cable for satellite, TV and telephones

'New' old product
In a new market — German confectionery (in the UK)
New packaging — Anything
New marketing — French wine competing with Australian wine

7 You might have identified a number of different factors here. Perhaps the most important general point to make is that price is particularly important if the other elements in the marketing mix are relatively similar across a range of competing products. For example, there is a very wide variety of toothpastes on the market, most of them not much differentiated from the others. The price of a particular toothpaste may be a crucial factor in its sales success.

8 The main problem is that, unless very detailed research has been carried out, the price elasticity of a particular product or service is likely to be unknown. As a theoretical concept, it is useful in gaining an understanding of the *effects* of price changes; but it is of little use as a practical tool in *determining* prices.

9 Monthly demand at £1.40 per unit = 220,000 units.

Monthly demand at £1.60 per unit = 200,000 units.

% change in demand $\dfrac{20,000}{220,000} \times 100\% = 9.09\%$

% change in price $\dfrac{20}{140} \times 100\% = 14.29\%$

Price elasticity of demand = $\dfrac{-9.09}{14.29} = -0.64$

6: Product, price and place operations

Demand is inelastic at a price of £1.40 per unit, because the price elasticity of demand (ignoring the minus sign) is less than 1.

10   The industry referred to is the financial services industry. When economic factors cause alterations in interest rates (one of the main 'costs' borne by building societies and banks, because of their interest payments to investors), the societies reduce or increase their lending rates (the price of their mortgage products). It is usual to see one of the larger societies leading the way, after which the others fall into line.

11   Your answers might include some of the following points.

   (a)   The middleman's margin reduces the revenue available to the producer.

   (b)   The producer needs an infrastructure for looking after the retailers - keeping them informed, keeping them well stocked - which might not be necessary in, say, a mail order business.

   (c)   The producer loses some control over the marketing of the product. The power of some retailers (for example, W H Smith in the world of book publishing) is so great that they are able to dictate marketing policy to their suppliers.

12   Prices are up to 50% below conventional retail outlets and shoppers can choose from a wide range of branded goods, that they otherwise might not be able to afford. They can also turn a shopping trip into a day out, as factory outlet centres are designed as 'destination' shopping venues, offering facilities such as playgrounds and restaurants.

Manufacturers enjoy the ability to sell surplus stock at a profit in a controlled way that does not damage the brand image. They have also turned the shops into a powerful marketing tool for test-marketing products before their high street launch, and selling avant-garde designs that have not caught on in the main retail market.

Now try illustrative questions 8, 9, 10 and 11 at the end of the Study Text

Part C
Managing marketing relationships

7 Relationships with Customers and Suppliers

Chapter Topic List	Syllabus reference
1 Setting the scene	-
2 The nature of the customer	3.1
3 Internal marketing	3.3
4 Types of outside resources	3.2
5 When to use outside resources	3.2
6 Competitive tendering	3.2
7 Management of external suppliers	3.2

Learning Outcome

Students will be able to understand and appreciate the marketing operations process and how it can be delivered through multiple relationships.

Key Concept Introduced

- Relationship marketing

Examples of Marketing at Work

- Customer care
- Scandinavian Airlines System
- Rentokil International
- Wang UK
- The NHS

1 SETTING THE SCENE

1.1 The syllabus emphasises the wider relationships businesses must nurture if they are to succeed. This chapter deals with some of those relationships. Section 2 considers the nature of the customer, emphasises the advantages to be gained from customer retention and discusses the concept of relationship marketing. Section 3 deals with internal marketing, a phrase which has a range of meanings.

Part C: Managing marketing relationships

1.2 The remainder of the chapter is concerned with the organisation's use of outside resources. Section 4 illustrates the wide range available and Section 5 offers some ideas on their applicability, including the possibility of establishing a 'virtual company'. Competitive tendering is an important type of outsourcing, with its own features and Section 6 deals with this field. Where external services are used, it is important that control is not abdicated; the client organisation must ensure that the contractor performs properly. Section 7 is about the management of external suppliers.

2 THE NATURE OF THE CUSTOMER

2.1 **The customer is central to the marketing orientation**, but so far we have not considered this important concept in detail. Customers make up one of the groups of **stakeholders** whose interests management should address. **The stakeholder concept suggests a wider concern than the traditional marketing approach of supplying goods and services which satisfy immediate needs**. The supplier-customer relationship extends beyond the basic transaction. The customer needs to **remain** satisfied with his purchase and positive about his supplier long after the transaction has taken place. If his satisfaction is muted or grudging, future purchases may be reluctant or non-existent and he may advise others of his discontent. Customer tolerance in the UK is fairly high, but should not be taken for granted.

2.2 **Not all customers are the same**. Some appear for a single cash transaction and are never seen again. Others make frequent, regular purchases in large volumes, using credit facilities and building up a major relationship. This variation will exist to a greater or lesser extent in all industries, though each will have a smaller typical range of behaviour. However, even within a single business, customers will vary significantly in the frequency and volume of their purchases, their reasons for buying, their sensitivity to price changes, their reaction to promotion and their overall attitude to the supplier and the product. **Segmentation** of the customer base can have a major impact on profitability, perhaps by simply tailoring promotion to suit the most attractive group of customers.

2.3 Many businesses sell to intermediaries rather than to the end consumer. Some sell to both categories; they have to recognise that **the intermediary is just as much a customer as the eventual consumer**. Examples are manufacturers who maintain their own sales organisation but appoint agents in geographically remote areas and companies who combine autonomous operations with franchising. While it is reasonable to give the highest priority to the needs of the ultimate consumer and insist on some control over the activities of the intermediary, it must be recognised that he will only perform well if his own needs are addressed. For instance, a selling agent who has invested heavily in stock after being given exclusive rights in an area should be consulted before further demands are made on his cash flow by the launch of a new product.

Customer retention

2.4 Variation in customer behaviour was mentioned above. The most important aspect of this variation is whether or not the customer comes back for more. Customers should be seen as potentially providing a lifetime of purchases so that **the turnover from a single individual over time might be very large indeed**. It is widely accepted that there is a non-linear relationship between customer retention and profitability in that **a fairly small amount of repeat purchasing generates significant profit**. This is because it is far more expensive in promotion and overhead costs to convert a non-buyer into an occasional buyer than to turn an occasional buyer into a frequent buyer. The repeat buyer does not have to be persuaded

7: Relationships with customers and suppliers

to give the product a try or be tempted by special deals; he needs less attention from sales staff and already has his credit account set up.

2.5 Today's highly competitive business environment means that customers are only retained if they are **very satisfied** with their purchasing experience. **Any lesser degree of satisfaction is likely to result in the loss of the customer.** Companies must be active in monitoring customer satisfaction **because very few will actually complain. They will simply depart.** Businesses which use intermediaries must be particularly active, since research shows that even when complaints are made, the principals hear about only a very small proportion of them.

Marketing at Work

Customer care

In the increasingly competitive service sector, it is no longer enough to promise customer satisfaction. Today, customer 'delight' is the stated aim for companies battling to retain and increase market share.

British Airways, which lists delighting customers among its new goals, says ensuring the safety of passengers and meeting all their needs drives everything it does. 'Other airlines fly the same routes using similar aircraft. What BA must do is provide a superior standard of efficiency, comfort and general service which persuades passengers to fly with us again and again,' says Mike Street, director of customer services at BA.

Kwik-Fit, the car repair group, is another company that has included customer delight in its mission statement. Its forecourt promises to deliver '100 per cent customer delight' in the supply and fitting of vehicle brakes, tyres and exhausts leaves little margin for mistakes - and none at all for making any customer unhappy. Staff attend courses at company-run centres covering 'all practical aspects of their work, customer care and general management techniques'. Commitment is encouraged by 'job security', opportunities for promotion and a reward package that includes profit-related pay and shares in the company.

Customer satisfaction is monitored via reply-paid questionnaires distributed after work is carried out and through a freephone helpline that is open 24 hours a day. Kwik-Fit also says its customer survey unit 'allows us to make contact with 5,000 customers a day, within 72 hours of their visit to a Kwik-Fit Centre.'

Financial Times, 25 November 1999

2.6 The most satisfactory way to retain customers is to offer them products which they perceive as providing superior benefits at any given price point. However, there are specific techniques which can increase customer retention. Loyalty schemes such as frequent flyer programmes, augment the product in the customer's eyes. The club concept, as used by Sainsbury and Tesco, offers small discounts on repeated purchases. The principal benefit of both these types of scheme, however, is the enhanced knowledge of the customer which they provide. Initial registration provides name, address and post code. Subsequent use of the loyalty card allows a detailed purchasing profile to be built up for individual customers. This enables highly targeted promotion and cross-selling later.

2.7 Research indicates that **the single largest reason why customers abandon a supplier is poor performance by front-line staff.** Any scheme for customer retention must address the need for careful selection and training of these staff. It is also a vital factor in **relationship marketing.**

Relationship marketing

> **Key Concept**
> **Relationship marketing** is defined very simply by *Grönroos* as the management of a firm's market relationships

Part C: Managing marketing relationships

2.8 Much has been written in recent years on relationship marketing. *Gummesson* suggests it is a 'paradigm shift' requiring a dramatic change in marketing thinking and behaviour, not an add-on to traditional marketing.' In his book *Total Relationship Marketing*, he suggests that the core of marketing should no longer be the 4Ps, but 30Rs, which reflect the large number of complex relationships involved in business. *Kotler* says 'marketing can make promises but only the whole organisation can deliver satisfaction'. *Adcock* expands on this by remarking that relationship marketing can only exist when the marketing function fosters a customer-oriented service culture which supports the network of activities that deliver value to the customer. The metaphor of marriage has been used to describe relationship marketing, emphasising the nature of the necessary long term commitment and mutual respect.

2.9 Relationship marketing is thus as much about attitudes and assumptions as it is about techniques. The marketing function's task is to inculcate habits of behaviour at all levels and in all departments which will enhance and strengthen the alliance.

2.10 The conceptual or philosophic nature of relationship leads to a simple principle, that of **enhancing satisfaction by precision in meeting the needs of individual customers**. This depends on extensive two-way communication to establish and record the customer's characteristics and preferences and build a long-term relationship. Adcock mentions three important practical methods which contribute to this end.

- Building a customer database
- Developing customer-oriented service systems
- Extra direct contacts with customers

2.11 Modern **computer database systems** have enabled the rapid acquisition and retrieval of the individual customer's details, needs and preferences. Using this technology, relationship marketing enables telephone sales staff to greet the customer by name, know what he purchased last time, avoid taking his full delivery address, know what his credit status is and what he is likely to want. It enables new products to be developed which are precisely tailored to the customer's needs and new procedures to be established which enhance his satisfaction. It is the successor to **mass marketing**, which attempted to be customer-led but which could only supply a one-size-fits-all product. The end result of a relationship marketing approach is a mutually satisfactory relationship which continues indefinitely.

2.12 Relationship marketing *extends* the principles of **customer care**. Customer care is about providing a product which is augmented by high quality of service, so that the customer is impressed during his transaction with the company. This can be done in ignorance of any detail of the customer other than those implicit in the immediate transaction. The customer is anonymous. **Relationship marketing is about having the customer come back for further transactions by ending the anonymity**. Adcock says 'To achieve results, it will be necessary to involve every department ... in co-ordinated activity aimed at maximising customer satisfaction'. The culture must be right; the right people must be recruited and trained; the structure, technology and processes must all be right.

2.13 It is inevitable that **problems** will arise. A positive way of dealing with errors must be designed into the customer relationship. *Deming*, the prominent writer on quality, tells us that front line sales people cannot usually deal with the causes of mistakes as they **are built into the products, systems and organisation structure**. It is therefore necessary for management to promote vertical and horizontal interaction in order to spur changes to eliminate the **sources** of mistakes.

2.14 It is inevitable that there will be multiple contacts between customer and supplier organisations. Each contact is an opportunity to enhance or to prejudice the relationship, so

7: Relationships with customers and suppliers

staff throughout the supplier organisation must be aware of their marketing responsibilities. Two way communication should be encouraged so that the relationship can grow and deepen. There is a link here to the database mentioned above: extra contacts provide more information. Confidential information must, of course, be treated with due respect.

Key accounts

2.15 So far we have considered the retention of customers as an unquestionably desirable objective. **However, for many businesses a degree of discretion will be advisable.** 'Key' does not mean large. A customer's **potential** is very important. The definition of a key account depends on the circumstances. Key account management is about managing the future.

2.16 Customers can be assessed for desirability according to such criteria as the profitability of their accounts; the prestige they confer; the amount of non-value adding administrative work they generate; the cost of the selling effort they absorb; the rate of growth of their accounts and, for industrial customers, of the turnover of their own businesses; their willingness to adopt new products; and their credit history. Such analyses will almost certainly conform to a Pareto distribution and show, for instance that 80% of profit comes from 20% of the customers, while a different 20% generate most of the credit control or administrative problems. Some businesses will be very aggressive about getting rid of their problem customers, but a more positive technique would be to concentrate effort on the most desirable ones. These are the **key accounts** and the company's relationship with them can be built up by appointing **key account managers**.

2.17 Key account management is often seen as a high level selling task, but should in fact be a business wide team effort about relationships and customer retention. It can be seen as a form of co-operation with the customer's supply chain management function. The key account manager's role is to integrate the efforts of the various parts of the organisation in order to deliver an enhanced service. This idea has long been used by advertising agencies and was successfully introduced into aerospace manufacturing over 40 years ago. It will be the key account manager's role to maintain communication with the customer, note any developments in his circumstances, deal with any problems arising in the relationship and develop the long term business relationship.

2.18 The key account relationship may progress through several stages.

- At first, there may be a typical adversarial sales-purchasing relationship with emphasis on price, delivery and so on. Attempts to widen contact with the customer organisation will be seen as a threat by its purchasing staff.

- Later, the sales staff may be able to foster a mutual desire to increase understanding by wider contacts. Trust may increase.

- A mature partnership stage may be reached in which there are contacts at all levels and information is shared. The Key account manager becomes responsible for integrating the partnership business processes and contributing to the customer's supply chain management. High 'vendor ratings', stable quality, continuous improvement and fair pricing are taken for granted.

3 INTERNAL MARKETING 12/98

3.1 Unfortunately, the term **internal marketing,** has been used in a variety of ways. It has, for instance, been adopted in the field of **quality management** where the concept of the

Part C: Managing marketing relationships

internal customer is used to motivate staff towards achieving quality objectives. **In its most common usage, internal marketing means the promotion of a marketing orientation throughout the organisation** and, in particular, creating customer awareness among staff who are not primarily concerned with selling. Hotel housekeeping staff, for instance, may rarely be seen by the guests, but their work makes a major contribution to the guests' perception of their welcome.

3.2 The achievement of such a widespread marketing orientation may involve **major changes in working practices and organisational culture**. The successful management of organisational change depends to a great extent upon successful communication and communication is a major marketing activity. 'Internal marketing' has therefore also come to mean the communication aspect of *any* programme of change and, even more simply, **the presentation by management to staff of any information at all.**

Internal marketing as part of marketing management

3.3 If we concentrate on the use of the term to mean the promotion of a market orientation throughout a business, we will see that a number of challenges may exist. The first is that we may well be looking at a **major cultural shift**. Even in businesses which have highly skilled and motivated sales teams, **there may be areas of the organisation whose culture, aims and practices have nothing to do with customer satisfaction**. Engineering is a good example. The old nationalised industries like British Railways and Post Office Telecommunications saw engineering effectiveness as their major goal, with customer service nowhere. A business which takes this view is unlikely to succeed, but achieving a change of orientation can be a long, difficult and painful process. It will involve a major change in culture and probably entail significant changes to the shape of the organisation, as departments which contribute little to customer service lose influence and shrink or even disappear as the cost base is cut.

3.4 **Organisational change**

(a) Measuring activities against contribution to customer satisfaction means that some areas of the organisation are likely to shrink. The process of **delayering** may be necessary. This utilises modern information technology systems to replace the communications relaying function of middle management. As this activity forms a large part of middle management work, the result is a much reduced requirement for general managers and an increased span of control. A **Total Quality approach** can also lead to staff reductions: if the organisation succeeds in improving initial quality, the need for people to handle complaints, claims and rework is much diminished.

(b) At the same time as these changes are being made, front-line sales and marketing capability will probably have to be enhanced. This is likely to involve more than just an increase in numbers. New methods of working will be introduced, including working in cross-functional teams. In particular, the natural partner of delayering is **empowerment**. Front line staff will take greater responsibility for delivering customer satisfaction and will be given the necessary authority to do so. Relationship marketing databases and staff will be installed and key account managers appointed.

3.5 Such restructuring of the organisation has **important human resources management (HRM) implications.**

(a) There are likely to be **redundancies**. Staff who cannot adjust to the new methods must be released with proper attention to both the legal requirements relating to redundancy and the organisation's policies on social responsibility.

7: Relationships with customers and suppliers

(b) **Recruitment** will continue, because of natural wastage, but it will probably be necessary to adjust recruitment policy and practice to reflect the new requirements. Recruits must be selected who will be able to absorb the new approach and respond to the necessary training.

(c) **Training** will become a major feature of the change management programme. As well as new recruits, existing staff must be educated in the new methods and approach. The Marketing Department may have an input here, or the task of inculcating the marketing orientation and ideal of customer service may be contracted out to consultants.

3.6 Research suggests that although the principles involved may be acknowledged by a large number of companies, **formalised internal marketing programmes in the UK are still fairly uncommon**. Initial findings make several other suggestions.

(a) Internal marketing is **implicit in other strategies** such as quality programmes and customer care initiatives, rather than standing alone as an explicit policy in its own right.

(b) Where it is practised, internal marketing tends to involve a **core of structured activities** surrounded by less rigorously defined ad hoc practices.

(c) To operate successfully, internal marketing relies heavily on **good communication** networks.

(d) Internal marketing is a key factor in competitive differentiation.

(e) Conflicts between functional areas are significantly reduced by internal marketing.

(f) **Internal marketing depends heavily on commitment at the highest level of management, on general, active, widespread co-operation, and on the presence of an open management style.**

Marketing at Work

Scandinavian Airlines Systems

Companies using this approach to great effect include SAS (Scandinavian Airline Systems), who have increased the involvement of employees in the decision-making process to achieve the highest levels of satisfaction, empowered them to make decisions appropriate to the requirements of particular customers, and trained them to feel a responsibility towards customers of all kinds. As a consequence, the company culture fosters a caring relationship internally and externally.

The marketing mix for internal marketing

3.7 **Product** under the internal marketing concept is the changing nature of the job. **Price** is the balance of psychological costs and benefits involved in adopting the new orientation, plus those things which have to be given up in order to carry out the new tasks. Difficulties here relate to the problem of arriving at an accurate and adequate evaluation of psychological costs.

3.8 Many of the methods used for communication and **promotion** in external marketing may be employed to motivate employees and influence attitudes and behaviour. HRM practice is beginning to employ techniques, such as multi-media presentations and in-house publications. Presentational skills are borrowed from personal selling techniques, while incentive schemes are being employed to generate changes in employee behaviour.

Part C: Managing marketing relationships

3.9 **Advertising** is increasingly used to generate a favourable corporate image amongst employees as well as external customers. Federal Express has the largest corporate television network in the world, with 1,200 sites,

3.10 **Distribution** for internal marketing means e-mails, meetings, conferences and physical means like noticeboards which can be used to announce policies and deliver policies and training programmes.

3.11 **Physical evidence** refers to tangible items which facilitate delivery or communication of the product. Quality standards such as BS 5750/ISO 9000, for instance, place great emphasis on documentation. Other tangible elements might involve training sessions, which would constitute a manifestation of commitment to standards or policies.

3.12 **Process**, which refers to how a 'customer' actually receives a product, is linked to communication and the medium of training which may be used to promote customer consciousness.

3.13 **Participants** are the people involved in producing and delivering the product, and those receiving the product, who may influence the customer's perceptions, are clearly important within the internal marketing process. Communications must be delivered by someone of the right level of authority in order to achieve their aims. The way in which employees act is strongly influenced by fellow employees, particularly their immediate superiors. Inter-departmental or interfunctional communications are likely to be least effective, because they have equal status or lack the authority to ensure compliance.

3.14 **Segmentation and marketing research can also be used in internal marketing**. Employees may be grouped according to their service characteristics, needs, wants or tasks in order to organise the dissemination of a service orientation. Research will monitor the needs and wants of employees, and identify the impact of corporate policies.

Problems with the internal marketing concept

3.15 Even effective use of inwardly directed marketing techniques cannot solve all employee related quality and customer satisfaction problems. **Research clearly shows that actions by the personnel department, or effective programmes of personnel selection and training, are likely to be more effective than marketing based activities**. In the UK retail sector, for example, while many large scale operations have begun Sunday trading, there has been significant resistance from employee organisations. Internal marketing would argue that employees should be persuaded by means of a well-executed communications campaign and by the offer of proper incentives. Although these strategies have been tried, they have met with little success, or, in the case of incentives, have been too expensive. Employers have solved the problem by specifically recruiting employees who are required to work on Sunday, and who may be paid slightly higher wage rates for the time in question. **Rather than internal marketing, external recruitment proved to be the solution**.

3.16 Claims by marketers such as *George*, *Berry* and *Parasuranam*, that marketing can replace or fulfil the objectives of some other functions are clearly overstated. However, the internal marketing concept has a major role to play in making employees customer conscious. The most effective and widely adopted programme at the moment appears to be TQM, although there are very few models of how internal marketing should be implemented currently available.

4 TYPES OF OUTSIDE RESOURCES

4.1 In the modern world, it is possible to outsource everything. Some examples are given below.

Manufacture

4.2 Outside resources can be used in the following areas.

(a) **Manufacturing materials**. These include raw materials such as iron ore, semi-processed materials such as sheet metal, and components such as solid state electronic devices.

(b) **Assemblies**. Items such as car headlights and wiring harnesses are usually outsourced.

(c) **Total outside manufacture**. Retailers buy-in their goods fully made, packaged and delivered by the manufacturers, who may well also offer stock control services including auditing and 'Just-in-Time' systems.

(d) **Packaging**. Some manufacturers, eg Boots, will sub-contract out the packaging and/or the filling of containers to local small firms.

(e) **Product design**. In the fashion garments industry it is quite usual for textile manufacturers to use outside designers, some of whom become internationally famous like Christian Dior and Norman Hartnell. Externally sourced design is increasingly used for industrial goods also. A large amount of software development is done in India, via the Internet.

Distribution

4.3 Many manufacturers will outsource storage to **warehouse space providers** and the delivery of their products to **transport specialists**. In international marketing, many exporters will use **overseas distributors** offering the full range of services from shipping to selling.

Finance

4.4 The great majority of incorporated bodies and charities are required by law to have an **independent audit**. Many small businesses purchase a variety of management accounting and financial management services from their auditors. **Factors**, who are usually wholly owned subsidiaries of banks, provide a range of services including a full sales ledger operation, and credit reference agencies sell detailed information about the creditworthiness and history of businesses of all types.

Marketing

Consultants

4.5 There are a great many management and marketing consultants in the UK. The CIM, for example, provides a comprehensive service. Some consultants specialise in design, research or promotion.

Marketing research agencies

4.6 Not many organisations have all the in-house facilities needed to cater for their total information requirements. Nearly all organisations find it necessary from time to time to outsource surveys to specialists.

Part C: Managing marketing relationships

Promotional agencies

4.7 There is a great variety of **promotional agencies** including advertising agencies and agencies specialising in sales promotion, in PR, in telesales/telemarketing. Within sales promotion there is a range of specialists in such areas as packaging design, POS display material, exhibition services, and mail-order.

Full-service agencies

4.8 **Full service agencies** supply the full range of marketing services.

4.9 In smaller companies, many of the functions associated with marketing may actually be sourced from outside the company. Obvious examples would be market research services, advertising, design of packaging, and specialist aspects of product testing (for example, sensory testing of new food products, or safety tests on new electrical goods). When promotional campaigns are being mounted, 'leafleting' is typically the province of small subcontractors as are teams who dispense free samples during in-store promotional exercises.

Human resources management

4.10 Much recruitment is outsourced, particularly where higher paid staff are concerned. Executive search agencies maintain databases to enable them to find top executives. There are many training consultants who will advise on, design and deliver a variety of training.

Marketing at Work

Rentokil International

Sir Clive Thompson, group chief executive of Rentokil International, talks to Michael Dembinski about the future of the outsourcing sector. Outsourcing's first wave affected those activities that were clearly non-core ; property service, catering, equipment maintenance, security, logistics. The next, intermediate, phase is to look at outsourcing information processing.

But there is more to come, says Sir Clive. 'The initial driver was *cost saving*; the next driver will focus more on *turning fixed costs into variable ones*. The next phase of outsourcing will happen as companies start considering what their *real* competitive advantage is - the core competence that differentiates them in the market. They may then outsource and thereby concentrate on what they consider to be their core competence. Perhaps general management of purchased resources. This would then give cost flexibility which is a huge advantage with variable volume'.

But for outsourcing to bite that deeply, companies must have enormous faith in the quality and consistency of their suppliers. 'This can only happen where the relationship between the company and the support company is based on credibility, integrity and long-term relationships' says Sir Clive.

CBI News, March 1997

4.11 The tendency to increased outsourcing is identified in the above extract leads to the concept of the 'virtual company' which owns very few tangible assets and employs very few people. Instead, it contracts out nearly all its activities and leases any assets which it needs. This works very well when the company's core competence is in fact its entrepreneurial and managerial ability.

5 WHEN TO USE OUTSIDE RESOURCES

5.1 A simple rule is to use outside resources when they can provide either of two things.

- Better service at an equivalent cost

7: Relationships with customers and suppliers

- Equivalent standard at a lower cost

5.2 The answer is, however, not usually as simple as this. Cost benefit analysis might imply outsourcing involves a degree of risk.

- The costs and benefits may not be as predicted.
- The outsourced service may be unsatisfactory in quality.
- The service provider may cease to trade, leaving a dangerous void.
- The service provider may betray trade secrets, undermining competitive advantage.

5.3 Sometimes organisations use outside resources such as design agencies in order to **gain new ideas and to avoid over-introspectiveness**. When deciding whether to develop and launch a new product, companies find it useful to seek a marketing research agency which will not only be more efficient in conducting surveys but also perhaps more objective. The cost of failure in launching new products is not only the loss of the investment itself but also the risk of loss of goodwill and trust in the market place.

5.4 Employing **advertising agencies** not only gives access to their expertise but may also improve the finances of a media campaign because of the commission which the media pay to bona fide agents only.

5.5 **The use of outside resources can add a great deal of flexibility to an organisation**. It reduces the need for investment and offers the possibility of greater profits.

5.6 Outsourcing also reduces the strain on the organisation's **limited human resources** and frees marketing management to concentrate on the more important strategic rather than tactical aspects of its marketing plans.

Action Programme 1

What are the main advantages of outsourcing?

---

6 COMPETITIVE TENDERING

Exam Tip
A question specifically about tendering was asked in June 1997. It asked you for some guidelines for a firm seeking to tender for local government contracts.
The topic could be examined from the opposite perspective, from a firm *receiving* competitive tenders, for example, from advertisers and market research consultants, if it wishes to outsource some of its activities.

The tradition of tendering

6.1 Traditionally, public authorities have attempted to ensure fairness in the process of obtaining bids by advertising publicly for tenders, and **allowing anyone who wishes to do so to submit an offer**. This method is very often employed, even when major constructional works are involved. The practice has been **strongly criticised**, however, for contracts of any magnitude, or for those in which special technical expertise is involved. **Often the low bidder is a firm which has neither the necessary financial backup, nor the technical know-how necessary**. The client finds that the firm selected is third-rate, while firms with

Part C: Managing marketing relationships

greater strengths are put off from bidding by the length of the tender list and the fear that their prices would almost certainly be undercut.

Selective tendering

6.2 **Selective tendering** means that only some firms are invited to bid. The difficulty which clients face is the way in which to make that selection in order to obtain a satisfactory completion of the job, while guaranteeing the fairness and appropriateness of the process of tendering. The aim is to achieve a balance between the price paid and the quality of the job. Two main methods are involved.

- Approved lists
- Pre-qualification

Approved lists

6.3 There are two ways of operating an **approved list.**

(a) Public advertising of the work with a statement that **bidding is restricted** to those already on the approved list for that category and value of work.

(b) **Invitations to bid** to firms already on the approved list, seeking to meet criteria of fairness and impartiality. This system inevitably causes difficulties and resentments because of the balances which have to be struck between fairness, efficiency and expediency. Only good judgement and diplomatic skills can resolve these problems.

6.4 **EU guidelines** state that in relation to **public works contracts**, all companies in any one of the EU countries should have the right to participate wherever in the EU these may be located. Evidence suggests that these guidelines are largely ineffectual, thanks to the forces which operate to favour local companies and distort the pre-qualification process. However, the legal requirement to advertise such contracts is still followed.

6.5 **International lending agencies** (ILA) such as the World Bank usually underwrite very large scale contracts, **but the bidder's contract is with the borrower, not the lending agency** itself. Preparing a tender, however, involves familiarity with the procurement **guidelines** which such agencies operate, since they will directly affect the terms under which the borrower contracts. These will typically include two important considerations.

(a) Agencies will wish to see due regard for **economy** and **efficiency** in the use of their loans

(b) Agencies are likely to require that **pre-qualification should be based entirely on the ability of firms to perform the particular work**. This should be assessed objectively using clear criteria.

- Experience and past performance
- Capabilities with respect to personnel and equipment
- Financial resources

6.6 Since the ILA guidelines require non-price factors such as time of completion, to be taken into account, specified in enquiry documents and expressed in monetary terms, the **lowest evaluated bid may well not be the lowest price bid.**

6.7 Guidelines on **bid price strategy** argue that the opening of bids should be public, and that no bidder shall be allowed to alter his bid after the first bid has been opened. The client may ask any bidder for clarification but should not ask any bidder to change the substance

7: Relationships with customers and suppliers

or price of his bid. **In many commercial situations, the reverse of these guidelines is followed.**

Pre-qualification

6.8 In order to tender, bidders may have to answer a questionnaire and provide extensive information.

- Previous experience
- Organisational structure, showing details of the operation, and its personnel
- Lists of facilities
- Accounts which illustrate financial health
- Names and histories of key personnel
- Project control and quality assurance methods
- Sub-contractors pre-qualification criteria

Emphasis varies widely and bidders will normally wish to address the potential client's particular concerns.

Evaluation

6.9 Evaluation of bids is normally formal and based on the following sorts of main heading criteria, each of which would be broken down into more detailed sub-criteria and **scored on a weighted basis**.

- **Reliability** (eg reputation, performance, finance)
- **Technical capacity** (eg equipment, expertise)
- **Managerial capability** (eg track record, staff qualifications, control mechanisms)
- **Project capability** (eg work schedules, sub-contracts, safety, standards)
- **Project experience** (eg similar projects successfully conducted)

Marketing at Work

Wang UK

In October 1994, Wang UK, the software and service company, won a key contract to become one of two service providers in the UK, and subsequently internationally, to computer systems giant Dell. Dell sells computer systems direct, so it relies on external partners for the service element which is so critical to its business reputation. The contract Wang won was worth £2 million a year, and is growing year on year by 20 to 30 per cent.

Dell was seeking a partner with European and international capability in order to build its business internationally and to provide continuity of service around Europe and beyond - in Australia, Mexico and North America. Also crucial was the ability of a potential partner to expand service offerings beyond simple warranty repair - network support, for example. Service is increasingly the area where value-added lies in the industry, and Dell had a clear idea of the range it wanted to offer.

Dell's first informal 'hands-off' evaluation of Wang would have focused on what it already knew about the supplier's references and the world market place. Bidders who can establish their 'referenceability' at this stage can move quickly to the front of the customer's consideration.

Stage two was the formal evaluation, when Dell moved a team into Wang's London headquarters in Isleworth to work with the Wang bid team and to look at all aspects of its organisation - technical skills, training, quality processes, geographic distribution and logistical capability. Only when it was satisfied that Wang could do the job did the process move to stage three: pricing the different areas of service required.

Chris Norton, Dell's customer services director for the UK, confirms that price was only one element in the decision to choose Wang. Other questions were:

- Cultural fit: could the organisations work together?

- Did Wang have the experience and credibility to undertake the work?
- Did Wang have the flexibility and ability to adapt and move as the business needs to be moved? Could Wang grow with Dell?

'In all three of these Wang scored highly, making price an important but secondary issue' says Norton.

Marketing Business, March 1997

7 MANAGEMENT OF EXTERNAL SUPPLIERS 12/99

7.1 Services upon which organisations depend to function properly must be well managed, so that the outside suppliers who are called upon to carry out these tasks are a key aspect of the overall functioning of the organisation.

Briefing

7.2 **Good briefing ensures good working relationships**. Bad briefing will lead to misunderstandings between client and supplier to the detriment of the ultimate customer. In the event of a dispute, a full brief will leave less room for doubt as to the requirements of the contract. There must be basic ground rules for briefing outside suppliers.

- To what extent do we take outside suppliers into our confidence?
- What do they need to know?
- Who will draw up the briefs?
- How often should the brief be reviewed?

Management of externally sourced factors

Control and review

7.3 Direct supervision of externally sourced staff and equipment will normally be the responsibility of the contractor, but the hiring company must maintain its own management input into the relationship. Costs, benefits and risks must be considered during the life of the contract as well as before it is let. **The company must be clear about what it wants to achieve from outsourcing and set quantifiable standards against which the contractor's performance can be reviewed.**

7.4 One or more managers should be charged with oversight of every important aspect of every contract. These managers should also maintain communication with the contractors and promote good relations between the parties. If performance is unsatisfactory, the contractor must be informed direct rather than via the operational staff so that effective corrective action is taken. If there is no improvement, the contractor cannot then complain that he did not know of the problem.

7.5 **Costs, risks and performance should be reviewed regularly** and the results reported to the senior managers responsible for outsourcing policy. A framework for review is given below (paragraph 7.9). The supervising manager should be particularly alert to developments which may affect the relationship, such as new legislation and changes in labour relations. For instance, the recent minimum wage legislation will undoubtedly affect the profitability of many contractors, and some will be tempted to evade it. No company conscious of its image would wish to be associated with such evasion.

Marketing at Work

The NHS

The privatising of public utilities within the UK provides a useful illustration of one of the dangers involved in working with external suppliers. The major managerial problems associated with management of, for example, the National Health Service has led to massive increases in the number of managers employed by the new 'Hospital Trusts', coupled with a reclassification and redeployment of health services. Yet, as a recent report revealed, there was also huge expenditure on the employment of management consultants in order to make recommendations concerning the most efficient deployment of the new management within the organisation.

Given the large scale of outsourcing, the newly developed structures, and a remit to develop efficient and competitive units based on competition within internal markets, this might seem like a logical move. However, a report suggested that there were a number of mistakes involved.

(a) Consultants were not briefed adequately. Too often, consultants would be called into 'fix' an organisation without real guidance as to the areas which needed to be addressed, and without any limits on the scope of the problem with which they were involved. As a consequence, the reports they produced were often inappropriate, unrealistic or ineffective.

(b) Consultants were given too much power. Managers employing consultants in these circumstances were inclined to delegate too wide a range of decisions to them.

(c) Public perceptions were not considered sufficiently.

7.6 **One of the main potential problems is lack of response to client input.** There are some mechanisms, such as staged payments and incentive structure, which attempt to address this issue by making the outsourced function responsible for meeting particular targets, and holding back payment. There is a tendency for this to be seen as somewhat excessive attention in smaller contracts, and there is a feeling that this is a somewhat draconian response if applied too insensitively. Control rests, ultimately, upon the market power of the client, and on the quality of the management control system operated within the client organisation.

7.7 Control might be applied selectively. Should a supplier who involves small or spasmodic expenditure be subjected to the same degree of control as a supplier the organisation uses regularly or extensively? The answer cannot depend on expenditure alone. The organisation could, for example, be making a relatively small spend with an agency on concept testing a proposed new product. However, this proposed new product could be vital to the organisation's future and therefore the agency could require stricter control than a dependable supplier of raw materials.

7.8 The nature of the control should perhaps be different **according to the nature of the product or service being bought**. For raw material suppliers, an organisation might have scientific tests on quality and maintain records of deliveries late/on time/before time. However, for an advertising agency, control might be more informal and based on frequent personal meetings.

7.9 **A framework for review**

- Supplier's name, address, telephone number
- Names and positions of contacts
- Description of types of goods and services supplied
- Total annual spend for last three years
- Splits of annual spends by types of product/service where relevant
- Number of years we have been trading with this supplier
- Perceived strengths and weaknesses of supplier
- Record of improvements made by supplier during trading period

Part C: Managing marketing relationships

- Record of growth of supplier: turnover, staff, number of branches
- List of alternative suppliers
- Perceived strengths and weaknesses of top three alternative suppliers
- Date of last review of this supplier
- Name/position of person conducting this last review
- Recommended date of next review

> **Exam Tip**
>
> Outside suppliers were examined in June 1996 in a general question concerning a company wishing to expand into new product areas. You had to prepare a brief to show how outside suppliers could be briefed and controlled. You could choose any industry you liked – a good opportunity to exploit your knowledge of your own company in this respect. Sections 1, 4 and 5 of this chapter would have helped you with this question.

Chapter Roundup

- Customers are stakeholders. This means that they should be valued and not taken for granted. They differ in their characteristics and can be analysed or segmented to increase profitability.

- Intermediaries such as agents and franchisees are also customers. They have their own different needs which must be considered.

- Customer retention is an important contribution to profitability since each customer can represent a lifetime's cash flow and creating a new customer requires far more promotional and administrative effort than retaining an existing one. The vital factor in customer retention is the skill and approach of the front-line staff.

- Relationship marketing is more than customer retention. It is the fostering of a mutually beneficial relationship by precision in meeting the needs of individual customers. It uses powerful computer database systems.

- Customers can be analysed for their value to the business. Key account management allows the most valuable customers to be given an enhanced service.

- Internal marketing has a range of meanings but the most useful relates to the promotion of a high level of customer awareness throughout the organisation using marketing communication techniques to change culture and deliver training.

- Almost any activity can be outsourced. Typical areas for outsourcing activities are manufacture, distribution, finance and marketing. Marketing activities which can be outsourced include consultancy, marketing research, promotion and 'full service'.

- As a general rule, the use of outside resources can be considered whenever external suppliers can provide better services at the same cost or equivalent services at a lower cost.

- Many contracts involve a process of tendering especially where contracts are awarded by public/state authorities, but is also of value in the private sector. Sometimes there is a prequalification stage.

- Good briefing provides a solid foundation for a successful working relationship.

- An organisation using outside resources must ensure that it puts mechanisms for control and review of external suppliers in place.

7: Relationships with customers and suppliers

> **Quick Quiz**
> 1. Give two examples of intermediaries (see para 2.3)
> 2. Why is customer retention important? (2.4)
> 3. What is relationship marketing? (2.8 and Key Concept)
> 4. What other management discipline makes a major contribution to internal marketing? (3.5)
> 5. Give four types of marketing resources which can be resourced externally. (4.5 – 4.9)
> 6. Why is outsourcing risky? (5.2)
> 7. How can an approved list system of competitive tendering be operated? (6.3)
> 8. How should outsourcing be controlled? (7.3 – 7.9)

Action Programme Review

1. (a) Cost savings

    (b) Specialism of the company

    (c) Accountability is tied to specific performance

    (d) Introduction of desirable outside qualities such as imagination and fresh ideas into particular sorts of activities

Now try illustrative question 12 at the end of the Study Text

8 Relationships with the Wider Public and Society

Chapter Topic List	Syllabus reference
1 Setting the scene	-
2 Ethics and social responsibility	3.4
3 Ethical codes	3.4
4 Social responsibility	3.4
5 Consumer and community issues	3.4
6 Green issues	3.4
7 Strategies for social responsibility	3.4

Learning Outcome

Students will be able to demonstrate the adaptation of marketing operations principles in a variety of contexts.

Key Concept Introduced

- Ethical issue

Examples of Marketing at Work

- Pampers Care Mats
- Ethics and the 4Ps
- Social responsibility
- Cause-related marketing
- Product contamination
- Green marketing

1 SETTING THE SCENE

1.1 In this chapter we focus on an area which is of increasing significance to marketers in the UK and in many other countries: the importance of marketing ethics and social responsibility. A lack of ethics can affect customer service and customer loyalty, both of which are central to successful marketing. In the second half of the chapter, we will develop the themes of social responsibility and the 'green' issue.

2 ETHICS AND SOCIAL RESPONSIBILITY 6/97, 6/98, 6/99

> **Exam Tip**
> Social responsibility is a regular question topic, having appeared in June 1999 in Part B, in the case study in December 1998 and in June 1998 in Part B. The December 1998 case study was, in fact, built around the concept of ethical trading.

2.1 **Social responsibility** requires that organisations will not act in a way which harms the general public or which is thought to be socially irresponsible. **Marketing ethics** relate to morality rather than society's interests. Morality is about right and wrong. Marketing ethics affect customers rather than society at large. Marketing ethics concern marketing decisions whereas social responsibility is about corporate decisions. It is because corporate decisions subsume marketing decisions that the **terms marketing ethics and social responsibility are often used interchangeably.**

The well-being of individuals and society

2.2 Critics of marketing argue that it is dedicated to selling products which are potentially damaging to the health and well-being of the **individual** or the **society** in which consumers live. Examples include tobacco, alcohol, automobiles, detergents and even electronic goods such as computers and video recorders. It has been argued that even seemingly beneficial, or at least harmless, products, such as soft drinks, sunglasses or agricultural fertiliser, can damage individuals and societies. In traditional societies, new products can disrupt social order by introducing new aspirations, or changing a long established way of life.

Marketing at Work

Pampers Care Mats

Proctor & Gamble has been forced to make an embarrassing U-turn on a newly-launched infant product, after fears were raised that it could suffocate young babies.

Pampers Care Mats, disposable mats on which infants can be placed while changing their nappies or to protect toddlers against bed-wetting, were launched last September. But P&G has been forced to put stickers on the packaging warning parents that they should not be used in cots for babies under 12 months old 'to avoid the risk of suffocation'.

P&G says it had to change the packaging because it had not realised parents would use the Care Mats in cots with young babies.

A spokeswoman says: 'We like to make sure our products are as safe as possible, which is why we stickered (the warning) as soon as we realised people were using them for cots.'

Marketing Week, 27 January 2000

2.3 How should the marketer react to these problems? There appears to be a clear conflict; what is profitable for a business organisation may well not be in the interest of the customer, or the society within which the transaction is taking place.

2.4 Ethics are the moral principles and values which guide thinking, decision making and action. It is to our ethical framework that we must turn when making decisions which involve moral dilemmas.

Part C: Managing marketing relationships

Ethics and the law

2.5 Ethics deal with personal moral principles and values, but laws are the rules that can actually be enforced in court. However, behaviour which is not subject to legal penalties may still be unethical.

2.6 For example, is it acceptable for the RJ Reynolds Tobacco Company in the USA to target Afro-Americans for a new brand of cigarette, while public health statistics show that this group has a high incidence of lung cancer and smoking related illnesses? The company maintains that this is still within the law but is it ethical?

2.7 We can classify marketing decisions according to ethics and legality in four different ways.

Marketing decisions according to legality and ethical status

Ethical but illegal	Ethical and legal
Unethical and illegal	Unethical but legal

A business may be operated on principles which are:

- **Ethical and legal** (eg the Body Shop)
- **Unethical and legal** (eg 'gazumping')
- **Ethical but illegal** (eg publishing stolen but revealing documents about government mismanagement)
- **Unethical and illegal** (eg employing child labour)

2.8 Surveys in both the UK and the USA show that the public think that business has poor ethical standards, and levels of trust are low. In the USA, 90% of respondents in a recent survey thought that white collar crime was 'very common', and more than three-quarters of the sample saw tumbling business standards as an important contributor to declining moral standards within society as a whole.

2.9 Different cultures view marketing practices differently. While the idea of **intellectual property** is widely accepted in Europe and the USA, in other parts of the world, ethical standards are quite different. Unauthorised use of copyrights, trademarks and patents is widespread in countries such as Taiwan, Mexico and Korea. According to a US trade official, the Korean view is that ' ... the thoughts of one man should benefit all', and this general value means that, in spite of legal formalities, few infringements of copyright are punished.

> **Key Concept**
> An **ethical issue** in marketing can be defined as an identifiable problem, situation or opportunity requiring an individual or organisation to choose from among several actions that must be evaluated as ethical or unethical.

Marketing at Work

Ethics and the 4Ps

(a) *Product issues.* When the French company Perrier discovered that its mineral water was in danger of contamination, they immediately withdrew all supplies, suffering huge losses. By acting ethically, the company's reputation was enhanced. Coca Cola dithered, played down the issue, denied liability and suffered a huge blow to its image.

8: Relationships with the wider public and society

(b) *Promotional issues.* It was because so many companies were acting unethically with regard to marketing communications that the Trade Descriptions Act 1968 came into being. However, the 'angle' on communications can be more subtle, such as the Spiller's Homepride Flour slogan 'Finer grains make finer flour'. The advertisements gave the impression that the flour was made from smaller grains whereas the grains were actually made larger by a process of coagulation. Upon challenge, Spillers claimed they were using the word 'finer' in the dictionary sense of being better.

Many think that persuading people to buy something they don't really want is intrinsically unethical, especially if hard sell tactics are used, or downright deception.

(c) *Distribution issues.* Some manufacturers have refused to supply retailers who do not carry out their bidding or as a means of manipulating the market.

(d) *Pricing issues. Knowing* collusion to fix prices is illegal. However, market forces tend to equalise prices and price leadership in oligopolistic markets is accepted.

3 ETHICAL CODES

3.1 **It is now common for businesses to specify their ethical standards. Some have even published a formal declaration of their principles and rules of conduct.** This would typically cover payments to government officials or political parties, relations with customers or suppliers, conflicts of interest, and accuracy of records. The Boeing Corporation has published such a code since 1964. Yet in 1990, it was charged with using inside information to win a US government contract and fined $5.2m.

3.2 Ethical standards may cause individuals to act against the organisation of which they are a part. More often, **business people are likely to adhere to moral principles which are 'utilitarian', weighing the costs and benefits of the consequences of behaviour. When benefits exceed costs, the behaviour can be said to be ethical.** This the philosophical position upon which capitalism rests, and is often cited to justify behaviour which appears to have socially unpleasant consequences. For example, food production regimes which appear inhumane are often justified by the claim that they produce cheaper food for the majority of the population.

3.3 The American Marketing Association has produced a statement of the code of ethics to which it expects members to adhere.

Code of Ethics

Members of the American Marketing Association (AMA) are committed to ethical professional conduct. They have joined together in subscribing to this Code of Ethics embracing the following topics.

Responsibilities of the Marketer

Marketers must accept responsibility for the consequence of their activities and make every effort to ensure that their decisions, recommendations, and actions function to identify, serve, and satisfy all relevant publics: customers, organisations and society.

Marketers' professional conduct must be guided by

1. The basic rule of professional ethics: not knowingly to do harm.
2. The adherence to all applicable laws and regulations.
3. The accurate representation of their education, training and experience.
4. The active support, practice and promotion of this Code of Ethics.

Honesty and Fairness

Marketers shall uphold and advance the integrity, honor and dignity of the marketing profession

1. Being honest in serving consumers, clients, employees, suppliers, distributors and the public.
2. Not knowingly participating in conflict of interest without prior notice to all parties involved.

Part C: Managing marketing relationships

3 Establishing equitable fee schedules including the payment or receipt of usual, customary and/or legal compensation or marketing exchanges.

Rights and Duties of Parties in the Marketing Exchange Process

Participants in the marketing exchange process should be able to expect

1 Products and services offered are safe and fit for their intended uses.

2 Communications about offered products and services are not deceptive.

3 All parties intend to discharge their obligations, financial and otherwise, in good faith.

4 Appropriate internal methods exist for equitable adjustment and/or redress of grievances concerning purchases.

It is understood that the above would include, *but is not limited to*, the following responsibilities of the marketer.

In the area of product development and management

- Disclosure of all substantial risks associated with product or service usage.
- Identification of any product component substitution that might materially change the product or impact on the buyer's purchase decision.
- Identification of extra-cost added features.

In the area of promotions

- Avoidance of false and misleading advertising.
- Rejection of high pressure manipulation, or misleading sales tactics.
- Avoidance of sales promotions that use deception or manipulation

In the area of distribution

- Not manipulating the availability of a product for purpose of exploitation.
- Not using coercion in the marketing channel.
- Not exerting undue influence over the resellers choice to handle the product.

In the area of pricing

- Not engaging in price fixing.
- Not practising predatory pricing.
- Disclosing the full price associated with any purchase

In the area of marketing research

- Prohibiting selling or fund raising under the guise of conducting research.
- Maintaining research integrity by avoiding misrepresentation and omission of pertinent research data.
- Treating outside clients and suppliers fairly.

Organisational relationships

Marketers should be aware of how their behaviour may influence or impact on the behaviour of others in organisational relationships. They should not demand, encourage or apply coercion to obtain unethical behaviour in their relationships with others, such as employees, suppliers or customers.

1 Apply confidentiality and anonymity in professional relationships with regard to privileged information.

2 Meet their obligations and responsibilities in contracts and mutual agreements in a timely manner.

3 Avoid taking the work of others, in whole, or in part, and represent this work as their own or directly benefit from it without compensation or consent of the originator or owner.

4 Avoid manipulation to take advantage of situations to maximise personal welfare in a way that unfairly deprives or damages the organisation or others.

Any AMA members found to be in violation of any provision of this Code of Ethics may have his or her Association membership suspended or revoked.

(Reprinted by permission of *The American Marketing Association*)

3.4 The CIM's code is as follows. How do you think it compares to the AMA's?

(a) A member shall at all times conduct himself with integrity in such a way as to bring credit to the profession of marketing and The Chartered Institute of Marketing.

(b) A member shall not by unfair or unprofessional practice injure the business, reputation or interest of any other member of the Institute.

(c) Members shall, at all times, act honestly in their professional dealings with customers and clients (actual and potential), employers and employees.

(d) A member shall not, knowingly or recklessly, disseminate any false or misleading information, either on his own behalf or on behalf of anyone else.

(e) A member shall keep abreast of current marketing practice and act competently and diligently and be encouraged to register for the Institute's scheme of Continuing Professional Development.

(f) A member shall, at all times, seek to avoid conflicts of interest and shall make prior voluntary and full disclosure to all parties concerned of all matters that may arise during any such conflict. Where a conflict arises a member must withdraw prior to the work commencing.

(g) A member shall keep business information confidential except from those persons entitled to receive it, where it breaches this code and where it is illegal to do so.

(h) A member shall promote and seek business in a professional and ethical manner.

(i) A member shall observe the requirements of all other codes of practice which may from time to time have any relevance to the practice of marketing insofar as such requirements do not conflict with any provisions of this code, or the Institute's Royal Charter and Bye-laws; a list of such codes being obtainable from the Institute's head office.

(j) Members shall not hold themselves out as having the Institute's endorsement in connection with an activity unless the Institute's prior written approval has been obtained first.

(k) A member shall not use any funds derived from the Institute for any purpose which does not fall within the powers and obligations contained in the Branch or Group handbook, and which does not fully comply with this code.

4 SOCIAL RESPONSIBILITY

4.1 **There is a growing feeling that the concerns of the community ought to be the concerns of business since businesses exist within society, and depend on it for continued existence. Business therefore has a moral obligation to assist in the solution of those problems which it causes.** Businesses and businessmen are also socially prominent, and must be seen to be taking a lead in addressing the problems of society. Enlightened self-interest is probably beneficial to business. **In the long term, concern over the damage which may result from business activity will safeguard the interests of the business itself.** In the short term, responsibility is a very valuable addition to the public relations activities within a company. As pressure for legislation grows, self-regulation can take the heat out of potentially disadvantageous campaigns.

4.2 Recent studies in the US have shown that between 25% and 40% of the financial community take a company's record in social responsibility into account when making investment decisions. Research in the UK suggests that, by 1993, the corresponding figure was around

Part C: Managing marketing relationships

10%, and rising. More and more, it is being realised that it is necessary for organisations to develop a sense of responsibility for the consequences of their actions within society at large, rather than simply setting out to provide consumer satisfactions. **Social responsibility involves accepting that the organisation is part of society and, as such, will be accountable to that society for the consequences of the actions which it takes.** Three concepts of social responsibility are **profit responsibility, stakeholder responsibility** and **societal responsibility**.

Profit responsibility

4.3 **Profit responsibility** argues that companies exist to maximise profits for their proprietors. Milton Friedman asserts:

> 'There is one and only one social responsibility of business: to use its resources and engage in activities designed to increase its profits so long as it stays within the rules of the game - which is to say, engages in open and free competition without deception or fraud.'

4.4 Thus, drug companies which retain sole rights to the manufacture of treatments for dangerous diseases, are obeying this principle. The argument is that intervention, to provide products at affordable prices, will undermine the motivation of poorer groups to be self-sufficient, or to improve their lot. Proponents of this view argue that unless the market is allowed to exercise its disciplines, groups who are artificially cushioned will become victims of 'dependency culture', with far worse consequences for society at large.

Stakeholder responsibility

4.5 **Stakeholder responsibility** arises from criticisms of profit responsibility, concentrating on the **obligations of the organisation to those who can affect achievement of its objectives**, for example, customers, employees, suppliers and distributors.

Marketing at Work

Social responsibility

In a new pamphlet for the Foreign Policy centre (patron: Tony Blair, the prime minister; president: Robin Cook, the foreign secretary), corporate identity expert Wally Olins argues that companies are failing to keep up with the changing demands of perception as the distinction between nations and companies becomes blurred. As companies take on many functions vacated by a retreating nation state, they must increasingly behave like countries if they are to legitimise themselves.

Corporate power on the scale of today is unprecedented, Mr Olins says. One man, Bill Gates, has more money than 135 of the United Nations' 185 members; Ford Motor Company has a greater global sales total than the combined gross domestic products of Greece, Ireland and Luxembourg. Consequently, companies must blend their public image with the governments whose wealth and power they dwarf. They must be accountable not just to shareholders, but to consumers and employees.

'Slogans like shareholder value are simply not good enough any more,' says Mr Olins. 'It is now incumbent upon companies to modulate their behaviour to recognise that economic value is insufficient. Consumers have enormous power. They will buy from organisations that match their expectations in both behaviour and product and will be able to destroy those that don't.'

Financial Times, 3 December 1999

Societal responsibility

4.6 **Societal responsibility** focuses on the responsibilities of the organisation **towards the general public**. In particular, this includes a responsible approach to environmental issues and concerns about employment. A socially responsible posture can be promoted by **cause**

related marketing, when charitable contributions are tied directly to the revenues from one of its products. An example is Procter and Gamble's support for the Special Olympics when particular products are purchased.

Marketing at Work

Cause-related marketing

Charities face a constant struggle to get both corporations and the general public to support their cause, which many say has grown worse since the launch of the National Lottery.

Generally, individual giving in this country has ground to a halt. Levels of giving are not falling, but we are not getting any more generous. But it's not all bad news. Corporate Britain is becoming increasingly generous.

The nature of corporate giving has changed, however. Corporate donations used to be made on a purely philanthropic basis. Today, that philanthropy has been finely tuned to ensure the giver is able to bask in the glow of is own generosity – it's called **cause-related marketing.**

But, says Barnardo's director of marketing and communications Andrew Nebel, this is no bad thing.

'It used to be that the target of a company's philanthropy was the choice of the chairman's wife. Now the selection of a charity is analysed carefully, which means the links, when they are made, are much stronger.

'It also enable charities to get access to larger budgets from, for example, companies' marketing departments or staff incentive schemes,' says Nebel.

Marketing Week, 16 December 1999

The social audit

4.7 Socially responsible ideas may be converted into actions through plans developed in the course of a social audit. Companies develop, implement and evaluate their social responsibility through a social audit, which assesses their objectives, strategies and performance in terms of this dimension. Marketing and social responsibility programmes may be integrated.

Action Programme 1

What do you think a social audit might involve?

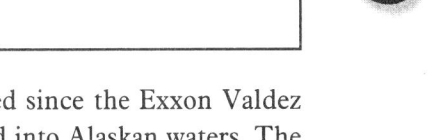

4.8 In the USA, social audits on environmental issues have increased since the Exxon Valdez catastrophe in which millions of gallons of crude oil were released into Alaskan waters. The **Valdez principles** were drafted by the Coalition for Environmentally Responsible Economics to focus attention on environmental concerns and corporate responsibility. They encourage companies to behave responsibly towards the environment.

- Eliminate pollutants, minimise hazardous wastes and conserve non-renewable resources

- Market environmentally safe products and services

- Prepare for accidents and restore damaged environments

- Provide protection for employees who report environmental hazards

- Appoint an environmentalist to their board of directors, name an executive for environmental affairs, and develop an environmental audit of their global operations, which is to be made publicly available

Part C: Managing marketing relationships

5 CONSUMER AND COMMUNITY ISSUES

5.1 The consumer movement can be defined as a collection of organisations, pressure groups and individuals who **seek to protect and extend the rights of consumers**. The movement originated in a realisation that **the increasing sophistication of products meant that the individual's own judgement was no longer adequate to defend against inappropriate marketing**.

5.2 The main consumer protection body is the **Office of Fair Trading**. The Director of Fair Trading has a number of roles.

- To promote competition
- To encourage the adoption of codes of practice
- To curb anti-competitive practices
- To issue licences under the Consumer Credit Act
- To administer the Estate Agents Act

5.3 As well as government bodies, there are voluntary associations. Chief of these in the UK is the **Consumers' Association** (CA).

(a) *Which?* magazine is published by the CA every month. It contains detailed reviews of products and services. Each product review features detailed breakdowns of the performance of competing products in a number of tests. Whilst readership of *Which?* magazine is limited, its findings are widely reported in the media.

(b) The CA provides its members with **legal advice**, even acting on members' behalf in some cases, against malpractice or poor service.

(c) **The CA also lobbies Parliament and ministers** on matters such as product safety, labelling, advertising honesty and so forth.

5.4 There are a number of other organisations and groups representing consumer interests.

- National Consumer Council (a government sponsored body)
- National Federation of Consumer Groups
- National Association of Citizen's Advice Bureaux

5.5 Some industries have panels of individuals appointed to represent the consumer interests. This is particularly true of utilities. There are consumer groups representing users of Railtrack services and London Underground for example.

5.6 **Consumer protection legislation**

- Trade Descriptions Act 1968
- Fair Trading Act 1973
- Unfair Contract Terms Act 1977
- Food Act 1984
- Weights and Measures Act 1985
- Consumer Protection Act 1987

Marketing at work

Product contamination

In 1982, the US healthcare products group Johnson & Johnson wrote the book on crisis management with its deft handling of the poisoned Tylenol affair. This week, Coca-Cola appeared to be tearing the book up in its response to an unfolding fiasco in Europe over sales of tainted Coke.

8: Relationships with the wider public and society

The partial withdrawal of Coca-Cola products from four European countries is likely to set the record for the biggest product recall yet by a packaged goods manufacturer. But a much greater cost could arise from the damage done to Cola-Cola's brand, meticulously managed over the past 113 years.

On Tuesday, the world's biggest soft drinks maker acknowledged that Coca-Cola products going mainly into the Belgian market had been tainted in two separate incidents. One involved the accidental injection of 'defective' carbon dioxide gas into some cola. In the other, the outside of soft drink cans was contaminated by a fungicide used to treat wooden shipping pallets.

But the admission came only after Coca-Cola had spent most of the preceding week assuring consumers that its products were safe. It made that claim as dozens of Belgian children were being taken to hospital, complaining of stomach cramps, vomiting and dizziness after drinking Coca-Cola products.

So far there have been no confirmed reports of any serious illnesses directly attributable to Coca-Cola's products, and Coca-Cola says no health or safety issues have been identified. But its proposed solution to the problem fell far short of what the authorities demanded.

Coca-Cola's plan was for a targeted withdrawal of the affected products. Instead, by yesterday, sales of nearly all Coca-Cola's canned and bottled products had been banned by the governments of Belgium and Luxembourg. And in France, where only the affected products were banned, some retail chains such as Carrefour removed all Coca-Cola products from their shelves rather than risk confusion.

Coca-Cola also earned hostile headlines in much of northern Europe. In the countries affected, it became the butt of cartoon jokes - such as one showing its trade-mark polar bear writhing in pain, and another changing its name to 'Coca-Colic'.

In terms of the textbook method of dealing with crises such as these, Coca-Cola seems to have broken nearly all the basic rules. One is to act quickly to recall the affected products. Another is to be open with consumers about what went wrong, and a third is to show contrition.

The textbook was devised by Johnson & Johnson 17 years ago. It acted after an extortionist tried to wring money out of the company by lacing capsules of its Tylenol painkiller with cyanide, and seven people died.

While the government was still considering what to do, and before the media had time to put the company on the defensive, Johnson & Johnson recalled all Tylenol products. That cost about $100m and it lost short-term sales. But it emerged from the episode with consumer confidence at a higher level than ever, and quickly regained its leadership of the painkiller market.

Financial Times, 17 June 1999

Community issues

5.7 Marketers and organisations are members of a community which expects them to contribute to its well-being. Areas which the marketer might consider as suitable for supporting community growth and increasing community satisfaction include education, the arts and disadvantaged groups. The organisation also has a responsibility towards its own employees which is recognised by modern employment protection legislation and health and safety regulations.

5.8 **Recognition of community issues can also have a long-term benefit for the organisation. It can generate goodwill and publicity and perhaps affect the attitudes of potential customers.**

6   GREEN ISSUES   12/97

6.1 **Public awareness of the connections between industrial production, mass consumption and environmental damage is higher than it has ever been,** with information flooding out through the mass media and sometimes generating profound public reaction. Modern marketing practice, then, needs to reflect awareness of these concerns, and is being changed by the issues that they raise. In particular, **food scares, when badly handled** (as in the case of BSE in the UK), **have caused great damage to primary producers and retailers.** When handled well (as, for instance, in the scare over the mineral water Perrier - see above), little

Part C: Managing marketing relationships

damage to sales is caused, and the company or industry may even emerge with an enhanced reputation.

Green concerns

6.2 The modern Green Movement is animated by concerns over pollution, overpopulation and the effects of massive growth on the finite resources of the earth. A series of ecological disasters, notably at the Union Carbide plant at Bhopal, India; the Chernobyl nuclear reactor in Ukraine; the Exxon-Valdez oil spill in Alaska; and the torching of the Kuwaiti oilfields at the end of the Gulf War highlighted links between business and environmental damage. According to green thinkers, conventional economics has failed to deal with the problems of overproduction. Green economists have tried to put together an **economics based on alternative ideas**.

- Monetary valuation of economic resources
- Promoting the quality of life
- Self reliance
- Mutual aid
- Personal growth
- Human rights

The impact of green issues on marketing practices

6.3 **Environmental impacts on business**

(a) **Direct**

- Changes affecting costs or resource availability
- Impact on demand
- Effect on power balances between competitors in a market

(b) **Indirect**. Examples are pressure from concerned customers or staff and legislation affecting the business environment.

Green pressures on business

6.4 Consumers are demanding a better environmental performance from companies. In recent surveys, it has been demonstrated that around three-quarters of the population are applying environmental criteria in many purchase decisions.

- **Green pressure groups** increased their influence dramatically during the late 1980s. Membership of the largest 13 green groups in the UK grew to over 5 million, with staff of over 1,500.

- **Employees** are increasing pressure on the businesses in which they work, partly for ethical reasons.

- **Legislation** is increasing almost by the day. Growing pressure from the green or green-influenced vote has led to mainstream political parties taking these issues into their programmes.

- **Environmental risk screening** has become increasingly important. Companies in the future will become responsible for the environmental impact of their activities.

6.5 **Sustainability** requires that the company only uses resources at a rate which allows them to be replenished and confines emissions of waste to levels which do not exceed the capacity of the environment to absorb them. **Policies based on sustainability have three aims.**

8: Relationships with the wider public and society

- To pursue equity in the distribution of resources
- To maintain the integrity of the world's ecosystems
- To increase the capacity of human populations for self-reliance

Green marketing

6.6 There are strong reasons for bringing the environment into the business equation. The green consumer is a driving force behind changes in marketing and business practices. In 1990 26% of all new products marketed in the USA were marketed using a green approach. Green consumption can be defined as the decisions related to consumer choice which involve environmentally-related beliefs, values and behaviour. There is extensive evidence that this is of growing importance to business.

- Surveys which indicate increased levels of environmental awareness and concern
- Increasing demand for, and availability of, information on environmental issues
- Value shifts from consumption to conservation
- Effective PR and marketing campaigns by environmental charities and causes

Of course, levels of greenness vary across the population.

Segmenting the green market

6.7 Profiles of green consumers show that the force of green concern varies. Many consumers have not resolved the complex, confusing and often contradictory messages which are being sent out by various interest groups in this area. Broadly, females are more environmentally-aware than males, and families with children are more likely to be concerned about making green consumption choices. The evidence also shows that consumers are becoming both more aware and more sophisticated in their approach.

6.8 Marketing diagnostics has developed a **typology of green consumers which identifies four main groups**.

- **Green activists** (5 - 15% of the population) are members or supporters of environmental organisations.
- **Green thinkers** (30%, including the activists) seek out green products and services, and look for new ways to care for the environment.
- **Green consumer base** (45 - 60%) includes anyone who has changed behaviour in response to green concerns.
- **Generally concerned** (90%) claim to be concerned about green issues.

6.9 A behaviourally-based **psychographic typology** by Ogilvy and Mather involves a range of factors. **Four categories of consumers are identified in terms of tendencies and characteristics going beyond environmental matters.**

(a) **Activists** (16%)

- Aware of the issue
- Likely to buy green products
- Concerned for their children
- Optimistic about technological change
- People oriented
- Home owners with children
- Conservative voters
- Likely to be upmarket consumers

Part C: Managing marketing relationships

  (b) **Realists** (35%)
  - The youngest group - those with young children
  - Worried about the environment
  - Consider profit and environmental protection as conflicting
  - Pessimistic about a solution
  - Sceptical about a 'green bandwagon'
  - Vote Labour

  (c) **Complacents** (28%)
  - Upmarket consumers with older children
  - Optimistic about mankind, business and government
  - Likely to see this as someone else's problem
  - Not very conscious of green issues
  - Right wing politically

  (d) **Alienated** (22%)
  - Less well educated, downmarket consumers
  - Young families or senior citizens
  - Unaware of green issues
  - Likely to see greenness as a fashion or a fad
  - Pessimistic about a solution
  - Left wing politically

6.10 Studies show that consumer behaviour varies in greenness according to the information which is available about the product, the regularity of purchase, the price-sensitivity of the purchase involved, their degree of brand loyalty to existing brands, the availability of substitutes and the credibility of green products.

6.11 **Successful green marketing**

- Understand the environmental issues which are relevant to the company, customer, products and market environment.

- Evaluate the degree to which green product attributes fit consumer needs.

- Develop strategies which identify and effectively meet consumer needs and competitor challenges in relation to green issues.

Marketing planning

6.12 Marketing plans need to be reconsidered in the light of **new environmental priorities**. Certain areas will require redefinition.

- Strategic product/market objectives
- Markets
- Market share, customer satisfaction and competitor comparisons
- Performance and technical aspects of product performance and quality

All of these aspects will have to be fitted within **a view of the company's performance which takes account of environmental responsibilities**. In addition, the traditional criteria for evaluating success or failure, and the parameters within which they operate, may well have to be redrawn.

6.13 **Timescales** also have to be lengthened considerably, since products are now evaluated in terms of their long-term effects, as well as the impact of the processes by means of which

8: Relationships with the wider public and society

they have been produced. Programmes designed to clean up environmental impacts often take a long time to become fully operational.

6.14 Getting marketing's 4Ps right leads to profit, according to orthodox ideas. Green marketing insists that the mix must be evaluated in the terms of **four Ss**.

- **Satisfaction** of customer needs
- **Safety** of products and production for consumers, workers, society and the environment

The Green Marketing Process
(from Ken Peattie, *Green Marketing*)

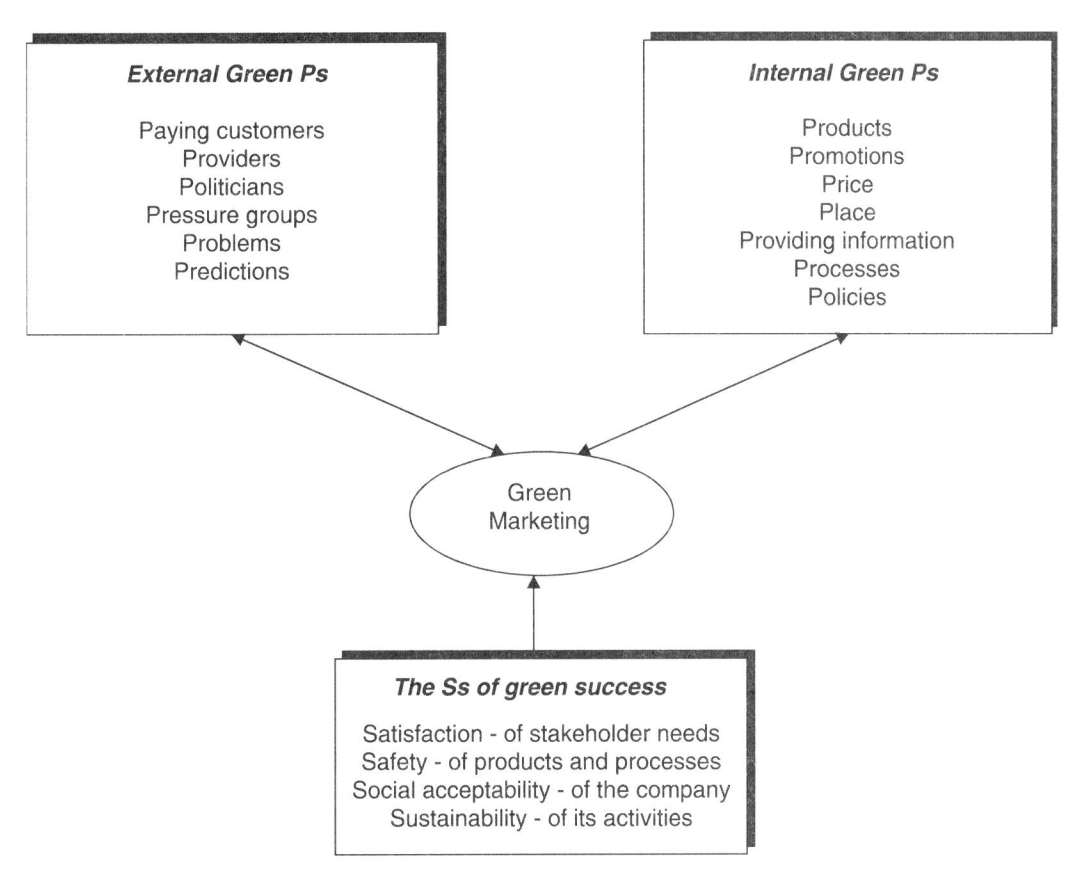

External Green Ps

Paying customers
Providers
Politicians
Pressure groups
Problems
Predictions

Internal Green Ps

Products
Promotions
Price
Place
Providing information
Processes
Policies

Green Marketing

The Ss of green success

Satisfaction - of stakeholder needs
Safety - of products and processes
Social acceptability - of the company
Sustainability - of its activities

- **Social** acceptability of the products, their production and other activities of the company
- **Sustainability** of the products, their production and other activities of the company

Marketing at Work

Green marketing

Being able to predict problems can produce great strategic advantages, but also some odd results. The problem of CFCs from aerosols, and their effects on the ozone layer, was known about from the early 1970s, and Johnson & Johnson abandoned the use of them in their products back in 1976. Consumer reactions to the product began in the late 1980s, and, of course, the firm was well prepared, but found itself in a very strange position, having to attach 'ozone friendly' labels to products which had, in fact, been modified more than ten years before.

This illustrates green marketing problems very well. Action is vital at the time when public *perceptions* threaten a product, rather than the manufacturer simply dealing with the environmental dangers which the product may pose. Green marketing practices will have to deal with more and more of these problems, and the old assumption that these worries are simply a 'moral panic' which will run its course and disappear is surely now revealed as wishful thinking.

Part C: Managing marketing relationships

Nevertheless, resistance to green marketing within many companies is likely to remain strong. It may be necessary for marketers to market ideas internally for these changes. New products, new communications strategies and messages, new 'clean' plant and technology, new appointments of staff skilled in these areas, and very broad changes in organisational culture will all have to be 'sold' to powerful individuals and groups within organisations. Obviously, the internal politics of business organisations need to be taken into account by green practitioners.

Action Programme 2

What are the implications of green issues for services marketing?

6.15 The **not-for-profit (NFP) sector**, since the profit motive has been blamed for generating wasteful and environmentally damaging over-consumption, would seem to be intrinsically greener. Free market enthusiasts argue that not having to make a profit is more likely to promote waste and inefficiency, since the discipline of competition is absent. Even within the NFP sector, there are likely to be varying factors at work, for instance government departments are more likely to feel a responsibility for the environment than smaller organisations.

Action Programme 3

You should, as part of your studies, read a quality daily newspaper so as to keep abreast of current marketing developments. But keep a special look out for articles about marketing and social responsibility. The examiner will be impressed if you are able to give up-to-date examples in your exam.

---

7 STRATEGIES FOR SOCIAL RESPONSIBILITY 6/98

7.1 An organisation can adopt one of **four types of strategy** for dealing with social responsibility issues.

Proactive strategy

7.2 A **proactive strategy** implies taking action before there is any outside pressure to do so and without the need for government or other regulatory intervention. A company which discovers a fault in a product and recalls the product without being forced to, for example, before any injury or damage is caused, acts in a proactive way.

Reactive strategy

7.3 A **reactive strategy** involves allowing a situation to continue unresolved until the public, government or consumer groups find out about it. The company might already know about the problem. When challenged, it will deny responsibility, while at the same time attempting to resolve the problem. In this way, it seeks to minimise any detrimental impact.

Defence strategy

7.4 A **defensive strategy** involves minimising or attempting to avoid additional obligations arising from a particular problem. There are several defence tactics.

- legal manoeuvring
- obtaining support from trade unions
- lobbying government

Accommodation strategy

7.5 An **accommodation strategy** involves taking responsibility for actions, probably when one of the following happens.

(a) Encouragement from special interest groups
(b) Perception that a failure to act will result in government intervention

7.6 It can be seen that **this strategy falls somewhere between a proactive and a reactive strategy**. McDonalds developed a nutrition-centred advertising campaign in an attempt to appease nutritionists and dieticians who were pressing for detailed nutritional information to be provided on fast food packaging. Action before the pressure arose would have been proactive; action after government intervention in response to the pressure would have been reactive.

Chapter Roundup

- Ethics are the moral principles and values which guide the thinking, decision making and actions of individuals and groups within society. Many of the most important ethical values form the basis for legislation which governs business activity in general including marketing. However, while ethics deal with personal moral principles and values, laws express the standards of a society which can actually be enforced in court. Ethics and legality are not necessarily congruent.

- Ethical issues can arise in relation to any of the elements of the marketing mix.

- Some businesses have published ethical codes, specifying the ethical standards to which they adhere and setting out the standards which they expect all their staff to meet. The AMA has also published a *Code of Ethics*.

- In the UK, there is a growing feeling that the concerns of the community ought to be the concerns of business. Social responsibility involves accepting that the organisation is part of society and, as such, will be accountable to that society for the consequences of its actions.

- Three key areas of social responsibility which have implications for marketers are consumer issues, community issues and 'green' issues.

- Green marketing is founded on *responsibility for the community* and *sustainability* - the idea that we must be aware of the need for resources to be marshalled and monitored so that the environment can continue to provide inputs and absorb the products of consumption.

- An organisation can adopt one of a number of different strategies for dealing with social responsibility issues.

Part C: Managing marketing relationships

> **Quick Quiz**
> 1. Distinguish between ethics and social responsibility (see para 2.1)
> 2. Give an example of a marketing operation which is unethical but legal. (2.7)
> 3. List the main areas covered by the AMA's *Code of Ethics*. (3.3)
> 4. What is profit responsibility? (4.3)
> 5. What is societal responsibility? (4.6)
> 6. What does the Consumers' Association do? (5.3)
> 7. What are the four 'green' character types in Ogilvy and Mather's psychographic typology. (6.9)
> 8. What are the four Ss of green marketing? (6.14)
> 9. What does a proactive strategy for social responsibility involve? (7.2)

Action Programme Review

1.
   - Recognising society's expectations and the rationale for engaging in socially responsible activity
   - Identification of causes or programmes which are congruent with the mission of the company
   - Determination of objectives and priorities related to this programme
   - Specification of the nature and range of resources required
   - Evaluation of company involvement in such programmes past, present and future

2. *Service providers* have traditionally thought that green issues are less relevant to them than to other types of business enterprise. Although service enterprises typically do have less environmental impact than other types of business, they still consume resources and generate waste. They still face the same choices in their selection of suppliers, their investments and their contribution to the welfare of staff and customers. In fact, the very proliferation of green marketing practices is creating a growing demand for business services such as environmental auditing, green training, waste management and pollution control specialists.

Now try illustrative question 13 at the end of the Study Text

Part D
Marketing operations in context

9 Business-to-Business Marketing

Chapter Topic List	Syllabus reference
1 Setting the scene	-
2 Business-to-business marketing	4.1
3 Target marketing in industrial markets	4.1
4 Marketing mix differences in industrial marketing	4.1
5 Competitive edge	4.1

Learning Outcome

Students will be able to demonstrate the adaptation of marketing operations principles in a variety of contexts.

Example of Marketing at Work

- Business loyalty schemes

1 SETTING THE SCENE

1.1 Business-to-business, or industrial marketing, is the first topic in the *Marketing operations in context* section of the syllabus, which has a 20% study weighting. Target marketing is likely to be easier in industrial marketing than consumer marketing because of the easy availability of large amounts of analysed data. This is discussed in section 3.

1.2 However, the marketing mix is likely to be very different, as shown in section 4, with a heavy emphasis on personal contact and product features. Industrial marketers must be prepared to seek competitive advantage where they can because product differentiation may not be possible. The nature of organisational buying can be a source of competitive advantage, if it is understood. This is covered in section 5.

Part D: Marketing operations in context

2 BUSINESS-TO-BUSINESS MARKETING 12/97

> **Exam Tip**
> The case study in December 1999 was based on business-to-business marketing. The first part dealt with the ways in which business-to-business marketing differs from consumer marketing. The second major theme was industrial buying behaviour and the concept of the Decision Making Unit. This topic had not previously appeared since December 1997. The December 1999 question required you to give your answer in the form of a script for a presentation.

2.1 Although many of the products involved in industrial markets are the same as those bought within the ordinary consumer markets, for example, motor vehicles, **the reasons they are bought will be quite different**. Buying motivations, the criteria which consumers apply, and the nature of the buying process itself will be quite different.

2.2 Organisational buyers are buying for their organisations, and what they buy is part and parcel of the business activity of the organisation involved - it is part of the process of earning a profit.

2.3 Industrial marketing involves widely varying products and services. It is not just about raw materials, or about the selling of specialised, heavy duty machinery or equipment.

Products

2.4 **Industrial goods and services are bought by manufacturers, distributors and other private and publicly owned institutions, such as schools and hospitals, to be used as part of their own activities, rather than for resale.**

2.5 Categories of industrial market

(a) **Capital goods** include such items as buildings, machinery and motor vehicles. Accounting procedures involve recognition of depreciation in their value over time.

(b) **Components and materials** include raw, partly and wholly processed materials or goods which are incorporated into the products sold by the company.

(c) **Supplies** are goods which **assist** production and distribution. They are not regarded as a capital investment, however; this would include small but important items such as machine oil, computer disks and stationery, and janitorial wares.

(d) **Business services** are services used by businesses.

2.6 Industrial products are **distinctive** in several ways.

(a) **Conformity with standards**. Industrial products are often bound by **legal or quality standards,** and as a consequence, products within a particular group are often similar. Differentiation, which is such a key dimension of *consumer* goods, is more difficult here. At the same time, buyers lay down their own specifications to which manufacturers must adhere.

(b) **Technical sophistication**. Many products in this area require levels of complexity and sophistication which are unheard of in consumer products. Often the industry standard gradually influences the consumer equivalent as, for instance, in the case of power tools in the DIY market. After-sales and maintenance contracts have become essential in certain areas.

(c) **High unit values**. As a consequence of (a) and (b), many industrial goods, particularly capital equipment, are very often extremely costly items. Even in the case of supplies, although the unit value of components and materials may be comparatively low, the quantity required frequently means that individual orders and total sales to individual customers usually have a very high value.

(d) **Irregularity of purchase**. Machinery used to produce consumer goods is not bought regularly. Materials used to produce the goods certainly are, but components and materials are often bought on a contract basis, so that the opportunity to get new business may not arise very often.

Characteristics of industrial markets

2.7 Three kinds of economic activities have been defined.

(a) **Primary or extractive industries** cover activities like agriculture, fishing, mining and forestry.

(b) **Secondary or manufacturing industries** include manufacturing and construction.

(c) **The tertiary sector includes the service industries**. Services are becoming extremely important within our modern economy and services marketing is exerting a big influence on the way in which marketing is developing.

The importance of marketing for the industrial sector

2.8 A marketing orientation is just as valid within the industrial sector as it is in the consumer goods sector. Customers seek answers to their problems. Industrial products must be full of customer benefits, providing answers to customers' problems rather than simply being 'good products'.

The marketing manager within the organisation

2.9 This implies a need for well co-ordinated activity, around a common, market-oriented, mission. Marketing management has several functions.

- It acts as catalysts within the firms.
- It informs technical management about market trends.
- It monitors competitive activity.
- It informs corporate planning decisions.
- It directs R & D.

They are not simply concerned with customers, but in linking and co-ordinating various activities within the firm.

Special practices

2.10 **Reciprocal trading** is evident in some markets where buying and selling firms engage in reciprocal trading agreements. This closes markets off for newcomers and restricts trading.

2.11 **Joint ventures** often involve large industrial and commercial organisations which pool their resources in order to accomplish particular contracts. This may be necessary because of the scale of the project, or because of cultural, legal or technical advantages which the co-operation confers on both parties.

2.12 **Consortiums** are more permanent partnerships.

Part D: Marketing operations in context

2.13 **Project management** involves special techniques to bring a single unique development to completion. Projects may involve research, design, manufacturing and logistic activities.

2.14 **Turnkey operations** may be similar to project management or may involve continuing responsibility to the customer for services and maintenance.

2.15 More and more **machinery is being leased rather than bought**. In the construction industry, leasing deals also involve lessors tying the machinery to exclusive purchasing of other items such as raw materials.

2.16 **Licensing** enables new products to be introduced to customers without the risks and high costs associated with the development and launch of a new product. It also significantly reduces the time to launch.

3 TARGET MARKETING IN INDUSTRIAL MARKETS

3.1 Business-to-business target markets tend to be easier to identify than consumer market segments, mainly because more data is readily available on businesses than on groups of people within the general public. Much information about industrial markets is published in government statistics. Production statistics, available monthly and quarterly for manufacturing companies, are broken down into ten major Standard Industrial Classifications (SICs), for example, SIC3 is metal goods, engineering and textiles. Each major heading is broken down into smaller groups. Under each heading is given such detail as number of employees, number of establishments, value of shipments, exports and imports and annual growth rates.

3.2 Distribution statistics are available for retail outlets by type giving turnover and number of establishments, for instance.

Action Programme 1
Find some examples of government publications which might provide a useful source of statistics.

3.3 Official statistics are also published by bodies such as the United Nations and local authorities.

3.4 **Privately published statistics**

- Companies and other organisations specialising in the provision of economic and financial data (eg the *Financial Times* Business Information Service, the Data Research Institute, Reuters and the Extel Group).

- Directories and yearbooks, such as Kompass or Kelly's Directory.

- Professional institutions (eg Chartered Institute of Marketing, Industrial Marketing Research Association, Institute of Practitioners in Advertising).

- Specialist libraries, such as the City Business Library in London, collect published information from a wide variety of sources.

- Trade associations, trade unions and Chambers of Commerce.

- Commercial organisations such as banks and TV networks.

- Market research agencies.

Buying in data

3.5 The sources of secondary data identified above are generally free because they are in the public domain. However, the information is non-specific and needs considerable analysis before being useable.

3.6 A middle step between adapting secondary data and commissioning primary research is the purchase of data collected by market research companies or business publishing houses. The data tend to be expensive but less costly than primary research.

3.7 There are a great many commercial sources of secondary data, and a number of guides to these sources are available.

- *The Source Book*, Key Note Publications
- *Guide to Official Statistics*, HMSO
- *Published Data of European Markets*, Industrial Aids Ltd
- *Compendium of Marketing Information Sources*, Euromonitor
- Various publications from *Overseas Trade Services*

3.8 Commonly used sources of data on particular industries and markets are:

- Key Note Publications
- *Retail Business*, Economist Intelligence Unit
- Mintel publications
- *Market Research GB*, Euromonitor

4 MARKETING MIX DIFFERENCES IN INDUSTRIAL MARKETING

4.1 **The industrial marketing mix differs from the marketing mix for consumer products.** Often industrial products are not packaged for resale, prices tend to be negotiated with the buyer and distribution tends to be more direct. The promotional mix is also generally different in that consumer goods are often advertised heavily on TV and in mass media whereas industrial marketing companies tend to restrict advertising to trade magazines.

4.2 **Much more reliance is placed on personal selling.** An industrial buyer purchase off the page, especially where capital goods are concerned. Whereas most FMCG are purchased on a self-service basis, industrial goods involve a great deal more personal contact. Industrial marketers also use **exhibitions and demonstrations** to quite a high degree when promoting their products.

Product

4.3 Most business-to-business marketing mixes will include **elements of service** as well as product. Pre-sales services may involve technical advice, quotations, opportunities to see products in action and free trials. After-sales service will include Just-in-Time delivery, service and maintenance and guarantees. Products will also be custom-built to a much greater degree than for consumer marketing mixes. Frequently, products will have to be tested to laid down conditions. Packing will be for protection rather than for self-service. Some of these elements can comprise a powerful differential competitive advantage. For example, ICI offers laboratory testing of various metals so that industrial customers can be assured of the one most suitable for given corrosive conditions.

4.4 When buying machine tools, **efficiency features** can be the most powerful buying motive. Other product-unique features may be the ease of or safety of operation. If an operator can

Part D: Marketing operations in context

manage two machines rather than one, his potential output is doubled. Training of operators is another service often provided by manufacturers of industrial equipment.

Price

4.5 **Price is not normally fixed to the same degree as in consumer markets**. Particularly where products or services are customised, price is a function of buyer specification. Price is negotiable to a much greater extent and may depend upon the quantity, add-on services and features and sometimes the total business placed per year. Retrospective annual discounts act as loyalty incentives. Mark downs and special offers as used in consumer markets have spread to industrial market pricing.

4.6 **Trade discounts** can apply in those cases where industrial and commercial goods are marketed through middlemen (see below on distribution). In some industrial markets, especially construction, prices are set under a **tendering system**.

Promotion

4.7 Within the promotional mix, personal selling is very important in business-to-business marketing. Some industrial products are quite complex and need explaining in a flexible way to non-technical people involved in the buying process.

4.8 Buying in business-to-business marketing is often a group activity and, equally, selling can be a team effort. Salespeople are expected to follow-up to ensure that the products are working properly and that the business buyer is perfectly satisfied. Where an industrial equipment manufacturer markets through an industrial dealer, the manufacturer's salesforce may be required to train the dealer salesforce in product knowledge.

4.9 The partnership approach is present to a much greater degree in industrial selling, where the buyer needs information and services and the seller is seeking repeat business in the long term.

4.10 The types of **media** used for advertising differ greatly from those in consumer markets. Mass media are rarely used. Advertising is usually confined to **trade magazines**, which reach more precise targets. Direct mail is used to supplement personal selling.

4.11 **Industrial exhibitions** are popular as a means of personal contact with particular target markets, and factory visits are used as a means of engendering confidence in the manufacturer's abilities and standards. More industrial marketers are using PR, through agencies, as a means of gaining favourable publicity in the trade media and to build up their corporate images.

Place (distribution)

4.12 Industrial marketers tend to deliver direct where agents are used, as in international markets. UK manufacturers will usually deliver direct to overseas business clients.

4.13 Sometimes, however, business to business distributors are employed, particularly for consumable and lower-value goods. **Business to business channels** are

- Manufacturer → Business buyer
- Manufacturer → Agents → Business buyer
- Manufacturer → Business distributor → Business buyer
- Manufacturer → Agents → Business distributor → Business buyer

4.14 **On-time delivery can be an extremely important requirement in industrial markets**, especially where valuable contracts can be held up for want of a relatively small piece of equipment. In such circumstances, the premium on delivery is so great that penalty clauses for lateness are invoked.

5 COMPETITIVE EDGE 12/99

5.1 When competing for business, the industrial product manufacturer is likely to have to conform to laid down standards or quote to tight specifications. **This means it is more difficult to gain a differential advantage in the product itself.** However, a variety of add-on services, such as technical advice pre-sale and rapid spares availability after-sales, can provide competitive advantage.

Buyers

5.2 The relationship with the industrial buyer may also provide competitive advantage and it is important to understand and exploit the customer's buying process.

5.3 **Organisational buying is a transaction between a number of individuals rather than an action by one person.** Buying decisions are likely to be made by a group called a **decision making unit** (DMU). The **purchasing officer** (PO) will usually be part of the DMU but may play one of a variety of roles. Small and routine purchases will normally be the PO's territory and other members of staff may make only small input. For larger or less frequent purchases the PO may lead the team or may be relegated to an **administrative** or **gatekeeper** role. Other members of the DMU will also vary in their influence and involvement.

- The **specifier** is very important and lays the ground rules for the buying decision, though this person may not have the final say. The specification process is often complete before sales negotiations commence and it may not be easy to influence the specifier.

- The **user** may be the same person as the specifier, but not necessarily. The user and the specifier may have different ideas about the good or service to be purchased and the sales person may be able to exploit such differences.

- The **finance** person decides what can be spent. Again, this person may play another role, since purchasing is often a matter of applying budgets and the budget holder may well be the specifier or the user. It is the role of the financier to ensure that value for money is obtained and to approve things like credit arrangements.

5.4 Differences between consumer behaviour and organisational buying can be summarised as follows from the viewpoint of the **buying centre**.

(a) At an organisational level, the decision process is a *group* buying process, in which the people involved make up the DMU or buying centre.

(b) The complexity of the products is usually greater.

(c) The needs of users are more varied and difficult to satisfy.

(d) The impact of an unsuccessful purchase decision poses much greater personal and organisational risks than the average consumer decision process, for both groups and individuals involved in the purchase.

(e) There is more interdependence between buyer and vendor in industrial markets because there are smaller numbers of goods and customers. Therefore, not only are

Part D: Marketing operations in context

sellers dependent on buyers for an assured outlet for their goods, but also buyers are dependent on sellers for the continued source of inputs for their processes.

(f) Post-purchase processes are much more important.

> **Action Programme 2**
>
> What external factors do you think influence organisational buying behaviour?

5.5 There are also, of course, **organisational** forces affecting buying.

Centralisation	The physical and managerial location of the decision-making authority.
Formalisation	The degree to which rules and procedures are stated and adhered to by the employees of the organisation.
Specialisation	The degree to which the organisation is divided up into specialised departments according to job function and organisational activities.
Organisational culture	Informal but influential habits, practices and attitudes.

Models of organisational buying

5.6 A number of models have attempted to deal with the complex relations between the factors involved in organisational buying.

The American Marketing Association model

5.7 The American Marketing Association model proposes that there are four main influences on organisational buying decisions.

- The inherent priorities of the buyer and the buying department
- Pressures applied to the buyer by the organisation
- Environmental influences on the buyer, including increased professionalism
- Environmental influences on the wider organisation and the way it does business

Departmental influences

	Within purchasing department	Between departments
Intra-firm influence	**Cell 1** **The Purchasing Agent** Social factors Price/cost factors Supply continuity Risk avoidance	**Cell 2** **The Buying Centre** Organisational structure Power/conflict processes Gatekeeper role (1)
Inter-firm influence	**Cell 3** **Professionalism** Word-of-mouth communication Trade shows, journals Advertising, PR, promotion Supplier purchase reciprocity	**Cell 4** **Organisational Environment** (2) Technological change Nature of suppliers Cooperative buying

Organisational influences

Notes

(1) The gatekeeper role is the buyer's reaction to pressure from other departments; the buyer tends to defend his territory.

(2) Research suggests that as technological change accelerates, the purchasing agent is less likely to be an important influence in the process. The nature of the supplier is also likely to influence the buying process, with larger firms presenting less risk to their customers, while smaller firms may be preferable to ensure continuity of supply.

5.8 While emphasising the importance of relationships, this model is not really able to predict outcomes.

The Sheth model

5.9 The Sheth model is based on the Howard-Sheth model of Consumer Behaviour (CB) which gives a central place to **learning** following behaviourist principles. This model illustrates the intricacy of the organisational processes involved, and suggests that the relationships between the individuals concerned in cell 2 of the American Marketing Association model may hold the key to understanding the process.

5.10 Three aspects of organisational buyer **behaviour** are identified.

- **Psychological environments** of the individuals in the buying decision
- Conditions which **precipitate joint decision making**
- Joint decision-making process and conflict resolution amongst decision makers

5.11 **Joint decision making**. The model recognises that a number of individuals, and often a number of different departments, are involved in the decision to buy. Purchasing agents, quality control engineers and production management, for instance, may be involved, and all have different backgrounds, expertise, and exposure to information. Individuals have very different requirements of the products involved, because of these differences.

5.12 Five main factors influence the psychological environments of individuals involved in organisational buying decisions.

- **Backgrounds** of individuals such as education and lifestyles
- **Information sources** available to them
- **The degree of active search** in which they are involved
- **Perceptual distortion** affecting the way they see the problem
- **Satisfaction with past purchases** - again, backgrounds will influence how satisfactory the performance of the product was judged to be

5.13 Factors precipitating **joint** rather than **autonomous** decision making can be divided into **product specific** and **company specific**.

(a) **Product specific** factors include perceived risk, type of purchase and time pressure. Each of these has implications for the degree of risk and joint expectations which the product is expected to satisfy.

(b) **Company specific** factors include company size, degree of centralisation, and company orientation. Clearly, the nature of the company, and the relationships between the individuals and departments involved will all bear on the way in which purchases are approached.

Part D: Marketing operations in context

5.14 This model does not examine autonomous buying decisions in any detail, but **concentrates on joint decision making**. Conflict is seen almost as a natural and inevitable aspect of such decision processes. Resolution is an essential aspect of organisational structure. There are four main ways in which this takes place.

- Problem solving
- Persuasion
- Bargaining
- Politicking

5.15 The first two of these are rational, and although time consuming, lead to good decisions, according to this model. The others tend to be used when there are irremediable conflicts between interested parties, and they lead to resolution of conflicts, but poor decisions are often made, since they imply that the requirements of some parties remain unsatisfied or frustrated.

Other ways of creating differential advantage

5.16 Other ways of creating differential advantage arise directly from the close relationship involved in industrial marketing. Here are some examples.

(a) *Product*

- Offer to finish product in any colour to match factory/warehouse decor
- Offer to add customer's logo to casings
- Emphasise the benefits of any unique product features

(b) *Pre-sales services*

- Technical advice
- Free demonstrations, perhaps at other customers' premises

(c) *After-sales service*

- Spares immediately available from stock
- Rapid maintenance and repair service
- Guarantees for longer periods than competitors

(d) *Price*

- Leasing arrangements made upon request
- Discounts for quantity
- Package prices for supply, installation and maintenance

(e) *Promotion*

- Sales engineers who take a partnership approach
- Video presentations
- Models and samples

(f) *Distribution*

- Direct delivery
- Just-in-Time service

Marketing at Work

Business loyalty schemes

Air Miles operates through many consumer outlets but has also developed its position in the business-to-business market with around 87 clients in the electrical and retail sectors, manufacturing, breweries and pharmaceuticals. One of its longest-standing relationships is with electrical wholesaler Newey & Eyre. Newey & Eyre began offering Air Miles in 1989 as part of its loyalty scheme. 'We felt that travel was one of the most powerful motivators,' says Ian Lund, national marketing manager for Newey & Eyre. 'We were also attracted by Air Miles' flexibility and the fact that the perceived reward is far greater than the cost.' The company identified a core group of customers from its 100,000-plus accounts who it felt could increase business substantially. Each one was approached and a target based on previous performances was agreed. Air Miles are awarded on the basis of incremental revenue which allows for clear performance measures.

'Business-to-business schemes can be easier to set up as there is a more tightly defined environment than consumer programmes,' explains business-to-business account director John O'Boyle. 'Depending on the model we can launch a business-to-business scheme in three or four months but each programme is based on return on investment. The key tenet is to deliver incremental revenue to the clients so Air Miles becomes almost self-funded as they are rewarded on increased spend.'

But, he adds, the modelling of a scheme is crucial. 'We look at individualistic programmes, look at the customers, their return on investment and margin, and we build a bespoke offer. In independent retailing, for example, the margin is so tight on food and drink and we cannot offer a scheme on the same basis as a dental parts manufacturer where competition is not so strong and margins are high.'

Also working in the business-to-business sector and with strategic partners is office supplies firm Pitney Bowes. As a Pitney Bowes customer you place an order for any equipment and you automatically become a Partners Club member. This entitles you to special deals an savings with Hilton National chain of hotels, BT, Budget car rental, Thorntons chocolates, H Forman smoked salmon producers and Linguaphone. Angie Reed, Pitney Bowes UK marketing manager, explains the strategic thinking behind the scheme. 'A franking machine, for example, is not a frequent purchase, so the idea of the scheme is for us to keep in contact with our customer, to keep our names in the frame. The club is an on-going business relationship. We keep in touch with mailings from a sophisticated database. It means from there we can also identify unmet needs, so we can see the equipment they may be lacking. The only measurement tool though is through uptake of special offers with the partners. It was arranged through our direct marketing agency CoAxis and it worked because each partner is a well-known name and it benefits them too, as we bring in extra business for them.'

Marketing Business May 1996

Chapter Roundup

- Industrial marketing, or marketing business-to-business, is different in nature from consumer marketing. Buying motivations (the criteria which consumers apply) and the nature of the buying process itself are quite different. There are four basic categories of industrial market.

    Capital goods
    Components and materials
    Supplies
    Business services

- Target markets for industrial marketing tend to be easier to identify than consumer market segments. Data is generally more easily available on businesses than on consumers. Sources include government and privately-published statistics.

- There are differences in the marketing mix for industrial marketing when compared to the characteristic mix adopted for consumer markets.

- Competitive advantage may be obtained from an understanding of the industrial *buying* process.

Part D: Marketing operations in context

> **Quick Quiz**
> 1. What are the four categories of industrial market? (see para 2.5)
> 2. Give four examples of non-government publications which could be used in targeting industrial markets. (3.4)
> 3. How does 'product' differ in industrial marketing when compared to consumer marketing? (4.3 - 4.4)
> 4. How does 'distribution' differ in industrial marketing when compared to consumer marketing? (4.12 - 4.14)
> 5. What are the four influences on organisation buying as identified by the AMA? (5.7)
> 6. What are the five factors which influence the *individuals* involved in organisational buying? (5.12)

Action Programme Review

1. Examples of government publications include:

   - The *Annual Abstract of Statistics* and its monthly equivalent, the *Monthly Digest of Statistics*. These contain a wide variety of data about manufacturing output, housing, population and so on
   - The *Digest of UK Energy Statistics* (published annually)
   - *Housing and Construction Statistics* (published quarterly)
   - *Financial Statistics* (monthly)
   - *Economic Trends* (monthly)
   - *Census of Population.* The Office for National Statistics publish continuous datasets including the *National Food Survey,* the *Household Survey* and the *Family Expenditure Survey*
   - *Census of Production* (annual). This has been described as 'one of the most important sources of desk research for industrial marketers'. It provides data about production by firms in each industry in the UK
   - *Employment Gazette* (monthly) giving details of employment in the UK
   - *British Business*, published weekly by the Department of Trade and Industry, giving data on industrial and commercial trends at home and overseas
   - *Business Monitor* (published by the Business Statistics Office), giving detailed information about various industries
   - *Social Trends* (annually)

2. These include the following.

   - *Political/legal.* Government attitude toward business; international tariffs; trade agreements and government assistance to selected industries; legal and regulatory forces at the local and national levels which affect the industrial decision-making process
   - *Economic.* Interest rates; level of unemployment; consumer and wholesale price index; growth in GNP. Changes in different economic conditions will impact different sections of the market in differing degrees
   - *Physical influences.* Climate, geography, locations, labour supply, choice of raw materials

Now try illustrative question 14 at the end of the Study Text

10 Services Marketing

Chapter Topic List	Syllabus reference
1 Setting the scene	-
2 Services marketing	4.2
3 Characteristics of services marketing	4.2
4 The extended marketing mix for services marketing	4.2
5 The importance of people	4.2
6 Service quality	4.2

Learning Outcome

Students will be able to demonstrate the adaptation of marketing operations principles in a variety of contexts.

Examples of Marketing at Work

- Radio 5 Live
- Quality in stockbroking

1 SETTING THE SCENE

1.1 The service sector has grown rapidly in recent years in the UK, both as an employer and in terms of its contribution to GDP. There are certain basic characteristics of service industries (sections 2 and 3) which differentiate them from other business operations. These characteristics mean that the successful marketing and delivery of services requires attention to areas not really covered by the 4 Ps: who gives the service (people); how the service is given (process); the environment in which the service is given (physical evidence). The nature of quality in services is complex. Section 6 discusses what it is and how to measure it.

Part D: Marketing operations in context

2 SERVICES MARKETING 12/99

> **Exam Tip**
> Services are an increasingly important area of the British economy and now account for more employment than the manufacturing sector.
> Services marketing was the subject of a Part B question in both December and June 1999.

2.1 There are a number of reasons why services marketing is more important today than in the past. These include the following.

(a) **The growth of service sectors in advanced industrial societies**. More people now work in the service sector than in all other sectors of the economy and the major contributors to national output are the public and private service sectors. Invisible earnings from abroad are of increasing significance for Britain's balance of trade.

(b) **An increasingly market-oriented trend within service-providing organisation**. This has been particularly apparent within the public sector with the advent of internal markets, market testing and the chartermark.

2.2 The public sector in Britain includes service provision in the legal, medical, educational, military, employment, transportation, leisure and information fields. Increasingly, there is a focus on profits in many of these areas. The private sector embraces not-for-profit areas such as the arts, charities and religious and educational organisations and includes business and professional services in travel, finance, insurance, management, the law, building, commerce and entertainment.

2.3 **Services: some definitions**

(a) ' ... those separately identifiable but intangible activities that provide want-satisfaction, and that are not, of necessity, tied to, or inextricable from, the sale of a product or another service.'
Donald Cowell, The Marketing of Services

(b) ' ... any activity of benefit that one party can offer to another that is essentially intangible and does not result in the ownership of anything. Its production may or may not be tied to a physical product.'
P Kotler, Social Marketing

2.4 Marketing services faces a number of distinct problems, and as a consequence, the approach adopted must be varied, and particular marketing practices developed.

3 CHARACTERISTICS OF SERVICES MARKETING 6/99

3.1 Characteristics of services which make them distinctive from the marketing of goods have been proposed. These are five major differences.

- Intangibility
- Inseparability
- Heterogeneity
- Perishability
- Ownership

Intangibility

3.2 Intangibility refers to the lack of physical substance which is involved with service delivery. Clearly, this creates difficulties and can inhibit the propensity to consume a service, since customers are not sure what they have.

'Ultimately the customer may have no prior experience of a service in which he or she is interested, nor any conception of how it would satisfy the requirements of the purchase context for which it was intended.'

Morden, The Marketing of Services

Shostack has suggested viewing insubstantiality as a continuum, as shown in the diagram below.

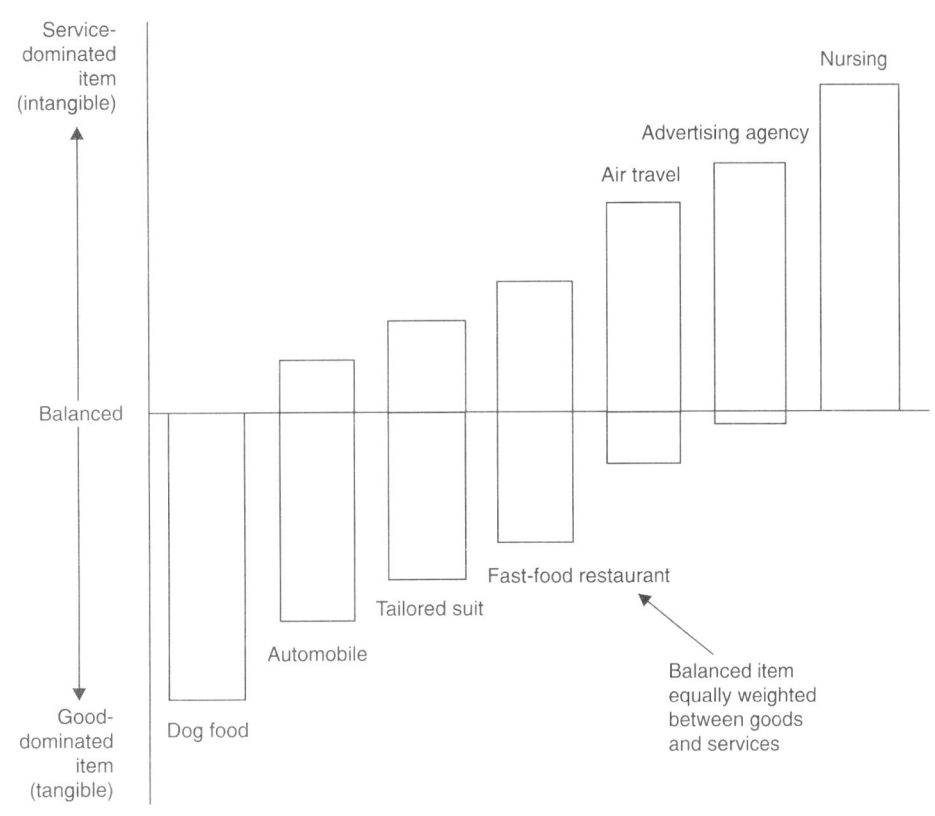

The Goods - Services Continuum

[Diagram showing a continuum from Good-dominated item (tangible) at bottom to Service-dominated item (intangible) at top, with the following items plotted from most tangible to most intangible: Dog food, Automobile, Tailored suit, Fast-food restaurant (Balanced item equally weighted between goods and services), Air travel, Advertising agency, Nursing.]

3.3 Shostack has also proposed that marketing entities are combinations of elements, which are tangible or intangible. A product then comes to be conceived as a blend of various elements, combining **material entities** (the aeroplane we are flying in, the airport lounge) with various sorts of **processes** (the courtesy of the airline staff, the frequency of services).

3.4 Clearly, for each service, the number, complexity and balance of the various elements involved will vary a great deal. What is experienced remains insubstantial, although many parts of the process (the machines, buildings and staff of an airline, for instance) are very substantial.

3.5 The consumer needs **information** to form some grounds for **judgement**, and to cut down **risk**. The marketer wishes to make the choice of the product safer and make consumers feel more comfortable about paying for something that has no physical form.

Marketing at Work

Radio 5 Live

BBC Radio 5 Live is to embark on its first major TV advertising campaign since the station launched six years ago. It is part of a new marketing strategy for the station.

A month-long TV and poster campaign breaks in mid-February and will attempt to woo new listeners to R5 Live, according to BBC Radio head of marketing Vanessa Griffiths.

Griffiths says: 'The station has strong loyalty among its core audience but minimal awareness outside of it. But R5 Live has massive potential to talk to millions more listeners.'

Part D: Marketing operations in context

The station has 5.6 million listeners and a 4.2 per cent share of listening, according to Rajar figures for the quarter ending September 1999.

Marketing Week, 20 January 2000

3.6 The intangibility may be countered in two ways.

- By the consumer seeking opinions from other consumers
- By the marketer offering the consumer something tangible to represent the purchase

3.7 Intangibility is a matter of degree and takes several forms.

- Intangibles making a tangible product available, such as delivery
- Intangibles adding value to a tangible product, such as house decorating, hairdressing, vehicles or plant maintenance
- Complete intangibility, such as entertainment or leisure services

Marketing implications

3.8 Dealing with the problems may involve strategies to **enhance tangibility**.

(a) **Increasing the level of tangibility**. When dealing with the customer, staff can use physical representations or illustrations to make the customer feel more confident as to what it is that the service is delivering.

(b) **Focusing the attention of the customer on the principal benefits of consumption**. This could take the form of communicating the benefits of purchasing the service so that the customer visualises its appropriateness. Promotion and sales material could provide images or records of previous customers' experience.

(c) **Differentiating the service and reputation-building**. This is achieved by enhancing perceptions of service and value through offering excellence in the delivery of the service and by promoting values of quality, service reliability and value for money. These must be attached as **values** to brands, which must then be managed to secure and enhance their market position.

Inseparability

3.9 A service often cannot be separated from the provider of the service. The **performance of a service often occurs at the same instant as its consumption**. Think of having dental treatment or going on a journey. Neither exists until actually consumed by the purchaser.

Marketing implications

3.10 Provision of the service may not be separable from the provider. Consequently, increasing importance is attached to **values of quality and reliability** and a customer service ethic which can be transferred to the service provision. This emphasises the need for customer orientation, high quality people and high quality training for them.

Heterogeneity

3.11 Many services face a problem of **maintaining consistency in the standard of output**. Variability of quality in delivery is inevitable, because of the number of factors which may influence it. This may create problems of operations management. For example, it may be difficult or impossible to attain:

(a) **Precise standardisation of the service offered**. The quality of the service may depend heavily on who delivers the service and when it takes place. Booking a holiday using standard procedures, may well be quite different on a quiet winter afternoon and on a hectic spring weekend, and may well vary according to the person dealing with the client.

(b) **Influence or control over perceptions of what is good or bad customer service**. From the customer's perspective, it is very difficult to obtain an idea of the quality of service in advance of purchase.

As a result, it is necessary to monitor customer reactions constantly and to maintain an attitude and organisational culture which emphasises three things.

- Consistency of quality control
- Consistency of customer service
- Effective staff selection, training and motivation

3.12 Other important matters

(a) Clear and objective quality measures

(b) Standardising as much as possible within the service

(c) The **Pareto principle** (80 percent of difficulties arise from 20 percent of events surrounding the provision of the service). Therefore, identify and respond most closely to these potential troublespots.

Perishability

3.13 **Services cannot be stored**. They are innately **perishable**. Performances at a theatre or the services of a chiropodist consist in their availability for periods of time, and if they are not occupied, the service they offer cannot be used later.

3.14 This presents specific marketing problems. **Meeting customer needs in these operations depends on staff being available when they are needed**. This must be balanced against the need to minimise unnecessary expenditure on staff wages. Anticipating and responding to levels of demand is, therefore, a key planning priority. There are two risks.

- Inadequate level of demand is accompanied by substantial fixed cost.
- Excess demand may result in lost custom through inadequate service provision.

Policies must seek to match demand with supply by price variations and promotions to stimulate off-peak demand.

Ownership

3.15 **Services do not result in the transfer of property**. In the case of purchasing a product, there is permanent transfer of title and control over the use of an item. An item of service provision is often defined by the length of time it is available.

3.16 This may very well lessen the perceived customer value of a service, and consequently make for unfavourable comparisons with **tangible** alternatives. Attempts have been made to overcome this problem by providing **symbolic** tangible items which can be taken away and kept. Car brochures, theatre programmes and the plethora of corporate giftwares such as golf umbrellas, pens and keyrings, are all examples of this.

Part D: Marketing operations in context

> **Action Programme 1**
>
> What are the marketing implications of the lack of ownership of a service received?

Marketing at Work

Quality in stockbroking

The following table shows the type of factors on which judgements are based in stockbroking.

Dimension and definition	Examples of specific questions raised by stock brokerage customers
Tangibles. Appearance of physical facilities, equipment, personnel and communication materials.	• Is my stockbroker dressed appropriately?
Reliability. Ability to perform the promised service dependably and accurately.	• Does the stockbroker follow exact instructions to buy or sell?
Responsiveness. Willingness to help customers and provide prompt service.	• Is my stockbroker willing to answer my questions?
Competence. Possession of the required skills and knowledge to perform the service.	• Does my brokerage firm have the research capabilities accurately to track market developments?
Courtesy. Politeness, respect, consideration, and friendliness of contact personnel.	• Does my broker refrain from acting busy or being rude when I ask questions?
Credibility. Trustworthiness, believability, and honesty of the service provider.	• Does my broker refrain from pressuring me to buy?
Security. Freedom from danger, risk, or doubt.	• Does my brokerage firm know where my stock certificate is?
Access. Approachability and ease of contact.	• Is it easy to get through to my broker over the telephone?
Communication. Keeping customers informed in language they can understand, and listening to them.	• Does my broker avoid using technical jargon?
Understanding the customer. Making the effort to know customers and their needs.	• Does my broker try to determine what my specific financial objectives are?

Zeithaml, Parasuraman and Berry, Delivering Quality Service

4 THE EXTENDED MARKETING MIX FOR SERVICES MARKETING

4.1 *Booms and Bitner* suggest that the standard 4P approach to the marketing of products should be extended for services by the addition of **three more Ps.**

- People
- Process
- Physical evidence or ambience

4.2 Services are provided by **people** for people. If the people providing the service are wrong, the service is spoiled. In the case of a bus service, a cheap fare, a clean vehicle and a frequent service can be spoiled by a surly driver.

4.3 Services are usually provided in a number of sequential steps. This is **process. The service can be spoiled or enhanced at any step in the sequence.**

4.4 Finally, there is the **physical evidence** or **ambience** which can be a maker or spoiler of experience of the service.

4.5 **An alternative approach identifies four extra Ps.**

- Personal selling
- Place of availability (operations management)
- People and customer service
- Physical evidence

Personal selling

4.6 **Personal selling** is very important in the marketing of services, because of the **greater perceived risk** involved and greater uncertainty about quality and reliability. The reputation of the supplier may be of greater importance, and the customer places greater reliance on the honesty of the individual salesperson. When consumers seek reassurance, personal contact with a competent, effective representative may provide the necessary confidence. Conversely, inappropriate selling may generate increased anxiety.

Place of availability

4.7 **Place of availability** is really covered by the distribution system, but there are special problems for services in **operations management**. The place and frequency of availability are key service variables but service resources must be used economically.

4.8 The level and quality of service are sensitive to the efficiency of the processes by which services are delivered. There are three key factors.

- **Capacity utilisation**: matching demand sequences to staff utilisation to avoid both the costs of overstaffing and the lost revenue of underprovision

- **Managing customer contact**, to avoid crowding and customer disruption, meet needs as they arise, and increase employee control over interactions

- **Establishing objectives within the not-for-profit sector**, for example, standards for teachers or medical staff

4.9 Interactions **between customers** are a key strategic issue. Customers often interact to gather information and form views about the service they are contemplating purchasing. Minimising exposure to negative feedback, and promoting the dissemination of positive messages about the service are important objectives.

People and customer service

4.10 For some services, the **physical presence of people performing the service is a vital aspect of customer satisfaction**. For example, staff in catering establishments are performing or producing a service, selling the service and liaising with the customer to promote the service, gather information and respond to customer needs. Customer orientation is needed in all sectors of organisational activity.

Part D: Marketing operations in context

4.11 Customers will tend to use cues to establish a view about the organisation from the demeanour and behaviour of staff. The higher the level of customer contact involved in the delivery of a service, the more crucial is the staff role in adding value. In many cases, the delivery of the service and the physical presence of the personnel involved are completely inseparable; here, **technical competence and skill in handling people are of equal importance** in effective delivery of the service.

> ### Action Programme 2
> All levels of staff must be involved in customer service. To achieve this end, it is vital for senior management to promote the importance of customer service. How do you think that this might be achieved?

Physical evidence

4.12 **Physical evidence** is an important remedy for the intangibility of the product. This may be **associated with the service itself**, (for example, credit cards which represent the service available to customers); **built up by identification with a specific individual** (a 'listening' bank manager); or **incorporated into the design and specification of the service environment,** involving the building, location or atmosphere.

> ### Action Programme 3
> What do you think that design can achieve in services marketing?

5 THE IMPORTANCE OF PEOPLE

5.1 As a consequence of the importance of **people**, service marketing organisations have certain common areas of emphasis.

(a) **Selection** and **training**

(b) Internal marketing to promulgate the **culture of service** within the firm

(c) Ensuring conformance with **standards**
- Behaviour
- Dress and appearance
- Procedures
- Modes of dealing with the public

(d) **Mechanising** procedures where possible

(e) Constantly **auditing** personnel performance and behaviour

(f) Extending the promotion of the service and its qualities into the design of service environments and the engineering of interactions between staff and customers and among the customers themselves.

Action Programme 4

The role of people in services marketing is especially important. What human characteristics improve the quality of client service?

6 SERVICE QUALITY

6.1 **Service quality** is a significant basis which customers use for differentiating between competing services. Second only to market share in the PIMS research (*Buzzell and Gale*, 1980), relative quality is a key contributor to **bottom line profit performance**.

6.2 **Quality can only be defined by customers**. It occurs where a firm supplies products to a specification that satisfies their needs. Customer expectations serve as standards against which subsequent service experiences are compared. When service performance falls short of customer expectations, dissatisfaction occurs.

6.3 There are two ways firms can gain from improving their quality of service.

(a) **Higher sales revenues** and improved marketing effectiveness brought about by improved customer retention, positive word-of-mouth recommendations and the ability to increase prices.

(b) **Improved productivity and reduced costs** because there is less rework, higher employee morale and lower employee turnover.

6.4 *Grönroos* introduced the concept of 'perceived service quality' in 1982 and extended this in the development of his widely cited model of service quality in 1984.

Grönoos (1984) Service Quality Model

```
    EXPECTED         Perceived Service Quality         PERCEIVED
    SERVICE                                            SERVICE
       ↑                         ↑ ↑
  Traditional marketing activities
  (advertising, field selling, PR,
  pricing); and external influence        IMAGE
  by traditions, ideology and
  word-of-mouth
                                        ↗       ↖
                              TECHNICAL         FUNCTIONAL
                              QUALITY           QUALITY

                               What?             How?
```

6.5 The model suggests that the quality of a given service is the outcome of an evaluation process where **consumers compare what they expected to receive with what they perceive that they actually received**. Consumer expectations are influenced by marketing mix activities, external traditions, ideology and word-of-mouth communications. Grönroos also suggests previous experience with the service will influence expectations.

Part D: Marketing operations in context

6.6 In terms of perceived service quality, Grönroos suggests there are two principal components of quality, **technical** and **functional**, with a third, **image**, acting as a mediating influence.

(a) **Technical quality** is what the customer is left with, when the production process is finished. For example, in higher education this would be perceived as the level of attainment and understanding achieved at the end of the course. This can be much more easily measured by the consumer.

(b) **Functional quality**, on the other hand, is more difficult to measure objectively because it involves an evaluation of **how the consumer receives the technical quality** in the interactions between customer and service provider and other customers. Grönroos' suggestion that **service quality is dependent both on what you receive and how you receive it** emphasises the importance of service interactions, contact employees and managing in the service experience.

6.7 **Image**. Grönroos also suggests that both expectations and perceptions are affected by the consumer's view of the company and by its image. If a consumer has a **positive image** of a university or lecturer but has a negative experience, for example a rather confused lecture, the consumer may still **perceive** the service to be satisfactory because he or she will find excuses for the negative experience. Correspondingly, Grönroos suggests that a **negative image** may increase perceived problems with service quality.

Quality gaps

6.8 *Parasuraman, Zeithaml and Berry* developed the most widely applied model of service quality in 1985. The researchers developed their model via interviews with fourteen executives in four service businesses and twelve customer focus groups. The executive interviews resulted in the idea of **five gaps** which are potential hurdles for a firm in attempting to deliver high quality service.

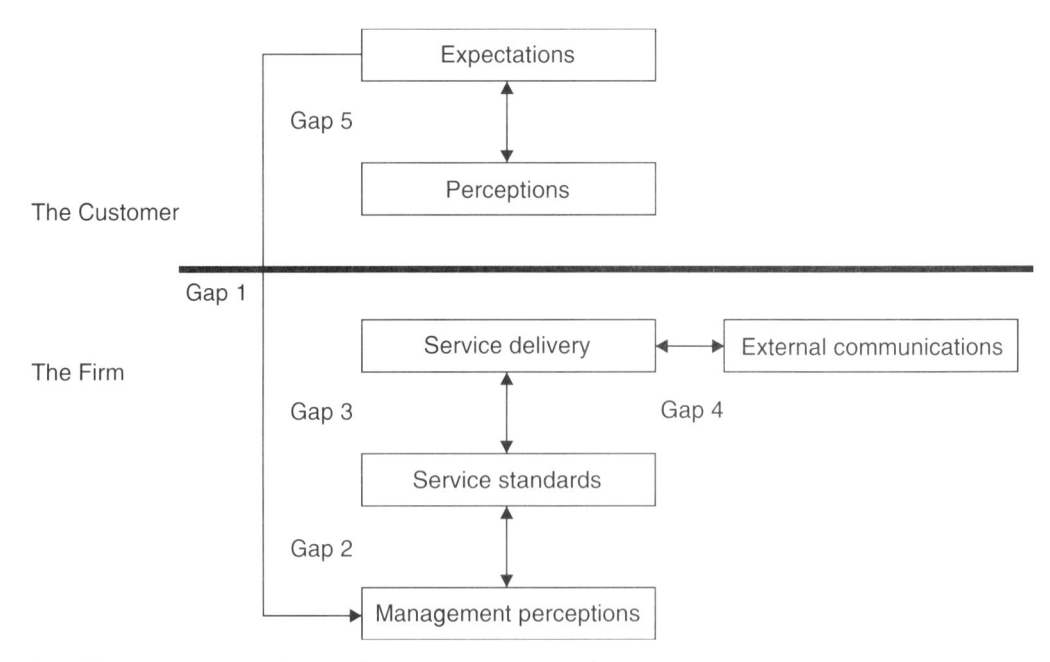

Gap 1: *Consumer expectations and management perceptions gap*

Essentially managers may not know what features connote high quality, what features a service must have or what levels of performance are required by customers.

Gap 2:   Management perceptions and service quality specification gap

Resource constraints, market conditions and/or management indifference may result in this gap.

Gap 3:   Service quality specifications and service delivery gap

Guidelines may exist but contact employees may not be willing or able to perform to the specified standards.

Gap 4:   Service delivery and external communications gap

Exaggerated promises or lack of information will affect both expectations and perceptions.

Gap 5:   Expected service and perceived service gap

This gap was defined as service quality. The authors argue that gap five is influenced by the preceding four gaps so if management want to close the gap between performance and expectations it becomes imperative to design procedures for measuring service performance against expectations.

6.9 In 1988, the researchers developed the SERVQUAL questionnaire which purports to be a global measure of Gap 5 across all service organisations. This measures the five generic criteria that consumers use in evaluating service quality.

1 *Tangibles*: physical facilities, equipment, appearance of personnel
2 *Reliability*: ability to perform the promised service dependably and accurately
3 *Responsiveness*: willingness to help customers and provide prompt service
4 *Assurance*: knowledge and courtesy of employees and their ability to convey trust and confidence
5 *Empathy*: caring, individualised attention

Respondents are asked first to give their expectations of the service on a seven point scale, then to give their evaluation of the actual service on the same scale. Service quality is then calculated as the difference between perception and expectations, weighted for the importance of each item.

6.10 Once a firm knows how it is performing on each of the dimensions of service quality it can use a number of methods to try to improve its quality.

- Development of customer orientated mission statement and clear senior management support for quality improvement initiatives

- Regular customer satisfaction research including customer surveys and panels, mystery shoppers, analysis of complaints and similar industry studies for benchmarking purposes

- Setting and monitoring standards and communicating results

- Establishment of systems for customers complaints and feedback

- Encouragement of employee participation, ideas and initiative, often through the use of quality circles and project teams

- Rewarding excellent service

Part D: Marketing operations in context

6.11 What evidence do you see of firms implementing quality programmes and continually improving service quality? How does your company, or one you have worked for in the past, measure service quality?

> **Exam Tip**
>
> Service quality was explicitly addressed in June 1997, as part (c) of the TSB/Lloyds merger mini-case. Had you been able to adapt your knowledge learned from section 5 of this chapter, you would have earned 20 marks.
>
> The key to the answer could be the use of *quality gaps*. Banks, particularly, labour under these problems. A bank's management will be pleased that 99.99 per cent of transactions are error free. However, the customer expects that 100 per cent of his/her transactions will be error-free and that errors which do creep in are dealt with speedily and effectively.
>
> Maintaining and improving service standards after the merger was another component of this half of the question and was largely specific to the mini-case. You could have structured your answer by distinguishing between technical quality and functional quality.

Chapter Roundup

- The extension of the service sector, and the application of market principles across many public sector and ex-public sector organisations, has made a large number of service providers much more marketing-conscious. Services marketing differs from the marketing of other goods in a number of crucial ways, and five specific characteristics of services marketing have been proposed.

- An extended marketing mix has been suggested for services marketing. Booms and Bitner suggested an additional 3Ps. Here, we have taken an approach which analyses an additional 4Ps.

- Service quality can be defined as the difference between what the customer expects and what he or she perceives him/herself to be receiving. Improved service quality leads to higher profits and is a key task for service marketers.

Quick Quiz

1. What are the five marketing characteristics of services? (see para 3.1)
2. What are the marketing implications of the intangibility of services? (3.8)
3. What issues arise from the perishability of services being marketed? (3.13 - 3.14)
4. How can the problems of lack of ownership be overcome in service marketing? (3.16, action programme 1)
5. What are the additional 'Ps' in the service marketing mix? (4.1, 4.5)
6. In what areas should rigorous procedures be applied to take account of the importance of people in services marketing? (5.1)
7. In what two ways can firms gain by improving their quality of service to customers? (6.3)
8. What is 'quality' in marketing terms? (6.2, 6.5, 6.8)

Action Programme Review

1. Possible marketing implications.

    (a) Promote the advantages of non-ownership. This can be done by emphasising, in promotion, the benefits of paid-for maintenance, and periodic upgrading of the product. Radio Rentals have used this as a major selling proposition with great success.

    (b) Make available a tangible symbol or representation of ownership (certificate, membership of professional association). This can come to embody the benefits enjoyed.

    (c) Increasing the chances or opportunity of ownership (eg time-shares, shares in the organisation for regular customers).

10: Services marketing

2   There must be continuous development of service-enhancing practice.

- Policies on selection.
- Programmes of training.
- Standard, consistent operational practices ('MacDonaldisation').
- Standardised operational rules.
- Effective motivational programmes.
- Managerial appointments.
- The attractiveness and appropriateness of the service offer.
- Effective policies of staff reward and remuneration.

3   Things design can do:

- Convey the nature of the service involved
- Transmit messages and information
- Imply aesthetic qualities, moral values, or other socio-cultural aspects of a corporate image
- Reinforce an existing image
- Reassure
- Engender an emotional reaction in the customer, through sensory and symbolic blends

4   The following are all dimensions of client service quality.

- *Problem solving creativity:* looking beyond the obvious and not being bound by accepted professional and technical approaches

- *Initiative:* anticipating problems and opportunities and not just reacting

- *Efficiency:* keeping client costs down through effective work planning and control

- *Fast response:* responding to enquiries, questions, problems as quickly as possible

- *Timeliness:* starting and finishing service work to agreed deadlines

- *Open-mindedness:* professionals not being 'blinkered' by their technical approach

- *Sound judgement:* professionals such as accountants dealing with the wider aspects of their technical specialisations

- *Functional expertise:* need to bring together all the functional skills necessary from whatever sources to work on a client project

- *Industry expertise:* clients expect professionals to be thoroughly familiar with their industry and recent changes in it

- *Managerial effectiveness:* maintaining a focus upon the use of both the firm's and the client's resources

- *Orderly work approach:* clients expect salient issues to be identified early and do not want last minute surprises before deadlines

- *Commitment:* clients evaluate the calibre of the accountant and the individual attention given

- *Long-range focus:* clients prefer long-term relationships rather than 'projects' or 'jobs'

- *Qualitative approach:* accountants should not be seen as simple number crunchers

- *Continuity:* clients do not like firms who constantly change the staff that work with them - they will evaluate staff continuity as part of an ongoing relationship

- *Personality:* clients will also evaluate the friendliness, understanding and co-operation of the service provider

Now try illustrative question 15 at the end of the Study Text

11 Charity and Not-for-Profit Marketing

Chapter Topic List	Syllabus reference
1 Setting the scene	-
2 Charity and not-for-profit marketing	4.3
3 Is marketing relevant to this sector?	4.3
4 Distinctive characteristics	4.3
5 The charity marketing mix	4.3

Learning Outcome

Students will be able to demonstrate the adaptation of marketing operations principles in a variety of contexts.

Examples of Marketing at Work

- Oxfam and the RSPB
- Charities and the government
- The Army

1 SETTING THE SCENE

1.1 The objectives of charities and not-for-profit organisations are different from those of most other commercial organisations. While they may carry on economic activities their main purpose is not profit maximisation (Section 2). Although the marketing concept does involve profit, marketing techniques, such as segmentation and targeting, can be applied by non-profit sectors to further their objectives (Sections 3 and 4).

2 CHARITY AND NOT-FOR-PROFIT MARKETING 12/96, 6/98

2.1 In the United Kingdom, charitable status is governed by statute law. For a body to qualify as a charity its **purposes** must fall within certain fairly widely defined categories such as the promotion of education or religion. The rather wider category of not-for-profit (NFP) organisations might be defined as organisations which do not have increasing the wealth of the owners as a primary objective, though the larger cooperative and mutual societies probably do not count as NFP bodies. Also, many NFP bodies undertake clearly commercial ventures, such as shops and concerts, in order to generate revenue. Neilsen

11: Charity and not-for-profit marketing

describes this process of undertaking a profit making operation, so that income will exceed expenditure, as 'piggy-backing'.

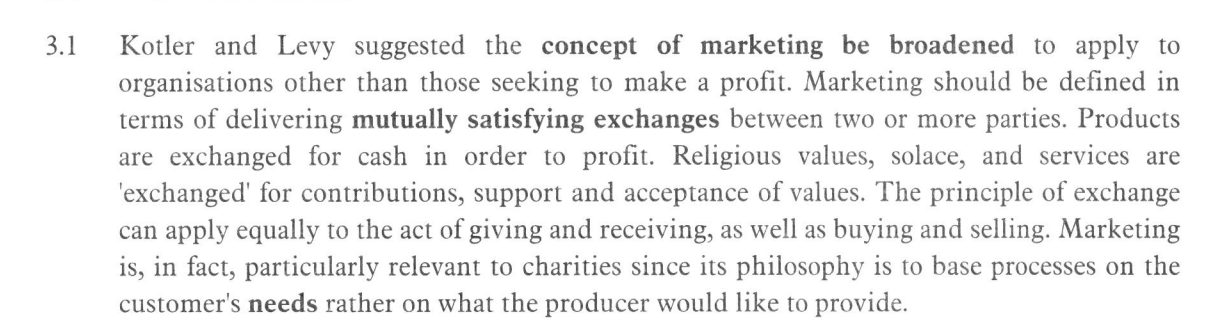

Marketing at Work

Oxfam and the RSPB

Oxfam operates more shops than any commercial organisation in Britain, and these operate at a profit. The Royal Society for the Protection of Birds operates a mail order trading company which provides a 25% return on capital, operating very profitably and effectively.

2.2 Bois suggests that we define NFP enterprises by recognising that their first objective is to be 'non-loss' operations in order to cover their costs and that profits are only made as a means to an end such as providing a service, or accomplishing some socially or morally worthy objective.

2.3 *Dibb, Simkin, Pride and Ferrell* suggest that non-business marketing can conveniently be split into two sub-categories.

   (a) **Non-profit organisation marketing,** for , examples, for hospitals and colleges.

   (b) **Social marketing** seeks to shape perceived beneficial social attitudes such as protecting the environment, saving scarce resources or contributing towards good causes.

3 IS MARKETING RELEVANT TO THIS SECTOR?

> **Exam Tip**
> A question in the June 1998 exam required you to write a case history which illustrated excellence in the practice of not-for-profit marketing. The examiner remarked that the question was poorly answered and give notice that this type of question would be set again. You should ensure that you prepare case study examples for each area of the syllabus.

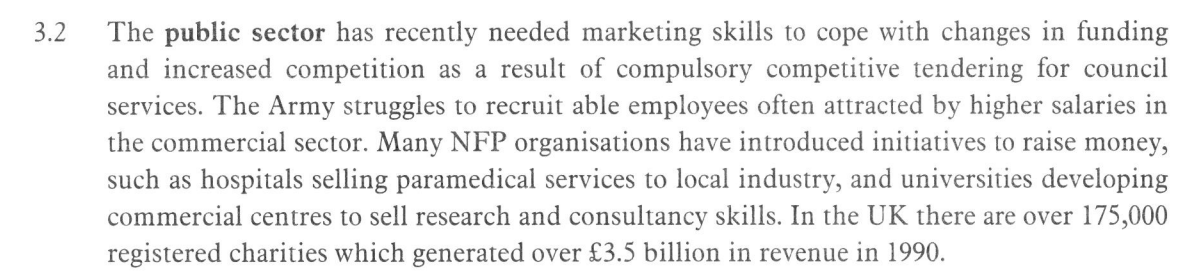

3.1 Kotler and Levy suggested the **concept of marketing be broadened** to apply to organisations other than those seeking to make a profit. Marketing should be defined in terms of delivering **mutually satisfying exchanges** between two or more parties. Products are exchanged for cash in order to profit. Religious values, solace, and services are 'exchanged' for contributions, support and acceptance of values. The principle of exchange can apply equally to the act of giving and receiving, as well as buying and selling. Marketing is, in fact, particularly relevant to charities since its philosophy is to base processes on the customer's **needs** rather on what the producer would like to provide.

3.2 The **public sector** has recently needed marketing skills to cope with changes in funding and increased competition as a result of compulsory competitive tendering for council services. The Army struggles to recruit able employees often attracted by higher salaries in the commercial sector. Many NFP organisations have introduced initiatives to raise money, such as hospitals selling paramedical services to local industry, and universities developing commercial centres to sell research and consultancy skills. In the UK there are over 175,000 registered charities which generated over £3.5 billion in revenue in 1990.

Part D: Marketing operations in context

Marketing at Work

Charity and the government

'Charity is one of the things the British seem to be very good at. Our parliament, judiciary and civil service may no longer be the best in the world, but few countries have quite such an array of impressive voluntary organisations such as the RSPCA and Barnardo's, Shelter and the National Trust. Few could have staged Live Aid, or the kind of disaster relief that OXFAM or Save the Children specialise in. Few have such a tradition of independent bodies, confidant (and rich) enough to criticise governments with impunity. On the surface this tradition remains remarkably strong. Charities have expanded their role as contractors to government in everything from community care to training, with surprisingly few hiccups. The decline of some of the older charities, such as the St John Ambulance or the Salvation Army, has been matched by the rise of others - Save the Children or the National Trust, and an explosion of new charities. In political terms the volunteer section has probably never had such a cross party support as it enjoys today.'

The Independent, 20 July 1996

3.3 Marketing management is now recognised as equally valuable to profit orientated or NFP organisations. The tasks of marketing audit, setting objectives, developing strategies and marketing mixes and controls for their implementation can all help in improving the performance of charities and NFP organisations.

Marketing at Work

The Army

In every market there are two indications that advertising is working: results and emulation by the competition. Saatchi and Saatchi's integrated campaign for the Army has achieved both in spades.

So far, as a result of the campaign, officer and soldier recruitment levels have risen, awareness is running at 95 per cent among 16-24 year-old men, and there is a significant improvement in the image of an army career.

The most recent estimates show that officer recruitment will easy hit its target for 1996-97 and is expected to be up 2.5 per cent year on year while soldier recruitment is expected to achieve a 25 per cent hike on 1995-96 levels.

This success has not gone unnoticed by industry observers. Leo Burnett's executive creative director, Gerard Stamp, said 'If quality of advertising was anything to go by, I think we'd all be joining the Army.' (Campaign, 6 September 1996.)

Where most direct campaigns seek to make a response easy, this one put challenges in the way of applicants such as giving readers the task of finding a photocopier to enlarge the too small coupon on one of the press ads.

The degree of difficulty of the challenges was adjusted to suit the type of applicant required and all elements of the campaign - which included TV, radio, direct mail, press, posters and a Website - emphasised the umbrella campaign theme, 'Be the best'.

In each case, communications were used as filters to ensure the best quality recruits were attracted and the poor quality ones discouraged. A key objective was to maximise the number of quality applicants. Coupled with this was the requirement to improve conversions from enquiry to enlistment, all against a background of falling enlistments until 1994-95, when Saatchis took over the account.

Campaign 14, February 1997

4 DISTINCTIVE CHARACTERISTICS

4.1 Whilst the basic principles are appropriate for this sector. Dibb *et al* suggest that **four key differences** exist related to objectives, target markets, marketing mixes and controlling marketing activities.

4.2 **Objectives** will not be based on profit achievement but rather on **achieving a particular response from target markets**. This has implications for reporting of results. The organisation will need to be open and honest in showing how it has managed its budget and

11: Charity and not-for-profit marketing

allocated funds raised. Efficiency and effectiveness are particularly important in the use of donated funds.

> **Action Programme 1**
>
> List possible objectives for NFP and charitable organisations.

4.3 **The concept of target marketing** is different in the not-for-profit sector. There are no buyers but rather **a number of different audiences**. A target public is a group of individuals who have an interest or concern about the charity. Those benefiting from the organisation's activities are known as the client public. Relationships are vital with donors and volunteers from the general public. In addition, there may also be a need to lobby local and national government and businesses for support. *Gwin* has identified five constituent groups.

- Resource generators
- Service users
- Regulators
- Managers
- Staff members

4.4 *Bruce* has identified four types of 'customers' for charities.

(a) **Beneficiaries** include not only those who receive tangible support, but also those who benefit from lobbying and publicity.

(b) **Supporters** provide money, time and skill. Voluntary workers form an important group of supporters. Those who choose to buy from charities are supporters, as are those who advocate their causes.

(c) **Regulators** include both the more formal bodies, such as the Charities Commission and local authorities, and less formal groups such as residents' associations.

(d) **Stakeholders** have rights and responsibilities in connection with charities and include trustees, managers, staff and representatives of beneficiaries.

4.5 Charities and NFP organisations often deal more with services than products. In this sense the **extended marketing mix of people, process and physical evidence** is important.

(a) **Appearance** should be business-like rather than appearing extravagant.

(b) **Process** is increasingly important; for example, the use of direct debit to pay council tax, reduces administration costs, thus leaving more budget for community services.

(c) **People**, whether employed or volunteers, must offer good service and be caring in their dealings with their clients.

(d) **Distribution channels** are often shorter with fewer intermediaries than in the profit making sector. Wholesalers and distributors available to business organisations do not exist in most non-business contexts.

(e) **Promotion is often dominated by personal selling** with street corner and door-to-door collections. Advertising is often limited to public service announcements due to limited budgets. However, the Army case study illustrates that this is not always true. Direct marketing is growing due to the ease of developing databases. Sponsorship, competitions and special events are also widely used.

Part D: Marketing operations in context

(f) **Pricing** is probably the most different element in this sector. Financial price is often not a relevant concept. Rather, **opportunity cost**, where an individual is persuaded of the value of donating time or funds, is more relevant.

4.6 **Controlling activities** is complicated by the difficulty of judging whether the **non-quantitative objectives** have been met. For example, assessing whether a charity has improved the situation of client publics is difficult to research. To control NFP marketing activities, managers must specify what factors need to be monitored and permissible variance levels. Statistics related to product mix, financial resources, size of budgets, number of employees, number of volunteers, number of customers serviced and number and location of facilities, may be useful.

5 THE CHARITY MARKETING MIX

5.1 Bruce points out that charity marketing is akin to service marketing and that the extended service marketing mix is appropriate. To the 7Ps he adds an eighth: **philosophy**. The guiding philosophy of the charity says what it is for and how it goes about its business. Clearly, just as the components of the normal marketing mix must be in harmony with one another, so too must they be in harmony with the charity's philosophy. It would, for instance, be inappropriate for an animal rights charity to own a battery egg production unit.

5.2 A charity's **products** include **ideas** as well as goods and services. Ideas are very important in fund-raising, pressure-group activity and communicating with the public.

- When a supporter provides money to a charity, the idea of what the money will be used for is a kind of product, providing satisfaction to the supporter.

- Pressure groups work, in part, by promoting new ideas into the public consciousness, so that bodies with power can be persuaded to take a desired course of action.

- Ideas can also be promoted to the public with the aim of changing their behaviour. Governments often take this approach, as, for instance, with energy conservation and road safety campaigns.

5.3 **Price** is very important to larger charities since sales of goods and services provide their largest single source of income. Proper cost accounting techniques must be applied where appropriate.

5.4 Since supporters are crucial to a charity's income and beneficiaries are the reason why it exists, **processes** must be as customer-friendly as possible. This is certainly an area where philosophy is important.

Action Programme 2

You have just joined a small charity which is currently without a formal marketing function. You have been asked to prepare a report which outlines the relevance of marketing in this sector.

11: Charity and not-for-profit marketing

Chapter Roundup

- NFP and charitable organisations are usually viewed as a single type, even though this is a varied sector containing both public and private operations.

- Marketing has a lot to offer this sector in terms of marketing auditing and research, the development of strategies to include a clear understanding of segmentation, targeting and positioning.

- Each element of the marketing mix can be used to achieve the organisation's objectives and marketing control can help to ensure these are achieved.

Quick Quiz

1. Define NFP marketing. (see para 2.1)
2. How do Dibb *et al* split NFP marketing? (2.3)
3. What are the four distinctive characteristics in this sector? (4.1)
4. What are the five constituent groups identified by Gwin? (4.3)
5. How might a charity use the tools of the promotional mix? (4.5)

Action Programme Review

1. Possible objectives include the following.

    - Surplus maximisation (equivalent to profit maximisation)
    - Revenue maximisation (as for a commercial business)
    - Usage maximisation (as in leisure centre swimming pool usage)
    - Usage targeting (matching the capacity available as in the NHS)
    - Cost recovery (minimising subsidy)
    - Budget maximisation (maximising what is offered)
    - Producer satisfaction maximisation (satisfying the wants of staff and volunteers)
    - Client satisfaction maximisation (the police generating the support of the public)

2. The charity has objectives which it wants to attain.

    Plans will be developed and implemented to achieve these non-profit objectives. The various publics to whom the charity will be communicating will need to be identified. This is in keeping with profit orientated organisations' application of marketing, namely, 'to identify, anticipate and satisfy customer requirements profitably' (CIM). Whilst the profit element is not included in our activities, we are still seeking to make the best use of our resources.

    The anticipation of our target markets' needs is vitally important. Our 'customers' in this sense are the people that the charity supports. Other 'customers' include the volunteers working for the charity. In return for their time, support and enthusiasm we must satisfy their needs for team-spirit, and social activities, for example. The donors to the charity will need to feel that their funds are being used wisely and for the purposes they intended. By satisfying the needs of our various stakeholders, we can satisfy our own goals.

    Charities are in the business of attracting volunteers and donors and developing a long term relationship with them. To achieve this, the development of trust is vital, and can be fostered through effective communications as in commercial markets.

    Part of our work is about education of the public, and choosing the correct communication channels and message is just as important as it is in advertising a bar of chocolate. The issues involved are more serious but the process is the same. The difference really lies in the results desired - one is to increase awareness, the other is to prompt action to purchase. Much commercial advertising is intended to increase awareness, change attitudes and increase knowledge. We will be using our communications in relation to the charity aims rather than profit objectives.

    Marketing has a valuable contribution to make in achieving the charity's goals. It emphasises the needs of the various customer groups and directs our attention towards satisfying their needs. We can do this by using the tools of marketing which include marketing planning, implementation and control and in

Part D: Marketing operations in context

particular the techniques offered by marketing communications, including advertising, direct marketing, sponsorship and public relations. A marketing orientation also emphasises the need for a quality service to achieve customer satisfaction and for relationship management to ensure loyalty and support.

Now try illustrative question 10 at the end of the Study Text

12 International Marketing

Chapter Topic List	Syllabus reference
1 Setting the scene	-
2 International marketing opportunities	4.4
3 Marketing information needs	4.4
4 Marketing environment differences	4.4
5 Regional trade alliances and markets	4.4
6 Product	4.4
7 Place	4.4
8 Price	4.4
9 Promotion	4.4
10 Structure choices	4.4

Learning Outcome

Students will be able to demonstrate the adaptation of marketing operations principles in a variety of contexts.

Examples of Marketing at Work

- Boeing
- Bicycles
- Market research in China
- Wal-Mart
- Language problems
- Mars
- JIT
- World cup
- Trade missions
- Tesco

1 SETTING THE SCENE

1.1 International marketing presents a new set of challenges (Section 2) for the marketer. First, the marketing information needs are great and cannot be satisfied as easily as at home (Section 3). The marketing environment is different, with each country having its own characteristic laws and culture (Section 4). Regional trade alliances between countries (Section 5) present a new set of difficulties and opportunities which must be addressed if

Part D: Marketing operations in context

the organisation's strategy is to be successful. Key decisions relate to adapting the marketing mix (Sections 6-9) and the means by which a firm will enter the overseas market (Section 10).

2 INTERNATIONAL MARKETING OPPORTUNITIES

> **Exam Tip**
> International marketing has been examined fairly regularly. Its first appearance was in a pan-European consumer marketing context in the 40-mark mini-case in December 1997. (This is the *Dockers* mini-case which appears as Q71 in our Practice & Revision Kit). It also featured in December 1995 (part of the *Ben and Jerry's* mini-case, Q66 of our Practice & Revision Kit).

2.1 Companies will enter into international marketing for a number of different reasons.

(a) **Growth**. If the domestic market is static or growth is slow, or if competition is excessively fierce, a company may seek to explore new areas within which it can hope to compete or operate without competition.

(b) **Economies of scale**. Since volume of output and unit cost are related, increased volume may lead to lower-than-competitive costs. Expanding into international markets may provide the level of sales necessary to benefit from economies of scale.

(c) **International competition**. Markets of all kinds are becoming globalised. International trade becomes a necessity. In many industries, those who are unable to compete globally may find themselves reduced to subcontracting for the main players.

(d) **National necessity**. Imports must be paid for with foreign currency, and exports provide the means of acquiring this currency. Governments typically encourage exports.

Marketing at Work

Boeing

Boeing has taken over McDonnell Douglas. While McDonnell Douglas is a large defence contractor, its commercial aircraft business, once a world force, was struggling to win 3 per cent of the world market. Boeing's take-over signalled the end of McDonnell Douglas as an independent maker of civil aircraft. It also promised to turn Boeing into the biggest defence and aerospace company on earth.

Boeing could not stand still. There are too many examples in aviation and other sectors of what has happened to companies that have tried to do that.

Last year, in a speech to managers, Condit (CEO) described his vision of what the group would look like in 2016, its centenary year. He told them that Boeing would be an aerospace company. It would not repeat earlier mistakes such as attempting to enter the train or boat-building business.

Second, he said, Boeing would be a 'global enterprise'. This would mean increasing the number of countries of operation.

One of the ways in which Boeing plans to increase its international exposure is through increased use of joint ventures. Boeing has worked with Japanese companies for years. McDonnell Douglas has links with companies such as British Aerospace through projects like the Harrier jump jet. Condit saw scope for joint venture projects in China, although the Chinese have chosen European partners instead of Boeing to develop a new 100-seat jet.

Financial Times, March 12th 1997

The analysis of international marketing opportunities

2.2 *Morden* suggested that international markets could be analysed under headings described as the 12Cs.

- Country
- Culture and consumer behaviour
- Concentration
- Communication
- Channels of distribution
- Capacity to pay
- Currency
- Control and co-ordination
- Commitment
- Choices
- Contractual obligations
- Caveats

2.3 Marketing into a 'foreign' marketplace presents quite specific problems which should not be under-estimated even when the markets involved appear very similar.

3 MARKETING INFORMATION NEEDS 6/97, 6/98

3.1 In order to develop an effective marketing plan, information about the markets into which the company intends to go is essential. In the case of domestic markets research would provide that information. International marketing research faces a number of challenges which mark it out from home research.

- Lack of secondary data and the difficulty of establishing comparability and equivalence
- Cost of collecting primary data
- Complexity of research design
- Co-ordination of research and data collection across countries

Secondary data

3.2 There is little comparability between countries' available data. For example, it is by no means easy to compare census data. Different countries gather it in different ways and at different time intervals.

- Every 10 years in the USA
- Every 5 years in Japan and Canada
- Every 27 years in Germany

Similarly, in ten reports on the economies of Eastern Europe, figures varied widely. For the old East Germany, reported GDP varied from $4,000 to $13,000 per capita.

3.3 Many countries do not collect **income data** at all. In some there is a tradition of independence and a suspicion of government interference, plus great cultural differences in attitudes to tax collection. **Education levels**, which may be used to measure socio-economic status, may be misleading since education systems vary between countries. Some countries collect data on non citizens, for example Germany and Switzerland. Others, for example Canada, collect data on religion, but this is regarded as a private and highly sensitive matter in many countries. Comparability and equivalence become sensitive issues when there are no ready agreements as to the definition of a household. Homosexual groups protested when recent research did not accommodate the idea of single sex 'family/household' groups. In some countries, single sex marriages are legally acknowledged. Definitions also vary for 'housewife'/'homemaker', socio-economic groupings, income brackets and customer profiles.

3.4 In addition, data may well imply quite different things, even when the same instruments are used in the data collection process. A cross-national comparison of consumer research

Part D: Marketing operations in context

measures showed that even with the same scales, measuring the same product attributes, different levels of reliability appear.

3.5 The marketing research process conducted internationally is more complex, but the basic approach remains the same as for domestic research. The key difference is in implementing some of the steps. For example, problem definition and development of research objectives may take weeks or months, and this depends upon choice of methodology, selection of respondents and decisions about time frame.

Marketing at Work

Bicycles

In a study of market research in Japan, Brizz looked at research objectives. For example, for a bicycle marketer, these will vary according to 'served needs' in different cultures/economies. In a western society, bicycles have to compete with product replacement threats from other 'youth leisure' products such as skis, footballs and the cinema. In less developed countries, the major competition could be motorcycles, mopeds, scooters or small cars, since this product is a major source of serious everyday transport.

Primary data collection

3.6 As noted above, for secondary sources of data in developing countries, both availability and reliability are major problems. Despite the expense, companies may have to commission primary data generation much earlier in a developing country research project. However, this has its own problems.

3.7 In the case of primary research, participation is often difficult to obtain. In many cultures, men will not discuss shaving habits with anyone, particularly women interviewers, while respondents in the Netherlands and Germany are unwilling to discuss personal finances. The Dutch are more willing to discuss sexual behaviour.

Marketing at Work

Market research in China

A survey of the vast Chinese market, published in *Marketing Business,* shows that market research is a new science in China but already there are a dozen or more groups in the Shenzhen Economic zone in Guangdong researching the buying habits of the Chinese public.

Marketing research is a new concept for some Chinese enterprises because consumers had no choice under a totally state-run system.

The public is bemused by the use of Western research techniques, based on focus groups, door-to-door interviews and broad surveys. Nobody has ever canvassed their views on any aspect of life in the People's Republic. The response tends to be enthusiastic with a reply rate to surveys at 60 per cent, high compared with the West.

3.8 Even the process of translation can be a major problem. In **back translation,** questionnaires are translated from the home language to the language of the country where they will be used by a foreign language speaker, then translated back to the home language by a bilingual who is a native speaker of the home language. In **parallel translation**, two or more translators translate the questionnaire and then the results are compared.

3.9 Methods of data collection may also vary between countries. For example, face-to-face interviews at home or work are very popular in the UK and Switzerland, while interviews in

12: International marketing

shopping areas are favoured in the Netherlands and France. The Japanese consumer prefers personal, face to face discussions to telephone or mail.

Research design

3.10 **Sampling techniques** may be less than perfect. Although probability samples are preferred, because errors can be taken into account, in many countries the market infrastructure and lack of data does not allow probability sampling to take place, because an adequate frame cannot be constructed from which the sample can be selected.

3.11 Overseas data is frequently aggregated, and consequently does not satisfy the needs of a firm which is focusing on one product. In this case, **market assessment by inference** becomes a useful tool. This approach uses **available facts about related products or other foreign markets** as a basis for deriving appropriate information.

According to *Reed Moyer*, three inference bases are commonly used.

- Inference based on a **related product**, for example replacement tyre market based on car ownership.

- Inference based on **related market size,** for example, a known need in one country may be used as a basis for countries with similar economic development levels, and consumption patterns, scaling statistics population ratio).

- Inference based on **related environmental factors** such as similar shifts in socio-economic variables.

In many cases, researchers can use multiple factor indices or proxies known to be correlated to the market potential for the product.

> **Exam Tip**
> Marketing information requirements were covered specifically in June 1997 and June 1998. In the June 1997 question you had to centre your report around an industry of your choice and a country of your choice.
> The June 1998 question was related to emerging markets and information on their attractiveness. Information is likely to be hard to get, so don't assume that you an automatically apply the same approach to marketing research in the overseas market that you use at home.

4 MARKETING ENVIRONMENT DIFFERENCES 12/99

4.1 Even between neighbouring countries such as France and Spain, or Zimbabwe and South Africa cultural differences can be very great. Marketing planning must consider the main aspects of cultural systems.

- Material culture
- Social institutions
- Belief systems
- Aesthetics
- Language

4.2 **Material culture** affects the following.

(a) The **level of demand**. For instance, the lack of electricity will restrict the demand for electronic items. An American firm set out to launch a best selling cake mix in the 1950s to Japan, only to find that Japanese kitchens were not equipped with ovens.

Part D: Marketing operations in context

- (b) **Quality and types of products demanded.** Difference in disposable income influences the kinds of goods demanded. Note also the **symbolic** importance of particular goods which may be used primarily for **display,** for instance, the popularity of comparatively expensive western cigarettes and sunglasses in Communist China.

- (c) **Functional characteristics.** Demand for snack food and the habit of 'grazing' has been stimulated in the UK by changes in the social roles of women, and in the activities which take place within the home.

- (d) The **nature of products demanded.** 'Menu meals' are a product intended to help women prepare quality food when they cannot spare time for shopping and cooking because many are now in full-time employment.

Marketing at Work

Wal-Mart

For most people, the announcement that Wal-Mart was buying Asda, the UK supermarket chain, was just another merger, another confirmation that modern business crosses national boundaries.

But Wal-Mart, on any conceivable criteria of the half dozen most successful companies of our times, is not global at all.

Almost all its employees work in the US. Almost all its sales are in the US and not comprehensively within the USA at that. It is only 10 years since the company targeted the north-eastern states at all, and it continues to encounter customer and community resistance there.

Wal-Mart is firmly based in mid-town America. The products they sell, from doughnuts to handguns, and the ways in which they are sold - 'You must be satisfied, our policy guarantees it' - are culturally specific. The Wal-Mart formula is American not only in its location but in its values.

In this, Wal-Mart epitomises the retailing business. Most retail formats remain assertively national.

No general retailer has yet made a real success of taking a domestic format overseas, and those who have come closest have placed their domestic format in an overseas niche - as when Marks and Spencer's English sandwiches became the favoured lunch of chic Parisians. There is still no more forceful reminder that the homogenisation of taste is still some way off than the contrast between a Wal-Mart supercentre and a Carrefour hypermarket.

John Kay, Financial Times, 23 June 1999

4.3 **Social institutions** give a society its distinctive form, and develop around particular aspects of the life experience such as the care and training of children, or coping with conflict or suffering. The form of social institutions has profound implications for the ways in which goods are regarded, since they provide the foundations for value systems, and through them, attitudes and behaviour.

- (a) **Social organisation.** Tightly knit family units, in which social roles are bound up with responsibility to the family, influence both the kinds of products demanded, and the ways in which purchase decisions are made.

- (b) **Political structures.** The political system sets the agenda for consumption through policy and example.

- (c) **Educational system.** Literacy is a key factor in promotional and advertising activity.

- (d) **Family or household roles.** Roles played by family members in decision making are one area in which culture shapes consumption. Also, the way in which the household is actually used and regarded are very important for consumption. For instance, the modern household actually forms the focus for leisure activity far more than it did in the past.

12: International marketing

4.4 **Belief systems** include **religious, philosophical, and political ideologies**. Generalised belief systems are all-pervasive, even in societies which consider themselves secularised. Our holidays and gift giving occasions are formed around the old religious calendar; the foods we eat reflect moral and aesthetic judgements as much as nutritional good sense. Many religions proscribe particular forms of consumption, such as coffee, alcoholic drinks, 'provocative' clothes and certain music. In Japan, claims to be 'superior' to other products would be regarded as shocking and in questionable taste.

4.5 **Aesthetics** and what counts as beauty or ugliness is tied into quite specific values which a marketer must be aware of in a foreign culture.

4.6 Marketing literature is full of examples of linguistic *faux pas*, such as the Vauxhall Nova, which means 'doesn't go' in Spanish. Advertising slogans need to beware of the pitfalls of the local **language**; successful slogans may not work in another language, or may be unintentionally funny or offensive.

Marketing at Work

Language problems

The marketing of 'Cue' toothpaste in French-speaking Canada failed because the brand name sounds exactly like a very rude French colloquialism. The number 4 (shi) in Japanese also serves as the word for death, and needs to be avoided. In India, numerology is also part of the everyday knowledge, so that numbers have meanings (6, for instance, is 'hijira', the eunuch).

5 REGIONAL TRADE ALLIANCES AND MARKETS

5.1 Trade between nations is of such significance that rules governing it have been established. Economic theory predicts mutual benefits for nations trading internationally but there are two opposing pressures.

- The desire to expand the domestic economy by selling to other nations
- The desire to protect indigenous sources of employment by restricting imports

Regional trading groups

5.2 Whilst the World Trade Organisation encourages free trade, the opposite force of protectionism has led to the creation of regional trading organisations, which seek to encourage trade between members but introduce hurdles to non-members. An example is the EU. These regional trading groups can take progressively more integrated forms.

- Free trade areas
- Customs unions
- Economic unions

5.3 **Free trade areas** have members who agree to lower barriers to trade amongst themselves. There is little other form of economic cooperation. Examples include Mercosur and the Andean Community in South America, and the North American Free Trade Agreement, comprising Canada, the USA and Mexico. In underdeveloped countries, attempts to form such associations have led to problems as members seek to protect their embryo economies, and fear the effects of free trade with member states.

Part D: Marketing operations in context

5.4 **Customs unions** not only provide the advantages of free trade areas, but also agree a common policy on barriers to external countries. Currently the EU is the leading example of this type of union, and is seen as the prototype for other unions elsewhere.

Economic unions

5.5 The ultimate step is the submission of all decisions relating to trade, both internal and external, from member states to the union itself. **In effect the members become one for economic purposes**. The EU has economic union as an aim. The effect of regional trade organisations, such as the EU is mixed. On the one hand, trade within the community will no doubt be easier and freer, opening up significant opportunities to importer and exporter alike. On the other hand, those outside the community will find it more difficult to compete on even terms due to the tariff barriers being introduced to protect members.

5.6 For a country like the UK, membership may bring mixed blessings.

(a) Over 50% of UK foreign trade is with other EU members, and the development of the EU will expand such trade and make it easier.

(b) However our largest market in terms of a single country is the USA, which takes some 13% of UK exports. The EU barriers to non-members such as the USA, may result in retaliatory action. The net result could be a trade war between the major economic blocs, and a diminution in world trade.

5.7 One significant effect of EU progress has been the rush of multinationals setting up assembly or manufacturing plant within one or more member states, rather than importing into the EU. Thus France, Germany and the UK have seen considerable inward investment from US and Japanese firms, trying to avoid the barriers being set in place from 1993. In the case of the EU, assembly is not sufficient. EU goods must be 80% sourced within the community to qualify as EU produced and thus avoid tariffs and quotas.

6 PRODUCT

To standardise or to customise?

6.1 Products successfully marketed within one country cannot necessarily be moved into an alien market without problems. Products have symbolic and psychological aspects as well as physical attributes. As a result, entry into a market with a different set of cultural, religious, economic, social and political assumptions may cause extreme reactions to a product concept or marketing mix.

6.2 The problem derives from an inherent tension between two important ideas in marketing. Target marketing and segmentation suggest that the way to maximise sales is to identify specific consumer needs and hence to **adapt** a product for a new foreign market. At the same time, it is impractical to create separate products for every conceivable segment, and it is more profitable to produce a **standardised** product for a larger market. This is resolved by considering the costs and benefits of alternative marketing strategies.

> **Exam Tip**
> The June 1999 case study included a review of globalisation and customisation strategies and their implications for the marketing mix.
> The examiner remarked that better answers used *Keegan's* adaptation model.

6.3 Keegan suggests there are five approaches to the problem of adaptation which are defined by decisions about the product and about promotion. They are summarised in the diagram below. **Extension** of product or promotion means that no significant change is made.

		PRODUCT	
PROMOTION		Extension	Adaptation	New
	Extension	Straight Extension	Product Adaptation	Product invention
	Adaptation	Communication Adaptation	Dual Adaptation	

(a) **Straight extension** has the advantages discussed in the next paragraph.

(b) **Product adaptation** is normally undertaken so that the product can either fulfil the same function under different conditions, as when an electrical device is adapted to conform to a different voltage, or to overcome cultural problems such as taste.

(c) **Communications adaptation** is a way of marketing an unchanged product to fulfil a different need as when garden implements are promoted as agricultural equipment in less-developed countries where plot sizes tend to be small. This can be very cost effective.

(d) **Dual adaptation** is expensive but applies to most products since there tend to be at least small differences in the ways they are used in new markets.

(e) **Product invention** is commonly used to enter less sophisticated markets where products must be simple and cheap.

6.4 **Arguments in favour of product standardisation**

(a) **Economies of scale**

(i) **Production**
- Plant confined to one country and used to maximum capacity rather than duplicated.
- Exporting rather than difficult licensing deals.

(ii) **Research and development**. Product modification is costly and time consuming.

(iii) **Marketing**. Promotion which can use the same images and theme in advertising is clearly more cost effective when only the soundtrack, or the printed slogan, has to be changed. Similarly, standardisation of distribution systems, salesforce training, aftersales provisions, and other aspects of the marketing mix can save a great deal of money.

(b) **Consumer mobility**. Finding a familiar brand name is important for the growing numbers of travellers moving across national boundaries.

Marketing at Work

Mars

Mars is posed to combine its confectionery, food and petcare divisions into a single pan-European business.

The changes take immediate effect in Europe, with the UK businesses following suit at a late stage under plans drawn up by Mars' European management team.

Part D: Marketing operations in context

In the UK, the Mars Confectionery, Pedigree Masterfoods and Seeds of Change businesses will eventually merge.

Mike Davies has been appointed UK vice-president for the petcare and food business. He replaces Sandra Blaza, who becomes European vice-president of personnel. Bill Ronald remains in charge of confectionery in his post as vice-president of UK snack food.

European petcare vice-president Ann Francke is overseeing a plan to combine petcare marketing operations in the UK and Europe.

It is unclear how the restructure will affect marketing at Mars Confectionery.

A Mars UK spokesman says: 'We want a more harmonised business in Europe, because the needs of our consumers are the same across the continent.

'We have international competitors, and it's also vital because central European countries want to be part of a single market. Our bigger markets, such as France and Germany, will not be integrated.

'The UK will definitely fall in line with the structure, but it's a very big market for us and we'll watch and learn what happens in Europe first.'

Marketing Week, 6 January 2000

(c) **Technological complexity**. The microelectronics market illustrates the inherent danger of diversity in technically complex products. Even the endorsement of powerful Japanese companies could not sustain the Betamax VCR system or non-standard PC systems. The international market selected VHS and IBM respectively.

Action Programme 1

What are the arguments in favour of product adaptation?

New products in international markets

6.5 Product ideas, both internally and externally generated, must be screened in order to identify potentially marketable and profitable products. Product screening may be carried out at a centralised location, although this poses the threat of alienating management at remote subsidiary plants where many ideas may originate. If this does cause problems, some measure of decentralisation in the screening process may be necessary.

Criteria for product screening

6.6 Products are screened against the firm's capabilities and characteristics.

(a) **Producing the product**. This may involve existing resources or involve diversification.

(b) **Marketing the product**. If this can be accommodated within existing marketing resources, then so much the better. Formulating a new system could involve substantial outlay and disruption.

(c) **Researching the new market**. This might involve the deployment of existing resources, particularly if (as is likely) the firm is already established, and operating in a related area. If there is no related market involvement, there is greater uncertainty and hence risk.

(d) **Marketing internationally**. Orientation to a specific market will reduce the economies of scale involved in multinational marketing. Products are likely to be rejected if they cannot be produced for international markets.

12: International marketing

(e) **Motivation to introduce and market the new product effectively.** What are the reasons for the new product being introduced and how well adjusted is the organisation to this process?

(f) **Organisational suitability to marketing the new product.** Are, for example, suitable support and maintenance systems available?

Product screening in practice

6.7 International firms exist partly because operations spread across several countries reduce overall risk. The more diverse the operations of the firm, however, the more difficult they are to co-ordinate.

A checklist for new products

6.8 Some factors can be assigned a variable weighting, since they are likely to be of varying importance in differing circumstances. Some are **critical**, and failure in these areas will **disqualify** a product from international marketing.

6.9 **Requirements for a new product**

- It must fall within a company's terms of incorporation (critical).
- It must be profitable in the short term.
- It must be profitable in the long term (critical).
- It must have a realistic payback period.
- It must be distinct from previously patented products (critical).
- It must be protected by patent or trademark in all overseas markets.
- It must comply with national safety standards.
- It must be compliant with regulations and profitable when taking account of import duties.
- It must be capable of being produced in a number of countries.
- It must be able to be introduced in either a standardised, or suitably adapted form.

7 PLACE

7.1 A range of factors affect the selection, establishment, and running of international distribution systems. A wide range of channels can be developed.

7.2 Using an **Export Management Company** (EMC) which handles all aspects of exporting can be an attractive option. It requires minimal investment and no company personnel are involved. The EMC already has an established network of sales offices, and extensive international marketing and distribution knowledge. From the company's point of view, however, there is a loss of control.

7.3 Another alternative is **export agents**. These provide more limited services than EMCs, are focused on one country and do not perform EMC marketing tasks but concentrate on the physical movement of products. The main problem here is that a company requires several agents to cover a range of markets.

Part D: Marketing operations in context

7.4 **Direct exporting** can be attractive. In-house personnel are used, but they must be well trained and experienced. Also, the volume of sales must be sufficient to justify employing them.

Import middlemen, or distributors who are experts in their local market needs, can play a key part, being able to source goods from the world market to satisfy local needs. They operate to purchase goods in their own name, and act independently of the manufacturer. They are able to exploit a good access to wholesale and retail networks.

Developing an international distribution strategy

7.5 As in domestic marketing, there must be **consistency of purpose** in the way in which elements within the marketing mix operate. **Four key strategic areas** are involved.

- Distribution density - exposure or coverage desired
- Channel length, alignment and leadership - number, structure and hierarchy relationships of the channel members
- Distribution logistics - physical flow of product

Distribution density

7.6 **Distribution density** depends on a knowledge of how customers select dealers and retail outlets, by segment. If less shopping effort is involved, as in the case of convenience goods, an extensive system would be appropriate. If more shopping effort is used, as in the case of premium priced goods, then a selective or exclusive system would be required.

Channel members

7.7 After strategy has been formulated, marketers must select **channel partners** capable of implementing the overall strategy. Since it can be difficult to change partners once contracted, this choice is very sensitive indeed. There are several important criteria for selection.

- Cost
- Capital requirement
- Product and product line
- Control
- Synergy

Cost falls into three categories. The **initial cost** of locating and setting up the channel **maintenance costs** such as employing sales people, paying travel expenses, auditing and controlling, the profit margin paid to middlemen, and **logistics costs** such as transportation, storage, breaking bulk and customs administration.

7.8 *W J Bilkey* found that the **least profitable approach to distribution was that of direct exporting** to retailers in the host country. The **most profitable involved selling to a distributor** in a country with its own marketing channels. **Capital requirements** here are offset by cash flow patterns. In order to arrive at the right decision, costs must be evaluated as between channels. For example, an import distributor will often pay for goods received before they are sold on to the retailer or industrial. An agent, however, may well not pay anything until payment by the end customer is received.

7.9 **Product and product line** is also relevant. Perishable or short shelf-life products need shorter channels, and this bears on costs and hence profits. High tech products require either direct sales effort or skilled and knowledgeable channel partners.

7.10 **Synergy** arises when the components of a channel complement one another to the extent that they produce more than the sum of their individual parts. Such synergy may arise if, for example, the chosen partner has some key skill which allows quicker access to the market.

Logistics

7.11 Logistics systems are expensive and can be very damaging to corporate profitability if badly handled. There are several areas which are crucial to international logistics.

- Traffic and transportation management
- Inventory control
- Order processing
- Materials handling and warehousing
- Fixed facilities location management

7.12 **Traffic and transportation management** deals primarily with the main mode of transport involved in moving goods. Three main criteria are employed in this choice - lead times, transit time and costs.

7.13 **Inventory control** relates cost with service levels. Inventory reduces potential profit by using up working capital; the management aim here is to reduce inventories to an absolute minimum.

Marketing at Work

JIT

Just-in-Time (JIT) deliveries of parts and components have become increasingly important. Rank Xerox used to keep buffer stocks of 40 days and an inventory of finished goods of 90 days. Now, many JIT parts and components are not kept in stock, and the company maintains a finished goods inventory of only 15 days. This is clearly a global trend in distribution systems as markets and money become increasingly squeezed by ever fiercer competition.

Retailing

7.14 There are certain key global trends in international distribution. **Larger scale retailers** are partly a consequence of economic development and growing affluence. Increasing car ownership, increasing fridge/freezer ownership and the changing role of women all encourage one-stop shopping. Tesco has shut down two-thirds of its small in-town stores (less than 10,000 square feet) in favour of larger stores. This is a global trend deriving from a reduction in distribution costs and increased sophistication of retailers.

7.15 **International retailers** like Marks and Spencer have developed for the same reasons. Companies saw limited growth opportunities at home, and moved to overseas markets. This allows manufacturers to build relationships with retailers active in a number of different markets. This internationalisation process is prompted by improved data communications, new forms of international financing, more open international markets and lower barriers to entry. In the EU for instance, the Single European Market motivates retailers to expand overseas, as they see international retailers entering their domestic markets.

Part D: Marketing operations in context

7.16 **Direct marketing** is growing rapidly all over the world using IT systems to bypass the wholesale - retail network, and go direct to customers.

7.17 **Information technology** has had an enormous impact. Computerised retail systems allow better monitoring of consumer purchases, lower inventory costs and quicker stock turns alongside a better assessment of product profitability. They also make it possible to extend JIT ideas into the area of retailing. Internet selling is widely expected to revolutionise business (though it depends on traditional fulfilment).

Communications

7.18 **Market communications** face additional barriers internationally. In developing an effective promotional mix, experience plays a key role. Costs and the overall effectiveness of measures are also important considerations. The elements to be considered are as follows.

(a) **Push-oriented strategy**. In a domestic setting, this emphasises personal selling. This may be more expensive if employed abroad since minor equipment or supplies in large UK firms may be 'major equipment' overseas and require more involved personal selling effort. Also a long non-domestic channel, involving many non-domestic intermediaries, increase costs, reduces the effect of personal selling, and poses severe control problems.

(b) **Pull-oriented strategy** is characterised by a greater dependence upon advertising and is typically employed for FMCG marketing to very large market segments. It is generally more appropriate for long channels where relatively simple products are being sold. However, not all countries have the same access to advertising media and the quality of media varies greatly.

8 PRICE

Getting the price right

8.1 Prices in foreign markets are likely to be determined by local conditions, with each market separate. The organisation's degree of control over pricing is likely to be higher if it has wholly owned subsidiaries in each of the markets and lower if it conducts business through licensees, franchisees or distributors.

> **Action Programme 2**
>
> Market conditions are the most important influence on pricing. What other factors do you think influence pricing?

8.2 The diversity of markets within a region is important. If markets are unrelated, the seller can successfully charge different prices. Pressures for price uniformity often come from large groupings such as free trade areas or the EU and from increases in international business activity. Companies can control price in several ways.

- Direct distribution to customers
- Resale price maintenance
- Recommended prices
- Agreed margins between parent and subsidiary companies
- Centralised control over prices within several subsidiary companies

9 PROMOTION

9.1 **Sales promotions** may be affected by different retailing norms and government regulations. For example, coupons, much used in the UK and the USA, are prohibited in Germany and Greece. Reduction in price promotions are often restricted to a percentage of full price. As a consequence, standardising sales promotion tools is extremely difficult. Sales promotions are usually handed over to local experts.

9.2 **Sports promotions and sponsorships are widely used**. The key methods involved are advertising during sports programming on TV, positioning of stadium or arena signs and sponsorship of individuals, teams or events. What type is used depends on the country involved, the circumstances and regulations which they apply. In Germany, for example, TV advertising cannot be used within sports shows so alternative approaches are needed.

Marketing at Work

World cup

During the 1990 football World Cup (in Italy), over the course of eight weeks, 24 national teams were watched by 15 billion viewers with 9 billion exposures for sponsoring companies. Major sponsors, including Coca-Cola, Mars, Gillette, Canon, Fuji-Film, Philips, Anheuser-Busch and Carlsberg, gained excellent exposure. It is important to choose the sport correctly. As the 1994 World Cup has shown, soccer still has limited commercial value in the USA. Sponsoring teams can be very powerful, as can linking with a sports star such as basketball player Michael Jordan (Nike).

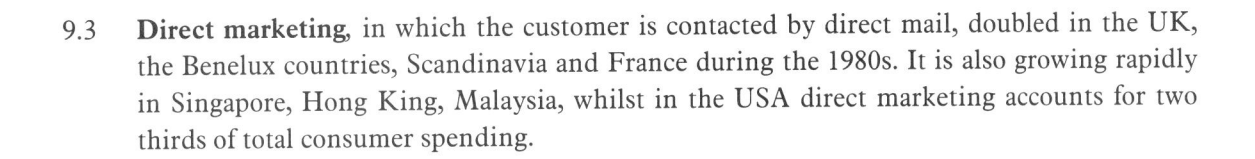

9.3 **Direct marketing**, in which the customer is contacted by direct mail, doubled in the UK, the Benelux countries, Scandinavia and France during the 1980s. It is also growing rapidly in Singapore, Hong King, Malaysia, whilst in the USA direct marketing accounts for two thirds of total consumer spending.

Advertising

9.4 Sources of **media problems**

(a) **Availability**. Media may be more important and effective in some countries than in others (for instance, cinema in India, radio in the USA), while there may be a lack of specific media in others.

   (i) **Newspapers** may not be widely available because of low levels of literacy, or even specific policies on the part of the government.

   (ii) **Magazines**, which are important for specialist products such as industrial machinery, may be very restricted.

   (iii) **TV commercials** are restricted, or even banned in many countries, for instance advertising specifically directed at children is banned in some Scandinavian countries. It is also sometimes very difficult to gauge effectiveness because of missing or incomplete MR data.

   (iv) **Billboards, direct mail** and other forms of promotion may be unfamiliar or ineffective (there is very limited usage of billboards in some formerly communist countries).

(b) **Financial aspects**. Costs may be very difficult to estimate in many countries, since negotiation and the influence of intermediaries is likely to be much greater. There may also be expectations of gift-giving in the negotiation process.

Part D: Marketing operations in context

(c) **Coverage of media (or reach of advertising message)**. This relates to the forms of media employed as well as the physical characteristics of the country. Inaccessible areas may rule out the use of direct mail, or posters; scarcity of telephones may rule out this form of advertising promotion. It may also be difficult to monitor advertising effectiveness.

10 STRUCTURE CHOICES

10.1 Section 7 dealt with distribution specifics. Here we are concerned with marketing at the strategic level.

When considering exporting for the first time a company has to decide upon the degree of involvement which is appropriate and the level of commitment. There are five basic alternatives when entering a foreign market.

- **Simple exporting**, often based on the need to dispose of excess production for a domestic market, is the commonest form of export activity.
- The second main form is **licensing** based on patents, designs and trade marks.
- **Franchising** is the third main option. It is very similar to licensing, in terms of advantages and disadvantages, ie there is minimal risk, but also modest returns. **Joint ventures** are more likely to produce good returns, but they are much riskier.
- **Trading companies** may be established in the target countries.
- **Manufacturing abroad** may be undertaken. This will require major investment.

Exporting

10.2 Exporting can involve minimum effort, cost and risk and is relatively flexible. Exporting can be direct to buyers or more normally through export organisations of various kinds. An export agent acts as an intermediary between buyers and sellers, taking a commission from the transactions. Export merchants/export houses buy products from different companies and sell them to other countries.

10.3 In most cases these export organisations have long-established contacts in foreign countries and a purchasing headquarters in, say, London. The exporter thus deals in English, under the English legal system, gets paid by a resident bank, is not involved in shipping and may not have to alter products in any way. It is simple and risk free, but naturally the rewards are not as potentially great as other options.

Marketing at Work

Trade missions

Trade missions do pay off. All you need is the right product, the right price - and the right contact. Here is a tale of missions to two cities - Eindhoven and Brussels - in which that old export maxim proved true.

Scarborough based Unison/TJP Electronics is on the way to new business after taking part in a mission of high tech companies from North Yorkshire to Eindhoven.

Organised by Yortek, North Yorkshire's association of high tech industries, the mission gave companies a low-cost opportunity to explore new markets in Benelux.

Unison/TJP Electronics, which specialises in the design and building of industrial washing and degreasing machines, met several new prospective clients, and appointed a local representative.

As a result, it has already quoted for orders worth more than £500,00. 'If we win only 50 per cent of them, we'll be very busy for the next few months, working to capacity,' says Terry Pickering, Managing Director.

12: International marketing

A trade mission from the West Country landed orders worth more than £300,000, following a visit to Brussels earlier this year. Another £200,000 worth of orders are anticipated.

The Devon and Cornwall mission was sponsored by Bond Pearce, Ernst & Young, Devon and Cornwall County Councils and the South West Chamber, and assisted by DTI and the British Embassy. Forty-seven companies took part, with interests ranging from waste processing and mining to jewellery manufacture, hi-tech design and marketing.

Overseas Trade, Dec/Jan 1997

Licensing

10.4 **Licensing** usually involves only a small capital outlay and this approach is favoured by small and medium sized companies. It is the least profitable method of entry, and has the least associated risks.

10.5 The licensee pays a royalty on every product item produced or sold in addition to a lump sum paid for the license. Licensing is used particularly when local manufacture, technical assistance and market knowledge offer advantages. It is an alternative to investing directly and is particularly advantageous if an overseas country should be politically unstable.

10.6 Licensing is also attractive for medium-sized companies wishing to launch a successful home market brand internationally. Fashion houses such as Yves St Laurent and Pierre Cardin have issued hundreds of licences and Löwenbrau has expanded sales worldwide without having to expend capital building its own breweries overseas.

Joint ventures

10.7 **Joint ventures** in Europe have become particularly prevalent since the advent of the EC. They involve collaboration with one or more foreign firms. They offer reduced economic and political risks and a ready made distribution system. Where there are barriers to trade, they may be the only way to gain entry to foreign markets.

10.8 Quite a number of vehicle manufacturers have initiated joint ventures or strategic alliances, including Rover with Honda, Chrysler with Mitsubishi and Alfa Romeo with both Nissan and Fiat.

Trading companies

10.9 This structure avoids involvement in manufacturing. A trading company simply buys in one country and sells to buyers in another country. It will sometimes also act as a consultant advising buyers and sellers on market conditions, quality/price issues etc. For example, long-established trading companies control much of the world's food market for commodities such as cereals or indeed any other items that are able to be stored in bulk and moved rapidly in response to shortages.

Direct ownership

10.10 Setting up a company in a foreign country may be appropriate if growth prospects and political stability make a long-term commitment attractive.

10.11 Manufacturing abroad requires major investment and is only justified by very heavy demand. However, it may offer advantages such as those below.

Advantages may include:

Part D: Marketing operations in context

- Lower labour costs
- Avoidance of import taxes
- Lower transport costs

but these may be offset by the degree of management effort required and higher levels of risk.

10.12 Multinationals will have directly owned subsidiaries in many countries. These can offer considerable operating and tax advantages. Some car manufacturers such as General Motors and Ford in the US actually import cars built by foreign subsidiaries.

Marketing at Work

Tesco

Tesco has become one of the leading retailers in Central and Eastern Europe, according to a new Euromonitor report, Retailing in Eastern Europe.

This has come about because of Tesco's purchase last April last year of 13 stores - six in the Czech Republic, seven in the Slovak Republic - from the US discount chain, K-Mart. It paid £76.7m.

Euromonitor reports that Tesco is active in Hungary, Poland and the Czech and Slovak Republics. In Hungary, it holds 74 per cent of the global food retailing chain, and plans to develop another 18 stores around Budapest.

In Poland, it holds 96 per cent of the local food chain, Savia. It has operated 36 shops there since 1995.

Its outlets in the Czech and Slovak Republics, says Euromonitor, are discount and department stores but Tesco plans to expand the food side of the business.

Another leading UK retailer, Marks & Spencer, opened its first store in Prague last October, has two others in Budapest, and, says Euromonitor, is studying the Polish market.

Overseas Trade, March 1997

Chapter Roundup

- International marketing is an increasingly important area of marketing. There is a range of specific problems to be addressed.

- In order to develop an effective marketing plan, information about the markets into which the company intends to go is essential. In the case of domestic markets, the normal step would be to undertake research which would provide that information. International marketing, however, requires a different approach to marketing research, and presents its own peculiar problems.

- The marketing environment is different in international marketing. Most aspects of cultural systems vary between countries, sometimes quite significantly.

- International marketing operations are affected by regional trade alliances and markets.

- Within the marketing mix, standardisation or customisation of the product must be considered.

- Distribution is a complex issue in international marketing, and a wide range of channels can be identified.

- Prices in foreign markets are likely to be determined by local conditions, with each market separate.

- Elements of the promotional mix must also be considered.

- There are five basic alternatives for structure when entering a foreign market.

Quick Quiz

1. Why do companies enter into international marketing? (see para 2.1)
2. What are Morden's 12Cs? (2.2)
3. What is the significance of material culture in international marketing? (4.2)
4. What are the two main opposing pressures on international trade? (5.1)
5. What are the arguments in favour of product standardisation? (6.3)
6. What is product screening? (6.5)
7. What factors influence the choice of channel members? (7.7)
8. Distinguish between a push-oriented strategy and a pull-oriented strategy. (7.18)
9. What media problems may arise in international marketing? (9.4)
10. What is licensing? (10.4, 10.5)

Action Programme Review

1. Arguments in favour of product adaptation

    (a) *Greater sales potential*, where this also means greater profitability, which it may not!

    (b) *Varied conditions of product use* may force a company to modify its product.

    - Climatic variations, for instance cars produced for dry climates may suffer corrosion in wet ones
    - Literacy or skill levels of users such as languages which can be used on a computer
    - Cultural, social, or religious factors such as religious or cultural requirements for food products like Halal slaughtering of New Zealand lamb for Middle Eastern Markets or dolphin-friendly tuna catching methods for Europe and the USA)

    (c) *Variation in market factors*. Consumer needs are in their nature idiosyncratic, and there are likely to be distinctive requirements for each group not met by a standard product.

    (d) *Governmental or political influence*. Taxation, legislation or pressure of public opinion may force a company to produce a local product.

2. Other factors

    (a) *Cost:* full cost of supplying goods to consumers. Relevant costs could include administrative costs, a proportion of group overheads, manufacturing costs, distribution and retailing costs.

    (b) *Inflation*, particularly in the target market and in raw material suppliers

    (c) *Official regulations*. Governments may well intervene in pricing policies. This may involve *acceptable* measures such as import duties and tariffs, and generally *unacceptable* measures such as non-tariff barriers, import quotas and price freezes. Price controls may also be used.

    (d) *Competition*. 'Price leaders' may well be undercut by competitors. The effectiveness of this policy will vary according to the significance of other marketing activities, and the capacity of competitors to match these.

Now try illustrative question 17 at the end of the Study Text

Illustrative questions and suggested answers

Illustrative questions

1   ENVIRONMENT (20 marks)   *32 mins*

Your company produces computer software for small businesses. In your role as marketing manager, you have been asked to prepare a report for your board of directors which explains how aspects of the marketing environment could affect the company's activities. Your report should cover aspects of the wider (macro) marketing environment.

2   SEGMENTATION (20 marks)   *32 mins*

Many organisations recognise the benefits offered by the careful application of market segmentation. However, exactly how the process works is less widely understood. For example, some managers regard the identification of target markets as the key stage in the segmentation process. Others are more interested in identifying appropriate segmentation variables with which to group customers. You have been asked to make a presentation to your organisation which explains the segmentation, targeting and positioning elements of the market segmentation process. Using examples from business to business markets to illustrate your explanation, draft a document which details the areas you intend to cover.

3   CONTROL AND EVALUATION (20 marks)   *32 mins*

You are employed as a journalist by a magazine read by marketing executives. The magazine recently published a reader questionnaire to help it to focus more closely on areas of interest to marketing executives. You have been asked to analyse the responses and choose a number of topics which could form the basis for future articles. In the first batch of replies, a recurrent theme is that, although companies are spending significant amounts on marketing activities, they seem to obtain very little in the way of feedback on those activities.

Prepare an article for the magazine which explains different approaches to marketing control and evaluation. Provide details of possible approaches to implementation in a retail environment and suggest who should be involved.

4   ANSOFF (20 marks)   *32 mins*

Lewis Upholstery manufactures and sells craftsman produced seating furniture for the home user. There is one showroom which features three-piece suites. The company attracts price-conscious customers by placing advertisements in the local newspaper which emphasise *buying direct from the manufacturer*. The Managing Director wants to increase sales and has employed a marketing consultant to assist.

As the marketing consultant, use Ansoff's growth matrix as the basis of your report. This should outline a number of specific marketing strategy alternatives and go on to recommend and justify the best alternatives to implement in the short and medium term.

5   IKEA (40 marks)   *64 mins*

Swedish furniture manufacturer and retailer IKEA was formed in 1943 by Ingvar Kamprad. Between 1954, when the first store opened, and 1990 the company underwent massive expansion from a single Swedish outlet to more than 80 spread through 21 different countries, with over 70% of revenue generated outside Scandinavia. The IKEA concept comprises large retail outlets (around 80,000 square metres) situated on the edge of sizeable towns and cities, selling a full range of furniture and furnishings. From beds to lounge suites, kitchen utensils to carpets, curtains, pictures and lighting everything the customer needs to set up and update the home. The stores also offer instore restaurant and child care facilities to make the shopping experience a pleasant one. To help in the selling effort, the company produces an extensive catalogue, giving details of the items for sale, prices, colours, measurements and availability. In 1990 alone, around 35 million US dollars were spent producing 40 million copies in 12 different languages.

IKEA operates with an up market brand image, linked to stylish and sophisticated Swedish taste, but its products are aimed clearly at the mass market. The company is not a market nicher and to maintain its growth must attract large numbers of customers of low as well as high incomes. To keep its prices low, IKEA must keep costs down. This is achieved by a clever combination of buying in bulk, making buying centres compete for orders, having large stores with self-service facilities and products which are flat packed, for self assembly at home.

Illustrative questions

The IKEA company mission is clearly stated 'We shall offer a wide range of furnishing items of good design and function, at prices so low that the majority of people can afford to buy them'. This philosophy is backed up by the following aims.

- IKEA should keep costs low and assist customers
- products should combine good quality, durability and be functional
- profit should be used to build and expand
- a keen understanding of the company's cost base must be maintained and good results achieved with careful investment
- energy must be concentrated carefully and time used efficiently
- simple solutions should be found to product and company problems
- IKEA should take responsibility and put things right
- IKEA should find alternative solutions to problems by experimenting

Currently IKEA seems to appeal particularly to customers aged in their 20s and 30s who are furnishing a home for the first time. These customers want their homes to look stylish and smart, but with relatively low disposable incomes must carefully consider price. The company is also keen to attract other customer types, from many different countries and of all ages and lifestyle stages. Although IKEA does not formally use demographics and psychographics to segment its market, it divides its markets into different geographical areas, each with a standard product range but having the flexibility to include products which match local, cultural requirements.

Answer the following questions with reference to the IKEA case.

(a) Briefly define marketing planning and say why it is important for IKEA to use it. (8 marks)

(b) How should the marketing planning process relate to IKEA's corporate planning? (8 marks)

(c) Describe the elements of a detailed marketing plan and show within this framework what types of information might be included in a marketing plan for IKEA. (20 marks)

(4 marks will be allocated for presentation.)

6 MODELS (20 marks) *32 mins*

Prepare a short paper on the value of behavioural models in seeking to understand the promotional process. Illustrate your answer with three different models. Specifically illustrate applications and limitations of each model.

7 HOW TO INTEGRATE PROMOTION (20 marks) *32 mins*

You are an officer of the Health Education Council, a government supported body and you are charged with a campaign to reduce alcohol consumption among young adults. In a memorandum to your manager state what relative emphasis you would place on each element of the promotion mix. Also set out how you would seek to integrate the campaign.

8 NEW PRODUCTS FOR GROWTH

Your company is seeking to develop a strategy which will enable the business to expand rapidly, growing turnover fourfold in four years. Prepare a statement for the board of directors that indicates the most appropriate methods of examining new and existing products in order to identify those most likely to enable the business to reach the growth goals outlined above.

9 PRICING POLICY *32 mins*

Construct a report to marketing management that explains the factors that should be taken into consideration when pricing for a product line.

10 PHYSICAL DISTRIBUTION AND MARKETING

The company in which you work is considering the idea that physical distribution should become a component part of marketing, rather than being the final delivery part of the production process. Your

Illustrative questions

Line Manager has asked you to prepare a report for the board of directors outlining how such an arrangement might improve service to customers.

11   SALES PROMOTION, HOOVER (20 marks)   *32 mins*

In 1992 Hoover, the manufacturers of electrical appliances, offered two free flights to America for customers who purchased Hoover goods in excess of £100. This apparent bargain immediately attracted thousands of customers and stocks were soon exhausted. Evaluate the advantages and disadvantages of this type of sales promotion campaign from the points of view of the manufacturer, the retailer and the customer.

12   OUTSIDE RESOURCES (20 marks)   *32 mins*

Outside resources can be used by companies wishing to buy-in particular skills when they need them. Your company is considering expanding its business into new product areas and feels it would benefit from expertise from outside resources. As marketing director, you have been asked to prepare a report which describes the types of outside resources which your business might use, suggests how outside suppliers should be briefed, and indicates how the progress of such suppliers might be controlled and measured.

13   ETHICS AND RESPONSIBILITY (20 marks)   *32 mins*

As a journalist for a business publication, you have been asked to prepare an article which explains the importance of marketing ethics and social responsibility in business today. Put together a draft document using appropriate examples to illustrate your arguments.

14   INDUSTRIAL MARKETING (20 marks)   *32 mins*

You are employed as a marketing manager by an industrial organisation producing moulded plastics for the car industry. Your managing director has asked you to prepare a presentation for junior marketing recruits explaining the characteristics of industrial marketing and how they apply to your organisation. Draft a document which details the areas you will cover in your presentation.

15   SERVICE MARKETING (20 marks)   *32 mins*

You have applied for a job with a small hotel company which is establishing a formal marketing function for the first time. As part of the interview process, you have been asked to make a short presentation which explains the characteristics of marketing in the service sector. Prepare some notes which detail the areas you intend to cover in your presentation.

16   CHARITY (20 marks)   *32 mins*

You have recently taken up a new position with a well-known national charity. Your job is to oversee and organise marketing activities for the charity. Your previous work experience has been entirely in the commercial sector so not-for-profit marketing is new to you.

Your new boss, the charity's director, has asked you to make some notes on the similarities and differences you expect to find between your new and old positions. Prepare a document which does this and explains how these contrasts will affect the marketing activities which you carry out.

17   MODES OF ENTRY (20 marks)   *32 mins*

You are a freelance journalist who specialises in writing articles on international marketing for a variety of publications. Decide upon the publication you wish to target and write a short article which explains the difference between structure choices such as exporting, licensing, joint ventures, trading companies and direct ownership. The article should also outline the factors which organisations should take into account when selecting which structure choice to adopt.

Suggested answers

1 ENVIRONMENT

> *Tutorial note.* The impact of the macro-environment on a computer software company forms the basis of this question. It is a relatively straightforward question requiring application of the generally well understood 'PEST' framework. The most important aspect of the question is the requirement to apply this framework to the context and provide interesting and relevant examples.

Report: Effect of Macro Environment on the Company
To: The Board of Directors
From: The Marketing Manger
Date: June 1996

Introduction

1. The Marketing environment defined

Every company is affected by both its internal and external environment. The external environment audit directs managers to consider the likely affects of political, economic, social and technological factors on the company's operations. In addition, customer, competitor, supplier and distributor activities should be monitored. Such activity is often referred to as MACRO and MICRO environmental analysis. This should highlight opportunities and threats for the organisation to consider in its planning activities.

The focus for this report is how aspects of the macro environment could affect our computer software company when selling to small businesses.

2. The external marketing environment

2.1 Political/Legal factors

The change of government at the last election has already resulted in some significant changes. The National Minimum Wage Regulations and the Working Time Regulations both require the keeping of records to prove compliance; there are opportunities for us here.

The government claims to support small businesses and the many regional programmes can be used to assist purchase. Regional priorities may be adjusted in the wake of Welsh and Scottish devolution.

The 1998 Data Protection Act has replaced the 1984 legislation and has wider implications for us and for our clients. The new legislation considerably strengthens the position of the individual in relation to others who possess data about him. Processing such data will be forbidden except in certain tightly controlled circumstances. We can add value to our products by providing good advice on the implications of the legislation.

The political environment further afield is also of interest. A lasting peace in Ireland could increase the viability of a sales subsidiary in that country. Similar international opportunities should be evaluated with consideration for political stability.

At a more tactical level we should be aware of the legal standards imposed by statutory bodies such as the Advertising Standards Association and the legal requirements of Acts such as Trade Descriptions and Health and Safety.

Economic factors

The local economy is very relevant to us and, more particularly, our customers. Whilst we are able to spread our risk through a national network, small businesses are much more dependent on the local economic climate. We should use local employment and economic indicators available through the HMSO and Monthly Digest of Statistics, to anticipate changes.

On the national scale, the economy should be evaluated on a regular basis. There is currently significant debate over interest rates, with tension between the Bank of England's brief to contain inflation and the sluggish performance of small manufacturing businesses. The possibility of adopting the Euro makes the effect of future monetary policy difficult to forecast.

Social and cultural factors determine people's basic assumptions and habits of thought. This is particularly important for us as we deal mostly with owner managed businesses. Larger organisations may display a greater tendency towards entirely logical decision making; the owner manager is more influenced by impressions and innate preferences. The crucial factor here is the imbalance in computer literacy between the generation which controls the budget and the generation which actually uses our product. We must offer the decision makers comfort and security while providing the operators with the facilities they need. References from satisfied customers will be invaluable.

Suggested answers

Conclusion

To conclude, effective environmental scanning systems and flexible, adaptive marketing planning processes are required by our company so we can avoid threats and exploit opportunities presented by the macro environment.

2 SEGMENTATION

> *Tutorial note.* This question asks students to demonstrate a sound understanding of the underlying principles and process of market segmentation. The application to the business to business context provides an opportunity for candidates to illustrate the concept's practical value.

Presentation: the market segmentation process

Structure of the presentation

1. Introduction
2. The three elements
2.1 Segmentation
2.2 Targeting
2.3 Positioning
3. Conclusions & Discussion

Materials for presentation

OHT, Flip chart, Pens, Handouts

1. Introduction

Good morning ladies and gentlemen. This presentation will last for approximately 45 minutes during which time I will outline the principles and benefits of the market segmentation process and provide a number of business to business applications of the concept. We should have time for questions and discussion at the end.

Market segmentation has been defined by Dibb et al (1994) as the process by which customers in markets with some heterogeneity can be grouped into smaller, more homogenous segments. Market segmentation is a process made up of three distinct activities: segmentation, targeting and positioning. Market segmentation allows a company to decide which groups of customers it can service most effectively and to design marketing mix programmes so that the needs of these targeted groups are then more closely met. Specific benefits include a better understanding of customers, a clearer view of the competitive situation and effective resource allocation.

2. The three elements of the process

2.1 Segmentation

Segmenting a total market involves the identification of variables which divide the market into sub-segments with similar characteristics.

Business to business markets, such as packaging, photocopier and computer markets, can be segmented with many of the bases used in consumer markets such as geography, usage rate and benefits sought. Traditional industrial market bases include customer type, use of product, customer size and purchasing procedures. So for example, a company selling protective packaging may segment their market by the customer types of consumer goods manufacturers, publishing companies and consumer durable manufacturers. They may further segment these by customer size and product application. So for instance packaging may be required for presenting the product, protecting each product or over-wrapping a group of products. The handling of books may require different packaging from tinned food and video recorders.

The base used to segment the total market should result in a group of customers who are:

(a) Measurable - Information on customer characteristics should be obtainable cost so that the marketer knows who is in the segment and therefore the size of the segment.
(b) Accessible - It should be possible to communicate effectively with the chosen segment.
(c) Substantial - Large enough to consider for separate marketing activity.
(d) Meaningful - customers who have different preferences and vary in market behaviour/ response to marketing efforts.

Once the market has been segmented, a more detailed profile of typical customers in each segment should be developed.

Suggested answers

2.2 Targeting

Following on from the segmentation process is the targeting process which involves evaluation of the attractiveness of each segment and the decision concerning which segments to target. A number of factors should be taken into consideration in evaluating segment attractiveness; the structure and size of the market, the company's brand and market share, the intensity of competition, production/marketing scale economies and the capabilities of the company in matching with the target markets' needs relative to competition. Following this, two targeting strategies are possible - the concentration strategy or the multi-segment strategy. So for example in the photocopying market if it were segmented on the basis of photocopying volume, a manufacturer such as Canon adopts a multi-segment strategy by targeting small, medium and high volume users whereas Kodak Copier business only concentrates on the high volume users.

2.3 Positioning

The final stage in the market segmentation process is that of positioning which involves selecting a position and signalling it to the target market. Positioning is the designing of the company's image so that target customers understand and appreciate what the company stands for in relation to its competitors. A number of strategies are available to position business to business products:

- Position on product features. Toshiba portable PCs are divided into three families according to screen technology.

- Position on benefits. This approach is similar to the previous one though the difference can be illustrated with the adage 'don't sell the steak, sell the sizzle'. For example, IBM have an advertising strap line that states, 'At IBM the last thing we'll offer you is a computer.' The copy goes on to offer solutions to business problems.

- Position on usage. Apple computers are often positioned on the desk top publishing capability needed by many businesses.

- Position on user. This associates the product with a user or class of users. So for example, ICL produce computers for retail organisations such as Boots and Sainsburys and position on the basis of specialisation for the retail user.

- Position against competition. With this approach marketers make either direct or indirect comparisons between their product and competitors products. When any computer company wins an industry award this is often used in advertising to differentiate themselves from the competition.

3. *Conclusions and discussion*

From the examples provided it should be apparent that all three stages of the market segmentation process are important. It is true to say that much more research has been conducted into segmenting consumer markets; however there are many effective applications of the concept in business to business markets as the examples provided illustrate. Any marketing manager in this sector should ensure that she or he is familiar with and able to apply the market segmentation process.

3 CONTROL AND EVALUATION

Introduction

In any control and evaluation process, a useful starting point would be a detailed breakdown of marketing expenditure for the last five years, together with a full review of current marketing control and evaluation procedures.

This would be followed by thorough audits of current marketing effectiveness (strategies, organisation, marketing operations etc) using the formats recommended by Kotler.

These documents will help readers with specific for their own operations, but for general purposes, I am assuming that the organisation is involved in all the marketing activities normally associated with a medium-sized or large company.

Suggested answers

The marketing control process in outline

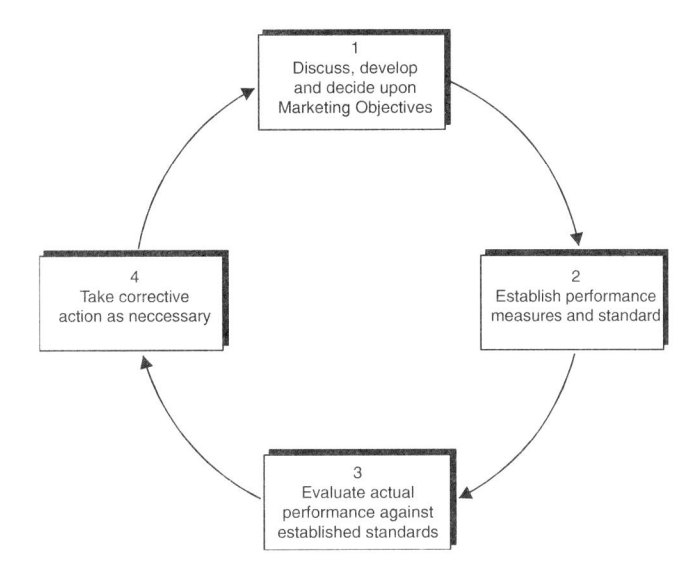

```
        ┌─────────────────┐
        │        1        │
        │ Discuss, develop│
        │  and decide upon│
        │Marketing Objectives│
        └─────────────────┘
       ↑                    ↓
┌──────────────┐      ┌──────────────────┐
│      4       │      │        2         │
│Take corrective│     │Establish performance│
│action as neccessary│ │measures and standard│
└──────────────┘      └──────────────────┘
       ↑                    ↓
        ┌─────────────────┐
        │        3        │
        │ Evaluate actual │
        │performance against│
        │established standards│
        └─────────────────┘
```

The following explanatory notes should be read in conjunction with the above diagram.

1   Marketing objectives

The starting point is the organisation's *marketing objectives* which should show clearly where it wants to be at or by particular points in time. Without knowing clearly where it wants to be, it cannot possibly establish the extent to which it is getting there or indeed whether it has arrived. Objectives should be achievable given prevailing market conditions and resources.

Realistic objectives will be based upon past performance moderated by internal and external audits, the latter supplemented, as necessary, by marketing research.

2   Performance measures

There are a number of *measures by which performance can be judged* and these should at least include:

(a) sales levels
(b) market share
(c) marketing costs
(d) profitability
(e) customer satisfaction

Performance standards can now be set at £x for the period, Y% market share and £z marketing costs, all set against a maximum number of customer complaints.

3   Evaluation

The organisation is now in a position to monitor and *evaluate actual performance* against these standards.

4   Corrective action

Where performance is below a tolerable level, the organisation should *take corrective action.* This may mean invoking contingency plans previously drawn up for this purpose.

Information will be needed at all stages of the process, ie information of the right type, in the right place and at the right time. The types of information the organisation should be seeking include:

(a) competitors market shares, strategies, products, prices etc
(b) sales by product, by area, by retail outlet, by week
(c) total market and forecasted trends. Market segments and brand positionings.

Different approaches to control and evaluation

Control methods can be formal or informal or a mixture of both. Some formal methods have been outlined above and are largely quantitative in nature. However, matters like brand image and customer satisfaction are more qualitative. Informal methods of evaluation and control include peer pressure, staff appraisal meetings and informal discussions.

Suggested answers

More detailed evaluation and control techniques for a retail company could include:

(a) mystery retail shoppers
(b) formal store checks
(c) retail audits
(d) consumer surveys
(e) on pack offer responses
(f) hall tests for presentation, packaging and so on
(g) taste tests and focus group discussion for new product introductions
(h) test marketing

Implementation

In a fully marketing orientated company everyone is involved directly or indirectly in marketing and therefore in marketing evaluation and control. This can be achieved by encouraging discussion and comments at meetings and through suggestion boxes. All staff should be asked their opinions and those of relatives and friends outside the company.

More specifically however, formal marketing evaluation and control procedures should be the responsibility of the marketing director, implemented downwards through marketing, sales and retail management/personnel. Advertising, PR and marketing research agencies would also play a part in the evaluation process.

4   ANSOFF

> *Tutorial note.* The Ansoff matrix is a key tool for generating a number of alternative marketing strategy options. This question therefore tests candidates' ability to apply this matrix and make decisions regarding the most appropriate options to select given the scenario presented. It is important to apply the theory to the specifics of the question. Note here that Lewis upholstery is probably a small business (no senior marketing staff, advertises in a local newspaper) and therefore has limited resources. Also, seating furniture is a shopping good which is probably purchased only after a good deal of planning and shopping around.

Report: Strategic options for increasing sales at Lewis Upholstery
To: Managing Director
From: Marketing Consultant
Date: December 1996

1. *Consultancy brief*: to outline a number of marketing strategy alternatives which will increase sales for Lewis Upholstery. To go on to recommend and justify the best strategy to adopt in the short and medium term.

2. *Ansoff matrix framework*: the matrix which will be used has been developed by Ansoff and covers four different routes to increased sales for any organisation. These include; market penetration, market development, new product development and diversification:

Suggested answers

PRODUCTS

	EXISTING	NEW
EXISTING MARKETS	**Market penetration** • More purchase and usage from existing customers • Gain customers from competitors • Convert non-users	**New product development** • Product modifications • Different quality levels • 'New' products
NEW MARKETS	**Market development** • New market sectors • New distribution channels • New geographic areas eg international marketing	**Diversification** • Horizontal integration • Vertical integration • Concentric diversification • Conglomerate diversification

Market penetration involves thinking about options to enable the company to sell more of its current products and services to current customers. According to Ansoff, this is the least risky option as the firm has experience in both areas. After this, market development is suggested. Here the company considers if there are any markets, distribution channels or customer segments who could be persuaded to buy the firm's current products. New product development is the third option, usually considered more risky than market development because the failure rate for launching and growing new product sales is high, particularly in the consumer products sector. Finally, diversification is a route to more sales but this is very risky because it entails getting involved in dealing with new markets and new products. Having outlined the basic tool, I will now apply the strategies outlined for each option in the matrix above to Lewis Upholstery.

3. Application to Lewis Upholstery

The firm has limited financial and marketing resources. While considering all possibilities, therefore, it may be that some will seem impractical.

3.1 Market penetration

3.1.1 More purchase and usage from existing customers: encourage repeat sales with sale offers, discounts on multiple purchases and setting up a database and mailing customers with relevant offers and supplementary product ideas. Train showroom staff in selling up and link sales techniques.

3.1.2 Gain customers from competitors: create differential advantage, emphasise 'custom made suites' and customers' ability to specify their requirements (style, fabric, finish etc.) and see them being made. Review the design and layout of the showroom - consider a re-launch day with free food and drink and prize draw. Reduce prices.

3.1.3 Convert non-users into users: increase promotion spend, use direct mail, yellow pages, local radio, sales promotion and step up efforts to gain local publicity. Another option is to offer existing and previous customers an incentive for recommendations to family and friends that results in an order.

3.2 Market development

3.2.1 New distribution channels: consider additional showrooms in the region. Consider manufacturing for a local or national retail chain. Mail-order catalogue or mail-order advertising would be an additional route to market.

Suggested answers

3.2.2 New markets: in terms of new market segments you could consider quality conscious rather than price conscious customers, emphasising 'craftsman manufactured' and 'tailor-made' thereby increasing profits perhaps rather than sales. Employ a sales person to target the business, hotel and leisure markets for reception suites and furniture.

3.2.3 New geographic areas: you could expand out of the local area and go regional, nationally or explore export markets. Marketing research would be advisable for these options.

3.3 Product development

3.3.1 Product modification: add 2 seater suites, arm chairs, stools, bedroom suites, garden chairs

3.3.2 Different quality levels: manufacture a value range, a standard range and a deluxe range

3.3.3 'New' products: add curtains, fabrics, tables, bookcases, lighting to range.

3.4 Diversification

3.4.1 Horizontal integration: moving into high quality suites, kitchen units, TV cabinets and tables for a made to measure premium market. Manufacture new products for pubs, sports centres and office reception areas.

3.4.2 Vertical integration is probably impractical as the minimum efficient scale for fabric manufacturing and the timber trade is beyond your investment capacity.

3.4.3 Concentric integration seeks marketing and technical synergy. An example might be to acquire or develop a fabrics business with an emphasis on soft furnishings and replacement made to measure loose covers.

3.4.4 Conglomerate: you may decide to change your business area completely and go into an entirely new, unrelated business area - catering for example. This would be highly risky.

4. *Recommendation and justification*

On the basis of risk, core competence and resource criteria, market penetration followed by product and market development seems sensible.

In the short term there exist a number of market penetration options which could be easily resourced and quickly implemented. You have a basic replacement demand, then you have new housing developments and friends and family of current customers. This will require more sophisticated marketing communications which I would be happy to help you with.

In the medium term, I would recommend you add products to your range which can be sold to current and new customers. It would be sensible to combine this with market development to begin to target more affluent, less price sensitive customers. The most successful position for small, niche companies is one of differentiation focus (Porter 1980, 1985) where you concentrate on high quality at a high price. It seems very possible that your company has the skills to do this.

Perhaps longer term the business market has potential, but as this requires both new products and developing an understanding of new customers I feel this is too risky at present. I look forward to discussing this report with you in due course.

5   IKEA

(a) Marketing planning is the regular, systematic, customer-centred and controlled series of activities a company will undertake to meet business objectives, secure long-term profitability and realise its product/market strategy effectively and competitively. Planning activity exists over the short term (1 year), the medium term (2 - 3 years), and the long term (3 - 6 years). Marketing planning is an essential management tool for IKEA to use because:

   (i) planning pre-supposes an organised and structured approach to business - essential for IKEA to stay competitive;

   (ii) marketing plans, effectively implemented, can be a spur to action for all concerned with their execution;

   (iii) marketing planning provides a market orientation to customers, and a control mechanism to keep corporate activity on track so that customer needs are continually satisfied;

   (iv) marketing planning helps stimulate the corporate vision, and as such may contribute to the creation of an open, action-centred culture;

Suggested answers

- (v) marketing planning focuses the organisation on the customer, and helps the organisation become more pro-active towards such constraining forces as economic and technical change.

(b) The marketing planning process should be fully integrated with the IKEA corporate planning process.

- (i) Marketing is an 'organisation-wide' function. Successful organisations realise everyone is marketer; that there are internal as well as external customers, and that successful marketing depends on the quality of relationships people have with each other and with customers.
- (ii) Marketing strategy is developed from corporate objectives and informs the corporate planning process.

The following approaches will facilitate the integration of marketing planning with IKEA corporate objectives.

- (i) Ensure marketing is represented at senior executive level.
- (ii) Create a culture where participation, motivation and self-development are encouraged, and where there is dedication to customer service.
- (iii) Ensure the management information systems within IKEA are linked to a market intelligence system, to facilitate speedy and reliable information flow back to the organisation.
- (iv) Develop marketing tactics from marketing strategy and test them against the requirements of corporate objectives.
- (v) The control mechanisms used to test the effectiveness of marketing planning should also be able to be used as tools to indicate to what extent corporate objectives are being achieved.

(c) The marketing plan will begin with a marketing audit which will examine in full the business environment of the firm, the internal marketing system of the firm, and the specific marketing activities which are currently being carried out. IKEA management will use the information gathered from this exercise to gain an overall picture of the firm's current trading and improve marketing effectiveness. Two specific marketing tools are used.

- (i) SWOT analysis - which will indicate to IKEA the company's current strengths, weaknesses, business opportunities and competitive threats.
- (ii) PEST analysis - which will indicate to IKEA the influences of political, economic, social and technical factors on the firm's business activities.

A number of key strategic questions emerge.

- (i) Who and where are our potential customers?
- (ii) When and where will they buy our products?
- (iii) Can we reach all of them with our existing or planned resources?
- (iv) Why do our customers buy from us, and do they have, any, as yet unsatisfied needs?
- (v) Who are our main competitors and what inducements to buy are they offering?
- (vi) What key external factors currently constrain our business activities?
- (vii) What key internal factors currently constrain our business activities?

The next component of the planning process are the assumptions and actions that IKEA management make and take in order to drive the planning process forward.

- (i) Timescales are placed on identified and agreed required actions.
- (ii) Marketing objectives are then set for IKEA over the short, medium and long terms. These should be quantifiable where possible. The objectives state what the company seeks to achieve with the products, and in the markets in which it trades.
- (iii) Marketing strategy is clearly set out. This enables IKEA management to set down the methods it will use to meet the marketing objectives.
- (iv) Marketing tactics will then be established; these will illustrate how the staff (who must deliver the plan) will carry out marketing activities.
- (v) A selling and sales management organisation will then need to be determined. This will consist of all the supporting activities and office structures needed to enable the marketing tactics to happen.

Suggested answers

Levels of planning

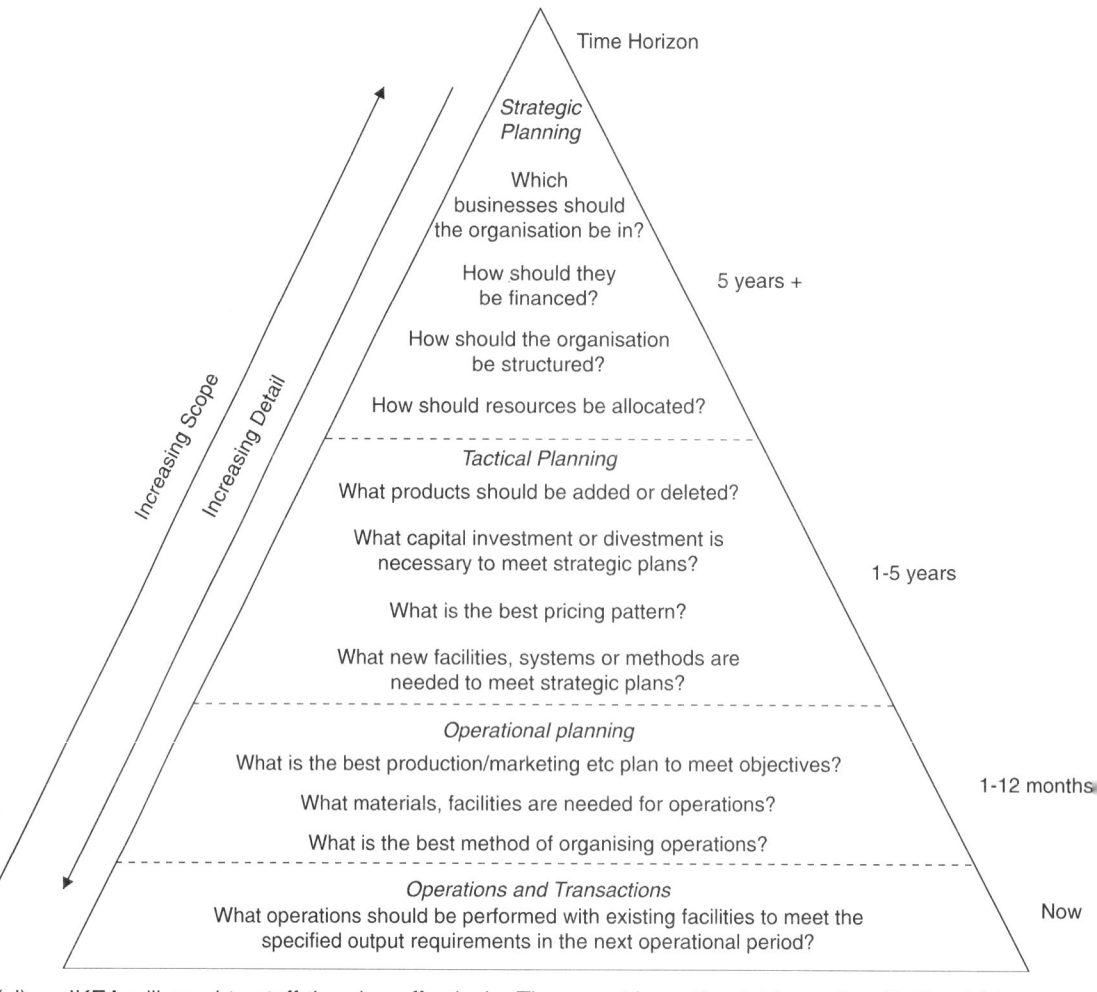

```
                    Time Horizon
                        /\
                       /  \
                      / Strategic \
                     /  Planning   \
                    /               \
                   /     Which       \
                  /  businesses should \
                 /  the organisation be in? \
                /                           \
               /    How should they          \     5 years +
              /     be financed?              \
             /                                 \
            /   How should the organisation     \
           /        be structured?               \
          /                                       \
         /    How should resources be allocated?   \
        /- - - - - - - - - - - - - - - - - - - - - \
       /           Tactical Planning                \
      /   What products should be added or deleted?  \
     /                                                \
    /   What capital investment or divestment is      \
   /      necessary to meet strategic plans?           \    1-5 years
  /                                                     \
 /       What is the best pricing pattern?               \
/                                                         \
/   What new facilities, systems or methods are           \
/      needed to meet strategic plans?                    \
/- - - - - - - - - - - - - - - - - - - - - - - - - - - - -\
/              Operational planning                         \
/  What is the best production/marketing etc plan to meet objectives? \
/                                                                     \   1-12 months
/  What materials, facilities are needed for operations?               \
/                                                                       \
/   What is the best method of organising operations?                    \
/- - - - - - - - - - - - - - - - - - - - - - - - - - - - - - - - - - - - \
/              Operations and Transactions                                 \
/  What operations should be performed with existing facilities to meet the \   Now
/   specified output requirements in the next operational period?            \
```

Increasing Scope / Increasing Detail

- (vi) IKEA will need to staff the plan effectively. They must have the right people with the right knowledge and skills in the right place at the right time to carry out the plan successfully.

- (vii) Contingency measures will need to be drawn up. These are used to address failures in expected outcomes, and are used as insurances against the product/market strategy not delivering the forecasted results.

- (viii) IKEA will need to have drawn up effective mechanisms for feedback and review. These are controls such as targets (individual objectives), budgets (used to finance the plan) and audits (used to test its effectiveness). Feedback information will feed both the marketing planning and corporate planning activities and will be used to initiate the next planning cycle.

6 MODELS

(a) *What are models?*

Because marketing systems are very complex it is necessary to represent them as models with a number of key elements displayed. These models are essentially simplifications of the real world but they do enable us to understand and plan the underlying processes. Although they are becoming increasingly scientific, many models used in understanding the promotional process are essentially empirical in character. Nevertheless they have proved useful.

(b) *Overall value of models*

Using models is of value for the following reasons.

- (i) They simplify complex situations.
- (ii) They allow postulation and measurement of actions.
- (iii) They can be used to support decision making and planning.

Suggested answers

(iv) They can be used for analysis purposes and to aid shared understanding in the marketing team.

(c) *Examples of models*

The three specific models we have chosen to use are:

(i) the AIDA model;
(ii) the (radio signal) communication model
(iii) the integrated marketing communication model.

(d) *AIDA model*

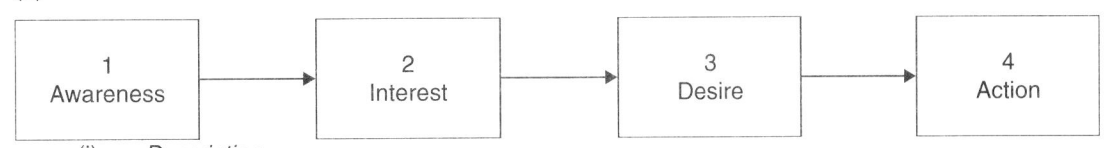

```
1 Awareness → 2 Interest → 3 Desire → 4 Action
```

(i) *Description*

This very simple model has stood the test of time since evolved by Strong in 1925. It describes the stages of consumer's behaviour as they move towards the final action which may be the purchase of goods or services. This model reminds us that a sale is not an instant process, rather it is the result of a number of individual stages. The consumer has to firstly be aware of the product/service. Secondly the consumer needs to have some specific interest in the product/service. Thirdly before the sale the consumer has to be motivated by having a particular desire for the product/service.

(ii) *Applications*

Though simple this model can be used to analyse plans and monitor all advertising campaigns. Its very simplicity is a powerful aid in this process. To start with it is necessary to know the awareness levels of your product/service in the target market. Then it is necessary to design the advertising campaign message to interest the target audience. Next various sales promotion incentives may be used to create desire for the product/service.

(iii) *Limitation*

At the same time as being a strength the simplicity of the four step AIDA process is a weakness, and more comprehensive models have been developed. Colley, in his 1960's book *Designing Advertising Goals to Measure Advertising Results* (DAGMAR) develops a more comprehensive response hierarchy with the following elements.

Awareness > Comprehension > Conviction > Action

(e) *(Radio signal) communication model*

The communication process

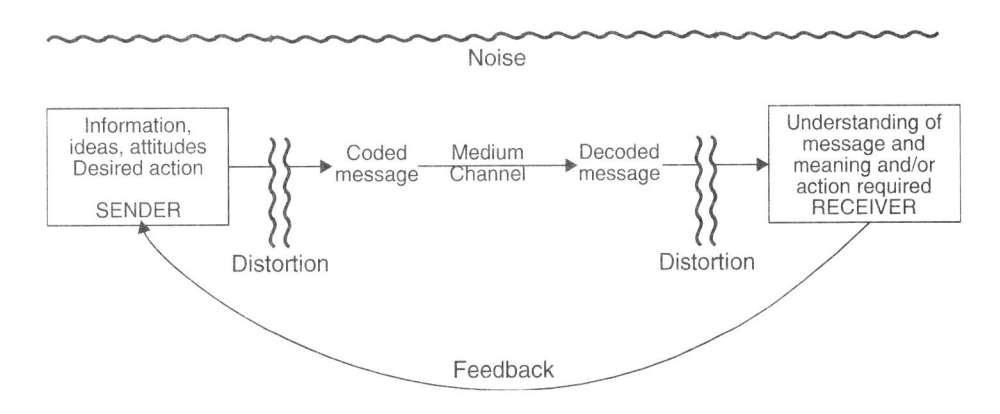

```
                              Noise

Information,                                            Understanding of
ideas, attitudes    Coded    Medium    Decoded          message and
Desired action  →  message   Channel   message  →      meaning and/or
                                                        action required
SENDER                                                  RECEIVER

           Distortion                   Distortion

                            Feedback
```

(i) *Description*

This model is clearly based on that of sending a radio or a telephone signal and can be used to emphasise that the communication process is more complex than it appears at first sight. For example, there may be 'noise' in the system. This may equate to the clutter of competing advertisements in the chosen media. The receivers(consumers) may also have to *interpret* what the message means to them. This is the 'decoding' process.

Suggested answers

(ii) *Applications*

Increasingly sophisticated advertising is being designed, in which the messages are minimised. They may be coded very cleverly in a colour scheme or by the use of a particular actor representing the product, for example the blonde Rutger Hauer dressed all in black representing Guinness or the puppy representing Andrex toilet tissue. The process of encoding/decoding is obvious in these examples.

(iii) *Limitations*

Like other models, the process of analysis is essentially a qualitative one which does not help with deciding on the absolute amounts of advertising spend. The model is also limited by the many other factors that it does not allow for but which are present in the market place, such as the degree of competitive reaction.

(f) *Integrated marketing communication model*

The integrated marketing communication process

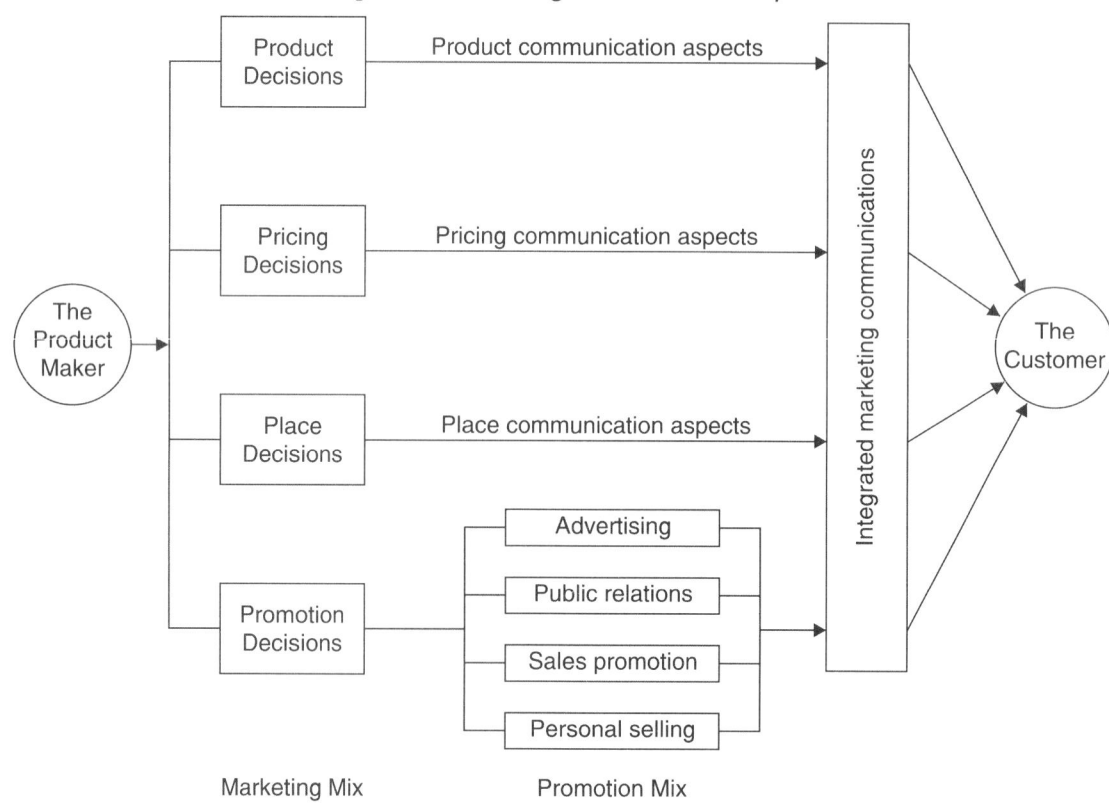

```
                    Product           Product communication aspects
                    Decisions ────────────────────────────────────►

                    Pricing           Pricing communication aspects        Integrated
    The             Decisions ────────────────────────────────────►        marketing           The
    Product ──────►                                                        communications ───► Customer
    Maker                                                                  
                    Place             Place communication aspects
                    Decisions ────────────────────────────────────►

                                          ┌─── Advertising ───┐
                    Promotion             ├─── Public relations ─┤
                    Decisions ────────────┤                      ├──►
                                          ├─── Sales promotion ──┤
                                          └─── Personal selling ─┘

                    Marketing Mix         Promotion Mix
```

(i) *Description*

This model, apparently comprehensive in nature attempts to depict the whole of the marketing communication process. It demonstrates that each element of the marketing mix can make a contribution to the communication process. It suggests that these elements must be integrated with the elements of the promotional mix. The whole process links the company with its customers in the most effective way.

(ii) *Applications*

Increasingly both agencies and clients recognise the need to integrate campaigns in the method described above. Each element can have a distinct role to play in the overall process. A synergistic combination is possible if the overall result is greater than the sum of the separate parts.

(iii) *Limitations*

Historically major patterns of communication may have been established by a company (for example advertising) and limited knowledge may prevent it from using other techniques such as direct marketing. The above model, though comprehensive, does not show how to make decisions about the relative proportion of each element of the overall mix.

Suggested answers

7 HOW TO INTEGRATE PROMOTION

Memorandum

To: Chief Executive
From: Information Officer
Date: January 1998
Subject: Reduction in alcohol consumption

In response to your request I set out my recommendations for the relative emphasis to be placed on each element of the marketing communications mix in the first year of our campaign.

(a) *Overall intention*

We should concentrate in the first instance on medium to heavy users. In this way we will avoid a head-on clash with committed users and alcoholics, yet ensure that there is overspill from our work into both the light and heavy user segments.

We should target the influential members of our target audience rather than attempt a widespread campaign that would dissipate our budget and minimise the effect.

The whole campaign should be co-ordinated around a positioning statement so as to ensure that we have consonance throughout.

(b) *Advertising (40% emphasis)*

The role of advertising is to inform, to persuade. It is necessary to target our campaign very carefully so as to hit the target audience, those with influence within the medium to heavy consumers of alcohol.

Trade press should be used to remind vendors of their legal obligations. More profit can be made from certain alternatives to alcohol, and this fact should be stressed.

Media advertising should focus not on the dangers of alcohol, but on the pleasure to be derived from the alternatives.

There should be a strong congratulatory element within the advertising (avoiding smugness) to reinforce the non-users and, in particular, those who have given up, or reduced their consumption.

(c) *Public relations (40% emphasis)*

PR should be our main weapon at this stage. We should endeavour to encourage prominent non-users of alcohol to mention the fact whenever possible without becoming strident nor appearing to preach.

Parliament should be lobbied to introduce legislation similar to that in place for smoking. Both government and opposition parties should be targeted, and individual MPs supportive of the cause recruited and supported.

Public media of regard, and particularly individuals who have an affinity with certain target segments, should be provided with case histories, and pertinent information in easy-to-use press packs.

Evidence of success in similar campaigns across the world should be compiled and used as appropriate in our briefings and press packs.

Non-alcohol events should be encouraged, and sponsorship such as the Milk Race should be supported.

Local pressure groups should be formed, and encouraged to be self-supportive within our overall promotional policy.

(d) *Packaging (Longer term emphasis)*

We cannot use packaging, since this is the province of the manufacturers. It is, however, a major target for our parliamentary lobby since we should endeavour to enforce government health warnings following the pattern established in the tobacco market.

(e) *Sales promotion (10% emphasis)*

We will develop sales promotion and point of purchase materials which will encourage moderation in consumption especially at critical periods such as Christmas and New Year.

Suggested answers

(f) *Contingency (10% emphasis)*

We should hold 10% of the budget as reserve to counter the expected reaction from the powerful alcohol industry and their established lobby. This budget should not be committed until six months into our campaign when we have assessed preliminary achievement and can decide where best to focus our effort.

(g) *Integration*

It is vital that we plan the above elements into an integrated campaign. We will use the same creative designs in all elements in a cost-effective manner. We will need to plan each stage so that they reinforce each other in a logical manner.

(h) *Summary*

This will be a prolonged campaign that must be sustained against great odds over a considerable period of time. To judge from the ASH campaign against smoking it may take ten years for the first effects to show in any marked way. However, the ASH curve of success was exponential. This is to be expected as attitude shift gains momentum, but we should not be too optimistic about immediate marked success. There are, after all, more committed users of alcohol than there are smokers, and the secondary effects of alcohol are less pronounced. It is nevertheless a campaign that must be undertaken, and one to which great numbers of the public will subscribe as it gains credibility.

8 NEW PRODUCTS FOR GROWTH

> **Examiner's comments.** 'Candidates who knew portfolio techniques were able to produce good answers here.' The most popular were Ansoff and BCG.

For presentation to:	The Board of Directors
Prepared by:	A Marketer
Date:	XX.XX.XX
Subject:	Examining new and existing products for greater potential

The four year time period enables us to consider the development of new products, support for products in growth markets, and divestment or repositioning of products that are in the decline phase of their product life cycle.

New product development process

The company is unlikely to achieve its goal unless it puts in place a process of new product development. These new products must be carefully researched, developed and if possible tested in the market place prior to launch.

Idea generation. This can be systematic or by chance. My recommendation is that the company adopts a systematic procedure to generate new ideas. The company should put in place a system for scanning its marketing environment to identify new opportunities. This should be supported by a systematic process of marketing research closely linked to the research and development process. New ideas can also be generated from employee suggestions, the research and development function or simply by observing competitive activity and listening to customers.

Screening of new ideas. The new ideas generated should be systematically put through a screening process. This process should analyse each idea in terms of its potential development, the market potential, financial resources required to develop the idea, its relevance to the overall strategic direction of the organisation, likely return on investment and the organisation's overall capability to market the product effectively.

Business analysis. This analysis involves a detailed evaluation of each idea with more comprehensive marketing research and testing of the concept, a detailed competitor analysis and a full analysis of the resource requirements that will be required to launch successfully and achieve sales targets. The market analysis should determine the degree of market attractiveness particularly the level of competitiveness, growth rates and longer term potential.

Test marketing. This is recommended although not always possible. The product can be tested either with one customer or in a particular region. It can involve simple trial or be supported by testing various marketing mixes to see which has the most effect on sales. This stage may require considerable

Suggested answers

investment and may need to run for several months prior to a decision being made to launch the product.

Existing product portfolio

It is recommended that the company assesses its current portfolio. The BCG matrix is a model that we can utilise to assist us in this process.

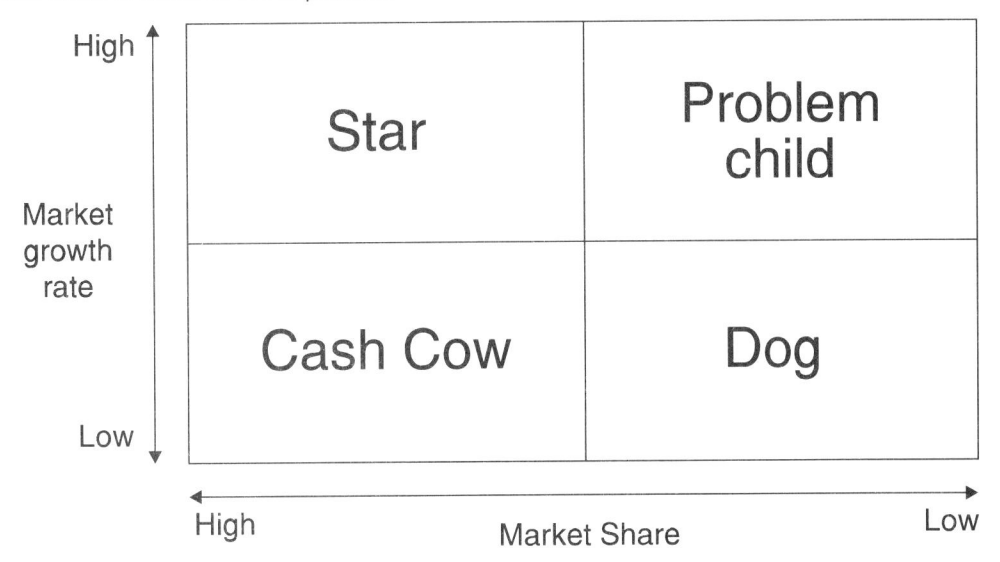

	High Market Share	Low Market Share
High Market growth rate	Star	Problem child
Low Market growth rate	Cash Cow	Dog

The matrix will enable use to identify our products' market positions relative to the competitors with the largest market share in the market we are operating in. It will also enable use to evaluate whether the products are in growing or mature markets. Finally, it will enable use to identify the balance of our overall portfolio of products and assess which products should be supported for growth (stars or possibly question marks), or divested to free up resources (dogs or possibly question marks). The matrix should also indicate whether the organisation's successful mature products (cash cows) are sufficient to generate the cash revenue needed to support those products than can help us achieve our goal of a fourfold increase in turnover.

The findings of this analysis will therefore require more detailed marketing research to identify those products that offer the most chance of growth. We may also consider the possibility of repositioning some of our products into new growth markets.

9 PRICING POLICY

Report

To: *The management*
From: *A Marketer*
Re: *Pricing policy of a product line*

A product line can be defined in terms of a 'broad group of products whose uses and characteristics are basically similar'. Such products can be differentiated by:

(a) Price
(b) Packaging
(c) Targeted customer
(d) Distribution channel used

A firm may have a line of products because it wishes to target a number of segments of the market, all of whom require different benefits. The following are the considerations you might make when detailing the influences on pricing of a product line.

(a) *Product quality.* If the firm is seeking a niche upper market segment and a reputation for quality then it may decide a high price is necessary (for example, the Caribbean cruise holiday market). This price may hold for all products in the line, yet there may be special offers for block bookings or during certain times in the year when demand falls.

(b) *Company image.* The firm may be seeking an exclusive image in the market place and may use pricing strategy in conjunction with public relations to achieve this, for example Marks & Spencer.

Suggested answers

(c) *Costs of production.* The firm will want to meet the full costs of production and make sustainable profits so pricing must reflect this. The bigger the operation, the bigger the scale economies available from production and marketing, particularly where products are very similar (thus permitting bulk manufacture/purchase of parts). This situation would help secure lower prices and increased competitiveness in a mass market.

(d) *Degree of standardisation of products.* An extension of (c) above, this implies that where products in a line are quite different in order to meet consumer needs, then the costs of the product and, therefore, the price, will have to be higher.

(e) *Desired level of profit.* A firm may willingly take losses on one line of product as long as the range of products meets the forecast profits target. It may price, therefore, to achieve this goal.

(f) *Desired level of market share.* A firm may set or alter prices as a promotional tool to realise market share goals.

(g) *To manage the portfolio effectively.* The firm may have a number of product lines in the market (or different markets) at the same times. Portfolio analysis may indicate that price changes to specific products in specific lines at specific times may realise more revenue from life-cycles; the firm is thus able to use pricing to manage profitability.

(h) *To market diversify.* The firm may be able, through lowering or increasing the price, to take its product line into a different market (upper or lower in income grouping). Some changes to the line (apart from price) would also probably be necessary in order to do this.

(i) *As a promotional tool.* A firm may use its pricing structure as a promotional tool to bring 'value for money' to the customer's attention. In order to increase added value it may additionally offer 'free servicing' as an added incentive.

(j) *To capitalise on novelty.* If the product line is new, and the market largely untapped, a firm may be able to harvest significant profits from the market over the short term by pricing up the whole line. Innovative products will command this competitive advantage until other, similar products enter the market, when the firm will need to reduce its profits to stay competitive. Such pricing up over the short term will additionally help cover the heavy research and development costs of innovation.

(k) *Price leadership.* Where a few suppliers dominate a market (an oligopoly), price competition is most unusual. Any reduction in price by one supplier is likely to be matched immediately by the others, so no benefit accrues. Price increases which are not matched rapidly erode sales. It is common in such markets for a price leader to emerge. This is likely to be a major player with a reputation for efficiency. The price leader indicates the current appropriate level of prices without using its leadership competitively.

Please raise any queries regarding this report with me.

A Marketer

10 PHYSICAL DISTRIBUTION AND MARKETING

> *Examiner's comments: summary/extracts.* Not a popular question, but well answered in the context of the role of distribution in *servicing customers,* such as order times, flexibility and so on.

REPORT

To: Board of Directors
From: A Candidate
Date: 4 December 1997

Introduction

The process of *physical distribution* is a key element of our marketing strategy in that we must ensure that our products reach the customer in the right quantity, at the right time and in perfect condition. In marketing text books it is described as the 4th P along with promotion, price and product. This report outlines the reasons why physical distribution should become a *component of marketing* and *not* as the *final delivery part of the production process*

The customer's perspective

It is important to consider the extent to which our organisation has adopted a customer orientation. Customers of our products are not concerned with *how* the product reaches the point of sale, only that

Suggested answers

it is available in the quantity and at the quality they require. If we see distribution as the final delivery part of the production process then we are in danger of adopting a production orientation The focus of our attention will be on the efficiency and effectiveness of our production and distribution systems and not on market factors and customer needs.

Competitive advantage

By focusing our attention on the market it is possible for the organisation to identify and assess new/innovative distribution opportunities that will achieve a competitive advantage. Such opportunities will range from transforming the channel structure through to tactical activities with our distribution channel. Distribution has until recent years had the least attention of the marketing mix elements but with increasing levels of competition and commoditising of products, its importance as both a strategic and tactical weapon are now being recognised.

Service and added value

The matching of the distribution process to our organisation's service marketing activities is an important consideration. Management of the distribution channel can provide many opportunities for improved service delivery ranging from stock management, order processing to guaranteed delivery. It is also important for us to identify our customers distribution problems and provide solutions that add value to our overall product offer.

Supply chain management

Our major customers require increasingly sophisticated channel management techniques to ensure our products maintain their shelf presence. Examples of these are the increasing importance of trade marketing activities and category management techniques as opposed to traditional product management activity. We also need to establish closer and stronger relationships with other distribution channel members to ensure that we maximise the efficiency and effectiveness of the *total supply chain* not just our final part in the chain. Many retailers are now adopting the concept of efficient consumer response (ECR) in trying to ensure that the distribution system works in a co-ordinated manner. Similarly, information technology is playing an increasingly important role in our customers stock handling and purchasing functions.

Integration of marketing strategy

The final argument for including distribution as a component part of marketing is the need to integrate our distribution activity with our total marketing activity. We must ensure that the promises we make in our communications are met by our distribution channel activities. Similarly our distribution strategy can reinforce our brand's positioning in the minds of the consumer. It is important that distribution is part of marketing's responsibility to ensure that our organisation maintains its competitive edge in the marketplace.

11 SALES PROMOTION: HOOVER

(a) *Background*

The Hoover sales promotion of 1992 can only be described as a disaster for the company. It subcontracted the organisation of the free flights promotion to a small company that apparently did not have the skills or knowledge to execute the whole scheme successfully. Many Hoover customers became annoyed and irritated about the travel arrangements (or lack of them) to which they thought they were entitled. Hoover then had to step in and commit substantial resources to meeting the promises made in the campaign. Customers, retailers and the company all became disillusioned by the campaign.

(b) *Definition*

The Institute of Sales Promotion definition is interesting:

'Sales promotion comprises a range of tactical marketing techniques designed within a strategic marketing framework to add value to a product or service in order to achieve specific sales and marketing objectives'

It is clear from this that sales promotions must have both tactical (short term) and strategic (longer term) implications. Clearly in the Hoover case the longer term image of the company has suffered major damage. The short term sales gain was quickly overtaken by the loss in reputation of the Hoover brand.

Suggested answers

A further more specific definition is that sales promotion consists of an offer to the customer that has tangible benefits not inherent in the normal product or service. These extra tangible benefits are added to help the company to achieve its marketing objectives.

Sales promotion has become particularly important in the 1990s for two important reasons. Firstly for economic reasons: sales promotion has been used to stimulate sales. Secondly because many products have increasingly had the characteristics of commodities, sales promotions have been used to distinguish one brand from another, or indeed, one retailer from another.

(c) *Evaluation from the manufacturer's viewpoint*

(i) *Advantages*

It is possible to examine the advantages of sales promotions to manufacturers by considering the stage reached in the product life cycle.

Life cycle position	Promotional intention
Launch	Awareness of new product
	Trial of new product
	Conversion to new product
Growth brand	Building penetration
	Increasing usage rate
	Retaining loyalty
	Tempting competitors' loyal customers
Established brand	Retaining loyal customers
	Tempting switchers
	Increasing weight of usage
Declining brand	Retaining loyal customers

The end result of these actions is to increase sales and profits for the manufacturer.

(ii) *Disadvantages*

The disadvantages to the manufacturer include the following.

- Substantial investments are required
- The process is a relatively uncertain one
- Things can go badly wrong, as in the case of Hoover.
- There can be adverse reactions to the brand.
- Continuing promotions destroy brand loyalty and can ultimately destabilise a market

(d) *Evaluation from the retailer's viewpoint*

(i) *Advantages*

Many of the reasons why manufacturers favour sales promotions apply equally to retailers. Manufacturers often stand the costs of the promotion and retailers benefit directly from increased store traffic, increased sales and higher profit levels.

During the 1990s sales promotions among retailers have become so common that customers expect them. Indeed they are built into the retailers' strategy. For example, in the DIY market, after a number of short term price discounting exercises particularly between B&Q and Texas, B&Q decided to institute a policy of every day low prices (EDLP). This has been extended to other companies in the Kingfisher Group.

The food retailers have regularly had sales promotions to gain store traffic and market share at the expense of the independent stores. This promotion was accentuated by the entry into the market by the continental discounters such as ALDI and NETTO. The leading supermarkets all now offer loyalty cards.

(ii) *Disadvantages*

The main disadvantage is that a price and promotion war develops and leads directly to loss of margins. Short term sales are gained at the expense of long term profitability.

Research has shown that sales promotions can lead to temporary brand switching and that sales can fall away again after the promotion has finished.

Suggested answers

(e) *Evaluation from the customer's viewpoint*

(i) *Advantages*

It can reasonably be argued that the customer is the main gainer in the sales promotion war. Among the advantages to the customer are the following.

(1) Lower prices; these have been in part responsible for keeping down the cost of living index.

(2) Sales promotion introduces a new product by encouraging trial and this can lead to better product performance.

(3) The tangible benefit, though not part of the inherent product, may itself be valuable. For example the *Sunday Times* has offered a free compact disc each week to readers of the newspaper. The CD's have greater value then the newspaper and are attractive in themselves building up eventually into sets of a substantial number.

(4) Strong brands are enhanced and weaker brands suffer. The brand leaders are able to develop improved products of benefit to the customer.

(ii) *Disadvantages*

Sales promotions have to be paid for ultimately. This may take the form of less competition as the market shares of the leaders grow. It may result in lower standards of service as margins come under attack. These are long term effects but in the short term promotions can go wrong causing the customer grief and aggravation.

However it appears that sales promotions are a technique loved by consumers and are likely to remain a growing factor in the marketing scene.

12 OUTSIDE RESOURCES

Tutorial note. This question tests candidates' breadth of understanding of dealing with outside suppliers. The application to an industry example of their choice provides an excellent opportunity for candidates to use their own practical marketing experience in this area.

Report: Dealing with Outside Resources
From: Marketing Director
Date: June 1996

1. Introduction

As a large brewing company we manage an extensive alcoholic drinks brand portfolio. We operate a very active new brands development programme. A significant part of the marketing division's role is to select and manage outside suppliers to support key activities.

2. Types of outside resources we could use

The organisation uses outside resources in a number of functional areas including brewing, operations, distribution, finance and marketing. This report will focus on the types of outside resources which could be used to support marketing activities.

2.1 Management Consultants could be used to undertake a major review of the new product development process, including the stages employed, the personnel involved and the key strengths and weaknesses of the process. We would expect a report clearly recommending how the company could implement an improved process. We would expect this investment to result in more brands being brought to the commercialisation stage and subsequently for new brands to build a significant market share.

2.2 Marketing research agencies would be vital for the market analysis and concept development and testing stages. We may wish to test market and again would require the services of a research agency.

2.3 Communication agencies (sales promotion, PR, advertising, direct marketing) are used on a continuous basis to support our current brand portfolio. Equally, we would need to involve them in any plans for new products as the launch would need to be supported with a communications plan. In turn these agencies would use the services of printers and designers.

2.4 Packaging design agencies could be used to ensure the visual appeal of the new drinks products was appropriate for the target market.

Suggested answers

2.5 Marketing training organisations are often used to improve the knowledge and skills of the marketing department.

3. *Briefing suppliers*

Once the decision has been made to buy-in the particular skills of the various agencies outlined, they need to be briefed. They can expect the following from us in our role as client:

(i) A statement of our requirements.

(ii) Setting these requirements in context by providing background information on the brewing industry, our company and the particular brand portfolio in which the new product will reside.

(iii) An opportunity to meet and discuss the brief.

(iv) An indication of the sorts of decisions influenced by the supplier's input and the likely uses of the their contributions.

(v) A broad indication of the budget available.

(vi) An indication of the timescales involved.

(vii) The number of competitive proposals sought.

(viii) An opportunity to discuss our reaction to the proposal before a final choice is made.

4. *Measuring and controlling supplier performance*

The final section of this report outlines how the progress of our suppliers might be controlled and measured. We should review performance against targets regularly and record the results. We would need a database containing the following information:

(i) Supplier's name and type of service provided

(ii) Estimated annual spend

(iii) Record of complaints/actions taken by supplier

(iv) Performance standard against targets

Rating on a scale of 0-10:
Quality, reliability, prices relative to competition, relationships, overall assessment

(v) Special terms and conditions, necessary controls

(vi) Recommended frequency of review

5. *Conclusions*

In the brewing industry the market research and communications agencies used will be key to gain consumer insight for new brand development and stretching and to build strong brand values with both consumers and the trade. Buying-in skills from outside resources not only builds in flexibility and choice related to the tasks and personnel involved, it most importantly allows our organisation to benefit from specialist skills and knowledge.

13 ETHICS AND RESPONSIBILITY

Title: Marketing Ethics and Social Responsibility: An Opportunity for Competitive Advantage or Simply Constraints on marketing decisions?

Marketing professionals are increasingly being influenced by a demand for higher standards in terms of ethics and social responsibility. Very recent examples of this trend include the positive publicity given to The Cooperative Bank when it severed ties with two fox-hunting associations, a peat extraction company and companies that test products on animals. In contrast, Ford experienced negative publicity for taking out black employees from photographs used in Eastern European advertising.

Ethic are concerned with a set of moral principles and values that act as a guide to an individual's conduct. Henderson has developed a matrix to illustrate the different positions a company can take towards this issue:

Suggested answers

1. Ethical and Legal	3. Ethical and Illegal
Ideal option - decisions are both legal and ethical	Decisions require a trade-off of legality in favour of ethical choices
2. Unethical and Legal	4. Unethical and Illegal
Decisions require a trade-off of ethics for legality	Decisions both illegal and unethical should be avoided

Positions 2 and 3 pose problems for marketing managers especially when operating internationally. For example, bribes in many African countries are often standard practice; managers have to decide whether to behave in line with local expectations or adhere to home country values. Many people consider it unethical to sell arms to oppressive nations but this practice is not illegal. Managers have to decide on the dividing line between acceptable and unacceptable behaviour. This comes into sharp focus when marketing to children and when marketing cigarettes and alcohol as the debate surrounding the advertising of Hooch, the alcoholic lemonade, demonstrated.

Another issue which highlights the importance of marketing ethics in business today is the opportunity it presents for developing a competitive position. The Cooperative bank in 1992 repositioned as 'the ethical bank' based on bank's core values of responsible sourcing and distribution of funds. A loss of £6m in 1991 turned into a profit of nearly £18m in 1993 following this repositioning.

Social responsibility is different from ethics. It refers to a company's obligation to maximise its positive impact and minimise its negative impact on society. However it is similar in the sense that it is also poses problems for marketers because society is made up of diverse groups and satisfying everybody is difficult. For example, airline companies tread a fine line between satisfying the needs of smokers and non-smokers.

Social responsibility can be usefully considered under three headings: consumer issues, community relations and green marketing. Many companies are now proactive in terms of responding to theses issues. Linking community relations and green marketing together, IBM have an environmental policy and community programmes plan which includes environmental improvement projects, software and teaching packs and secondees to the Department of Environment. ICI have significantly reduced their hazardous waste since 1990, Bass Brewers use CFC free cellar coolers and The Body Shop regard all three areas as vitally important.

Marketing ethics and social responsibility are both constraints on marketing decisions and opportunities for competitive advantage as the following headlines illustrate,

'Hoover doesn't keep its promises'

'Perrier re-calls all bottles, no harm done'

Gas flares and oil pipelines above ground in Nigeria, coupled with the Brent Spar controversy have earned Shell a tarnished reputation and provoked consumer protest while the Cooperative Bank has turned around its fortunes on the basis of its sound ethical policies.

The real question that therefore remains is, 'can a company in the 1990s afford not be ethical and socially responsible?

14   INDUSTRIAL MARKETING

Presentation: Characteristics of Industrial Marketing
By: Marketing Manager
To: Junior Marketing Recruits

Equipment: Slides, Handout

1. Introduction

Welcome! Over the next few minutes I would like to outline a number of key characteristics of industrial marketing as they particularly pertain to our industry - moulded plastics. The aims of this presentation are twofold:

- to outline the distinctive features of marketing to major motor manufacturers
- to consider in what ways the marketing mix is distinctive for industrial plastics products

Suggested answers

Let me ask you a question. How quickly did it take you to decide on your last car? On the model, the colour and whether you should pay extra for metallic paint? - Probably a long time, it wasn't a very quick decision. This should start you thinking about the distinctive characteristics of complex products and the type of marketing required.

2. *Distinctive features of marketing to major motor manufacturers*

2.1 Characteristically our products are bought when needed; this is known as derived demand. Our plastic dashboards are ordered when consumers buy our customers' cars. Our sales are therefore dependent on the fortunes of the car industry.

2.2 The purchase quantities are usually large

2.3 Target marketing is simpler as there are a small number of customers and readily available SIC codes and trade directories such as Kompass.

2.4 Typically our components are technical in nature and therefore high value. This results in a high risk purchase which requires long term contracts with our customers and a good MkIS to monitor re-buy situations of our competitors' customers.

2.5 The type of product affects the buying process our customers employ. In situations where we are tendering for new business the process is likely to take a number of months. The stages are likely to be problem recognition, general need description, product specification, supplier search, proposal solicitation, supplier evaluation and selection, order-routine specification and performance review. Later this afternoon you will meet one of the buyers from Ford who has agreed to outline their buying procedures for you.

2.6 Purchasing departments of major motor manufacturers are large and staffed by highly professional buyers. The decision-making process outlined is not down to one individual but to what is referred to as a 'decision-making unit'. This is made up of users, buyers, approvers, influencers and deciders. When marketing to the motor manufacturers the concerns and questions from all these people must be addressed. They each have different priorities. Buyers will be concerned with how much our products cost and how soon we can deliver. An assembly manager will be more concerned with the quality and how easily it can be inserted onto the line. All members of the DMU will have opinions and they will depend upon their background, past experience of the product and their perceptions and personality.

Our marketing must address their concerns and influence their decisions in favour of this company.

3. *Marketing approach*

3.1 Relationship marketing is vital. This involves a focus on retaining customers through building trust and commitment. Communication, shared values, joint projects and building in switching costs are all factors we consider. The role of the key account manager is vital. S/he needs to be an excellent communicator, problem solver and negotiator and be able to build a number of relationships spanning the different functions of both companies. We have a very good relationship with Ford and they provide us with testimonial information to use when trying to win new accounts.

3.2 The traditional marketing mix is also very important. The product is technical and purchase involves higher risk which means a greater use of services, for example the provision of technical advice and technical specifications. Price is negotiated and new orders are often put to tender. We need to consider legal & economic constraints, cyclical demand, administered, bid and negotiated pricing approaches. In distribution we mainly supply direct except for a small amount of smaller component business which is handled by distributors. With the advent of Just-In-Time manufacturing issues related to production, transport, storage and inventory holding are vital concerns. Finally, promotion focuses upon personal selling through our key account managers. The remainder of the budget is spent on trade press advertising, the use of exhibitions, trade promotion and publicity.

4. *Conclusions*

I hope this presentation has highlighted a number of distinctive characteristics of industrial marketing and how these influence our approach with customers and the emphasis placed on the different elements of the marketing mix. Are there any questions?

Suggested answers

15 SERVICE MARKETING

Presentation Notes on Services Marketing

By: A. Candidate
Audience: Interview Panel
Equipment needed: Slides, Handout

1. *Introduction*

Good morning ladies and gentlemen. Over the next 30 minutes I would like to outline a number of key characteristics of marketing any service and then relate these to the particular task of marketing an hotel. I'll be happy to take questions at the end of the presentation.

2. *Aims of presentation*

(a) To outline the distinctive characteristics of marketing an hotel service

(b) To consider in what ways the marketing mix should be extended when marketing the services of an hotel

3. *The characteristics of services*

Intangibility

A significant characteristic of services is the relative dominance of intangible attributes in the make-up of the service product. A service is a deed, performance or effort not a product which can be seen, touched and taken away. This makes it difficult to evaluate before purchase and means that customers do not own the service.

How can the hotel manage this intangibility?

We need to use tangible cues to service quality and manage 'physical evidence'. For example, our staff should look professional which includes a hotel uniform and attention to personal grooming. The decor in the rooms should be spotless and follow the hotel's overall decorative identity. The food we serve should be of a high standard and offer our guest variety.

Inseparability

Services have simultaneous production and consumption which emphasises the importance of the service provider and therefore the role of our contact personnel. The conference organiser and the waiter, in our customers' eyes, is the hotel.

Consequently, selection, training and rewarding staff for excellent service quality is very important. The consumption of the service often takes place in the presence of other customers, as in the restaurant, therefore enjoyment is not only dependent on the service provider but other guests as well. It is important to identify and reduce the risk of possible sources of conflict. For example our restaurant layout should provide reasonable space between tables and smoking areas.

Heterogeneity

This characteristic can also be referred to as variability, this means that it is very difficult to standardise the service our guests receive. The receptionist may not always be courteous and helpful, the maids may not remember to change all the towels and so on. Due to inseparability a fault such as rudeness cannot be quality checked and corrected between production and consumption.

This again emphasises the need for rigorous selection, training and rewarding of staff. Evaluation systems should be established which give our customers the opportunity to report on their experiences with our staff. In addition we must ensure that our processes are reliable. For example, the way we book in guests, organise their keys and deal with checking-out. No hotel is perfect, however it is important for any service delivery failures to be responded to immediately.

Perishability

Consumption can not be stored for the future, once a hotel room is left empty for the night that potential revenue is lost.

This makes occupancy levels very important and it is necessary to match supply with demand. For example if our hotel is busy in the week but not at weekends, a key marketing task is to provide incentives for weekend use. To cater for peak demand we can employ part-time staff and multi-skill full time staff. We can also use reservation systems in the restaurant and beauty salon to smooth out demand and ensure that if our customers have to wait that comfortable seating in the reception is provided.

Suggested answers

3. The extended marketing mix

The marketing mix for products is the well known 4Ps of product, price, place and promotion. For service marketing we add three additional Ps to our tool kit: physical evidence, process and people.

Physical evidence is used to manage the essentially intangible nature of the hotel service. As previously stated, smart staff, an impressive lobby and interior design for all areas of the hotel is important to establish an appropriate position and signal this to customers.

Managing processes helps to deal with the inseparability and heterogeneity characteristics. If standards and processes are adhered to a consistent level of service can be delivered. For example receptionists need to be trained to deal with demanding business people and cleaning staff need to prepare rooms to a consistent standard.

Probably the most important element of the services marketing mix is people. Hotel staff occupy a key position in influencing customer perceptions of service quality. Without training and control, employees tend to be variable in their performance which in turn leads to variable service quality and customer satisfaction.

4. Conclusions

Key professors in the field of services marketing, such as Bateson, Zeithaml and Bitner, all suggest that there are three key jobs for service marketers; managing differentiation, managing productivity and managing service quality. Should I be successful in my application today, I too would make these three issues my top priority for the hotel.

Does anybody have any questions?

16 CHARITY

Managing the marketing activities for a charity may seem radically different from that of managing marketing in a profit-orientated enterprise. However, marketing a charity may offer a more creative arena for marketers and often considerably greater challenges.

Goals

Often goals of business organisations are formulated in quantitative statements; for a non-profit organisation, goals may be stated in contribution value terms, or in terms of levels of support over a given period.

Structure

Within business organisations, there is usually a formalised structure of operating. In charities, more of an informal approach may prevail; there may be many more 'interests', perhaps individual (rather than collective groupings as with business) with a lack of agreement about how to move the charity forward. Opinion leaders in charities may have no formal management training, or may be retired; they may possess a fixed mindset and be highly resistant to change. Hence charities may be fairly slow moving organisations with fixed norms of operating.

Results

One can measure the effectiveness of business organisations by the bottom line result - profit. In a charity, no such measure exists and it can therefore be very difficult to measure results.

Intervention

With a charity, the effects of management intervention are largely unknown, as most charities operating today are structured for social ends rather than for strategic reasons, like most business organisations. Businesses are often structured into levels of hierarchy and accountability. Charities are frequently much more informally structured.

Possible objectives for a charity

(a) Surplus maximisation (equivalent to profit maximisation).
(b) Revenue maximisation (as for businesses).
(c) Usage maximisation (maximising the number of users and their usage).
(d) Usage targeting (matching the capacity available).
(e) Full cost recovery (minimising subsidy).
(f) Partial cost recovery (minimising subsidy).
(g) Budget maximisation (maximising what is offered).
(h) Producer satisfaction maximisation (satisfying the wants of staff).

Suggested answers

Marketing principles and charities

(a) *Strategic visioning.* As with a firm, a charity would have specific ideas of what it wanted to achieve, though these may not be as explicit or formalised as with a business organisation.

(b) *Marketing audit.* A charity would want to find out how effectively it had been operating but would probably do this in an ad hoc way, and not conform to the marketing audit procedure followed by many firms.

(c) *SWOT and PEST.* Unless a charity is particularly well organised and led by a marketer or someone with contemporary industrial/commercial experience, then it will largely be more re-active than pro-active. It may have a knowledge of the factors constraining it, but its knowledge of itself in terms of efficiency and effectiveness may not enable quality management.

(d) *Marketing objectives, strategy and tactics.* Although staffed by committed individuals, charities usually operate in the short term; rarely are objectives and strategies formally set. Tactics seem to evolve and staff are motivated on the basis of progress made.

(e) *Control, feedback and review mechanisms.* Periodic committee meetings and annual reviews facilitate progress and results communication; very rarely are there clear channels or identified mechanisms for performance measurement as with business enterprises.

17 MODES OF ENTRY

Tutorial note. Candidates should be able to define each of the alternative international market entry methods included in the question and clearly explain the difference between these structure choices. The second part of the question tests their ability to suggest factors which are important in making this international operations decision.

Article: Marketing Business, UK marketing practitioners, members of CIM.

Title: International Marketing - What Level of Involvement?

Articles abound in the marketing and general management press urging managers to exploit international marketing opportunities. But how should organisations go about entering foreign markets and what are the choices?

Many market entry methods are available, each with a different level of involvement in terms of risk and control. Phillips, Doole and Lowe provide a useful ladder of options:

Levels of involvement ↑

Wholly-owned subsidiary
Company acquisition
Assembly operations
Joint venture
Strategic alliance
Licensing
Contract manufacture
Direct marketing
Franchising
Distributors and agents
Sales force
Trading companies
Export management houses
Piggyback operations
Domestic purchasing

For this article we shall consider the differences between exporting, trading companies, licensing, joint ventures, and direct ownership:

Suggested answers

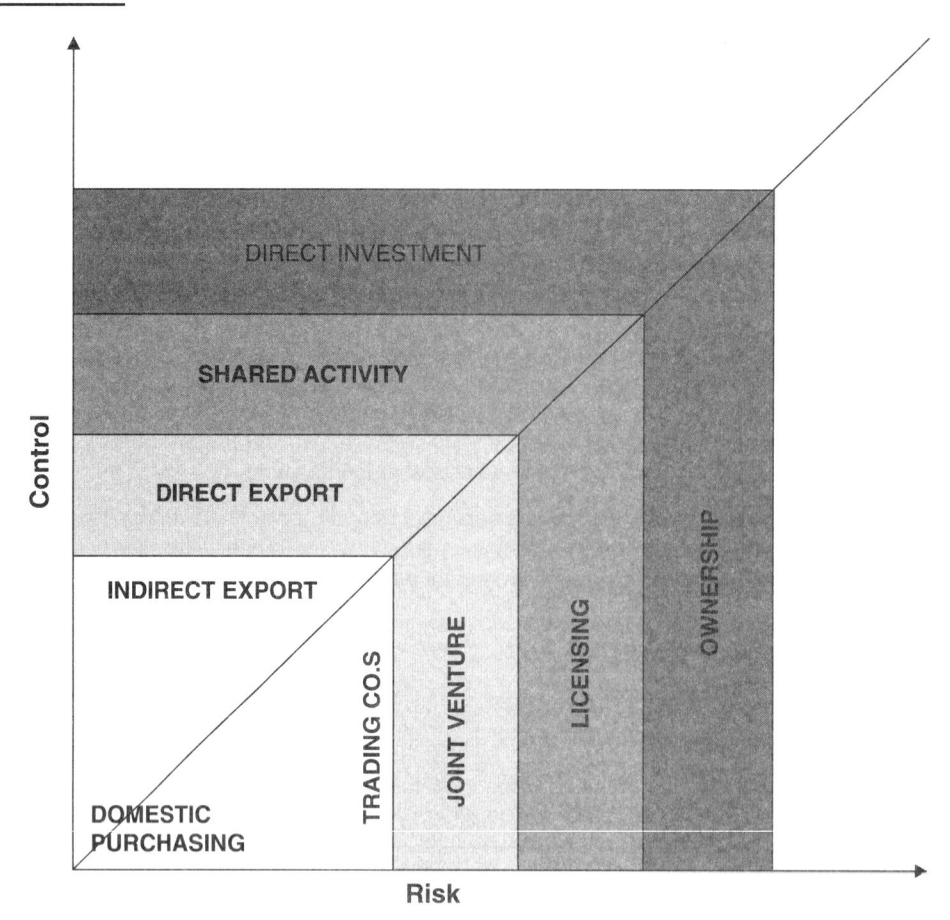

Exporting: involves minimum effort, costs and risk. Indirect exporting is the simplest and cheapest form of market entry and involves having your products sold overseas by others. This includes domestic purchasing, piggyback operations, export merchants & houses and using trading companies which will be discussed in more detail further on. Most small companies start this way as costs and risks are low, however this is at the expense of control over how the goods are marketed overseas. Direct exporting is the next step taken where a company wishes to secure a more permanent long-term place in international markets and begin to exercise more control. The disadvantage with this is that whether using agents, distributors, franchising or direct marketing, the level of investment required increases because the marketing, distribution and administration costs are borne by the company.

Trading Companies: represent a form of indirect export and involve a company selling their products to the trading company who buy in one country and sell to buyers in another country. Much of the world's food is sold internationally in this way and they are strong in managing counter-trade activities. The problem with using trading companies is the lack of control and experience which the firm will miss out on.

Licensing: also involves relatively low levels of investment and is a form of management contract in which the licensor confers to the licensee the right to use either patents, trademarks, copyrights or product/process know-how. A lump sum and royalty is paid by companies who use one of these; for example, many Disney characters are licensed to companies who use the characters on fabrics and games aimed at children. It can be an attractive form of market entry in politically unstable countries and for medium sized firms wishing to launch a successful brand abroad.

Joint ventures: are prevalent since the advent of the EC. It involves the shared ownership of a specially set up new company for marketing and/or manufacture of products overseas. This can be a significant feature of licensing, the difference with joint ventures is that each company takes an equity stake in the newly formed firm and control is usually split equally. May be used due to government restrictions on foreign ownership in countries such as China and South Korea and where complementary technology skills can speed up development. For example, vehicle manufacturers have initiated a number of joint ventures or the similar structural form, strategic alliances, including Rover with Honda and Alfa Romeo with Nissan and Fiat. Costs of single sourcing and strong competition encourage joint ventures; however differences in aims and objectives and the substantial increase in investment required are the disadvantages with this form of market entry.

Direct ownership: is often the choice where commitment is high and long term and the country is politically stable. In this type of situation direct ownership becomes attractive as control and profits are

Suggested answers

highest. Direct ownership can involve assembly, wholly owned subsidiaries or company acquisition. Multinationals such as Kodak have directly owned subsidiaries in many countries and import products from foreign subsidiaries.

Factors to take into account in selection of the options

In making the market entry choice a number of factors should be taken into consideration: level of resources available, degree of control required, amount of commitment, particularly from senior management, risk of losing proprietary information, size, stability, competitiveness of overseas market, government restrictions and incentives, marketing strategy & objectives for international operations and, of course, the company's existing level of foreign market involvement. Very often the final decision is based on the risk/return equation and, in reality, related to taking advantage of opportunities that present themselves, which cannot always be planned.

List of Key Concepts and Index

List of key concepts

Advertising, 108

Brand positioning, 57
Brand, 164
Business environment, 17

Consumer buying behaviour, 94
Contribution, 185
Control, 64
Culture, 96

Direct costs and overheads, 184
Direct marketing, 136

Economic theory, 171
Environment, 17
Equilibrium price, 171
Ethical issue, 224

Gap analysis, 37

Market segmentation, 45
Marketing planning, 4
Motivation, 98

Price elasticity of demand, 172
Product life cycle concept, 150
Public relations, 125
Public, 126

Reference groups, 97
Relationship marketing, 207

Sales promotion, 121
Situation analysis, 9
Sponsorship, 132
Strategic planning, 4

Telemarketing, 142

Index

12Cs, 275
4Ps, 29, 235
7-Up, 58

A
ABZ Ltd, 5
Accessibility, 46
Acorn targeting classification, 54
Active publics, 127
Administered marketing system, 194
Adoption model, 101
Advertising, 22, 74, 108, 212
　objectives, 108
Advertising and taboos, 110
Advertising effectiveness, 111
Advertising industry, 22
Advertising to children, 68
Advertorials, 132
Aerospace, 17
Aesthetics, 279
After sales service/technical advice, 190
AIDA, 101
AIDS, 110
Air Miles, 251
Airline industries, 17
Alcohol, 223
All-issue publics, 127
Allocating, 115
American Marketing Association, 225
American Marketing Association model, 248
Analysis of opportunities and threats, 11
Andean Pact, 279
Anheuser-Busch, 287
Ansoff, 29
Apathetic publics, 127
Apple Tango, 105
Approved lists, 216
Army, 268
Arts sponsorship, 134
Asymmetric cost moves, 23
Attitudes, 100
Automobiles, 223
Avis, 58
Avon cosmetics, 192
Aware publics, 127

B
Back translation, 276
Baker's dozen, 124
Balance of power, 118
Baron et al, 115
BCG matrix, 157
Beliefs, 95, 100
Benetton, 110
Betamax VCR, 282
Bhattacharya, 76
Bicycles, 276
Bilkey, 284

Black, 127
Black and Moss, 128
Blair, Tony, 113
Blind spot moves, 23
Body Shop, 41, 224
Boeing, 274
Boeing Corporation, 225
Booz, Allen and Hamilton, 161
Boston Consulting Group, 42
Boston Consulting Group (BCG) growth-share matrix, 157
Brand, 164
　beliefs, 95
　image, 164
　life cycles, 153
　name, 20, 164, 182
Branding, 164
Brands, 164
Breakthrough products, 40
Briefing, 109
British Rail, 7
British Telecom, 80
Brizz, 276
Budget, 113
Business loyalty schemes, 251
Business Monitor, 252
Business services, 242
Business to business communication, 130
Business-to-business markets, 103

C
Calvin Klein, 100
Campaign briefing, 109
Canon, 287
Capital expenditure projects, 30
Capital goods, 242
Cash Cow, 158
Cause-related marketing, 229
Census data, 275
Centralisation, 77
Centralised organisation, 77
CFCs, 235
Chain of distribution, 188
Channel design decisions, 190
Channel dynamics, 194
Channels of distribution, 74
Charity, 266
Cigarettes, 224
Cinema industry, 38
CK One, 100
Class, 97
Closing the sale, 118
Coalition for Environmentally Responsible Economics, 229
Coca-Cola, 123, 134, 287
Coding, 92
Community issues, 231
Company benefits, 117

Company mission statement, 7
Competition, 175, 291
Competitions, 123
Competitive advantage, 39
Competitive bidding, 176
Competitive moves/response models, 23
Competitive positioning strategies, 59
Competitive strategies, 39
Competitor performance, 71
Competitor responses, 23
Competitors' actions and reactions, 179
Complex decision-making, 94
Components and materials, 242
Computers, 21, 137, 223
Concentrated marketing, 57
Consortiums, 243
Consultants, 219
Consumer buying behaviour, 94
 factors influencing, 96
Consumer issues, 230
Consumer markets, 103
Consumer mobility, 281
Consumer Protection Act 1987, 230
Consumers' Association, 230
Contractual marketing systems, 194
Control action, 75
Copyright, 224
Corporate hospitality, 134
Corporate identity, 130
Corporate marketing systems, 194
Corporate objectives, 8
Corporate strategic plans, 5
Corporate strategy, 37
Corrective action, 76
Cosmology, 279
Cost, 284
Cost leadership, 39
Cost-focus strategy, 41
Cost-plus pricing, 181
Coupons, 122
Coutts, 7
Creative briefing, 109
Creative development research, 111
Creative ideas, 110
Credit Agricole, 7
Credit cards, 136
Crest, 58
Crisis management, 143
Critical mass, 40
Criticisms of the practical value of the PLC, 154
Criticisms of the product life cycle, 153
Cues, 100
Cultural changes, 20
Cultural differences, 277
Cultural factors, 25, 96
Customer analysis, 24

Customer care, 207
Customer loyalty, 137
Customer service, 30
Customisation, 190

DAGMAR, 101
Database applications, 139
Database marketing, 138
Database systems, 21
De Lorean, 62
Decentralisation, 77
Decentralised organisation, 77
Decision making
 consumer, 94
Decoding, 92
Defence, 17
Defensive moves, 23
Deliberate strategies, 37
Dell, 217
Demand, 175, 176
Demonstrations, 116, 117
Detergents, 223
Dhalla, 153
DHL, 58
Dibb, 94
Differential benefits, 117
Differentiated marketing, 57
Differentiation, 39
Diffusion of innovation, 163
Direct attitude survey, 177
Direct distribution, 189
Direct exporting, 284
Direct mailings, 130
Direct marketing, 286, 287
 budget, 140
 components of, 136
Direct response, 137
Direct selling, 191
Directories, 244
Distribution density/intensity, 284
Distribution for internal marketing, 212
Distribution strategy, 193
Distributor characteristics, 190
Diversification, 42
Divisional marketing, 84
Dog, 158
Downstream drift, 187
Drive, 100
Drucker, 34
Drug companies, 228

Early cash recovery objective, 181
Earnings per share, 34
Economic environment, 18
Economic influences, 19
Economic trends, 19

Index

Economic unions, 280
Economies of scale, 281
Educational sponsorship, 134
Effectiveness of advertising, 111
Effectiveness of the marketing mix, 73
Elasticity, 172
Emergent strategies, 37
Employee newsletters, 130
Environment
    definition, 17
Environmental analysis, 11
Environmental factors, 9
Environmental risk screening, 232
Equitable Life, 132
Ericsson, 14
Ethics, 223
Ethnic minorities, 48
EU, 285
EU guidelines, 216
European Union, 19
Evaluation of performance, 69
EverReady, 23
Exclusive distribution, 194
Export Management Company, 283
Exporting, 288
Extractive industries, 243
Exxon Valdez, 232, 229

Fair Trading Act 1973, 230
Family, 21, 97
Family branding, 166
Family characteristics, 48
Family Expenditure Survey, 252
Family life cycle, 49, 98
Feedback, 93
Fido Dido, 58
Financial control information, 67
Financial resources, 31
Financial services, 20, 85
Fixed assets, 31
Focus/nicheing, 39
Food Act 1984, 230
Forecasting, 37,
Forecasts, 76
Fragmented industries, 53
Fragrances, 100
Fragrances for men, 100
Franchising, 190, 288
Free movement of goods, 19
Free trade areas, 279, 286
Friends of St James Norland Parish Church, 139
Fuji-Film, 287
Fulfilment, 142
Functional organisation, 81

Gap analysis, 37
Gaps in the market, 59
General Electric (GE) Business Screen, 42, 157, 159
Geographical organisation, 81
Gift purchases, 182
Gift with purchase, 123
Gillam, 118
Gillette, 287
Glaxo and the arts, 134
Going rate pricing, 181
Golden Wonder, 123, 144
Graham, 196
Green issues, 231
Green market, 233
Greenwich Air Services, 42
Grocery market, 124
Growth strategies, 41
Grunig and Hunt, 126
Guarantees, 117

Habit, 94
Harvesting, 158
Heinz, 125
Hennessy Cognac, 58
Hertz, 58
Herzberg, 99
Heterogeneity, 254, 256
Hidden objections, 118
Hierarchy of effects, 101
Hierarchy of objectives, 102
Hospitable moves, 23
Hospital Trusts, 219
Hot-issue publics, 127
Household Survey, 252
Howard-Sheth model, 26
HRM practices, 211

IBM, 282
Improved products, 40
Income effects, 180
Indirect distribution, 189
Industrial and consumer distribution channels, 193
Industrial goods and services, 242
Industrial markets, 55
Inelastic demand, 173
Inertia, 95
Inflation, 179, 291
Information gathering, 115
Information search, 95
Information technology, 286
In-house magazines, 130
Initial concept testing, 162
Innovators, 164
Inseparability, 254, 256

Index

Institute of Public Relations, 125
Institute of Sales Promotion (ISP), 121
Intangibility, 254
Intellectual property, 224
Intermediaries, 191
   objectives, 179
   customers, 181
Internal appraisal, 11, 12
Internal marketing, 209
International
   channels, 195
   competition, 274
   distribution strategy, 284
   lending agencies, 216
   marketing, 274
   retailers, 285
Inventory control, 285
Ipana toothpaste, 154

JICNARs scale, 47
JIT, 285
John, Elton, 140
Johnson & Johnson, 235
Johnson's Baby Shampoo, 58
Joint products, 182
Joint ventures, 243, 288
Just in Time, 285

Kanban, 197
Kepner, 36
Key factor, 11
Kickers, 62
Kotler, 59, 74, 93, 95

Labour force, 31
Laggards, 152
Lancaster, 78
Language differences, 20
Language problems, 279
Latent publics, 127
Lavidge and Steiner, 101
Leaded petrol, 58
Lead-free petrol, 58
Learning, 100
Leasing, 244
Leverage moves, 23
Levi Strauss, 139
Licensing, 244
Life style segmentation, 50
Lifestyle, 98
Limited decision making, 95
Limiting factor, 11
Lists, 140
Lobbying, 130
Long Wotsits, 144
Loss leaders, 180, 182

Low cost air carriers, 171
Low involvement decision making, 94
Lufthansa, 114
Lung cancer, 224
Luxury hi-fi, 178

M form organisation, 84
Mailing lists, 140
Making the channel decision, 191
Management team, 31
Managing the product portfolio, 156
Manufacturing abroad, 288
Manufacturing industries, 243
Market
   background, 113
   development, 41
   level plans, 9
   management, 83
   penetration, 41
   penetration objective, 180
   performance ratios, 72
   research in China, 276
   segmentation, 53
   share performance, 71
   skimming objective, 181
   test, 177
Marketing
   activities, 28
   and social responsibility, 229
   characteristics of services, 254
   departments, 80
   director, 80
   environment, 28
   mix, 73, 104
   objectives, 28
   planning, 234
   research, 212
Marketing Science Institute, 154
Marketing strategy, 37
Market-led organisation, 78
Mars, 281, 287
Mars Light, 10
Maslow, 99
Mass market approach, 45
Massingham, 78
Matrix management, 84
Measurability, 46
Media
   characteristics, 113
   databases, 102
   menu, 129
   problems, 287
   relations, 130
   scheduling, 114
Merrosur, 279
MFI, 58
Mission statement, 7

Index

Models
    of consumer behaviour, 101
Models of customer behaviour, 26
Money off, 122
Monitoring, 23
Monitoring customers, 71
Morden, 275
Mortgage market, 42
MOSAIC, 54
Mothercare, 57
Motivation, 98
Multi-branding, 166
Multi-channel decisions, 193
Multiple products, 180
Mystery shoppers, 124

National Food Survey, 252
National Health Service, 219
Nationalism, 17
Need identification, 116
Need recognition, 95
Negotiation, 118
Neutral moves, 23
New product pricing, 179
Newey & Eyre, 251
NHS, 219
Nielsen's Homescan panel, 124
Noise, 93
Not-for-profit sector, 236
Nuclear family, 136

Objections
    dealing with, in personal selling, 117
Objectives, 8, 121
Objectives of an organisation, 4
Odd number pricing, 182
Offence moves, 23
Office of Fair Trading, 230
Official regulations, 291
Ogilvy and Mather, 233
Oliver, 196
One coin purchase, 182
Opening, 116
Opinion leaders, 97, 128
Opportunities, 18
Order fulfilment, 142
Organisational buyer behaviour, 249
Organisational buyers, 242, 247
OTC medicines, 194
Ownership, 254, 257
Oxfam, 267

P&G and Excite, 145
Packaging, 168
Packaging innovations, 169
Panel research, 112

Paper industry, 195
Parallel translation, 276
Pareto principle, 257
Patents, 224
Penetration' prices, 73
Pepe, 110
Pepsico Food International, 123
Percentage fill, 31
Perception, 100
Perishability, 190, 254, 257
Perrier, 231
Personal factors, 98
Personal selling, 75
    advantages and disadvantages, 120
Philips, 287
Physical evidence, 212, 260
Pitney Bowes, 251
Place of availability, 259
Planning cycle, 7
Pocket calculators, 40
Pogs and Tazos, 123
Policy statement, 45
Political change, 17
Political environment, 17
Population trends, 47
Porsche, 58
Porter, 39
Portrait, 55
Post purchase evaluation, 96
Post-testing, 74,
Pre-qualification, 217
Presentations, 116
Press agentry, 125
press releases, 129
Pre-testing, 74, 111
Price, 170
Price discrimination (or differential pricing), 181
Price elasticity of demand, 172
Price leadership, 183
Price setting in practice, 174
Pricing, 73, 170
Primary and secondary objectives, 8
Primary data collection, 276
Primary financial objectives, 34
Prizes, 123
Problem Child, 157
Problem identification, 116
Process, 212
Procter and Gamble, 229
Product, 149
    characteristics, 190
    choice, 160
    contamination, 230
    life cycle, 150, 153
    line, 285
    line pricing, 182

Index

line promotion objective, 181
manager, 82
mix, 156
offer, 170
screening, 282
standardisation, 281
testing, 162
Product-based organisation, 82
Productivity, 65
product-led organisation, 79
Product-market strategy, 72, 73
Professor Robin Wensley, 151
Profit responsibility, 228
Profitability, 34
Programme sponsorship, 132
Promotional budgets, 102
Promotional tools
choosing, 102
Psychographic segmentation, 50
Psychographic typology, 233
Psychographics, 50
Psychological factors, 25
Public, 126
Public information, 125
Public opinion, 128
Public purchasing, 19
Public relations, 125
definitions, 125
techniques, 128
Publicity, 125
Publics
types of, 127
Pull-oriented strategy, 286
Purchase decision, 94, 96
Push-oriented strategy, 286

Quality connotations, 179
Quality control, 30
Quality in stockbroking, 258
Quality policy, 162
Quantitative testing, 111
Quantum price, 182

R&D expenditure, 30
Radio 5 Live, 255
Rank Xerox, 285
Ranking objectives, 36
Readiness moves, 23
Real-life pricing, 186
Receiver, 92
Reciprocal trading, 243
Recommended retail price, 181
Reduced price, 122
Reed Moyer, 277
Reference groups, 97
Reference selling, 117

Regional trade alliances, 279
Regional trading groups, 279
Reinforcement, 100
Rentokil International, 214
Research
creative development, 111
Resource allocation, 9
Response, 93, 100
Response rate, 141
Retail banking, 85
Retailers, 136, 193
Return on capital employed, 34
Return on investment, 34
Ritz-Carlton hotel chain, 139
RJ Reynolds Tobacco Company, 224
Rolls Royce, 57
Royal Society for the Protection of Birds, 267
RSPB, 267

Safeway's logistics, 188
Sales positions, 115
Sales promotion
objectives, 121
Sales promotion objectives, 121
Sales promotions, 287
sales-led organisation, 78
SAS, 211
Satellite TV, 21
Scandinavian Airlines Systems, 211
Schweppes Europe, 77
Schweppes reorganisation, 77
Screening new product ideas, 161
Segmentation, 212
Segmenting consumer markets, 46
Segmenting industrial markets, 55
Selective attention, 93
Selective distortion, 93
Selective distribution, 193
Selective recall, 93
Selective tendering, 216
Selectivity, 93
Selling process, 116
Sender, 92
Sensitivity, 180
Service providers, 238
Services marketing, 253
Servicing, 115
Shareholders and PR, 130
Sheth model, 249
Shipping, 17
Shostack, 255
Single European Market, 20, 47, 285
Single parent families, 136
Single-issue publics, 127
Situation analysis, 9
Sizer, 38
Skimming prices, 73

Index

Social and cultural environment, 20
Social class, 97
Social class (socio-economics), 47
Social factors, 25, 97
Social institutions, 278
Social responsibility, 228
Social Trends, 252
Societal responsibility, 228
Socio-economic classification, 21
Socio-economic groups, 21
Sock Shop, 41
Special Olympics, 229
Sponsorships, 287
Sports promotions, 287
Sports sponsorship, 134
St James Norland Parish Church, 139
Stakeholder responsibility, 228
Standard benefits, 117
Star, 157
Stimulus, 100
Strategic implications of the product life cycle, 155
Strategic planning, 4
Strategy development, 9
Strengths and weaknesses analysis, 11
Subsidiary objectives, 35
Substantiality, 46
Sunday trading, 212
Superior strength moves, 23
Supermarkets, 180
Supplier characteristics, 191
Suppliers, 179
Survivors, 164
Sustainability, 237
SWOT ANALYSIS, 11
SWOT analysis., 11
Synchronisation, 196
Synergy, 285

Tactical planning, 4
Tailor-made promotion, 124
Tango, 110
Tarantino, 110
Target market, 46, 113
Target pricing, 181
Tazos, 123
Technological complexity, 282
Technological environment, 21
Telemarketing, 142, 143
Telephone, 137
Television advertising
  cost of, 136
Tendering, 215
Tertiary sector, 243
Tesco, 113, 290
Test marketing, 163
Thornton's chocolates, 189

Tie Rack, 41
TJP Electronics, 288
Tobacco, 223
Tolerance limits, 75
Tracking studies, 112
Trade Descriptions Act 1968, 230
Trade exhibitions, 130
Trade missions, 288
Trade promotions, 124
Trademarks, 224
Trading companies, 288
Traffic generation, 143
Traffic/transportation management, 285
Transport, 20
Tregoe, 36
Trial order, 117
Two-way asymmetric model of PR, 126
Two-way symmetric models of PR, 126

Unauthorised use of copyrights, 224
Undifferentiated marketing, 57
Unfair Contract Terms Act 1977, 230
Union Carbide, 232

Valdez, 229
Variances, 75
vertical marketing system, 194
VHS, 282
Video recorders, 223
Videos, 129
Virgin, 38
Virgin and the grim reaper, 99
Virgin Atlantic, 99

Walkers, 123
Wal-Mart, 278
Wang UK, 217
Weights and Measures Act 1985, 230
Which, 230
Wholesalers, 193
Wilson, 96
Working capital, 31
World Bank, 216
World cup, 287
World trends, 19
Wotsit (How long is your), 144

Yearbooks, 244
Yuspeh, 153

CIM Order

To BPP Publishing Ltd, Aldine Place, London W12 8AA
Tel: 020 8740 2211. Fax: 020 8740 1184

Mr/Mrs/Ms (Full name) _____
Daytime delivery address _____
Postcode _____
Daytime Tel _____ Date of exam (month/year) _____

		5/00 Texts	9/00 Kits	9/99 Tapes
CERTIFICATE				
1	Marketing Environment	£17.95 ☐	£8.95 ☐	£12.95 ☐
2	Customer Communications in Marketing	£17.95 ☐	£8.95 ☐	£12.95 ☐
3	Marketing in Practice	£17.95 ☐	£8.95 ☐	£12.95 ☐
4	Marketing Fundamentals	£17.95 ☐	£8.95 ☐	£12.95 ☐
ADVANCED CERTIFICATE				
5	The Marketing Customer Interface	£17.95 ☐	£8.95 ☐	£12.95 ☐
6	Management Information for Marketing Decisions	£17.95 ☐	£8.95 ☐	£12.95 ☐
7	Effective Management for Marketing	£17.95 ☐	£8.95 ☐	£12.95 ☐
8	Marketing Operations	£17.95 ☐	£8.95 ☐	£12.95 ☐
DIPLOMA				
9	Integrated Marketing Communications	£17.95 ☐	£8.95 ☐	£12.95 ☐
10	International Marketing Strategy	£17.95 ☐	£8.95 ☐	£12.95 ☐
11	Strategic Marketing Management: Planning and Control	£17.95 ☐	£8.95 ☐	£12.95 ☐
12	Strategic Marketing Management: Analysis and Decision (9/00)	£24.95 ☐		

SUBTOTAL £ _____

POSTAGE & PACKING

Study Texts

	First	Each extra	
UK	£3.00	£2.00	£ ____
Europe*	£5.00	£4.00	£ ____
Rest of world	£20.00	£10.00	£ ____

Kits/Passcards/Success Tapes

	First	Each extra	
UK	£2.00	£1.00	£ ____
Europe*	£2.50	£1.00	£ ____
Rest of world	£15.00	£8.00	£ ____

Grand Total (Cheques to *BPP Publishing*) I enclose a cheque for (incl. Postage) £ _____

Or charge to Access/Visa/Switch
Card Number ☐☐☐☐ ☐☐☐☐ ☐☐☐☐ ☐☐☐☐

Expiry date _____ Start Date _____
Issue Number (Switch Only) ☐☐
Signature _____

We aim to deliver to all UK addresses inside 5 working days. A signature will be required. Orders to all EU addresses should be delivered within 6 working days.
All other orders to overseas addresses should be delivered within 8 working days.
* Europe includes the Republic of Ireland and the Channel Islands.

CIM – Advanced Certificate: Marketing Operations (5/00)

REVIEW FORM & FREE PRIZE DRAW

All original review forms from the entire BPP range, completed with genuine comments, will be entered into one of two draws on 31 July 2000 and 31 January 2001. The names on the first four forms picked out on each occasion will be sent a cheque for £50.

Name: _____   Address: _____

                                                                                                              _____

How have you used this Text?
(Tick one box only)
☐ Home study (book only)
☐ On a course: college _____
☐ With 'correspondence' package
☐ Other _____

Why did you decide to purchase this Text?
(Tick one box only)
☐ Have used companion Kit
☐ Have used BPP Texts in the past
☐ Recommendation by friend/colleague
☐ Recommendation by a lecturer at college
☐ Saw advertising
☐ Other _____

During the past six months do you recall seeing/receiving any of the following?
(Tick as many boxes as are relevant)
☐ Our advertisement in the *Marketing Success*
☐ Our advertisement in *Marketing Business*
☐ Our brochure with a letter through the post
☐ Our brochure with *Marketing Business*

Which (if any) aspects of our advertising do you find useful?
(Tick as many boxes as are relevant)
☐ Prices and publication dates of new editions
☐ Information on Text content
☐ Facility to order books off-the-page
☐ None of the above

Have you used the companion Practice & Revision Kit for this subject?   ☐ Yes   ☐ No

Your ratings, comments and suggestions would be appreciated on the following areas.

	Very useful	Useful	Not useful
Introductory section (How to use this text, study checklist, etc)	☐	☐	☐
Setting the Scene	☐	☐	☐
Syllabus coverage	☐	☐	☐
Action Programmes and Marketing at Work examples	☐	☐	☐
Chapter roundups	☐	☐	☐
Quick quizzes	☐	☐	☐
Illustrative questions	☐	☐	☐
Content of suggested answers	☐	☐	☐
Index	☐	☐	☐
Structure and presentation	☐	☐	☐

	Excellent	Good	Adequate	Poor
Overall opinion of this Text	☐	☐	☐	☐

Do you intend to continue using BPP Study Texts/Kits?   ☐ Yes   ☐ No

Please note any further comments and suggestions/errors on the reverse of this page.

Please return to: Kate Machattie, BPP Publishing Ltd, FREEPOST, London, W12 8BR

CIM - Advanced Certificate: Marketing Operations (5/00)

REVIEW FORM & FREE PRIZE DRAW (continued)

Please note any further comments and suggestions/errors below.

FREE PRIZE DRAW RULES

1. Closing date for 31 July 2000 draw is 30 June 2000. Closing date for 31 January 2001 draw is 31 December 2000.

2. Restricted to entries with UK and Eire addresses only. BPP employees, their families and business associates are excluded.

3. No purchase necessary. Entry forms are available upon request from BPP Publishing. No more than one entry per title, per person. Draw restricted to persons aged 16 and over.

4. Winners will be notified by post and receive their cheques not later than 6 weeks after the relevant draw date. Lists of winners will be published in BPP's *focus* newsletter following the relevant draw.

5. The decision of the promoter in all matters is final and binding. No correspondence will be entered into.